"Michalis Psalidopoulos integration of two centuries Greek economic history with the history of economic thought is done in a paradigmatic way. The book lays stress on the dissemination of ideas of major economists and schools of economic thought, and the way these ideas were perceived and implemented in Greece either to stimulate economic growth or to deal with the harsh reality of economic slowdowns. The book extends the analysis and applied policies to the great recession of 2007 that affected Greece more than any other country."

Lefteris Tsoulfidis, *Professor in the Department of Economics, University of Macedonia*

A History of Modern Greek Economic Thought

Tracing the evolution of economic ideas in the context of the economic history and economic policy issues in Greece, this book examines the history of modern Greek economic thought from the War of Independence from Ottoman rule in 1821 until the present.

The book explores how native, religious-oriented economic thought was secularized and merged with different economic discourses during successive historical periods. It traces how the dissemination of French and German economic thought in the 19th century was followed by British and US influences in the 20th century. The institutionalization of economics as a discipline in the 1920s and its internationalization after 1971, with their effects on the emergence of modern mainstream and heterodox thought, are also discussed. Finally, reference is made to contemporary Greek economic thought in the frame of European Union economic thinking.

This book will be of interest to readers in the history of economic thought, economic history, intellectual history, Greek history, and modern European history more broadly.

Michalis Psalidopoulos is Chief Consultant at the Institute for Hellenic Growth and Prosperity of the American College of Greece and Professor Emeritus for the History of Economics at the National and Kapodistrian University of Athens, Greece.

The Routledge History of Economic Thought

A History of Australasian Economic Thought
Alex Millmow

A History of American Economic Thought
Mainstream and Crosscurrents
Samuel Barbour, James Cicarelli and J. E. King

A History of Czech Economic Thought
Antonie Doležalová

A History of Slovak Economic Thought
Julius Horváth

A History of Brazilian Economic Thought
From Colonial Times through the Early 21st Century
Edited by Ricardo Bielschowsky, Mauro Boianovsky and Mauricio C. Coutinho

A History of Colombian Economic Thought
The Economic Ideas that Built Modern Colombia
Edited by Andrés Álvarez and Jimena Hurtado

A History of Economic Thought in France
Political Economy in the Age of Enlightenment
Edited by Gilbert Faccarello and Claire Silvant

A History of Economic Thought in France
The Long Nineteenth Century
Edited by Gilbert Faccarello and Claire Silvant

History of Modern Greek Economic Thought
Michalis Psalidopoulos

For more information about this series, please visit: www.routledge.com/The-Routledge-History-of-Economic-Thought/book-series/SE0124

A History of Modern Greek Economic Thought

Michalis Psalidopoulos

Routledge
Taylor & Francis Group
LONDON AND NEW YORK

First published 2024
by Routledge
4 Park Square, Milton Park, Abingdon, Oxon OX14 4RN

and by Routledge
605 Third Avenue, New York, NY 10158

Routledge is an imprint of the Taylor & Francis Group, an informa business

British Library Cataloguing-in-Publication Data
A catalogue record for this book is available from the British Library

ISBN: 9781138220256 (hbk)
ISBN: 9781032738116 (pbk)
ISBN: 9781315413419 (ebk)

DOI: 10.4324/9781315413419

Typeset in Times New Roman
by Deanta Global Publishing Services, Chennai, India

Contents

Acknowledgments

The present study sums up research done over a period of 30 years, during which I had the privilege to interact with and learn from top historians of economics at History of Economics, European Society for the History of Economic Thought, and History of Economic Thought Conferences in the UK. Writing this study proved to be a challenge because of the word limit I had to respect and my aim to provide readers and future researchers with a full picture of the topic.

To keep the list very short, I would like to thank by name Craufurd Goodwin and Bob Coats for their friendship and generous support in my early research. I wish they were both among us to read this book. I would also like to thank my Greek brothers in arms, young and old, with whom we are devoted to the teaching and study of the history of economic thought in our country.

A special thanks goes to Yorgos Stassinopoulos, Adamantios Syrmaloglou, and last but not least Nicholas Theocarakis with whom we either exchanged ideas, coauthored papers, or shared rare books and articles. I am also indebted to Spiros Branis who read the entire manuscript and provided comments and suggestions, to Julianna Fassoulopoulou and Kostas Alexiou for their assistance, and the team at Taylor and Francis for their patience and support. The usual caveat applies.

Michalis Psalidopoulos
Athens, 30/9/2023

List of Abbreviations

AMAG: American Mission for Aid to Greece
AOS: Anotaton Oikonomikon Symvoulion (Supreme Economic Council)
AOKE: Archeion Oikonomikon ke Koinonikon Epistimon (Archive of Economic and Social Sciences)
ASOEE: Anotati Scholi Oikonomikon kai Emborikon Epistimon (Highest School of Economic and Commercial Sciences)
ASVP: Anotati Scholi Biomichanikon Spoudon Pirea (Highest School of Industrial Studies Pireaus)
ASVTh: Anotati Scholi Biomichanikon Spoudon Thessalonikis (Highest School of Industrial Studies Thessaloniki)
AUTh: Aristotelian University of Thessaloniki
Drs: Drachmas
EEC/EU: European Economic Community/European Union
EEPO: Elliniki Etaireia Politikis OIkonomias (Greek Society for Political Economy)
EEPOS: Elliniki Etairia Politikon kai Oikonomikon Epistimon kai Statistikis (Hellenic Society for Political Economy and Statistics)
EKDO: Epitheorisis Koinonikis kai Dimosias Oikonomikis (Review of Social and Public Economics)
EOPE: Epitherorisis Politikon kai Oikonomikon Epistimon (Review of Political and Economic Sciences)
FT: Freedom of Trade (Eleftheria tou Emporiou)
GHS: German Historical School
GSPE: Greek Society for Political Economy
IFC: International Financial Control
IOBE: Idryma Oikonomikon kai Viomichanikon Erevnon (Foundation of Economic and Industrial Research)
IMF: International Monetary Fund
KEPE: Kentro Programmatismou kai Oikonomikon Erevnon (Center of Planning and Economic Research)
KKE: Kommounistiko Komma Ellados (Communist Party of Greece)
KOMEP: Kommounistiki Epitheorisi (Communist Review)
LMU: Latin Monetary Union
NBG: National Bank of Greece

NO:	Nea Oikonomia (New Economy)
OECD:	Organization for Economic Co-operation and Development
OEEC:	Organisation for European Economic Co-operation
OJPD:	Official Journal of Parliamentary Debates
UoA:	University of Athens
UNRRA:	United Nations Relief and Rehabilitation Administration

Introduction

0.1 Setting the Stage

Joseph A. Schumpeter, writing about the history of economic analysis from the 1790s to the 1870s, identified a rapid professionalization process in economics during that period, compared to the past. The study of economics was promoted internationally, a rising tide of textbooks mostly exemplifying, popularizing, or paying lip service to Smithian economics were published, and economic periodicals and scientific journals appeared advancing the dialogue and the exchange of ideas between concerned citizens. Governments in all European countries accordingly backed the economic interests of their business classes and did their best to protect them (Schumpeter 1954, 380).

Thus, economics became a separate academic field in the early 20th century, with neoclassical economics forming the core of the discipline, especially after Alfred Marshall instituted the Economics Tripos in Cambridge in 1905. Historical, empirical, and institutional research methods were also used, whereas Marxism in its various forms had its own sympathizers. Then came Keynesian economics and in the wake of post-World War II developments, economics became increasingly mathematized and internationalized, with the result that any existing variants of national thought in economics existing until then gave way to a "universal" way of approaching and analyzing economic issues.

Schumpeter's statement and subsequent developments apply to Greece too, a country that, despite its economic backwardness in the 19th century, could count on a wealthy diaspora all over Europe. The ideals of the French Revolution and what Schumpeter defined as political liberalism (1954, 394) were a moving force during the Greek War of Independence and the 19th century was the century of nation-building in all countries in the periphery of Europe. National independence and the drive to follow the paradigm of Europe's more developed economies went hand in hand in the realm of ideas with the coming of age of liberalism, protectionism, and, at a later stage, socialism.

In 1830, modern Greece was still a newborn state (Clogg 2002; Dakin 1972; Koliopoulos & Veremis 2002). As a result, next to native thinkers, it absorbed economic ideas and theories from Europe's more developed countries. Striving to become rich and prosperous, Greece followed its own route to modernity. At first, a coalition of power between the royal house and landed interests led the Greek state

DOI: 10.4324/9781315413419-1

to an effort to expand its borders to include all Greeks living under Ottoman yoke. Emphasis was given to the introduction of modern institutions and to the need to foster the economic development of the nation. Many Greek intellectuals traveled and studied abroad, after 1870 mostly in Germany, at a time when classical political economy was giving way to neoclassicism and to protectionist ideas. Socialist ideas, either in relation to Marx or in line with other egalitarian platforms, were also disseminated. Not one, but many paths for growth were propagated to ensure personal liberties, freedom, and economic growth.

As economic liberalism in its various forms was, since the beginning of the 19th century, disseminated from the core European countries to the newborn states of Southeastern Europe, these countries first adopted a liberal approach in economic management. Soon, however, both Greece and its neighbors found it difficult to raise living standards (Psalidopoulos & Mata 2002). In fact, a modern scholar has described the process of economic life in 19th-century Southeastern Europe as "evolution without development" (Palairet 1997). Historical statistics reveal that economic growth rates in this region were considerably lower than those of Western Europe, with the income gap between the two growing instead of closing (Maddison 1995). Liberalism did not bring quick industrialization and economic convergence (Berend & Ranki 1982; Lampe & Jackson 1982), so the German Historical School seemed, after 1870, to offer a better research agenda and developmental policy framework to reach long-awaited goals. This led politicians and public opinion in Southeastern Europe to become more interventionist in their economic policies around the *fin de siècle.*

The imposition of an International Financial Control (IFC) in 1897, after the Greek default in 1893, furthered the tendency of Greek economists to study in developed Germany. More importantly, it also contributed to Greek economic policy becoming more streamlined, rigorous, and delivering compared with the recent past. Thirteen years of imposed austerity strengthened economic fundamentals and allowed Prime Minister Eleftherios Venizelos in 1910 to lead Greece to modernity with his far-reaching new-liberal social inclusive policy. This was accompanied by the full institutionalization of economics at Greek universities and tertiary education schools after 1920.

Wars were fought and borders were redrawn in Southeastern Europe in the second decade of the 20th century. The deluge of World War I and humanitarian assistance given to Greece by the League of Nations and other donors after the Asia Minor catastrophe in 1922 led to renewed debates and controversies among Greek economists, whose numbers grew substantially. During this time, economics made its distinct presence felt in the Greek university system and so did demand and supply analysis and neoclassical economics in general. Industry took off, becoming an important sector of economic activity based on investments, government support, and low labour costs. Moreover, a central bank, the Bank of Greece, was created in 1928, and big infrastructure projects were inaugurated to assist growth and prosperity, amid a large supply of labor that boosted profitability and industrial development. Monetary stability and the limits of government action were extensively discussed. The world economic depression after 1929 led Greece to default in 1932 and turned economic policy, as in other countries, to protectionism. Economic activity was heavily regulated until the outbreak of World War II. It was in this setting that Keynes' General Theory became initially known and was discussed among Greek economists. This discussion continued until the mid-1960s.

Occupation by the Axis powers between 1941 and 1944 had devastating effects on living standards and the currency. This situation was partially amended by Greek efforts, the generous British, and mostly American aid from 1947 to approximately 1962. The Anglo-Saxon approach to economics thus became essential for policy-makers and students. The process was further cemented with developments in the 1960s that included the creation of two important economic research centers, one co-financed by foreign assistance, the Center of Planning and Economic Research (KEPE), and the Research Department of the Bank of Greece.

Returning to the early post-World War II era, a civil war took place in Greece between 1946 and 1949, ending with a communist defeat. The economy rebounded after the successful devaluation of the currency in 1953 and got a further boost from the association agreement with the European Economic Community (EEC) of 1961. High rates of Gross Domestic Product (GDP) growth and low inflation set the basis for higher living standards during the next 20 years. Greek economists now started to follow postgraduate studies in the UK and the USA before returning to Greece. The Economics degree after a full four-year study was inaugurated in 1971, and economic education adjusted fully to international standards. At the same time, the university system expanded with new faculty and more students joining it. Economics in Greece became thereafter fully internationalized.

The collapse of the fixed exchange rate regime of the Bretton Woods system in 1971 changed the setting in which Greek economic policy was operating. The economy had transitioned from agricultural to industrial, with services being also very important. The full accession of the country in the European Communities (EC) in 1981 led to a steady decline of both primary and secondary activities. EC membership provided Greek access to European funds, and these "softened" somehow the permanent passivity of the balance of payments of the country. These funds provided liquidity in the economy and elevated the government and local authorities as primary agents in economic affairs. The last two decades of the 20th century saw the economy slipping into double-digit inflation and growing debt, developments that were partially reversed around the turn of the century to allow Greece to become a Eurozone member in 2002. Negative developments in the form of budget deficits, balance of payments disruptions, and a high external debt resumed and led, after the meltdown following the global financial crisis of 2008, to Greece facing financial trouble and turning to the EU and to the International Monetary Fund (IMF) to avoid a default. Austerity and three Memoranda of Understanding (2010–18) between Greece and its partners led the country to stand on its own feet, fighting to cover ground lost after 2010. These developments were and are still discussed by an ever-growing community of economists, with all schools of economic thought present and engaging in scientific exchanges over the hearts and minds of Greek citizens.

The present volume aims to contribute to an understanding of the evolution of economic thought in modern Greece from 1830 to the present, while at the same time discussing the economic history of the country and economic policy issues that made Greek economists react and offer theoretical as well as practical policy advice to their governments. Individual chapters narrate the slow emergence of an economic discourse blended with ideas imported from abroad. These ideas were based on certain trends or schools of thought and came from France, Germany, the UK, and later the USA at different historical periods. After a century of contributions, economics in Greece was institutionalized. Another 50 years later, the internationalization of economics followed, and the discipline became fully modern. We identify both major and lesser-known Greek economists in this process and explore their contributions, focusing on influences stemming from possible studies abroad. As these economists frequently held government positions of various ranks and influence, we also discuss their works, demonstrating their alignment with certain schools of economic thought. The book closes with issues in contemporary Greek economic thought and its relation to European Union economic thinking, making the whole prior analysis a key to better understanding current economic exchanges and developments.

0.2 Methodology

Two methodological approaches have been followed by historians of economics following the path-breaking works by Thomas Kuhn (1962), Imre Lakatos (1970), Paul Feyerabend (1970), and Scott Gordon (1991). These were rational reconstruction, the effort to seek antecedents of modern economic theory in past thinking, and historical reconstruction, the quest to investigate how economic concepts and analysis evolved out of concrete historical problems analyzed by economists (Rorty 1985; Wade Hands 2001; Blaug 1980). Roger Backhouse (1988) pioneered the approach that links economics with economic policy. The present author sees in a historical reconstruction that applies economic thought to concrete country circumstances a bigger merit, the main reason being that the purpose of the present work is not to hail those Greek economists who contributed to abstract economic analysis and classify them in a particular school of thought. It is to reconstruct how they analyzed the economic problems of their epoch and how they led slowly and steadfastly to the formation of camps and schools of thought. The evolution of economic thought in a particular country poses problems that need to be approached in a historical setting to be understood and explained.

In recent decades, and due to the opening of the history of economics to history of science and to influences from other social sciences, the landscape of methodology has grown richer, with innovative approaches contributing to a more inclusive understanding of the evolution of economic ideas. A major new approach has been lately suggested by Keith Tribe (2019), which influenced the study that follows. By focusing on the "word" articulated, in our case, by Greek economists and their effort to engage in discussion and debate, we identify their messages, and pay attention to their arguments and thoughts as they were disseminated through books, pamphlets, and newspaper articles. We gain thus their insights that reveal the environment in which they were active. Indeed, as we are about to see, economics in Greece was born from the ashes of religious and absolutist thought and those who professed themselves as economists need to be "listened" to in what they wrote and said until at least economics became institutionalized. This took enormous efforts. "Words" lead to "messages" and these to the formation of "schools" of economic reasoning and thought, for they create "communities" of thinkers. Public knowledge leads slowly to science, to replicable knowledge, to the forming of communities, and to certain career structures for those involved in public life and participating in these exchanges. In this process, the embeddedness of economics in law and the moral sciences started being questioned, resulting in the institutionalization of economics in the 1920s and the introduction of commercial education. Students trained in different streams of thought during this period accumulated standard qualifications and later appeared in public, advancing proposals based on economic theory. Half a century later, the internationalization of economics in Greece followed.

The task of studying the history of economic thought over two centuries in any country is challenging. It requires a multi-faceted reading of mentalities and institutions, the inclusion of novel ideas and their brewing with older, established views and opinions, whereas attention is needed to the inclusion of mechanisms of foreign influences and the dissemination of "superior" knowledge in the country in question. These questions have been reviewed in the past in pioneering articles by George Stigler (1965), William Grampp (1965), and Robert V. Eagly (1968).

To study the evolution of modern Greek economic thought, we extensively use "process analysis" as suggested by Craufurd Goodwin in his path-breaking article (Goodwin 1972), which distilled insights gained by his joint investigation with I. Holley (1968). Goodwin's approach inspired the works by Coats and Colander (1989), and by Perry and Tobin (2002).

Goodwin formulated a framework whose basic feature was the understanding of the effect economic theory had on society as a sum of various social processes taking place simultaneously and mutually affecting each other. He distinguished four social processes relevant to the unveiling of relationships between economic theory and society. These include: (i) the formulation or acceptance of abstract economic theory by individuals or research groups working mainly in academic institutions, (ii) the conduct of economic policy by the acting government and its relation to certain economic theories, views, and agendas, (iii) the expression of views either for or against current economic policy by academics, vested interests, in scientific clubs, professional journals, or in the media, and (iv) economic activity in society, understood as a wide range of acts pursued by private interests and related to processes i) to iii. Goodwin proceeded to link these processes with each other to demonstrate the channels through which economic theory and society are intertwined in one country.

This model is of substantial help when dealing with questions concerning the dissemination of economic thought across nations and the relationship between economic thought and policy, which can be understood in terms of a continuous interrelation between economic theory and policy in one country and the rest of the world.

0.3 Developments in the Greek Economy: A Brief Outline

Greek economists referred extensively to existing problems and policy issues. The following is intended as a crash course in what will be referred to in the following chapters.

Modern Greece broke away from the Ottoman Empire in 1821 and was recognized internationally as an independent state in 1827. Its borders (and accordingly population) expanded through negotiations and wars in 1864, 1879, 1912–14, 1922, and 1947. Border expansion had been proclaimed as a state goal since 1843 as the "Megali Idea" (Great Idea), the aim of which was to include all Greeks living in Southeastern Europe within the same borders. This Idea lost relevance after the Asia Minor catastrophe in 1922.

Initially, independent Greece had a (Greek) governor from 1827 to 1830, then became a Kingdom (with a Bavarian and later a Danish sovereign) from 1830 to 1922, followed by a Republic from 1923 to 1935. In the period 1835–74 it became a kingdom once more, to return to a republican form of governance after 1974. The country lived under absolute monarchy until 1843 and a constitutional one after that. The Royal house intervened regularly in political life and often went against the will of the voting majority, more importantly up to 1875, during World War I, and during the 1960s. Three times in its history, Greece was governed by a dictator, in 1926 for six months, during 1936–40, and more recently in the period 1967–74.

The protective powers (Britain, France, Russia) and a Greek elite consisting of tax collectors, bankers, and tradesmen under the stewardship of the Royal house blocked, for the period up to 1910, the development of productive relations, thus keeping progressive civil society at bay. The service of the Loans of Independence of 1830 to the Royal house was both a reason for frequent foreign intervention in political developments and a restriction in policy planning. Greece defaulted in 1827, 1843, 1893, and 1932. The country was under the close surveillance of an International Financial Control from 1897 to 1940 to repay its debts. The Control was relaxed after 1944 and ended officially in 1976.

As territory and population expanded continually until 1922, Greek GDP rose steadily but at far lower rates than those experienced in the West, around 1% annually in constant prices between 1833 and 1911 (Maddisson 1995; Kostelenos 2003; Mitchell 1978). The Greek economy was mainly agricultural until the middle of the 20th century, with commerce being an important sector of economic activity and shipping a sector that was, since the beginnings of the newborn state, internationally competitive. Industry came of age in the interwar years and took off after 1953 and up to 1980.

The "long" 19th century witnessed a slow transition of Greek rule from the Ottoman norm to a modern democracy. Many features of the Ottoman economic administration were carried forward by the Greek state for many decades, especially the handling of land property and the tax system. Property rights were given to peasants in three steps in 1836, 1871, and finally in 1917.

Before and after independence, taxes were collected by landlords and local nobles, mostly in kind and in very seldom cases in money. The aim of the peasants was autarchy/self-production throughout the 19th century. With the aim being the production of value in use and not value in exchange, the development of private initiative and of self-interested individuals was late in becoming the norm of economic life. The renting of taxes to landlords was terminated around 1917. An Agricultural Bank was created in 1928 to assist primary producers. After 1945, agriculture rebounded and continued contributing to Greece's exports, but because of its small scale and high production costs, it started gradually losing competitiveness. Association and later accession in the European Union shrank its contribution to Greek GDP from 30% in 1970 to 5% in 2020 (Bank of Greece 2020).

Despite certain initiatives, little was done for the encouragement of industry until 1922. The world economic exhibition in London in 1851 and the idea of progress through industry led to limited government initiatives in 1863, 1871, and especially between 1877 and 1880, when a special committee to assist industry was active. A tsunami of supportive measures for the secondary sector were introduced in the interwar period, making it important. Industry rebounded after 1945 and came to contribute no less than 30% of GDP in 1970. However, it lost ground after 1981 when European competition became more pronounced, and its share gradually shrank to 12% of GDP (Bank of Greece 1992).

Tourism became important after the 1970s and started contributing significantly to GDP, whereas shipping was a more permanent source of foreign exchange for the country. Seamen sent money to their families, and shipowners invested in various local economic activities and in the building sector.

The tax system relied heavily on indirect taxes (Dertilis 1993; Mitrofanis 1992). A stamp tax, and a tax on buildings, on professions, and on movable wealth were introduced quite early. Agriculture was seen as the most significant tax base, and in 1881 the tax on ploughing animals was introduced (Perakis 2000). The quest for an appropriate direct taxation was articulated and led, in 1909, to the introduction of the income tax. This was followed by another law in 1919 and a further one in 1955. Wage earners and pension holders are the main contributors of the income tax. Amendments update the existing legislation, with the ratio of direct to indirect taxation being between 3.5 and 6.5 today.

The Greek monetary system has undergone many changes since independence. After the failed attempt to introduce the phoenix, the drachma was created in 1833. A commercial bank was called into life in 1841, the National Bank of Greece (NBG). It succeeded over time, despite shortcomings, in imposing the drachma as a legal means of payment and became the main banking house of issue of drachmas. It was a stronghold of political power and attracted criticism from other banks because it was reluctant to grant credits to peasants.

Another major task of monetary policy was the convertibility of the drachma. At times of low levels of income, the currency was officially convertible. In 1867, Greece joined the bimetallic system of the Latin Monetary Union (LMU) but could not meet its requirements in practice until 1882 and only for a short while. Convertibility was enacted again in 1928 when the Bank of Greece was inaugurated, and it kept the drachma convertible until the default of 1932. The Bank of Greece dominated in the economy and reached formal independence once it became a member of the Eurosystem in 2002.

Foreign trade and the international economic relations of Greece were quite liberal. The balance of payments was a primary cause of concern. The trade balance was always negative, with the balance of services (invisibles) partially covering this deficit. Foreign lending (which at times was impossible), capital inflows, and direct foreign investment assisted in reaching the desired equilibrium. Tariff systems were introduced in 1830, 1857, 1867, 1885, and 1923, with only the last one aiming at protection (Andreou 1933; Kofinas 1901). Post-World War II tariffs were again protective of economic activities in a soft manner. Greece became a member of the General Agreement on Tariffs and Trade (GATT) in 1950. Tariffs were gradually dissolved after 1961 and especially after 1981, because of the agreements between Greece and the EEC/EU. Tariff policy toward non-EU countries is currently shaped according to European rules and arrangements.

0.4 Economics as an Academic Discipline in Greece: A Brief Outline

The evolution of economics as an academic discipline in Greece has gone through three distinct phases.

The first and longest one started in 1837 with the inauguration of a chair in Public Economics at the Law School of the University of Athens (UoA) and not the School of Philosophy. It was renamed Political Economy in 1863. A second one in Public Finance was established in 1885, but it was not fully operational until 1902. Next to professors, *ifigites* (readers) were giving lectures, thus contributing to a broader knowledge offered in economics to law students. The bottom line, however, remained that the discipline was not a "serious" examination topic.

The second period when economics was institutionalized started in the early 1920s, approximately 20 years after the introduction of a separate economics degree at Cambridge and the London School of Economics. UoA started awarding a *ptichion* (bachelor's degree) in economics to law graduates, who sat for an extra year of study. The same happened with the Law School of the University of Thessaloniki (Auth) (which was inaugurated in the mid-1920s).

A third institution devoted solely to commercial and business studies was the Highest School of Economics and Commercial Sciences (ASOEE) in Athens, founded in 1921. The School was renamed the Athens University of Economics and Business (AUEB) in 1990. During the first 50 years of its existence, most students chose the accounting/business degree and sought employment in the private sector.

Other universities offering courses, but not degrees in economics, included the Panteios School of Political Sciences (modeled after the Paris École des Sciences Politiques) since 1933, a school renamed as Panteion University in 1990. In the 1930s the Highest School of Industrial Studies, a semi-public school for professional education in Piraeus, came into life and offered evening economics courses. The school became entirely public and has operated full days since 1960. In 1990 it was renamed the University of Piraeus. In 1948 a Highest School for Industrial Studies was established in Thessaloniki but started operating only in 1957. In 1990 it was renamed the University of Macedonia. In the 1990s, economics departments were established at the Universities of Crete, the Aegean, Ioannina, Thessaly, and Thrace.

The curricula of studies everywhere, despite carrying some innovative elements, were at first oriented in Law, but emancipated themselves from legal studies over time and especially after 1971. This year marks the start of the third period of Greek economics, its internationalization. An autonomous degree for economics was introduced, and the content of studies, which was until then descriptive and rather old-fashioned, changed gradually to a new normal. Economics Departments were separated completely from Political Science and from Law, and a new generation of mostly UK or US educated economists conquered Greek academia. They were familiar with a mathematical approach to economic problems and quantitative methods in economic research.

In 1982, a new university law canceled existing chairs and brought all academics under the header of a specific department. Numerous university positions were advertised, and new universities were inaugurated. This enormous change, after decades of institutional constraints to become both an academic and to study economic science, thoroughly altered the landscape of economic education in Greece. The curricula of studies were changed to reflect the new situation, and in a further act of reform after the mid-1990s, postgraduate programs and degrees were introduced.

Thus, Economics as a discipline in Greece reached international standards.

1 Before 1821

1.1 Economy and Society in Greek Space from the Middle Ages to the War of Independence

Following the fall of the Byzantine Empire in 1453, the Greek Orthodox subjects of the Ottomans were recognized as a religious community (millet) under the auspices of the Patriarch in Constantinople. The Patriarch was responsible for the subordination of the Christians, and non-Islamic religions enjoyed relative autonomy and toleration at times when religious wars were fought among European peoples in the West.

The Greek Church pioneered education. The language it espoused was the Greek of the testament, not the spoken language. This issue, between a *katharevousa* (purist) and a *demotiki* (spoken) language, would become very crucial for Greek society after Independence and would remain ongoing until the late 20th century. Under Patriarch Gennadius, the "Patriarchic Academy of Constantinople" opened its doors to educate the oppressed, and with the passing of time academies were opened in Smyrna, Kydonies, Ioannina, and other cities. The Church was at first the keeper of knowledge. Later, after the French Revolution, it became less tolerant of dissent. When the War of Independence started in 1821, the Patriarch was, despite his harsh condemnation of the uprising, found liable and executed by the Ottomans.

The Ottomans were concerned with ruling and with military enterprises. For the running of their administration, they hired, among others, the services of Orthodox Christians, called "Phanariotes," Orthodox Greeks living in the capital district bearing this name. Important Phanariotes were Panagiotis Nikousios and Alexandros Mavrokordatos, who served in the 17th century as Great Interpreters (translators) for the Sultan for 40 years, respectively.

The Phanariotes were not the descendants of the Byzantine aristocracy, and their positions were lucrative. They developed an interest in the preservation of the status quo in the Empire, and they became so powerful that they were assigned by the Ottomans to govern the regions of Wallachia (38 princes) and Moldavia (36 princes). Some of these aristocrats moved quicker than others in the 18th century to liberal values and practiced in the regions under their jurisdiction an administrative way of governing opposed to the ecclesiastical administration. Those who lived in the Danubian principalities were exposed to modern, European ideas. They

DOI: 10.4324/9781315413419-2

participated in secret societies and debated about the future of a liberated Greece. For this reason, some of them were persecuted by the Turks after the outbreak of the revolution.

With the passage of time, a merchant class of Orthodox subjects emerged and rose to prominence in the 18th century by leveraging the treaties of Karlowitz (1699), of Küçük Kaynarca (1774), and of Jassy (1792). At first poor and half-educated, these merchants were men of rural origin who underwent a transformation. They settled all over Europe, forming networks of diaspora Greeks, and were exposed to French rationalism before and after the French Revolution more than others. After 1789, they were eager to work for the cause of national independence.

Shipping flourished in the Mediterranean and the Aegean Seas, with the islands of Hydra, Spetses, Psara, Chios, and others being home to very successful vessel owners. At first, subject to taxes and to constant contributions to the Sultan, they could negotiate a special status after the above-mentioned treaties and thrive economically (Harlaftis 1996).

An impoverished agricultural class survived through subsistence farming facing oppression from Greek primates, usurers, landlords, and tax collectors for the Ottomans. These landlords hated seeing their power and relative wealth diminish in a free, independent Greece.

In the following subchapters, we shed light on the impact of Greek Orthodox religious teaching on Byzantine economic thought and on the Ottoman approach to economic administration, to gain a first sense of economic mentalities and beliefs from 1453 to approximately 1766. We set this date because in that year, *Logic* written by Evgenios Voulgaris was published, an important work for the dissemination of modernist ideas in Greek space, ten years before the publication of the *Wealth of Nations*. We will then proceed to the debates between Greek Enlighteners and the Orthodox Church as they evolved between that date and the outbreak of the Greek revolution.

1.2 East Christian Fathers and Byzantine Economic Thought

The Greek Orthodox tradition in economic thought had its roots in the works of Basil of Cappadocia, John Chrysostom, Gregory of Nazianzus, and Gregory of Nyssa, who were active between the second and the fifth centuries CE. These influential figures pioneered "a minimalist-retreatist position on economic activity and advanced a monastic understanding of economic life, that should be applied to civilian life too" (Gordon 1975, 92). They advocated for private property and the accumulation of wealth, but with a strong emphasis on communal benefit. Income inequality was criticized, the ethical value of work was celebrated, and usury was explicitly condemned.[1]

When Constantine the Great declared his Byzantine Empire Christian, the teaching of the Fathers became sacrosanct. In their interpretation, "oikonomia" had the metaphysical meaning of moving through work from a low to a high standard of value. The motives of economic activity were self-interest and altruism. Private property was accepted, but there were limits to it, due to humans' tendency to become potential sinners. Church landowning was sanctioned, as monasteries were operating in a Christian manner. Excessive private property and wealth accumulation were condemned, along with avaricious behavior.

The laborer was hailed as a creator of valuable commodities essential for survival. The value of goods was tied to a human perspective, rather than their intrinsic nature. It was a responsibility of man to provide for himself and to support self-sufficiency in his community.

Agriculture was emphasized with a call for more altruistic behavior from landlords. Retail trade, especially in holy places, was discouraged. Money was equated with precious metals, and its hoarding was deemed morally questionable and economically unsound. Almsgiving and charity were proposed as solutions to scarcity. Society was divided into three classes: the poor, the middle class, and the rich. The poor were subdivided into *ptochoi* (indigents) and *penites* (paupers). The Fathers advocated for reduced taxes and no fines for the poor.

In the Orthodox Church, Greek identity centered around religion rather than the ancient Greek past. The preservation of language sustained Greek consciousness at a spiritual level. The teachings of the East Christian fathers continued during the Byzantine Empire. Various clergymen, philosophers, and authors attempted to go beyond delivered wisdom and questioned developments in economic life. Between God and Mammon, one had to follow the former, forgive the indebted, and love one's neighbor as oneself. Hybris in the form of wealth and luxurious life were condemned.[2]

Efstathios of Thessaloniki, for example, depicted progress as a journey from savagery to civilization, diverging from the notion of a struggle between man's fall and salvation. Georgios Gemistos or Plethon even proposed protectionist policies as an instrument for the Peloponnese region to compete with Italian products (Woodhouse 1986). Other authors delved into market dynamics, arguing favorably for labor as a measure of price.

Alexios Makrembolitis addressed the causes of poverty in 1343 and attributed inequality to the abandonment of Christian morality, criticizing rulers and Church leaders for societal confusion in the form of *ataxia* (disorder) and *synchesis* (confusion). While he didn't advocate radical change, he condemned the cruelty of tax collectors and customs offices (Laiou et al. 2013; see also Magliulo 2022, ch. 2).

To conclude, the East Christian tradition shared the condemnation of interest with the Western Church. The latter, however, underwent a transition after Luther and the commercial revolution that East Christian thought was late to follow and adapt to (Langholm 1992). Eastern Christianity remained closely tied to sacred texts, and economic realities were very slowly accepted by the Orthodox.

1.3 Economic Thought in the Ottoman Empire

The economy of the Ottoman Empire was centered around agriculture, bolstered by military expansion and revenue extraction from oppressed populations. However, the defeat of the Ottomans in the Battle of Vienna in 1683 marked a turning point, as Western economic expansion challenged Ottoman stability (Pamuk

1987; Inalcik & Quaetert 1995). Trade played a significant role in the Ottoman economy, but sea trade however and exchanges with other countries never took the form of extended transactions. The advent of steamships further marginalized the Empire, impeding its ability to leverage hard-won past military advantages. Industrial development remained stunted, but living standards held up until the onset of the industrial revolution. Government banking lagged, relying on private financiers until the mid-19th century, leading to inflation and social unrest. Uneven taxation burdened peasants, who increasingly sought through enlightened intellectuals a new national identity and political rights.

There is "a great gap" (Schumpeter 1954, 73) in our understanding of non-European economic thought that extends to the Ottoman Empire. Lately, this gap has been filled by two contributions about the evolution of economic ideas, mentalities, and policies throughout the centuries of Ottoman power (Genç 1994; Ermis 2013). The economy of the Ottoman Empire was "embedded" in the social system, a fact that was reflected in Islamic economic thought (Özveren 2002, 129). In general, Islamic teaching[3] exhibited skepticism toward markets, and rulers were taught how to administer prices and legislate to strengthen central power.

The basic channels that affected economic policy, and implicitly economic thought, in the pre-Tanzimat period were Ottoman merchants, Ambassador letters, and foreign officials. Foreigners were particularly significant in importing liberal ideas in Turkey at first through newspapers published locally; however, this took place only in the 19th century.

According to Mehmet Genç, the basic principles according to which the Ottoman State was organized were (1) *provisionism*, i.e., the uninterrupted supply of goods to the internal market, particularly the urban population; (2) *traditionalism*, a tendency to preserve existing conditions; and (3) *fiscalism*, the maximization of treasury income (1994, 60). Moreover, the Ottoman State relied on a policy of extensive accumulation, by adding new territories, but this came to a halt in the late 17th century. Provisionism entailed mercantilist policies in reverse, since a steady supply of goods in the Empire required the encouragement of imports and the curtailment of exports. The halt of territorial expansion created a fiscal crisis, since state needs kept increasing, partly due to the need to strengthen the army. This led to an intensification of the tax-farming system. Bureaucrats and the military subcontracted the raising of taxes to lower levels in the social hierarchy, thus creating more political problems. The systematization of tax-farming, which included the artisanal classes, led to subdued economic activity by the tax farmers who could not become entrepreneurs. Therefore, the industrial development of the Empire remained elusive. The weakening of the Ottoman State by the commercial treaties with the Western Powers continued after the creation of the modern Greek state, through the promulgation of the Hatt-i Şerif of Gülhane in 1839 and the Hatt-i Hümayun of 1856, which increased foreign intervention in the Ottoman Empire, at a time when ideas associated with economic liberalism were being disseminated.

Recently, Fatih Ermis (2013) underscored the pre-capitalist nature of Ottoman economic ideas. Ottoman thought drew from Aristotle, Islam, Sufism, Byzantine,

Iranian, and other traditions. Ermis highlighted three concepts: humorism, the notion of the circle of justice, and the concept of the household economy.

Humorism categorized Ottoman society into four classes, each associated with bodily humors. Blood was associated with scholars, yellow bile with merchants, black bile with peasants, and phlegm with bureaucrats. Striking the right balance between these four parts of society had to be the aim of the good ruler. Regulation featured prominently, with administrators maintaining price ceilings and market supervision for social harmony. Tensions, however, arose with the practice of Ottoman bureaucrats toward the 18th century (Ermis 2013).

Ottoman economic thought left a profound impact on its subjects. The all-encompassing tax state, extensive administration, and limited space for individualism shaped the populace's perception. Only cosmopolitan Greeks, merchants, and shipowners could challenge this norm, seeking alternative economic theories. The practice of the Ottoman Empire relied on the extraction of resources from the enslaved and arbitrary economic interventionism. This practice withered away with the emergence of nationalism in South-Eastern Europe.

1.4 Revival of Greek Thought: The Enlightenment, Korais, the Greek Orthodox Church, and Early Economic Thought (1766–1821)

1.4.1 Overview

During the Enlightenment era, the prevailing notion of divine law, which bestowed political legitimacy upon monarchs as God's earthly representatives, was fundamentally challenged. Enlightenment thinkers advocated that power was an inherent aspect of nature and belonged to the people, who were to regulate everyday life by means of a social contract. People shaped nations that were organized into states with written rules for the exercise of power, and the nation-state was the sole source of power and political control. From Locke to Hume and from Rousseau to Condorcet, these ideas dominated educated social strata and upcoming economic forces (Hutchison 1988). The French Revolution sent a universal message of freedom and emancipation and gave prominence to the emotional bond between a people and the nation.[4]

Enlightenment ideas made their way to Greek merchants who resided in colonies across Europe. After the treaties that gave them privileged status as Christians in Oriental trade, they began to accumulate big profits and concurrently became more conscious of their historical role as terminators of the oppressing Ottoman rule. This process took on a new quality after 1789. Similarly, the class of shipowners also embraced Enlightenment ideas. Agriculture, however, continued to grapple with economic backwardness and relentless exploitation through taxation by both the Ottoman administration and the Orthodox local lords.[5]

The fall of Byzantium to the Ottomans had a profound impact on Greek intellectual developments. While it meant that Greece missed out on the full impact of the Renaissance, there were still notable efforts toward a renaissance within the Greek mind. The establishment of the Patriarchal Academy and similar educational institutions in various cities, including Venice, Naples, Genoa, Budapest, Vienna,

Leipzig, Odessa, and Moscow, contributed to this intellectual revival and to the gradual distancing of philosophy from theology (Zakynthinos 1976; Henderson 1970, 13). From 1780 onward and up to the outbreak of the Greek Revolution, intellectual life was quite vital, experiencing a certain eclipse thereafter for the next 30 years.

The late 18th century and the lead-up to the Greek Revolution marked a period of intellectual vibrancy. Enlighteners such as Alexandros Mavrokordatos, Methodios Anthrakitis, Panagiotis Kodrikas, Evgenios Voulgaris, Iosipos Moisiodax, Athanassios Psallidas, Benjamin Lesvios, Nikiforos Theotokis, Rigas Feraios, and Adamantios Korais stand out in importance, as they produced works which transmitted modernist ideas (Kitromilidis 1999; Psimmenos 1988; Argyropoulou 1995). Philosophy began to enrich and, in part, to abandon, its attachment to the work of Aristotle. Rationalism and empiricism emerged in manuscripts of Enlighteners, who initially did not collide with the world of Orthodox tradition.[6]

Other Greeks traveled around Europe searching for the best schools or teachers to get an education. They went to the Universities of Padua, Vienna, Paris, Pisa, and Halle. Printing presses in Vienna and Venice produced books in Greek that were then sent all over the Empire to educate not only Greeks, but Bulgarians and Romanians as well.

The emergence of a diaspora middle class of Greeks in Europe paved the way for a significant shift. Once these merchants won their economic independence, they started aspiring for national freedom and supported authors who propagated rationalism, and, to some extent, anticlericalism (Stavrianos 2000). This marked the beginning of a conflict between clerics, who clung to tradition, and laymen, who embraced modern science and modern thought. There were also diverging views about language, with the church sticking to the archaic language of the testament and the laymen becoming vernacularists.

A new turn of events became visible among Greeks with the dawn of the 19th century. In 1796, Dimitrios Darvaris published *True Road to Happiness* and a translation of Xenophon's *Oeconomicus*, thus reminding contemporary Greeks of the wisdom of ancient economic thought. At the international level, after the French Revolution, the relationship between France and the Ottoman Empire initially remained stable, despite efforts to prohibit the sale of French books in Ottoman lands. Then, the French annexation of Corfu in 1797 blew up French-Turkish relations, and anything associated with French ideas in the Ottoman Empire became equated with treason. The French capture of Malta and Napoleon's Egyptian expedition brought French-Ottoman relations into total eclipse. Rumors of a possible Greek uprising were disseminating in the Empire.

The diffusion of Enlightenment ideas and the introduction of "western" sciences continued as a major project of the Diaspora Greeks, mostly in France, Austria, and the Danubian Principalities. According to Zakynthinos (1976, 152–79), between 1766 and 1820 an abundance of books was translated into Greek. These included Voltaire's *Memnon* and Rollin's *Histoire Ancienne* as well as the works of Locke, Montesquieu, Condillac, Beccaria, Genovesi, Mably, and Rousseau (Kitromilidis 1996; Gedeon 2010).

Literary periodicals appeared in the second decade of the 19th century: *Logios Hermis* (1811–21), *Melissa* (1819–21), *Kalliope* (1819–21), as well as the newspaper *Ellinikos Telegraphos* (1812–36). This activity drew the ire of the Church and provoked an ecclesiastical opposition to this "new learning" in the curriculum of Greek schools. The most outspoken opponent of the Orthodox Church's approach was Adamantios Korais. However, before turning to this pillar of Greek thought, reference should be made to Rigas Feraios/Velestinlis.

1.4.2 Rigas

1797 was the year that Rigas Feraios/Velestinlis was executed by the Austrians in Vienna due to his propagation of the uprising of the oppressed in the Ottoman Empire.

Rigas Feraios was a revolutionary who envisioned a multinational democratic state in place of the Ottoman Empire. He used the terms "class" and "*tagma*" (battalion) as early as 1790 in his novel *School for Delicate Lovers* and articulated in his *New Political Administration* the rights of man. These included equality, not a slave status, and the right to live and to possess estates. Estates were private property and were inherited by children and other descendants.

According to articles 18 to 20 of Rigas' manifesto, one may work as a servant, but he can't be treated as an object. No land is taken from anybody without compensation, and taxes are a public good. There is a right to demand information from the imposers about the spending of taxes by those who pay them. His *Thourios* (Battle Hymn) was a call for an uprising all over Southeastern Europe. He famously pleaded that it is "better to live one hour of free life, instead of forty years serfdom and prison." It was for this agitation that he was finally executed together with his comrades.

1.4.3 The Church

The Patriarchate began, as we saw, after 1790 to openly condemn "French ideas." Geopolitical changes added to this new situation. As forementioned, the French Revolution sparked attacks on the Patriarchate's part towards the Enlightenment, beginning with an act of great importance, i.e., the denunciation of Voltaire by Eugenios Voulgaris in 1790 (Zakynthinos 1976, 169–72).

Christian apology, authored by Athanassios Parios in 1798, was a work which aimed to function as a preventive medicine to Voltaire's "poison." The writer's goal was to reiterate that the Orthodox people had to embrace their faith and obey their oppressor. The deposition of kings, the search for regimes of liberal freedoms, and the questioning of the dominant religion were absolutely condemned. The above reflected the words of Patriarch Gregory on the so-called foolish "wisdoms" of Europe. Authors, such as Plato, Aristotle, Newton, and Descartes, as well as sciences, such as mathematics, drew believers away from metaphysical matters and were to be avoided. The Enlighteners were *antitheoi* (antigodly) and supported *morosophia* (stupid sophisms) (Petrou 1992, full text in Clogg 1969).

The next work bearing the seal of the Patriarchate was *Fatherly Teaching* (1798), authored by Anthimos of Jerusalem (although sometimes attributed to Athanasios Parios, as well), which was aimed at condemning *Thourios* by Rigas Feraios. Here, liberal pursuits were once again condemned and Orthodox Christians were called to voluntary slavery, as well as to faith and submission to their oppressor.

In 1802, Parios in his *Antiphonisis* (Riposte) brought ecclesiastical conservatism to new heights, stigmatizing those who sent their children to Europe to be educated in philosophy. The works of Copernicus and Newton were declared by him untrustworthy for the Church.

Patriarch Gregory V himself claimed that "the Platos and Aristotles, the Newtons and Descartes, triangles and logarithms lead to indifference in matters divine" (cited by Mathas 1837, 280); therefore, the Church anathematized French godlessness. The Western system of liberty was unchristian, a fake freedom that allowed everyone to pursue their selfish interests, a system of anarchy and disorder, where individuals exploited each other.

An extreme example of this way of arguing was an order circulated in 1818 when the clergy recommended to Phanariotes to hate Roman Catholics, to forbid marriages between Orthodox and Catholics, to fast 195 days per year, to promote pilgrimage to Jerusalem, and to "declare that the concept of political liberty had been inspired by the devil, whereas the Sultan's empire existed by God's grace" (Zallony 1824, 133).

1.4.4 Korais

The response to the teaching of the Church came from Adamantios Korais with his *Brotherly Teaching* (1798). According to Korais, the author of *Fatherly Teaching* was an enemy of the Greeks since he was ignorant of all the things the Orthodox suffered under the Ottomans on an economic, political, and social level. Korais stressed that Paul the Apostle asked for the submission of Christians to legitimate rulers, not to violent suppressors of freedom like the Ottomans. At the same time, Korais admitted mistakes on the part of Byzantine rulers, which weakened the empire, turning it into a lame duck.

He emphatically highlighted the fact that individual freedom, mocked in *Fatherly Teaching* as an invention of the devil against the Bible, was instead applauded in the latter. Christianity, he went on to say, believed in a free and autonomous individual, and the Bible was full of quotes standing for democratic egalitarianism. Korais used some of these to expose and condemn religious prejudice while at the same time promoting liberty and democracy.

Korais propagated *metakenosis*, the "transfusion" or "decanting" of western ideas of rationalism and liberal humanism into Ottoman Greece through translations of European books into modern Greek. He believed in the revival of Classical Hellenism, that would bring Greeks closer to ongoing developments in the contemporary European political and social mind (Papaderos 1970). He constructed a literary language designed to synthesize the ancient Greek of the Church texts with the spoken language, a language that would appeal, in his view to all social classes. He believed that through this the amorphous Greek ethnographic group could easily transform itself into a nation-state. Greek nationalism, plus human betterment, liberty, equality, and justice, were his goals. He reminded his contemporary Greeks that they were the descendants of the ancient Greeks.

Korais himself translated into modern Greek and published in 1802 and in 1823 Cesare Beccaria's *Dei delitti e delle pene,* a clear case for the rule of law and against absolutist arbitrariness. As the editor of the *Greek Library* (Elliniki Vivliothiki), a multi-volume collection of books in Greek, Korais made a more decisive appearance in the international scene with his *Mémoire sur l'état actuel de la civilization dans la Grèce* (1803). In it, he called for a moral revolution. The Greeks were making progress in the economic sphere; they amassed "richesses extraordinaires" out of shipping activities and had achieved luxury in social life through progress in education. He called on Europeans to not mistrust the Greeks, but to support them in their dawning struggle. He stressed that the Greek clergy was not reactionary in its entirety. He informed that through commerce the Greeks accumulated wealth, with the Ottomans not being able to understand, due to their backwardness and their inherent distrust, the international and local economic developments. Hydra and Chios thrived; their population rose, as did their residents' education. In continental Greece, Souli was setting the example of free morale. If the sympathy of the Greeks before 1789 was guided towards Russia and England, he said, after that landmark year, it was directed towards France. Greek scholars considered the French advances to be successes of the Enlightenment; they were long directed towards education, they were growing in numbers, and they disseminated knowledge. It was about time that French public opinion supported the difficult struggle of the Greeks.

Korais knew Jean Baptiste Say personally but didn't delve into economic issues. For him, two classes were important in society: the nobles and those who cultivated their land. A good administration could soften injustice in society, but not create equality between men, he thought. Total equality was for him not natural; only equality before the law could lead to better governance. Monarchy, on the other hand, could give birth to tyranny and was a form of government that needed to be controlled through a constitution.

One cannot easily evaluate the extent of this confrontation. The assumption that each side preserved its points, with the illiterate Greek peasants remaining closer to the word of the official Church, is reasonable. While the enlighteners witnessed the Patriarchate recommending to the enslaved to kiss their oppressor's hand, the Orthodox Church saw in the western (Catholic/Protestant) liberty system an illegitimate situation causing anarchy and agitation and possibly threatening to question the political position of the Patriarchate in the Ottoman system of power.

1.4.5 Hellenic Nomarchy

The anonymous Greek writer of *Hellenic Nomarchy* (1806)[7] was a fervent admirer of Korais and a vocal critic of the clergy. The book undertook a bold assessment of the then current situation and was not optimistic in its tone. The author underlined the role of education, the need to escape ignorance, and the importance for everyone to develop his personal ethic. Human happiness depended on good administration, he claimed, and concluded that, since Byzantium became Christian, the means of human emancipation were limited, instead of expanding (81). Sciences atrophied, schools closed, and until recently the works of priests were the only texts available to study and acquire literacy. Living conditions were shameful, with farmers living worse than animals (96) and craftsmen working for 18 hours per day (97). Causes of this backwardness were to be found among the ignorant priesthood and the absence of excellence in society (108). The anonymous author went on with his critique against the clergy (121 ff.), who stood in the way and hid the path towards Greek liberation (141). He had a negative view of merchants because they were, in his view, too selfish. The new teachers of the nation were the intermediaries of the future reality for Hellenism (145). The Ottoman state was withering away (163).

Following Quesnay's classes de citoyens, he defined the classes as the nobles (who were ignorant and idle), the Church (which was also ignorant and hid under the umbrella of sainthood the greatest lies), the peasants (who were the class to respect, the pillar of political happiness, and who were living lives worse than animals), and the technicians and the sellers (either in their own work place or through travels).

Regarding economic matters, the analysis of the anonymous author does not exhibit familiarity with the dominant economic approaches in Western Europe, like mercantilism, physiocracy, or the classical school of political economy.[8] Thus, nature, nurture, and "luck" were considered as causes of difference among people (19). Luck, according to the author, was to be blamed for the differences between the rich and the poor. Money was just "numericals" (113); it just facilitated exchanges and, besides the essentials for living, it came into existence for the acquisition of luxury goods (114). The invention of money was harmful to the people and damaged their morals. In this respect, commerce did not open productive paths.

1.4.6 Commercial Initiatives

Books on economic matters before the creation of the Greek State were not specialized in political economy. Financed by rich merchants, they were commercial handbooks or books on commercial arithmetic and weights, measures, and foreign exchange conversions (Sklavenitis 1991).

In the first decade of the 19th century, the translation of Joseph Nowack's *Grundriß der Handlungsgeschichte*, originally published in 1799, was translated into Greek thanks to a donation by the merchants of Constantinople. This work is the first case of deification of commerce as a profession and as a foundation of economic activity and prosperity circulating in Greek. Novak's book was a statement for the social domination of the merchants, regardless of their nationality or the specific work they accomplished. It didn't, however, link trade to mercantilist thought. Neither did Nikolaos Papadopoulos' *The Gainful Hermis: Encyclopedia of Trade*, in five volumes, published in Venice in 1815, also financed by the "big merchants of Constantinople." Papadopoulos' book was fashioned after dictionaries such as Malachy Postlethwayt's *Universal Dictionary of Trade and Commerce*. This work served aspiring merchants in multiple ways by informing them through innumerable entries on raw materials and objects of possible commercial interest.

At the same time, Papadopoulos published *Ermathini, or a business study* (1815). This was an extensive study discussing theoretical issues about commerce before examining specific ones on external and internal trade. In the closing part of the book, more general problems regarding the prosperity of society are discussed, as well as the role of banks and shipping, in combination with the priorities of commerce.

Discussing the skills necessary to promote commerce, Papadopoulos mentioned Adam Smith and the importance of the division of labor for society, a term attributed by Papadopoulos in Greek as *polycheiria* (lots of hands) (131).[9] However, here too, as was the case in *Hellenic Nomarchy*, the mention is not accompanied by an understanding of the rationale of the Great Scott. Papadopoulos missed the point of the division of labor almost completely and went on to argue that for goods to be cheap, apart from the division of labor, other ingredients include cheap materials, low interest rates, low wages (and hence low taxes on workers and cheap wage goods), and freedom of trade. In other words, the argumentation does not fit in the system of classical analysis, but the division of labor is a condition for inexpensiveness and, as such, leads to a feeling of pleasure among consumers.

Summing up the evolution of economic thinking shortly before the War of Independence, one can argue that in pre-revolutionary Greece there was a classic debate between rationalism and metaphysics, which influenced certain circles of intellectuals and erudite Greeks. In existing texts, we find fragments of general principles of a new economic and social organization, however without an exhaustive treatise that analyzes the present in Greek space and the prospect of its future. The aim of Enlighteners was the "transfill" of a new way of perception of socio-political life to Greeks. Their first goal was the political independence of the Greeks, and the economy came second. It remained a fact that the residents of the geographical space that would ultimately be liberated were traditional farmers, and not cosmopolitan merchants. Therefore, they were, in their majority, attached to Orthodoxy, rather than to theories which they had not yet met in their economic practice. The Enlightenment, consequently, lost momentum and its intellectual vigor went through an eclipse in the 1820s. Realities of nation-building under given internal and external restrictions had entered the scene (Henderson 1970).

Notes

1 See Karayannis (1994) on the Fathers' views on the redistribution of income as well as the monumental compilation of sources edited by Bougatsos (1980) on the Fathers' views about the "just" society.

2 See the pioneering analysis of economic thought during the Byzantine era by Angeliki Laiou in Laiou and Morrison (2007). See also Barker (1957).

3 On the Mediterranean tradition in economics and on Islamic economics, see Baeck (1994) and Ghazanfar (2003).
4 On economic thought in France during that period, see the collective volume edited by Faccarello and Steiner (1990).
5 On the economic history of Greece before 1821, see Andreadis (1939, vol. I, 883–721). See also Angelomati Tsougaraki (1990) for the reports of foreign travelers to Greece during the same period.
6 Henderson (1970) includes a full list of names of these authors. Out of 36 enlighteners (13 clerics and 23 laymen), 21 were teachers.
7 On this tract, see Karayiannis and Ithakissios (1999).
8 Hutchison (1988), Schumpeter (1953).
9 See Theocarakis (2018, 471–527).

2 French Ideas and German Cameralism (1821–62)

2.1 The Decade of Turmoil (1821–33)

The year 1821 stands as a momentous turning point in Greek history, signifying the nation's courageous defiance against Ottoman dominance. This seminal event challenged the decision emanating from the 1815 Vienna Congress and was masterminded by the Filiki Eteria (Society of Friends). This secret society was initiated in Odessa and united merchants, notables, clergymen, and landowners residing in South-Eastern Europe, rallying behind the ideals of liberty and freedom. The rule of law was hailed and compared to the reality of Ottoman tyranny. There was no recruitment from Paris, London, or Amsterdam and most members shared the idea that Orthodox Russia would not abandon the Greeks.

The military theater bore witness to a mixed outcome. The Battle of Dragasani (in present-day Romania) ended in dismal defeat, casting a shadow over the quest to liberate regions bordering Central Europe and the West. Conversely, the Peloponnesian uprising charted a triumphant course, albeit marked by internal strife among the Greek factions. The intervention of Egypt in 1826 at the behest of the Ottomans further complicated matters. Concurrently, the European continent saw the emergence of a robust philhellenic movement, especially pronounced in Britain, where an outpouring of solidarity bolstered the Greek revolutionaries. The Battle of Navarino in 1827 saw the Great Powers siding with the Greeks and prevailing, thus paving the way for the birth of an independent Greece. Ioannis Kapodistrias, a former Foreign Affairs Minister for the Czar of Russia, assumed leadership of the free Greeks.

The exigencies of the moment cast a shadow on Greece's economic landscape. A pall of desolation descended as agricultural output withered, monasteries faced pillage, and meager revenues were the norm. To surmount these trials, the quest for external financing intensified. The loans of Independence were brokered in 1824 and 1825 under the aegis of the London Philhellenic Committee that included Benthamites, Lord Byron, and other eminent Britons. These loans, beneficial to creditors, found purpose in bolstering military pursuits (for details, see Levandis 1944). Their service stalled after 1827, with Britain not pushing the Greeks for their repayment due to the negative publicity over their terms (*The Times*, 24/10 and 28/11/1826). Despite the insolvency of the not-yet-existing nation-state, the Great Powers offered a new loan to the Greek king they chose to govern the country, after

DOI: 10.4324/9781315413419-3

the assassination of Kapodistrias. The question of the repayment of these loans and of Greek debt in general would have major consequences for the economy until 1879 and later (Psalidopoulos 2019).

In the following pages, we will first refer to the economic aspects of the Greek constitutions of the revolutionary period. Then we will focus on the diffusion, by means of translations, of mostly French economic liberalism into Greece during the "long" decade of 1820, while making remarks on Bentham's utilitarianism and Saint-Simonian industrialism, which were disseminated in the country through British and French intellectuals. We will close with the aborted efforts of Kapodistrias to build a state and end up with the contribution of the German traveler Friedrich Thiersch concerning the country's economic future.

2.1.1 Constitutions

As we saw, the spiritual movement and the inquiries of intellectuals for the next "economic day" of Hellenism were remarkable. The first constitutions drafted by the Greeks after 1821 (of Epidavros, of Astros, and of Troezena) resulted from the specific power correlations among the notables participating in them. All constitutions expressed the quest for egalitarianism, human rights, and private property. They emphasized anti-absolutist governance rather than popular democracy.

On economics, they declared the basics like the issue of money, the authorization to enter loans through collateralization of national lands, and the process to create a budget and observe its implementation. Special mention was made of the need to distribute the tax burden in a just way. These clauses were repeated in all drafts (Pavlopoulos 2022; Bredimas 2021). Governor Ioannis Kapodistrias introduced the so-called Hegemonic Constitution in 1827, a centralized form of governance under his authority, that met its demise with his assassination. The reins of power then passed to Bavarian prince Otto von Wittelsbach as King of Greece, who governed as an absolute ruler until 1843 and constitutionally thereafter. The first political parties in the country were the English, the French, and the Russian.[1] Over time, Otto followed a pro-Russian policy, distanced himself from Britain and France, and had to abdicate in 1862.

2.1.2 Benthamites

Returning to the beginning of the 1820s, we witness the activation of the followers of Jeremy Bentham in Greece and mainly the exchange of opinions between him and Greek intellectuals (Papageorgiou 2012). The utilitarian philosophy of Bentham, the principle of seeking maximum pleasure with minimum pain, and its recognition as a reality of economic behavior in legislation, were not yet incumbent in British public services, as they would become later.[2] Bentham was interested in the "export" of his ideas to countries beyond his own, so, between 1823 and 1826, heated exchanges by means of correspondence and physical presence took place in the Greek context between Benthamites and Greeks. This initially intense intervention was preceded by the attempts of the London Philhellenic Committee to broker the Loans of Independence (Rosen 1992. See also St. Clair 1972). After 1827 and due to the inability of the Greeks to service them, the influence of the Benthamites in Greece withered.

Bentham's main goal was to provide a complete and rational code of law-governing society. For Bentham, happiness in society came first, and distribution of wealth came second. He "bombarded the new revolutionaries in France" to instruct them on how to make French society happy (Harrison 1983, 226). The same motive led him to endorse and influence the revolting Greeks (Halevy 1928). Lester Stanhope and Edward Blanquiere were the Benthamites on the spot. The inability of the Greeks to deliver at the constitutional level and the quarrels surrounding the loans of Independence alienated Bentham and distanced him from the Greek revival.

2.1.3 Translations

While utilitarianism permeated Greek space, three French books were translated, two of which were of a strict economic nature, sharing an intense liberal character. So were the translations of books by Benjamin Franklin.

Fragias Fournarakis translated Benjamin Franklin's *Poor Richard's Almanac.* The book was published in Paris. In 1831, Franklin's *The Way to Wealth* was translated by Ioannis Manesis in Triest. It is worth noting that both books were translated into Greek from the French, and not the English original.

In 1825, Fournarakis translated Pierre Claude François Daunou's treatise about human rights (Daunou 1825). Daunou was a well-known member of the Girondin parliamentary group in the French assembly and analyzed individual rights and the way the state ought to guarantee them. The individuals turned from zealots and slaves to subjects and citizens, according to Daunou. The safety of persons, ownership, industry, morale, and consciousness were the foundations of the new world order, while the judiciary had to be discrete and independent, and the fortunes created in economic life inviolable. Individual ownership was declared by Daunou as the foundation of the independence of the citizens and the nation-state. The writer asked the government to balance its budget and limit its economic activity, to "stop tightening what is already tied," as he characteristically put it. In other words, he recommended laissez-faire.

The next translation was that of Georgios Chrysiidis in 1828 and regarded the work of Jean-Baptiste Say, *Catechism of Political Economy*, a popular work which was particularly widespread across Europe (Tribe 2003). Chrysiidis confronted the vocabulary he was called to attribute in Greek with a great deal of fantasy, making the book a difficult read. He held praises beyond Say, also for Smith and Sismondi. Between the greedy and the prodigal, it was the latter who did wrong in society (97). It was better for any government to be able to borrow instead of having to borrow (117), and public consumption was crowding out private expenditure and should be kept to a minimum (112).

Chrysiidis dedicated his translation to Governor Ioannis Kapodistrias, believing that he would adjust his policies towards the teachings of Say. However, the Governor's priorities were different, and the translation could not function as a compass for his actions. A third translation followed later, just before the arrival of King Otto in Greece.

2.1.4 Kapodistrias

Kapodistrias faced huge economic problems in a homeland ruined by war and sought practical solutions (Woodhouse 1973). His understanding of the economy was based on his Russian experience, where economic thought remained captive by local circumstances that did not favor the democratization of society (Zweynert 2002).

Despite his Ionian feudal/democratic origins, the Russian experience must have influenced him substantially. Unfortunately, he outright despised theoretical economists as his possible advisors and asked for practical command enforcers and good administrators for the country's public finances. As he wrote, "I'm not looking for a dogmatic or for an economist (in the French version of the letter, *économe politique*) but for an industrious man."[3] His attempts were left hovering between Anglo-French hostility towards him and resistance on the part of Greek landlords, who were afraid of losing the tax-collecting rights they held under Turkish rule. A clash emerged. Kapodistrias tried to centralize power. He dismantled the powers of local communities, an institution that had existed during Ottoman times. Having been a Minister of an autocratic government, he was not a liberal intellectual, but an "incorruptible and patriotic" man (Stavrianos 2000, 291).

His plan to create a new state included education, social care for orphans and victims of the prolonged war of independence, the introduction of a new currency, and the creation of a bank (Loules 1985). On the one hand, he didn't allow the implementation of democratic rule, and on the other, he didn't call for elections that would legitimize his plan to resurrect Greece. His plan to grant property rights to peasants and an envisaged land reform didn't materialize. In vain, he asked for a loan from the Great Powers and was in constant contact with Swiss banker Jean Gabriel Eynard about Greek finances. In 1831, he was assassinated by Greek landlords. After two years of anarchy, the Bavarians took over.

2.1.5 Droz

Political rival of Kapodistrias and later judge Anastasios Polyzoidis translated in 1833 the book of Joseph Droz, *Political Economy, or Principles of the Science of Wealth*. The book was dedicated to King Otto, who was called to follow its teachings as a monarch. Polyzoidis accepted that until then the science of wealth, Economics, had not set foot in Greece. He expressed the hope that it would soon become the property of the people and that the transplantation of right ideas in the economy would lead to prosperity. In his extended introduction to the book, he demonstrated familiarity with authors and streams of thought in England and France. He considered François Quesnay to be the father of economics, but he emphasized the work of Smith and the importance of productive labor for the wealth of a nation. Laissez-faire was declared by him an axiom of right economic management. He addressed himself to diaspora Greeks in particular, inviting them to share their wealth with the poor fatherland (κε.).

For Droz, the first and foremost author that one needed to read was Say. He recommended then Storch, Tracy, and Mill, and if in more need, Malthus and Sismondi (χιξ-χιιξ). Of particular interest was chapter E (102) about legislation meant to regulate working conditions. These regulations were, according to Droz, a catastrophe for the development of industry, harmful for the consumers, and of no value for the right education of workers. Another point worth underlining was his critique of Adam Smith's condemnation of non-productive work (381). Society had, for Droz, a need for services, and these contributed to society's well-being. Economics was a moral science, and wealth was not the end but just a means to move to a higher level.

Despite its impressive circulation (around 500 subscriptions), the book of Droz could not be utilized by the Bavarian regents, adherents of absolutism, and the hope of Polyzoidis did not materialize. But it left fertile ground for the future.

During the same year (1831) a shortened version of Emmerich de Vattel's *Law of Nations* was translated, a demanding treatise investigating the rights of nations and their relation to natural law. Unfortunately, and due to political developments leading to Bavarian rule, this publication didn't have any impact.

2.1.6 Thiersch

Until 1833, there was no study by a Greek author suggesting what should be done from an economic viewpoint so that the newly founded state could stand on its own feet. What was not done by a Greek author was introduced that year by a German in the French language.

Philologist Friedrich Thiersch played a role of mediator in Greek political disputes between 1827 and 1831, recorded the wealth-producing resources of the country, and made suggestions for the organization of the economy with a comprehensive plan for the economic overhaul of Greece, written after his return in Germany. His extensive book is a work of practical solutions to the problems of the country, solutions based on the latter's wealth-producing sectors, agriculture, shipping, and commerce. His correspondence with selected persons (Thiersch 1972, v. B΄, 52–344) certifies a genuine philhellene, with a complete plan and strong opinions.

Thiersch gathered important, if unchecked, information on all the issues that had to be addressed by the political authorities, including exhaustive accounts of raw materials, various resources, salt pans, fish farming, as well as the basics of government revenue and payments. After presenting the Greek condition, he went on to make policy proposals. Indeed, Thiersch's treatise should be considered a landmark for economic thought and policy in Greece.

It was necessary for the state to be powerful and regulatory. Its primary duty was the imposition of law and order. Its second duty included taking care of agriculture, the fundamental revenue-generating sector of the economy. The public (former Ottoman) lands had to be distributed to the landless peasants. As Thiersch said, the agricultural problem "is the most pivotal of problems" (Thiersch 1972, 12). According to his estimations, there was an aggregate of 120,000 farm households, only 20,000 of which possessed property titles. He also thought that all landless people should become landowners, therefore he proposed a land distribution plan, in which the state would provide farmers with low-interest credit to buy property titles. Land should also be given for free to freedom fighters. Furthermore, new farming methods should take the place of existing plows. Thiersch also recommended the differentiation of agricultural products, which would facilitate the achievement of autarky and limit imported agricultural goods to a minimum. Another important step would be the import of animals to improve/restructure livestock farming. Thiersch also contemplated the demographics of Greece, considering the population density to be low (Petropoulos 1981, 155–75). At this point, he agreed with the Saint-Simonians and encouraged the relocation of Greeks and foreigners to the free state.

Taxation on agricultural production should help monetize the economy. Thiersch explicitly criticized the renting of taxes (1972, 35–8) and the view that communities and local authorities knew the collective interest better. It was clear to him that tax collectors unbearably oppressed farmers and contributed to the reproduction of the structures of Ottoman rule.

The state had to improve – in fact: to create – infrastructure. It also had to set up a land register. In addition, it should lay the foundation for an industrial policy which would go beyond the export of products in which Greece already had a comparative advantage. Trade and the maritime industry were economic branches of immense importance towards the development of Greece. Thiersch also gave a detailed account of how Greek shipowners managed to thrive despite Ottoman tyranny (1972, 170–7). He condemned regionalism and rejected the opinion that communities practiced self-management and the democratic distribution of resources (1972, 182–3). Tariffs and customs regulations should be aimed at strengthening external economic relations, while at the same time avoiding unilateral actions which would trigger commercial retaliation on the part of third countries. Unlike many of his compatriots, Thiersch was an advocate of free trade, which he believed was in the best interest of Greek shipping.

In the monetary sector, a new national currency had to be introduced to smooth a complicated situation, whereby Venetian, Spanish, Austrian, and Turkish coins circulated and were used all together in transactions because of maritime activities. Thiersch believed that if his proposals were implemented and deployed by a sound administration, after 1840 Greece would enter a development trajectory which would give the country the status of a sovereign power of the southeastern Mediterranean region (1972, 252).

It is true that, despite the magnitude of his work, Thiersch did not delve into the details of how he intended to achieve all these policies in a newly founded state, which was just emerging from tyranny. It is also true that his plan required funding: from the construction of roads to building schools and port warehouses, not to mention the funds necessary for lending to farmers and financing the introduction of a new monetary system. Although not perfect, what Thiersch proposed was still a plan. The fact that this plan was totally ignored by the Regency, Otto, and the Greeks is deeply saddening.

In conclusion, Thiersch's book comprises the first important attempt to record data, define challenges ahead, and offer suggestions for the economic development of free Greece. Unfortunately, his contribution was ignored by his compatriots, who started their economic and political administration of Greece in the year of publication of his book.

2.1.7 Saint-Simonians and D'Eichtal

During the early 1830s, Greece witnessed the quick rise and fall of followers of Henry de Saint-Simon, who came to the country to promote their economic ideas.

Saint-Simon was, as already known, an initially rich adventurer who created after the French Revolution a salon devoted to sciences. His aim was the study of society on a scientific basis. A positive empirical science was for him possible. In his *Du Système Industriel* (1821) he propagated that society was an organism governed by natural laws. It had to be an industrial society where the rulers would be general directors who would oversee all societal processes. Banks giving credit to society were indispensable for the progress of the nation (Jacoud 2010). Saint-Simon is generally credited for the scientific move from the renaissance/enlightenment path toward positivism and for his proposal for the creation of the credit mobilier (Manuel 1956; Ionescu 1976). He formulated a utopia of centralized social organization, based on industrialization which would replace Christianity as a creed in society. His teaching found many fanatical supporters who, as apostles, carried the ideas of their teacher across Europe.

In the beginnings of the 1830s, Saint-Simonians settled in Greece, headed by Gustave D'Eichtal, and sought to materialize Saint-Simonian teachings. Other prominent members were Francois Graillard, who became chief of the gendarmerie, and Jean Roujeux, personal secretary of Minister (and later Prime Minister) Ioannis Kolettis. However, relatively soon, as happened with the Benthamites, and not being able to find a free scope of action under Otto's regents, they were disappointed, giving up on their attempt.

D'Eichtal, a political ally of Ioannis Kolletis, too, was appointed in 1834 at the newly created Bureau of Public Economics. Ioannis Soutsos, the future professor of political economy at the University of Athens, was also part of the team. The functions of this Bureau were enormous, as it was envisaged to coordinate and provide funds for development projects that would lead to the economy taking off. Its budget, however, was extremely slim, and this involved dependence on regent Armansberg for their daily work. The Bureau tried to solve the question of individual land property. D'Eichtal's idea was that the land should be distributed to Greek fighters, but also to foreign investors who would settle in the country. The application of his plan opposed the plans of Armansberg, who condemned the preaching of Saint-Simonian beliefs. He diminished the budget of the Bureau, no personnel to assist its activities was hired, and it was led into an impasse. The law on the endowment of 1835 gave property rights to a limited number of fighters, and the whole process stopped for political reasons, namely, the alliance between the Regency and Greek tax collectors. The efforts to create a land register were abandoned.

In an autobiographical book, d'Eichtal described the Greek economy, the disasters of the 1820s (D'Eichtal 1974, 28), and the undue borrowing of the residents of Athens following a decade of armed struggle. He described the plan to transfer settlers to Greece as a foundation of an alliance between France and England on the Eastern Question in general (45). Following the abolition of the Poor Laws in England in 1834, he expected that many of the British poor, no longer supported by public help in their own country, would accept to come to Greece. D'Eichtal planned for them to settle in the regions of Elia and Messenia (46), but he admitted that "the introduction of foreign settlements in Greece is difficult." "Greeks do not love foreigners," he said (69). At the same time, he condemned the still ongoing plundering of monasteries, stressing that the Ottomans had respected the latter and yet they were disdained/trespassed by the Bavarians (75). He was impressed by the alternate cultivation of fine plots of land by peasants, instead of the use of dung as fertilizer, despite its existence (71). This proved the ignorance of farmers on important matters for them. He was also astonished when he saw the sick being read the Bible by a priest to recover, instead of receiving medical care (85). Which nation ever happened to be in the situation of Greece, he wondered (81), and he stood for the provision of all kinds of help to it.

The attempt of the Saint-Simonians to "export" their ideology to Greece failed. D'Eichtal himself, upon returning to France after 1836, became a pioneer in the advancement of Greek-French relations until his death.

2.2 Economy and Society (1833–62)

As already mentioned, the Great Powers named Bavarian Prince Otto von Wittelsbach King of Greece in 1833, guaranteeing at the same time a loan of 60,000,000 gold francs to be handed out to the Bavarians in three installments. As Otto was still a minor, a Regency took over until 1837, granting him access to unlimited power then. In 1843 his government declared official bankruptcy since it couldn't service the first two installments of the loan.[4] Otto was forced after an uprising to grant a constitution in 1844 that gave the voting privilege to all male Greeks. Despite this commitment, Otto continued his absolutist way of governing. In the 1850s he distanced himself from Britain and France, came closer to Russia, and openly espoused the Megali Idea. During the Crimean War, Britain and France blocked the harbor of Piraeus for three years to avert any Greek involvement in the conflict against the Turks (Kofas 1981). Thereafter, a Financial Commission was set up to investigate the ability of Greece to repay the loan to the Great Powers. Otto's throne was shaken, and he was terminated by both the Greeks and the Great Powers as the country's leader in 1862.[5] He was succeeded by King George I of the Danish house of Glücksburg in 1864. A new constitution of "crowned democracy" was passed upon George's arrival, making provisions for a unicameral parliamentary system.

To understand the environment in which the Greek economists of the time developed their ideas, it is necessary to recall that when Greece became a nation-state, the country had only 600,000 inhabitants of which over 90% were illiterate. Greece was, in today's terminology, a fragile state. The period until 1862 is considered as one of very modest economic progress (Soutsos 1861). It nourished, however, the preconditions for a moderate economic take-off, that started after 1864 and lasted until the end of the century. It also witnessed the publication of some remarkable books on economic topics.

During Otto's time and beyond, the economy was mainly agricultural. Only 20% of peasants were given property rights in 1835 through a bidding process that excluded the poor peasants (Vergopoulos 1975). Out of 120,000 families working as peasants, only 20,000 were proprietors. There were bigger and smaller landlords, and the government, having inherited Ottoman property, was a big landowner too. A continuous political strife was being fought around land distribution to the peasants (McGrew 1985).

Taxation was also an issue of great political relevance. As early as 1856, the Minister of Finance Alexandros Kondostavlos had conceded that "the tax system is anomalous" and blamed an inefficient administration for "delays" that resulted in far lower tax revenue than the projected level.[6] Politician Alexandros Koumoundouros, speaking in 1857, claimed that the tax system "contained elements in open contradiction with the principles of our country."[7] The tax system could be transformed for the better, if public land were to be distributed to peasants after the establishment of its true value through a land register. This would enable the government to calculate taxes on a realistic basis and not on arbitrary assumptions. Despite these sound proposals, nothing happened.

In the meantime, industry couldn't take off despite some privileges awarded to merchant-industrialists. In 1867, there existed only 24 industrial units in the country with only 331 HP (Agriantoni 1986, 417). Economic policy towards industrialization was liberal indeed. When in 1837 a committee for the encouragement of Greek industry was called into life, its statutes declared that "under no circumstances will the production of a good be encouraged if it is going to be more expensive than a foreign product of the same quality" (Psalidopoulos 1994, 17). The Briton Ricardo prevailed over the German List, despite Bavarians being so familiar with the latter.

Because of the lack of government funds, little happened for infrastructure. Between 1828 and 1852, only 165 km of roads were built, that is, less than 7 km per year. Money was scarce, and interest rates were as high as 40% for loans for the acquisition of grain (Evelpidis 1952). Tariffs for imported goods remained low after their imposition by Kapodistrias in 1830, and the system was reformed in 1857, focusing on revenue rather than protection of national business interests. In short, political power remained oligarchic. Between 1833 and 1853, Otto installed 39 different Prime Ministers, and his kingdom did not evolve into a modern civil state.

2.3 Cameralism in Practice

Any dissemination of ideas associated with French-borne economic liberalism until 1833 receded with the imposition of Bavarian rule in Greece.[8]

The Regency led by Armansperg, von Maurer, and von Heideck held sway from 1833 to 1837. Despite access to valuable data collected by Thiersch, their economic policy did not reflect this knowledge. Instead, Greece experienced the imposition of German cameralism, the administrative approach that flourished in German states during that period.[9] Cameralism was less a comprehensive economic theory and more an administrative practice geared toward securing resources and revenue for the ruling authority.

Cameralists, working closely with monarchs, acted as financial managers and bureaucrats, sometimes at the expense of other economic players. This approach took root in Greece and receded after 1862. However, its legacy endured – an administrative method of tackling economic challenges with little regard for economic theory.

2.3.1 Regents

During the Regency's tenure, the primary focus was on maintaining law and order, overshadowing economic development. Funds from the loans of the Great Powers were spent to establish a Bavarian monarch guard rather than bolstering the nation's economy. Land distribution remained restricted, no land register was drafted, and taxation continued to take place through tax collectors and, most importantly, not in money, but in kind. This solidified a political alliance between the throne and landlords.

Among the Regency figures, Armansperg emerged as a central player. Maurer, who fell into disrepute and later left, criticized the lack of economic progress under Armansperg (Maurer 1976, 344–58 and 585–605). Armansperg, a supporter of the Zollverein in Bavaria, but lacking protectionist plans for the Greek economy, survived thanks to his ability to bridge British interests with the priorities of the Regency (see Pipinelis 1932, 192–3).

The Regency focused on building a new army and a gendarmerie. Their efforts to shape the state led to the introduction of various laws and institutions: a Penal Code and a Procedural Law were introduced, a Statute of the Courts of Justice and Notary Offices were set up, and the Council of State was founded. In a further step and in accordance with decisions of the first assembly of the Greeks in Epidavros, the six-volume codex *Hexabiblos* of Armenopoulos, dating back to the Byzantine days, was fully reintroduced in the legal order. This was practically a backward-looking step, as it didn't have customary law as practiced among transactors as a basis. Elements of the existing French commercial code were also included in the existing legal edifice, making the whole legal system a complicated mix of temporary and very old procedures.

A new currency, the drachma, was introduced, related to gold and silver, but there was no effort to elevate it to a legal means of exchange. This clearly points to the cameralist approach of a top-down establishment of structures for the exercise of centralized political power and societal control without care for implementation. Herder's romantic nationalism and the need for the safety and domination of the king underpinned his "model kingdom" (Skopetea 1988).

The Regency shaped policies for the immediate present focusing on administrative/organizational matters. It was short-sighted. In the economic sector, no breakthrough action was taken. The Bureau of Public Economics was incapacitated before it could start delivering. No Regency accountability ever took place, nor did it look after the future. Tax revenues remained stuck at around 12.5 million drachmas per year and expenses were also stable at around 14 million drachmas (About 1855, 202). State deficits steadily increased and were partially covered by the Great Powers loan, a fact that led French author Edmond About to the famous statement that Greece "lives under full bankruptcy since the day it was born" (About 1855, 200). He also provided insights about the paradoxical situation of Greek public finance consisting of a planned and an administrative budget, without any concern for convergence between their respective figures. Strong (1842) confirmed the fiscal imbalances in Greece and provided further evidence in line with the one cited by About.

2.3.2 Otto

Otto, or Othon in Greek, had Christian August Banfield, professor of philosophy in Copenhagen, Berlin and finally Bonn (on him see Collison-Black 1987, 182) as his tutor when he was a young monarch, but it doesn't seem like he learned much economics from him. He was absorbed by party politics. A fierce political struggle between the autochthons (the native Greeks) and heterochthons (the Greeks whose origins were outside the borders of the Kingdom) over the possession of political offices shadowed political, as well as social, life. King Otto tried to manipulate these conflicts for his own benefit, but this kind of politics turned out to be ineffective since it cultivated feelings of resentment from both sides that ultimately called his tenure into question.

The attempts of the King to impose the drachma as a lawfully circulating currency were kickstarted in 1842, with the creation of the National Bank of Greece(NBG) (Stassinopoulos 2000). In the course of time, interest rates fell from 30% to 12–15%, but remained as high as 40% for acquiring seed for cultivation. The whole plan was beset by challenges arising from the limited understanding of monetary principles. In breach with every European practice, drachma coinage saw the coins incorporating 100% of the precious metal, meaning no seigniorage was included, so they disappeared from circulation. This had further adverse consequences for the monetization of the economy. Thereafter, and instead of changing this policy, drachmas were no longer coined. Ultimately, this monetary anarchy and undermining of exchanges was terminated after many decades of NBG action. The relevant discussion in the Senate in 1845 is revealing of the senators' ignorance of the fundamental principles of monetary policy (Psalidopoulos 2010). As a result, Spanish doubloons, Austrian thalers and "zwanzig," and Mexican piastres were circulating among traders, adding to currency anarchy and the undermining of exchanges. The fiscal system remained the one inherited from the regents, and public revenue remained at the same levels for years.

The year 1842 was a year of economic downturn and speculative actions by financiers Paramithiotis and Wright. In this impasse, the need for the third installment of the loan from the Great Powers was substantial, but a decision on their part to disburse was not forthcoming. Before proceeding to this step, the Powers demanded a detailed agreement on the repayment of the first two installments. They also demanded the creation of a committee on public savings that would possibly suggest expenditure cuts. In this setting, Otto's government stopped repaying the loan to the Great Powers, declaring thus bankruptcy. This act caused resentment in London and Paris, but not a catastrophe for the finances of the Great Powers.

The Bureau of Public Economics was not reactivated by Otto. Trade agreements with various European countries were sealed. The organization of tariff houses was slightly improved. A cotton mill from Vienna was imported to assist efforts to produce clothing, explorations about minting in the Lavrion region were introduced, and initial investigations/efforts to dry watered surfaces in Kopais were undertaken.

The still unresolved domestic economic problems found a substitute in foreign policy issues. Instead of economic progress and development, Otto based his political survival on the possibility of expanding the borders of his model kingdom. However, this policy lacked political rationalism and an agreement between Otto and the Powers. The latter didn't want to see the Ottoman Empire dissolve in a way that could threaten their national interests in the region and the existing international world order.

Before and during the Crimean War in the 1850s, Otto sided, as already mentioned, openly with the Russians, thus provoking an economic blockade of Greece under the pretext that Greece didn't serve its public debt. After its end, a Financial Control Committee was forced upon Greece to investigate the "right" amount of a yearly repayment of the Loans of Independence. The amount proved to be quite modest, just 800,000 drs per year, but the whole process was seen by the citizens as a humiliation for Greece and the issue shortened Otto's stay in the throne (Laskaridis & Syrmaloglou 2019).

2.4 "Greek Economics" Is Born

2.4.1 Greek Cameralists

The legislative industriousness of the Regency established a tradition, followed by Otto and his favored Greek administrators. Many of the Greeks who occupied public offices had been educated in Bavaria from 1826 onward. In his exceptional study, Konstantinos Kotsowilis (1995) lists 98 students in Munich between 1826 and 1844, 14 of whom obtained a PhD. These students returned to join the Greek public administration, disseminating the spirit of German cameralism within Greek administrative practice. The most prominent of these (on economic affairs) included the translator of Droz Anastasios Polyzoidis, NBG Governor, and prominent politician Pavlos Kalligas, Konstantinos Dosios, and Stamatios Proios.

In other words, the groundwork laid by the regents and the mentality of governing by means of legal provisions imposed on households and businesses was not contested. It was incorporated by Otto and his administration by the Greeks, the result being anything but an economic take-off for the country. On the other hand, neither did it lead to a backsliding. The country kept up the same tortuous and protracted pace towards development, maintaining a semi-feudal social structure, saving economic development and progress for an undefined future when the expected national integration would be complete.

2.4.2 Palaiologos

During the first decade of Bavarian cameralism, books started to be published touching upon economic topics. They all shared a practical approach in their discourse, while avoiding theoretical and philosophical arguments. In 1833, the first such textbook by a Greek appeared. It was Gregorios Palaiologos who wrote *Agricultural and Household Economics*. The book was meant to educate the literate among the Greek peasants and serve as a textbook at the newly established agricultural school for the education of Greek farmers in Tiryns in the Peloponnese. A second, more applied and practical volume of the book was published in Athens in 1835. In his report to the Regents on "Agriculture and Industry," Palaiologos started from the fact of a very low level of commercial activities in the country due to the industry being nonexistent and agriculture still in an embryonic state. The country was thus forced to buy foreign products to serve its needs and, worst of all, the money to acquire them came from borrowing and not from exports. The creation of many national farms for the education of peasants and of a factory producing equipment needed for cultivation were, for Palaiologos, indispensable. Better education and improvement of techniques were of paramount importance. A committee to steer the whole process was recommended by him with a focus on agriculture. Industry would enter the scene later, for Palaiologos, for the processing of agricultural raw materials and products.

Other books of a "practical" nature followed. First in line was *Wealth* (1837), an anonymous 32-page pamphlet of combined lessons in geography, history, and science applied to trade, the arts, and industrial occupations. Georgios Mavrokordatos (1838) compiled a volume of laws governing Greek Commerce, and so did Konstantinos Platis (1840). Nikolaos Vryonis published two books about shipping and the science of shipping, respectively (1831 and 1839). Two other authors, Konstantinos Melas (1848) and Georgios Naftis (2 vols, 1859 and 1860), wrote about commerce and principles governing the business of trade. Finally, Sergios Raftanis (1853) offered traders a manual that computed easily interest rates and thus assisted commercial decisions.

These books covered all fields of economic activity. They reproduced practical knowledge, indicating at the same time the necessity of an interested public for self-education and the need to approach empirical activities with some basic "authority knowledge" about running a business.

On the popularization front, Georgios Polimeris with his two books promoting Benjamin Franklin's contributions is worth mentioning. The first book (1839) was published anonymously and consisted of biographies of Benjamin Franklin and

Adamantios Korais. It also included some quotes from *Poor Richard's Almanac* for Greek juniors. The second one (1849) was a more extended version of *The Way to Wealth*, advancing the values of thrift and saving and stressing the need for the individual to work to avoid destitution and poverty. Franklin followed William Petty and stressed that the origins of wealth were set in labor and hours worked, thus signaling to youngsters the need to enter the labor market to become prosperous (Theocarakis 2018).

Another book that received attention during this period was the textbook by Pierre-Henry Suzanne, *Principes Généraux d'Économie Publique et Industrielle* (1849). It was written in the form of conversations between a father and son. The author, a professor of mathematics and not an economist, reproduced in an elementary fashion what was at that time basic knowledge in France about the reality of economic life. A total of 168 citizens had subscribed to buy the book. King Otto bought 40 copies and another 20 were purchased by the Ministry of Education. Suzanne's dialogues didn't delve into theoretical issues. They started with work, pleasure, and sacrifice to achieve goals, and moved to production, expenses involved with it and how to keep them at bay. The pricing of goods was discussed with emphasis on practicalities. How to set up a business, its location and bookkeeping were also analyzed. Thrift and the avoidance of luxury were said to be essential for a profitable business. The book was full of anecdotal suggestions that even included ways to make animals bulkier and more capable to assist cultivation (128).

2.4.3 Senior in Greece

In 1857, Nassau Senior, the classical economist, visited Greece and Turkey (Senior 1859). In his diary, he confessed that he wanted to study the economic backwardness of these countries and the reasons behind it. He painted a bleak outlook for Greece, were King Otto to remain in power based on what he saw and on the results of 24 interviews he conducted in Athens – 14 with British citizens and 10 with Greeks. Senior found the country's infrastructure in a primitive condition; the enforcement of law and order in the countryside was, for him, inadequate; the tax system unjust, and the new tariff system of 1857 hurt businessmen involved in import trade. To top it all, Otto's governments had been incapable of balancing the budget. Senior described a country in agony. He saw wealth wanting to get transformed into capital, possibilities for future growth, he stressed however the obstacles underlying this process. These had to do with an administration giving privileges and monopolies to whomever the King and the governing administration pleased. Political offices were breeding houses of corruption and, unfortunately, citizens could not change this situation. They tried to solve their problems with personal intermediation with authorities instead of political action. The Church was following the typical ritual instead of turning the Christian word into social practice. Those who couldn't survive under the rule of the king became brigands.

On the economic front, Senior criticized the lack of infrastructure because it raised transport costs and prices. He learned with surprise that the license to supply

Athens with water was not given because the king couldn't find somebody he could entrust with this profitable business. Similar backward conditions prevailed in the tax system and agriculture was not given high economic priority. These facts were, for Senior reasons of future concern. He noticed that Greeks were not rich, but neither were they destitute and this was a reason for optimism. On the other hand, the lack of reforms could lead to a political explosion. The political developments that Senior prophesied occurred a couple of years after his return to Britain.

2.4.4 Economics at the Ionian Academy

The Ionian islands were, as of 1815 part of the British Empire (Gekas 2016). Feudal relations prevailed in these islands, which had undergone periods of Italian, Ottoman, and French rule. Liberalism was a driving force for intellectuals to demand self-determination and unification with Greece. Moderate and radical Ionian Greeks fought toward this goal, which finally materialized in 1864 (Alysandratos 2006).

The Ionian Academy was the first Greek University established in 1827 in Corfu. Its purpose was to educate the Ionian Greeks in Law, Theology, Medicine, and Philosophy. Economics was not entirely missing from the curriculum, but it did not have a specialist to teach it.

The person who taught some economics and produced a short theoretical treatise on the topic in 1846 was philosopher (and later politician) Petros Vrailas-Armenis, with his *On the Subject and the Limits of Political Economy*. For Vrailas-Armenis, economics as a new science did not possess universally accepted limits and a clearly defined subject of study. It dealt with man not as a moral and thinking subject, but as a materialistic one, suffering pain and welcoming pleasure, striving through work toward utility. Individual utilities were added up to produce social utility, and it was through industrial works that social utility was maximized. This Benthamite approach, if combined with intellectual and moral considerations, led to wisdom and synthesis. Economics was, after all, the science of social wealth, but wealth had, for Vrailas-Armenis, to be first defined in a universally acceptable way. Wealth consisted of many things that had value in use and exchange value. Scientists, judges, philosophers, and other similar professions contributed to a wealthier society indirectly, but the production of wealth was the production of goods and services, and therefore economics dealt with whatever was useful and satisfied the material needs of the people.

Having accepted the principle of productive labor, Vrailas-Armenis indirectly moved on to express Saint-Simonian views and called for government attention to industry. He used Saint-Simons' parable and depicted society as nonexistent if there was no industry. Culture by itself could not thrive in a country, and intellectuals with their ideas and politicians with their plans could not make citizens happy. Industrialists were needed to make a country prosperous. Vrailas-Armenis was thus expressing hope that the wealth possessed by Greeks would somehow find its way to get invested in industry. However, this would materialize gradually and not by government order.

Another professor who was assigned to lecture on economics 15 years later was Othon Pylarinos, a professor of Roman law. In his 1860 introductory speech *Inaugural Lecture in Social Economics,* he defined his task as an "investigation of man in all his phases of social development" (4). In ancient times there were nations scared of wealth, he claimed, and the development of many economies was often slowed down by mistakes of economists and politicians. In modern times, he continued, wealth was the goal of societies and religious beliefs shouldn't interfere with business decisions.

Pylarinos started his historical investigation of economic doctrines from St. Simon and Fourier and stressed that they were both against human idleness, but also against the inheritance of fortunes (10). Smith and Quesnay were also important for their economic creed and the definition of it as an economic moving force. Another important economist quoted was Say with his overall optimism about the economic future of nations if private property was allowed to thrive.

Pylarinos drew the attention of his students to developments in Italy and in Germany and believed that the study of economic thought in these countries would be of value when analyzing Greece's economic problems (13). In Greece, and due to Ottoman serfdom, there was a disdain for work by laymen and nobles and an infantile situation with machines (13). However, the situation was improving steadily, social interests were in harmony (28), and private freedom, equality, and world peace were guarantees for economic progress (22). Moving on to politics, he defined the Eastern question as an economic one (25). The Powers wanted not to see their economic interests harmed were the Ottoman Empire to dissolve. The last part of his lecture was devoted to methodology. He defined the historical approach as the best way to learn economics (31). This method "leads to an infallible road" (32), and only with its assistance could questions such as the protection of industry, laws against luxury, and abundance or shortage of currency be discussed. The relation between Labor and Capital should also be approached through the historical method and practical solutions should be applied to all economic problems.

After the Ionian islands became part of Greece, Pylarinos was transferred as a professor to the University of Athens, but he resigned after two years and didn't continue his investigations in economics.

2.5 Ioannis Soutsos: From Constitutional Discourse to Economic Liberalism

Ioannis Soutsos, a central figure in Greek academic life during the 19th century, emerged as the most prominent advocate of economic liberalism (Kountouris 1998; Ithakissios 1992; Psalidopoulos & Stassinopoulos 2009). He held the sole academic position in political economy in Greece from 1837 to 1890 and exerted his influence through teaching, writing, and active involvement in various facets of Greek society. His aristocratic background, liberal ideals, and French influences shaped his contributions to economics in Greece.

Born in Constantinople in 1804 to a notable Phanariot Greek family, Soutsos was immersed in an environment of political and diplomatic activity (Goudas

1874, 153–81). His father was named ruler of Moldavia for a brief period in 1802 and his brother, Nicolaos Soutsos [Sutu], served as prince in Romania, developed a Romanian social consciousness, and is regarded as a major figure in economic liberalism and a popularizer of classical economics in that country. After receiving private education in Constantinople and Bucharest, Soutsos embarked on a journey of self-education. At the age of 19, he read and translated Say's *Treatise on Political Economy* in the process of his self-education as an economist (Sklavenitis 1994). He studied in Geneva close to Pellegrino Rossi. In 1832, he moved on to Paris and attended courses at the College de France, during the last year of Jean Baptiste Say's tenure there. No hard evidence exists on whether he attended Say's courses.

Upon settling in Greece in 1833, he was appointed as a judge at the Council of the State. In this capacity, he helped draft laws and contributed to the creation of the legal foundations of Greece. He was also briefly active in the Bureau for Public Economics during D'Eichtal's tenure. When the University of Athens (named then as Othonian University) was founded in 1837, he was appointed an honorary professor and, from 1842, at the age of 38, a full professor of "public economics." From 1859 to 1864, he returned as a director at the briefly reactivated Bureau for Public Economics and later to the Council of the State.

In 1867, he was appointed as a full professor of "political economy" and remained active in teaching until his death in 1890. He also served as a member of the Committee for the Encouragement of Greek Industry, as a consultant to the NBG, as a rector of the University of Athens (1847–8), and as an expert in parliamentary committees. His participation in the committee for the taxation of agricultural production in the early 1880s was very instrumental. He also contributed to the organization and implementation of the population census in Greece in 1861. In a country where university life was highly affected by everyday politics and widespread sympathies were rare, Soutsos succeeded in remaining very popular. His 50th anniversary as an academic, in 1887, was celebrated enthusiastically by colleagues, students, and graduates, but unfortunately, his legacy was forgotten after his passing.

Soutsos was a prolific writer. He started publishing in 1843 when he proposed (much to his credit, alone, in an absolutist environment) the adoption of a draft constitution that was based on the supremacy of civil society and economic liberties.[10] From 1847 onward, Soutsos concentrated on economic works which elevated him to a beacon of economic liberalism in Greece. His economic ideas evolved over many years. It took him almost 14 years after his first appointment to produce *A Treatise on the Production and Distribution of Wealth* (1851). This was followed by *An Essay on Economic Reforms* (1863), a *Textbook of Public Finance or Theory of the Budget* (1864), and then, his two-volume magnum opus, *Plutology* (1868–69). Soutsos also wrote other policy-oriented books and articles. As we will see, he arrived at theory after having dealt intensively with practical issues. For this reason, we will approach his contributions as they were articulated over time.

2.5.1 Constitution

Against the background mentioned above, Soutsos made his first intervention in the public sphere, publishing his proposal for the new constitution (Soutsos 1843). This was a courageous step from a conscious citizen. His draft drew heavily from the French and the Belgian constitutions and was meant to serve as a platform for discussion in the national assembly. He offered 70 articles, as well as three additional clauses accompanied by comments and arguments.

Equality before the law was of paramount importance to Soutsos. Privileges of persons, associations, or monopolies were incompatible with equality and should be abolished. The institution of private property should form the basis of economic life and be guaranteed. Possible expropriations were permitted for Soutsos if the public benefit stemming from nationalization had been proven first, and second, if the property owner had been compensated for the loss they suffered (10). Without the fulfillment of these two criteria, properties would become "the loot of the mighty" (10), he stressed.

He suggested a constitutional monarchy where respect for personal freedoms and of political and economic rights for everyone would be the basic rules (7). The transition to democratic rule should, according to him, be gradual, a sign of his cautiousness and conservatism. In his words, "as far as legislation is concerned … we should proceed slowly" (35). He identified the chief impediment to economic progress as the inadequate assignment of property rights to the peasants (10). The extensive possession of landed property by the state deprived resources from private initiative. Without secure property rights, he continued, private property "falls prey to the stronger, and the laborious energy is seriously damaged" (57). His proposal was passed in the constitution, but without a time plan for implementation, which delayed land reform until 1871.

The central administration should impose accountability on local communities to "put an end to the scandalous management of municipal resources" (57). He proposed that taxation should be decided by parliament and that the central government ought to be limited. In his words, "the number, the division and the interrelations of ministries should be arranged by law, and not arbitrarily" (14). These proposals found a place in the new constitution but in practice they were bypassed through many special laws that later governments enacted (Dertilis 1951, 357).

Soutsos considered the publicity of court proceedings as crucial for the impartiality of the judges and the judicial system. He also insisted on the publicity of discussions in both Chambers as prerequisites for control of members of parliament (27–28). An important section of Soutsos' draft consisted of the issue of the establishment of two Chambers (Senate and Chamber of Deputies) (32–47). He was a fervent supporter of the existence of two Chambers, as long as they "ensured the society for the most reasonable and advantageous conduct of laws" (35). The existence of only one parliament meant that the constitution might face hazards. A Senate should have as a mission to balance the power between the King and the Chamber of Deputies (39). The democratic legality of both chambers was one of the most frequently debated themes at the national congress (Petropulos 1968,

493–95). It was without doubt for Soutsos that Senators should be elected, and the King should not have the right to nominate and appoint whomever he pleased (43). His proposal on this issue did not find its place in the constitution, which gave the King the authority to appoint the members of the Senate he chose and grant them lifelong tenure (Article 70; cf. Svolos 1972, 120). In the following years the Senate did not fulfill its constitutional function and vindicated Soutsos' fears. The chamber was dissolved after Otto's abdication.

The constitution of 1844 was a compromise between the ruling elite and the king. The proposals made by Soutsos were only partly accepted, and the political situation in the country did not change for the better. The King, despite his oath to respect the new constitution, continued his absolutist way of governing, and public resources were not spent on productive expenses.

2.5.2 Soutsos and the Megali Idea

Soutsos was, as almost all Greek intellectuals, a supporter of the Megali Idea. In 1853, at the onset of the Crimean War, he fervently refuted a study/proposal by an anonymous author, suggesting a coalition government of Ottomans and Greeks instead of achieving the goal of the Megali Idea. In his 1853 *Reply of a Greek to an Easterner*, Soutsos was particularly critical of the appeasing policy of the Anglo-French towards the Ottomans and stressed that the institutions of Turkish absolutism were not compatible with those of European countries and of Greece.[11] The goals and aspirations of Greece as a civilized country could not endure coexistence with the Ottoman Empire. The Megali Idea was a noble cause. In his meetings with the classical economist Nassau Senior (1859, 351), he precisely defined the faults and errors of economic policymakers in taxation and monetary issues, while expressing optimism for the years to come. Total independence from the Ottoman Empire was instrumental in achieving Greek economic take-off.

2.5.3 **A Treatise on Production and Distribution of Wealth**

Fifteen years after his first appointment as a university professor, Soutsos published a 480-page study titled *A Treatise on Production and Distribution of Wealth* (1851). This study was an optimistic call to transform economic knowledge into human practice and reach prosperity.

For Soutsos, Political economy had both a direct and an indirect objective as a science. It dealt with the creation and growth of wealth on the one hand, and the inclusive development of all productive classes and forces on the other (κδ). Industrial improvement and political liberation led nations to an unprecedented prosperity; therefore, economics needed to be introduced as a science in society to analyze present economic conditions and point to reforms needed for future growth (11). Political economy was a mixed, dynamic, and experimental science that investigated all phenomena in society that were relevant from the point of view of economic utility and the full satisfaction of human needs. Soutsos argued that liberal principles should operate within a constitutional society and that "in practice, the application of these absolute theories is suspended or altered by the elements of nationality, time, distance etc." (1851, 3; see also his 1882, 12). He also believed that "we have to consider these elements, and not claim the direct application of unconditional principles" (1851, 4).

He proceeded to discuss value in use and value in exchange and concluded that supply and demand determined, for each given time and space, the valuation of commodities at a rate that reflected scarcity, tastes of consumers, and availability (228–36). Utility was determined under the influence of social circumstances. Ricardo and his law of productive expenses offered an alternative way for Soutsos to approach price determination, but this approach had, for him, the disadvantage of not being able to explain short-term changes in value and prices (440–42). Soutsos also distanced himself from Sismondi and the view of the latter about the negative effects of technological improvements on employment. Indeed, he focused on the short term both for price determination and the distribution of income (29). This led him to see land rent as the difference between the market price of agricultural products and the cost of their production. On profit, he didn't engage in any discussion about income shares being claimed by landowners and capitalists and didn't mention the possibility that industrial profit might have a declining tendency due to competition.

Wealth had different meanings among economists: It was the affluence of useful commodities, the saved stock of future production processes, the creations of human labor, and finally, the creation of values of exchange for human transactions. Production referred, for Soutsos, to both commodities and services, and money was defined as the means that made the result of the production process possible (36–52).

The part devoted to production started with a chapter about agriculture in different modes of production. Then came labor as a factor of production, and even if Soutsos quoted Adam Smith and his definition of productive labor, he remarked that labor could either produce goods or offer services (137–50). In any case, the division of labor was proclaimed as the process that guaranteed the efficient use of capital. A discussion about thrift and luxury followed, with Soutsos indicating a middle way of sailing between these two extremes. Returning to agriculture, Soutsos quoted extensively the French discussion and the contribution of Hippolyte Passy about its importance and underlined the need for big farms for best production results (215–28).

Exchange was a distinct concept and not to be identified with trade. Exchange presupposed the use of money, and this instrument ensured that short-term deviations between supply and demand could be overcome (230–36). The functions of money were discussed, including its velocity and advantages in international transactions. Then came an analysis of credit and, more extensively, of the banking system, in its different forms and functions (271–343).

The last chapter of this section was devoted to population issues. Malthus was discussed and given credit for his theory, but Soutsos regarded that his approach faced its limits in human behavior. Poverty was not the result of overpopulation. Human experience proved that raised living standards prolonged the duration of life; therefore, sexual self-restraint was not necessary if the economy would continue to grow (345–89).

The paragraph about the distribution of income started with the views of Nassau Senior and Pelegrino Rossi on the topic. Wages differed, according to how easy or difficult/dangerous a job could be and could be distinguished into real/money or necessary/market-determined. According to differences in real situations, a different determination of wages could be computed, Soutsos argued.

Land rent was not an interest for the possession of landed property, nor was it a form of tax imposed by nature. Here, according to Soutsos, the physiocrats and Ricardo offered diverging explanations of its volume. Industrial profits were not proportional to the capital invested and depended on time, place, the needs of citizens, and external circumstances. Industrial capital once invested in means of production could not be easily transformed into other forms or become liquid again. The interests of the workers were not opposed to the interests of the industrialists (453–62). However, the fluctuation of wages reflected changes in industrial profits, and progress was registered in places and countries where the accumulation of wealth brought higher levels of prosperity.

In a concluding chapter, Soutsos juxtaposed the British class system with one where agriculture was not in the hands of an aristocracy. Using examples from past civilizations, he left the road open to prosperity for every country where the authorities would introduce all necessary reforms to adjust the economy to the high ideal of prosperity for all. In short, his approach was pre-classical and optimistic if the economic system were allowed to perform without government impositions (470–80).

2.5.4 Soutsos and Ricardo's Theory of Distribution

In 1861, in an article in *Journal des Economistes*, Soutsos explicitly rejected the theory of distribution by Ricardo as a clearly theoretical construction, incompatible with Greek empirical realities.

The aim of this article was to report to a French audience the economic development of Greece in the last 30 years. There was progress, Soutsos claimed, but not to the desired level. Scarcity of labor and capital didn't allow industry to gain ground. Interest rates were as high as 20%, he stressed (374). Agriculture suffered from the lack of property rights and infrastructures. Fertile lands distant to city or community centers were left uncultivated, and prices of cereals were determined by those of imported cereals from Odessa. Greek peasants cultivated land that had easy access to markets, provided that the cost of production was low (375). The agrarian population had no capital and mechanical forces employed in industry were nonexistent, a totally different situation from Britain. Therefore, peasants were "incapable to cultivate the most fertile land as it is in need of big advance payments" (375). Greece couldn't be compared with a developed European state; it could not profit from explanations given to economic issues by foreign economists, who were basing their models on their country's experience (376). Land rent was not determined in Greece as it was in other countries and since most peasants didn't have property rights, they could not profit from it and couldn't transform it into demand for industrial goods or any other use (380).

Soutsos went on to discuss trade, shipping, and the role of the government. Education was of paramount importance for the Greeks with the existing agronomical and commercial schools in need of expansion. Policies for the future should concentrate on expanding land property to peasants, improving infrastructure, lowering interest rates, better administering the nation, and finally avoiding policies that accommodated the administration and the tax collectors in daily economic transactions.

2.6 The Consequences of Cameralism: The Administrative Tradition

The main reason for the slow and shaky development of Greece until 1862 and beyond was the absence of capitalist-friendly economic reforms and the small area of the kingdom. Otto's tenure did not soften the social and economic hardships of the Greeks. The core principle of his rule was his consistency with the Megali Idea, which protected him from potential internal challenges. There was no planning for growth and increasing public resources. Dependence on the third installment of the loan granted by the Great Powers was absolute, paving the way for political extortion against the country.

Cameralism had, in the meantime, sealed the approach of Greek public service towards economic affairs. The economy was developing, as mentioned above, at a slow pace as part of an insufficient administrative practice. Cameralism did not inherit any bibliographic references of importance to Greece. There were no pamphlets, monographs, or written documents from the policymakers, except for Maurer. Cameralism was not introduced in the "Othonian University" as an academic discipline; it was just practice, and this dimension brings us to the distinction between "good" and "bad" cameralism, which Andre Wakefield made in his work (2012).

According to Wakefield, the good cameralist does not simply record and manage what already exists. Instead, he tries to improve and increase the stock of wealth, from which he is to draw revenue for his boss. He uses numbers and processes empirical data to reap the seeds of welfare, which he himself implants in the economy. He doesn't just manage losses but improves the sources of revenue. On the contrary, the bad cameralist simply manages what already exists, without fantasy or innovation in his daily routine. He secures his stay in the halls of the ruler by means of intrigues and flatteries.

For the reasons mentioned above, we consider the Greek case under Otto as an example of bad cameralism. It infused an administrative practice according to the short-term wishes of the sovereign and hindered action based on what economic theory suggested about the conduct of economic policy. This practice unfortunately continued after 1862.

Notes

1 On the Greek political system and its evolution, see Hering (1992).
2 Much later, Bentham's hedonism was to influence the neoclassical school through the work of W. S. Jevons. It is worth noting, however, that for Bentham, state legislation was

fundamental in achieving the highest possible degree of happiness for the citizens of a country, not the free market.

3 See references in Psalidopoulos (2013).

4 For the political scene of the decade 1833–43, see Petropulos (1968). For a discussion of developments in the Greek economy during the same period, see Petropulos (1981).

5 For a full description of the interchange between Otto and the Great Powers between 1830 and 1838, see Parish (1838).

6 See the Report on State Budget for the Financial Year of 1856.

7 See the Report on State Budget for the Financial Year of 1857.

8 For the political developments, see Pipinelis (1932), Turcynski (2009), and Schoenhaerl (2017), who cover the political, social, and financial developments during the whole 19th century.

9 See Small (1909), Seppel and Tribe (2017), Nokkala and Miller (2019), and Tribe (2017). Cf. Wakefield (2012).

10 Another publication on the same topic published in 1846 was a translation of *On the Constitutions of Free People* by Sismonde de Sismondi.

11 He devoted his introductory lectures at the University in 1853, 1854, 1858, and 1859 to the same subject. They were reproduced in the periodical Pandora.

3 The Age of French Economic Liberalism (1862–97)

3.1 Overview of Economic and Social Developments

After an interregnum of a constitutional assembly between 1862 and 1864, George I of Denmark was accepted as the new King of Greece. The Ionian Islands were given by the British to Greece as a "gift" and thus a first step toward the implementation of the Great Idea was registered. Several publications appeared in the same period dealing with economic issues

The power coalition between the new King and landlord/tax collectors' interests remained intact. Policies continued to be administered on an ad hoc basis without due respect for the postulates of political economy, and reforms were delayed. Growing expenditures were met with government loans from the NBG. Banks (and sociétés anonymes), due to their political weight, did not pay any taxes (until 1877). In general, the tax system retained most of its arbitrariness until 1880 when the tax on ploughing animals substituted the individual tax rate for Greek peasants on gross production from Ottoman times.

Universal male suffrage was explicitly introduced in the constitution of 1864,[1] while voting, despite the occasional complaints about the handling of procedures and results,[2] was acknowledged as the democratic means of solving political disputes. The political system remained fragile throughout the 19th century.[3] Traditional, pre-modern patterns of government were gradually abandoned over several decades.

Despite the political change and the foundation of a liberal constitution, the political situation, corruption, and inefficiency continued to dominate the administration and the public sphere (Carabott 1997). Even though the new political élite made extensive use of liberal rhetoric (Kitromilidis 1988, 13–15, 19), its practice in economic matters retained a blend of nepotism and localism (Legg 1969).

During the 1863–80 period, primary production contributed steadily over 70% of GDP, and the corresponding figure for the handicraft/industrial sector remained under 9%. Services provided 18% to 22% of GDP (Kostelenos 2003). Things however changed after 1879 with the incorporation of (the rich in agricultural resources) region of Thessaly in the Kingdom of Greece. In the same year, the settlement of the public debt took place and thus access to external finance during the times of the "age of capital" in Britain was achieved. The huge wave of public lending after 1880 and the introduction of a new tariff system in 1884 stirred the economy, led

DOI: 10.4324/9781315413419-4

to growth, but also to fiscal derailment, which brought Greece to bankruptcy in 1893. An International Financial Control was forced upon Greece in 1897, and the country entered, as we will see, a new era.

3.1.1 French Liberal Thought

This whole period coincided with the dominance of French economic liberalism in Greece (See the anthology of French economists offered by Leroux & Hart 2012). This was an outcome of friendly political relations and cultural bonds between Greece and France and the fact that Greek economists mostly cited their French counterparts, above all Paul Leroy Beaulieu and Michel Chevalier. Last but not least, the influence of Ioannis Soutsos was extremely important.

In the first half of the 19th century, liberalism still possessed many national characteristics. It was not a unified doctrine but rather fragmented and sectarian (for France, see Haney 1927, 600–8). The tradition of state authority from the times of absolutism was too strong in some European countries, and liberal politicians and intellectuals were initially too divided and weak to challenge absolutist thinking and practice on all fronts.

Continental European liberal economists followed different liberal creeds instead of British classical political economy. The works of Smith, Ricardo, and Mill were read and made an impact in the rest of Europe, but not everyone agreed with their methodology and analysis (Ruggiero 1927). British classical political economy was founded on a model based on three classes in society and favored productive labor and industry against landowning interests. It espoused the labor theory of value and a distribution of income analysis that was logically consistent, but at the same time, due to the wages fund doctrine, hard to defend politically in times of rising citizen consciousness. Therefore, French, German, and Italian economic liberalism around the middle of the 19th century differed from the British. So did Greek liberalism of the times.

All liberals in Europe were united in their dislike for arbitrary authority, defending individual freedom, and the need for free expression of views. Constitutionalism, economic liberalism, and utilitarianism mixed in different variations in these countries, whereas the plea for government noninterference and the push for enfranchisement was common in all (Plamenatz 1973, vol. 3, 36–61).

The father of French economic liberalism was Jean Baptiste Say. For Schumpeter, Say was a policy-oriented economist rather than a model builder. Methodologically, he was close to a non-naive empiricism and critical of Ricardo's deductive method (Schumpeter 1954, 492; see also Forget 1993; Poitier and Tiran 2003; Schoorl 2013). His successor at the College de France, Pellegrino Rossi, the mentor of Ioannnis Soutsos, on the other hand, was effective in teaching, a good expositor, made no scientific discoveries, had no doctrinal following, and his politics eluded his economics. His teaching was "diluted Ricardianism plus a little Say" (Schumpeter 1954, 511).

French economists adopted a practical approach in their analyses, avoiding the strict class approach of the British. Charles Dunoyer and Frederic Bastiat accepted the thrust of the results of classical political economy (for an overview see O'Brien 2004), but optimism in the place of the British stationary state plus the natural law tradition were present in their works, as well as in the publications of authors such as Michel Chevalier and Paul Leroy Beaulieu. These works were known to Greek economists and were adapted in the process of seeking explanations for the economic backwardness of the country.

The appeal of French economic thought in Greece started to wane after the French defeat in the Franco-Prussian War of 1870–1. Germany's rise to economic importance and political power set an example for latecomers in development in South-Eastern Europe. The older and the younger Historical School started attracting the attention of students and citizens in general (Grimmer-Solem & Romani 1999; Grimmer-Solem 2003). This process was gradual, and after 1897 the German Historical School (GHS) gained superior fame in Greece.

In the following subchapters, we will review the economic literature during the transition from King Otto to King George, starting with proposals advanced by Greek economists during the period of the inauguration of the new king. We will present exchanges in parliament about economic reforms in fiscal and monetary issues to demonstrate that parliamentarians were aware of what had to be done but couldn't find the majority to implement it. We will also examine the controversy over free trade and protection in the country. We will then explore the role of Ioannis Soutsos and other academic and non-academic economists of importance, such as Aristidis Economos, Nikolaos Gounarakis, and Ioannis Zografos. Finally, we will refer to the popularization of economics and to the early socialist and romantic critiques of economic and social developments.

3.2 Contributions to the Economic Future of Greece (1861–3)

A remarkable occurrence around the years of Otto's abdication was the publication of many books and pamphlets devoted to the question of the economic future for the country. After decades of relative silence, economists felt like intervening and making their voices heard. These authors were Diamantopoulos, Soutsos, Sotiropoulos, Trikaliotis, Chalikiopoulos, Vlachos, and Efmorfopoulos.

3.2.1 Diamantopoulos

Argyrios Diamantopoulos demanded the revamping of the existing tax system and taxation on net revenue (1861, 6). In his capacity as a parliamentarian, he stood for the creation of a land register regardless of how costly and difficult this could be. It was important from an economic point of view that the farmers could accumulate even small savings. These savings would enable them to invest in new equipment and thus, in the medium-term, production would grow. Another important reform should be, for Diamantopoulos, taxing net agricultural, and not gross income, as was the case. The existing situation was unbearable for him and the argument that his proposal meant the downsizing of state revenue was countered with a plea that the majority should understand how wealth is created. "Let us leave the productive forces of the nation inviolable, so that national wealth grows and with it, tax revenue" (12), he argued. The need for government revenue should not become an obstacle for private initiative and entrepreneurial plans.

3.2.2 Chalikiopoulos

Panagiotis Chalikiopoulos, a businessman, man of letters, and politician, wrote a two-volume *Thoughts about Greece* that was published in Athens in 1863. The book opened with the declaration that his interest concerned the state of agriculture in the country. Negative developments had to be identified and the question, "Where should the development of the country start?," answered by every concerned citizen (4).

Absolute monarchy had done nothing for the farming sector and until then constitutional monarchy didn't deliver either, due to political clientelism. Society was divided into two camps. On the one side there were the working-class people and the farmers who paid taxes, and on the other side the idle ones, men of leisure, united in groups and striving for the support of the government (7). Without agriculture, neither industry nor trade could flourish (11). Economic legislation was complex and the tax system antiquated (12). Shipping on the other hand was productive and could assist agricultural exports if these existed.

Greece needed, for Chalikiopoulos, a progressive government based on a new administrative organization. Unnecessary public personnel should be laid off and government expenditure should be channeled to infrastructure and education (18). With the incorporation of the Ionian Islands into Greece, what was needed was new legislation based on their unity with mainland Greece instead of keeping two separate legal foundations, because some vested interests thought it appropriate (20). The lack of an agricultural bank and the neglect of the NBG to assist farmers gave space to usurers, who exploited the peasants, while at the same time the usurers entertained close connections to the governing elites.

In the second volume of his treatise, he repeated similar arguments in a more extensive manner: Greece was poor because the government, due to its inability to repay its loans, didn't possess public creditworthiness, had no capital to invest, and was totally passive from an economic point of view. Because of the lack of widespread private property, of accumulated capital, and of the ignorance of both the governed and the governing, bad laws were in effect, and the regrettable outcome was stagnation (16).

A new loan to repay the old and start anew was a possibility, if the repayment rate could be fixed at 1 million drachmas (drs) per year (28). On the other hand, Chalikiopoulos was afraid that the current administration could not hold spending below revenue. It would be tempted, according to him, to spend any consolidation loan on consumption. Development should start from the primary sector and farming should follow scientific advice (29). The deficit in the balance of trade and the importation of foodstuffs was proof of any existing grave problem (31–2). Greece, a coastal country, lacked proper transport means and ports. "Greece resembles a piece of unclean and unshaped metal," he concluded (32).

For Chalikiopoulos, it was necessary to maintain currants, cotton, silk, and olive oil as primary activities (38), as well as to create an agricultural bank. That bank would lower interest rates (47) and ought to be private because of possible corruption and political scandals if it were public (45). With insistence and rigor, he stressed the need for private property in agriculture (48–57). If peasants didn't own their land, there was no motive to improve cultivation and production. The wealth creator was not the community, but the individual, he stressed. Governments "shouldn't interfere in things like agriculture, industry, and trade" (52), according to his words. There was, however, a need for a ministry of agriculture that would gather and spread useful information among the farmers and assist them in their daily activity (63). The government should always think twice before public expenditure. Why should citizens pay taxes, if they didn't get back anything in return, he asked? (60). Challenging the supporters of the Megali Idea, he stressed that "if we want a big fatherland, we need to master the smaller one" (61).

Chalikiopoulos called Otto's government "a bloodsucker" (69) and was sad to state that taxation in Greece was still Turkish. Citing Emile de Laveleye, he claimed that Greeks paid higher taxes per capita than the English or the French (82). He also quoted Adam Smith and the latter's remark that increased trade between the provinces and the cities was a sign of economic growth. A land register was a top priority but not an excuse for the postponement of the introduction of a better tax system.

Education, finally, was above all, and progress in the country without better education was impossible. The abdication of Otto should be the starting point of reforms that would help the economy take off (88–91). Unfortunately, his hope that times of reforms had entered the stage was premature, and the influence of this well-grounded proposal remained limited (Syrmaloglou 2016, 39–49). Two decades later, he was sad to admit that little progress had been made toward what he had recommended in the past (Chalikiopoulos 1880).

3.2.3 Sotiropoulos

Sotirios Sotiropoulos was a civil servant before becoming a parliamentarian in 1863, a Minister of Finance, and Ultimately a Prime Minister in 1893. He wrote extensively on Greek agriculture and taxation.

His study on land taxation was published in Athens in 1861 and was divided into three parts. In the first, Sotiropoulos described the land tax system in its actual situation. Right from the beginning, Sotiropoulos distinguished enlightened (27–30) from ignorant agriculture (31–50), the first reaching out to science and improvements and the latter staying stuck in the past in terms of food supply and taxation. Subsequent chapters dealt with the state of various agricultural products, before the author turned to his main theme, the encouragement and promotion of agriculture. He endorsed "philanthropic taxation" (248) and the promotion of infrastructure and education among the peasants. A parliamentary democracy was incompatible with the existing Ottoman taxation system. The tyranny of the latter was expressed through the taxation of gross production and in kind instead of in money. Thus, taxation became in the eyes of the citizens “a violent contribution, a taking away of the bread from the mouth” (250), that led to alienation and social tension between the countryside and the cities and held back economic growth. Of equal importance could be “the representation of agriculture in the government” (305–10), which would defend its interests and promote its prosperity. The introduction of a series of agricultural laws in the spirit of reforms suggested by the author would improve existing conditions and signal a change of attitude of state authorities toward this vital sector for the development of the whole economy.

In the second part, the draft law of Koumoundouros and other proposals were discussed, and the question “Why didn‘t these proposals succeed in passing parliament?” was posed. It also included a discussion of the land register in Greece and its desirability. Even if the land register was a necessity, this would prove a difficult task demanding at least 20 million drs, a sum not easy to extract as revenue. Waiting for its introduction, and then proceeding to reform the tax system, would be a mistake for Sotiropoulos.

In the third part, Sotiropoulos proposed the splitting of arable land into separate distinguishable categories. A flat tax per acre, according to the product that was cultivated, could be introduced, and then the farmers should declare what product they cultivated in what piece of land. This would be a first important step in the right direction (56), he recommended.

His study about changes in land taxation (1867) was also divided into three parts. The first recapped the faults of the existing system and drew heavily on his 1861 book. Jean Baptiste Say and his negative views about decimation were used as arguments in favor of abandoning the existing and moving to a new system. The existing tax system in the Ionian Islands introduced by the British could be used as a guide for the rest of the country. The tax system of France and other European countries was discussed and offered as a guide to a better Greek one for the near future.

3.2.4 Efmorfopoulos

Leonidas Efmorfopoulos, a well-known Syros citizen and a trader, proposed, as a member of the Constitutional Assembly, the abolition of custom offices in Greece. He later headed an Economic Society with this objective.

In his *On the Abolition of Custom Houses in Greece* (1863), he calculated net customs receipts at approximately 3 million drs and made a rough division of the 250,000 living households in Greece into 150,000 poor ones and 100,000 wealthy ones. If the wealthier households could be made to pay 40 drs per year as a direct tax, not a large sum for Efmorfopoulos, the government could offset the loss of tariff receipts by one million drs. He accepted the arguments against direct taxes in general but thought that the introduction of a direct tax to be paid by every professional could be absorbed by the economy without any allocative disturbances. Efmorfopoulos opposed a flat tax reduction for people working in the agricultural sector. According to him, a distinction should be made between big landowners and small peasants. The latter should be granted tax reductions, not the former. His proposal was not accepted by parliament.

3.2.5 Trikaliotis

Information about Stamos Trikaliotis is scarce. He studied philosophy in Leipzig and taught political economy at the University of Athens as an ifigitis since 1865.

In his *On the Organization of a System of National Production and the Ways to Do It* (1863), he was critical of laissez-faire and doubted the sincerity of its advocates (2). He started with the axiomatic thesis that "Wherever we look (in Europe) we encounter the necessity of government foresight and determination toward organizing national production" (3) and praised Colbert for his role in the economic development of France (4–5). Greece should follow the same path and organize its economy. Implementing laissez-faire without first framing economic activities in a proper institutional setting led according to Trikaliotis to "paralysis of the nation" (5). He used the examples of Turkey, Jamaica, Ireland, and India that were forced by England to accept laissez-faire with negative economic results for their citizens, whereas the countries that followed Colbert's recommendations developed their productive forces.

He estimated that in every European country at least 80% of workers were offering productive work and propagated the need for Greece to imitate this tendency and exploit all its productive resources to maximize national production. External trade was beneficial if a country would first exhaust its productive potential. The new political start of 1864 was a chance to alter this situation and follow a policy of exploiting raw materials to contribute to the well-being of the citizens. A primary necessity for Trikaliotis was the definition of the interests of the people. These called for the distribution of property rights to all interested citizens. Then, government should provide through public works means of transport, communication, and infrastructure so that private property might thrive, enriching the nation and elevating its image abroad Since Greeks were known not to possess capital, the government ought to encourage the creation of cooperative financial activities and support them with capital (32). Citizens would thus be happy to pay taxes as they would have the income to do so.

In a follow-up publication, *Treatise on the Most Suitable Economic and Political Organization for Greece* (1865), he defended himself against accusations that he was a protectionist (1865, 68). He was not a natural law advocate either, he claimed (4). "Organization and discipline, cooperation and individuality, responsibility and freedom go hand in hand in the social world" (6) and Greece needed a new boost. The organization of the economy he envisaged included public and technical education, distribution of the land to the cultivators, inauguration of state industrial plants, reform of the tax system, building of highways, and creation of an agricultural bank. In other words, he favored what every economist in Greece espoused at that time. Cooperation and recognition that despite differences in social status, capital and labor shared the same goal, to see the country prosper, was his credo.

3.2.6 Soutsos

Ioannis Soutsos seized the opportunity to indicate the necessary steps the national assembly and the new dynasty should take to create more favorable economic conditions (Soutsos 1863). He proposed reforms in three fields: public finance, agriculture, and foreign lending.

One of the first priorities of the new political leadership should be to reform the tax system. After a detailed analysis of the existing tax system, Soutsos concluded that it was unfair and very ineffective. Unfair because the imposition of taxes on gross production, instead of net, violated the principle of proportional taxation, and ineffective because the collection of taxes had been rented to private individuals, who aspired to their own enrichment and regarded the taxpayers as an "object of speculation" (1863, 13), nourishing thus a situation unfavorable to economic activity. Tax collectors didn't pay taxes for the profit they were making, and peasants didn't have a chance to invest in improvements (14). They were obliged to pay a larger share of the increasing output, something that was condemned by esteemed authors like J. B. Say (18). Soutsos proposed therefore the disposition of national land to cultivators, stressing emphatically the advantages of private property: "the private interest is the vitalizing element of human industry" (104). The land should be distributed, free of charge or through deeds of sale, for cultivators and small proprietors to become owners. This proposal had matured enough in political circles, but it took another decade for Prime Minister Koumoundouros to pass it through parliament. As is generally acknowledged, this act increased investments in agricultural production (McGrew 1985, 212–14).

Expenditures not considered productive and not satisfying public needs should be abandoned, according to Soutsos. Furthermore, taxes should be as light as possible, thus helping the creation and reproduction of productive capitals. Ultimately, the distribution of taxes should follow the principle of proportionality and correspond to the total income of each person. Taxation should be universal and offer a feeling of justice to citizens (242). The central question, for Soutsos, was whether the imposed taxes were fair and equal to the necessary governmental expenditure, meaning the application of a balanced budget.

Soutsos also asked for the establishment of a land register. Since most of the population were peasants, income could, according to him, be estimated through this tool. The land could be classified according to its fertility and a tax, levied on net profit and payable in money, estimated (19). He also saw the possibility that the tax should burden a whole agricultural community, which would then divide it per capita according to property shares owned by its inhabitants. The tax could also distinguish between land close to the community and land in more mountainous locations. This system would be fairer than the existing one. Along with reforms in housing and profession taxes, it guaranteed constant revenues for the Treasury and a better framework for economic activity. Moreover, he proposed that fertile land should be taxed more heavily, and this measure could facilitate the reduction of embezzlements and of government corruption. Furthermore, credit institutions in the form of an Agricultural Bank should be inaugurated and assist in the financing of agricultural activities.

Positive effects would be felt in the economy from the improvement of infrastructures, as the times called for reforms in the international economic relations of the country. It was necessary, according to Soutsos, to resume annual interest payments on foreign loans. This was a pre-condition for the convertibility of the currency, which was needed to facilitate trade. Public debt should be settled with the Great Powers in such a way that restrictions imposed by debt repayments would not hinder a sound economic policy. Creating a balanced budget, through the cutting of expenses, could be assisted through a funding loan that would allow the regular settlement of past foreign debts. However, Soutsos was afraid that this new loan could create euphoria among statesmen and give them the wrong impression that huge and unreasonable expenses could be carried out. That would be, according to him, the worst scenario for the Greek economy (123).

3.2.7 Apostolopoulos

As the first years of the new king were disappointing, a disillusioned Kostantinos Apostopoloulos, director of the agricultural school of Tyrins, wrote a treatise *On Agriculture in Greece and the Agricultural School in Tyrins* (1868) to ring the bell again for much-needed reforms.

He gave a detailed account of the history and development of the School of Tiryns and its activities from 1829 to 1868 (23–89). He also offered as an introduction a brief account of the current state of the primary sector in the Greek economy and demanded from the start "respect for agriculture" (5). Necessary steps for improvement included the creation of agricultural schools, the creation of agricultural banks, the introduction of a proper tax system, and the creation of infrastructure (7). He stressed that usurers demanded 20–50% for loans, thus destructing the peasants. The policy deficiencies were listed exhaustively (17), and the call was made to change the existing impasse.

To conclude, the dawn of a new period after 1862 made economists rush to recommend reforms and the need for a new economic policy. They all favored a better tax system and policies to promote agriculture. Implementation of their recommendations was slow in coming despite their convincing analyses.

3.3 Economists in Parliament

Following Fetter (1980, 6), one can define a parliamentary economist as one who, in addition to having been elected, has either published something related to an economic problem or declared himself a political economist or simply spoken about economic issues in the chamber (see also Gordon 1976).

Between 1865 and 1910, a total of 54 governments were formed in Greece, with an average term in office of about 10 months (see Dakin 1972). Certain biographical works deal with the careers of MPs who were bankers, such as Efthymios Kehayias (Evlambios 1930–1) and Pavlos Kalligas (Masson-Vincourt 2000). Other authors have written on issues of general interest and tried to ascertain how parliament reached consensus or remained split on a certain course of action (Vergopoulos 1978, Dertilis 1980).

Between 1862 and 1910, and according to a sample of 179 sessions, a total of 64 economists in parliament served the country (Psalidopoulos & Syrmaloglou 2008). Most economists in parliament were lawyers by profession. Other professions included academics (19%), bankers and bank employees (14%), civil servants (11%), landowners (8%), and journalists (4%). More than half of the sample, approximately 67%, had studied Law either at the University of Athens or abroad. 55% of the total, 33 in number, had studied in Europe, some of them in more than one country. Nineteen had studied in France, especially Paris (Breton & Lutfalla 1991; Schumpeter 1954). Seven had undertaken studies in Italy, with the University of Pisa attracting half of them.[4] Thirteen had studied in Germany, with the universities of Heidelberg and Munich attracting parliamentarians who also followed academic careers. An important fact to note is the complete absence of parliamentarians with a British education.

The study of the interventions of members of parliament reveals that the economics-literate parliamentarians were aware of problems and dead-ends in the Greek economy. They were, however, not able to pass the legislation needed to assist the economy deliver better results.

Members of the constitutional assembly of 1862–4 faced the reality of not being able to enforce the collection of overdue and current taxes.[5] Athanasios Petsalis warned the deputies, who sought to circumvent this situation by requesting new loans to keep expenditures rolling, that the resources of governments were taxes, not loans. "The Assembly should not rush and accept the principle of loans, because it could destroy the economy,"[6] he stressed, averting a plea for a new loan.

The parliament was thus forced to devise new taxes. Discussion on the nature of possible new taxes raised questions such as equity, principles, and progressiveness of taxation.[7] The assembly debated these issues extensively, but no consensus could be reached. A proposal for raising the tax on professions was met with vociferous objections. Charilaos Souidas argued convincingly that a flat rate profession tax hit Athenian businessmen less than those active in the provinces, as the former enjoyed a bigger turnover.[8] Progressive taxation was a necessity, he thought, as well as taxation of net, not gross, income. In a semi-populist outburst, Professor Pavlos Kalligas stated: "I, as a big landowner, do not pay taxes,"[9] thus demanding the taxation of landowning income.

These arguments provoked a riposte from Athanasios Rontiris, a supporter of agriculture, who regarded agriculture and the shipping sector as the only real industries of the country.[10] Tax was a reward for security ensured by the government, he argued, but governments had little regard for the security and well-being of peasants. Taxing agriculture led to the decline of population, he stressed; at the same time, he rejected demands that privileges should be awarded to the industry, urging that a more rational distribution of the tax burden should be enacted before any consideration of raising existing taxes.

In 1865 Koumoundouros repeated that "The existing tax system is barbarous" and was prompted to ask parliament once more to consider his land distribution proposals.[11] Land distribution proposals materialized finally six years later in 1871. Koumoundouros was also a pioneer in an active role of government in the development process, admitting that prudent governments limit their public spending with an eye to the limits of national production. On the other hand, deficit spending to construct infrastructural works like public buildings "is the seed of sure and continuous treasures," a "positive and non-transformable capital." Therefore, in his view, voices demanding the curtailment of central government action in the economy were wrong. An "economization of resources" through less public expenditure could not lead to higher rates of growth, he added.[12]

In his capacity as a former Minister of Finance, he informed the assembly as early as 1863: "We have a deficit here and, regardless of how we economize, we cannot cover it. Therefore, you must admit the raising of existing taxes,"[13] however, he could not convince his colleagues. This inability to reach consensus was not new in Greek politics. Despite diagnosis, no suitable cure could be agreed.

Koumoundouros' claims were solid, for despite economic progress, tax receipts stood for about 15 years at the same level of around 14 million drachmas.[14] This was an indication that, for political reasons, administrations were lenient with local communities and did not extract more revenue from a rising National Income.

Dimitrios Christidis argued in the Assembly for a more liberal approach. "Do not tell me," he said, "that what is good for the private economy has no application for the public."[15] Since delays and arrears raised the deficit, Christidis continued, it was imperative for the country to economize, meaning to cut expenditure. No fundamental differences in economic affairs could be observed between the private and the public sector, and this clearly demonstrated that they should be run on the same principles. "No two ways to economize exist in the world, as there do not exist two truths for the same thing," he stressed.[16] Christidis was a supporter of commerce and felt that trade was adversely affected by taxes: nations that imposed obstacles to trade for no apparent reason were doomed to backwardness and poverty, he argued.[17]

A similar interest-specific approach was articulated when parliament debated a tax on buildings.[18] Diomidis Kyriakos insisted that such a tax should be rejected by arguing that while elsewhere in Europe the labor class was in a desperate condition and property was in the hands of the wealthy – who could thus well afford to pay for their real estate – in Greece, on the contrary, the majority of the population owned their own homes. But such houses were extremely small and run-down, little better than hovels; therefore, this tax was for him unjust, since it fell on the shoulders of the poor.

Efthymios Kehayias, Minister of Finance at the time, countered this view by appealing to no less than Adam Smith, who, in Kehayias' interpretation, believed that this tax burdened the rich,[19] thereby making it appropriate to impose this levy on homeowners in Greece. The tax was finally introduced eight years later, when the pressure for more revenue was extremely pressing.

In the period from 1864 to 1879, fiscal and monetary policy were frequently discussed, yet little breakthrough legislation was enacted, apart from the 1871 land reform.[20] This step, however, was not accompanied by an important corollary demanded by practitioners and academics: a land register. Despite the widespread acceptance of its importance (Diamantopoulos 1861, 7) and its necessity as an objective base for computing agricultural income, the land register did not materialize. Administrators blamed this failure on the high cost of setting up this endeavor, whereas politicians sought to act as guardians of rural voters.

A similar situation existed in the banking sector, with many speakers advocating greater competition and the curtailment of the dominance of the NBG, but to little avail. During the spring and summer of 1864, parliament debated the pros and cons of a land bank proposed by Evangelis Valtatzis and modeled after the French Credit Mobilier. A year earlier, on 17 May 1863, Athanasios Rontiris had drafted a memorandum, suggesting either the creation of an agricultural bank or the creation of a section for agricultural credit within the National Bank of Greece. Alexandros Koumoundouros led the camp that favored greater competition in banking, claiming that "privilege is stagnation" and stressing that "competition is the father of life and of the development of man and society."[21]

Pavlos Kalligas and Efthymios Kehayias, on the other hand, in lengthy speeches, used their expertise as bankers to oppose the project. The new bank would also have the privilege to issue land bonds, and this, they feared, would raise interest rates. European experience, they pointed out, showed that regulation of the market by intermediaries, such as the NBG, was more in line with the immediate needs of the Greek economy.[22] Their arguments followed their former successful efforts not to allow the creation of an agricultural bank, with the argument that the NBG hosted a department of agricultural credit (session 16.12.1861), and to successfully oppose the creation of a land bank (session 18.5.64, where Kehayias disputed that he was opposing the proposal due to his former affiliation with the NBG).

Kehayias defended the adoption of the bimetallic system of the LMU on the 10 April 1867; however, since however the country could not enforce it due to its inability to have a convertible currency, he returned to the topic on 13.11.1869 and remained a vocal advocate of this system, as it put Greece on the same monetary footing as other continental European states. Finally, on 1 November 1882, Greece joined the Union, but due to the renewed introduction of inconvertibility in 1885, it withdrew from it again. By then, silver was losing the war against gold, with the latter becoming the prime precious metal.

On the fiscal front, the balancing of the budget was accepted both by the government and the opposition. The Minister of Finance, Dimitrios Christidis, underlined the necessity of a balanced budget, equating it with creditworthiness.[23] Budget deficits would not disappear unless new taxes were introduced, contended Sotirios Sotiropoulos, a speaker of the opposition at that time, who stressed the need to expand production and extract more revenue from a larger income pie. "The economic condition of nations is not judged based on its debt only," he claimed.[24] Credit plays a role too and credit is given to an expanding economy with a promising future.

The short-term needs of the Greek treasury brought about a reshuffling of existing taxes. Kehayias, now the Finance Minister, was accused of transforming parliament into "a cabinet of taxing laws and decrees."[25] Agricultural products such as currants, silk, and other products saw their tax rates rise from 10% to 15%, without any substantial improvement for Greek finances. Ways to attract foreign capital were therefore sought and tax breaks were given to the Italian-owned company in Lavrion, based on the belief that they acted as a "bait" for much-needed investment in the country.[26] At the same time, the opposition favored the nationalization of extractive industries that were characterized as "national capital."[27] However, this legislation did not mark a turning point in foreign direct investment. By the end of the 1870s, parliamentary economists had learned one truth: the taxpayer, especially the peasant, was economically exhausted, and Greek taxation was regressive since professionals and certain social strata still paid no taxes at all. In 1877, therefore, a profession tax was introduced, and Societes Anonymes were made to pay a modest 2% tax on their profits.

In this context, Charilaos Trikoupis started building up his political profile. In 1876 he stressed that "it is an economic policy error when we cover the deficits of the regular budget with loans."[28] Nevertheless, the needs of the government took a priority, and indirect taxes were easily handled to generate revenue. Trikoupis declared himself an opponent of progressive taxation and indicated measures he himself would adopt a decade later. He pleaded for more protective tariffs, and a new tax on ploughing animals, which he justified as being more in line with a developmentalist agenda needed by the country. Sotiropoulos, who was his main opponent at the time, countered this view based on his experience and knowledge of market conditions. "Old taxes are like old shoes," he said, "they do not squeeze the feet."[29] A modest income tax for all would be better instead of the Talmudic Greek tax laws. In Sotiropoulos' view, progressive taxation would be accepted by society if combined with a reform that would simplify the relationship between the taxpayer and the government.[30]

Theodoros Deligiannis, the Trikoupis' main rival, accused the government of wrongdoing: "We follow the curing of disease without trying to find the reason of the illness," he claimed, speaking about the financial difficulties faced by the government.[31]

Epaminondas Deligiorgis lamented the absence of an industrial sector that was the sole guarantee for economic progress. The country needed capital and a low-cost labor force, but such a development could not take place with higher taxation. Instead, he argued, it was necessary to introduce expenditure cuts and proceed to the downsizing of the government.

This divergence of opinions led the Koumoundouros government in 1880 to relegate the issue to a bipartisan committee. The committee members were Sotiropoulos, Soutsos, Chalikiopoulos, and Zografos. This was the first time ever that four prominent Greek economists sat together and contributed to the betterment of the economic legislation of the country. They proposed unanimously the introduction of an income tax and other reforms (for the full report see Zografos, vol. 1, 1925, 233–64), but the result was disappointing. The tax was not introduced.

Their inability to convince the parliament speaks for the strength of vested interests as opposed to science and reason.

After 1879, the pressure to reform the tax system softened somewhat. The Trikoupis era began and coincided with the renewed possibility for Greece to obtain foreign loans. The inclusion of Thessaly in the state shortly thereafter gave new impetus and perspectives for development.

Ioannis Valassopoulos was assigned as an MP to update the chamber about taxes in 1880. Valassopoulos suggested, as many others before him, the introduction of an income tax. Citing Soutsos, he pointed to citizens who were industrialists, traders, and bankers that were taxed either not at all or only minimally. He argued that existing taxation was responsible for imports of foreign grain and should be replaced with some other tax. There was a need for the government to improve the country's infrastructure, and Valassopoulos favored public works and the building of railways to achieve this goal.[32]

Thrasyvoulos Zaimis, on the other hand, repeated the classic liberal objections to this developmentalist thinking. New taxes and economies were prerequisites for future growth, while possible foreign loans to cover deficits would be disastrous for the economy. It was therefore pressing to cut expenditures.

It was at this time that Trikoupis found the majority to enact three important laws: the tax on ploughing animals, the renewal of the NBG monopoly on the issuing of banknotes, and the new tariff system of 1884. Koumoundouros, now his opponent, objected on the basis that if the existing land tax was too heavy it would be more sensible to lower it, rather than abandon such a solid tax altogether in favor of a brand-new tax that might bring less revenue than expected.[33]

It should be noted that during Trikoupis' premierships in 1882–5 and 1886–90, a railway system was built, as was the Corinth canal that facilitated commerce greatly. At the same time, however, internal and foreign lending reached unprecedented heights, and the tax system, despite the reform that took place, was not delivering the expected revenues. The annual budgets appeared to be balanced, but there was no ex-post review of government activity. Moreover, from the early 1880s, the service of the public debt absorbed around 50% of regular revenues. This situation led to serious financial difficulties and to bankruptcy, which was declared by Trikoupis himself in 1893.

Trikoupis and his followers gave only scant consideration to arguments by the opposition, convinced that their policy was implementing changes and preparing the nation for the achievement of the Megali Idea. Only the convertibility of the drachma was a weak side of his policy. As Trikoupis himself put it on one occasion, "Capital is concentrating only where the currency has the value that is accepted by the general market of the people and not the one that is determined by law."[34] His opponent, Deliyiannis, agreed with him. As he admitted, "forced circulation is a disease that eats the economic flesh of nations."[35] But both men could not find a bipartisan solution to this problem. Convertibility was reintroduced in 1885, but it was abandoned after just six months and some years later, as we already mentioned, the currant crisis and the mounting interest on debt led to default in 1893.

Greek economists, as we saw, divided over this policy. Trikoupis and his followers were, for the liberal camp, outcasts, guilty of unsound financing of the state. The only dream they shared with him was his dream for national integration. For the followers of the German road to economic power, Trikoupis was on the right track when, among other things, he introduced the new tariff system in 1884, which was more protective of Greek industry.

The conclusion that springs from this inquiry is that all economists in the Greek parliament were basically of a liberal persuasion. They awarded national aspirations priority over sound economic fundamentals. Their views on fiscal policy over a fairly long period reveal that they were hesitant to adopt reforms, afraid to alter the status quo, and more inclined to accommodate the tax system instead of reforming it. On the monetary front, they supported convertibility, but were shy to recommend the restriction of monetary circulation or the termination of the practice of government loans from the NBG.

Greek parliamentary economists resembled Schumpeter's consultant administrators (Schumpeter 1954, 159). They were mostly practitioners and familiar with the business of governing. Their ideas and activities focused mainly on how to run and manage the short term, which always imposed its necessities over the long term. The mentality inherited from the years of Bavarian rule had left its mark on their actions, or rather their slow reaction, to necessary reforms. This came to an end with default in 1893.

3.4 Free Trade versus Protectionism

There is no doubt that the most important issue that made economics a distinct field of expertise in the 19th century and the hottest topic of discussion all over Europe was the issue of free trade versus protection (Augello & Guidi 2001, 11–12, 60, 76, 98–9, 117, 132, 188–9).

The political change in Greece in 1864 provoked the creation in March 1865 of the "Society for the Freedoms of Trade" (thereafter, the Society) by Leonidas Efmorfopoulos. This was to remain the only association of economists in Greece in the 19th century. For political reasons associated with political developments, the Society soon lost momentum and, in December 1867, it dissolved.

The Society was founded in Hermoupolis, the main town of the island of Syros in the Aegean Sea. The town became an economic center when merchants settled there in large numbers after 1821 and housed the biggest Greek port until the early 20th century. In a short time, trade brought to Syros an affluence not previously known and came to dominate social life. It was here that the first effort to create an insurance fund for shipbuilders materialized (in 1858), as well as the first strike in modern Greece was registered (in 1879).

The settlers of Hermoupolis demanded as early as 1838 that the port of Syros be declared "free of tariff charges" but had no success. The request was revived shortly before the 1857 slump and reached publicity in parliament, where Efmorfopoulos sat between 1862 and 1864 (Grapsas 1948).[36] Efmorfopoulos demanded in parliament the abolition of all trade restrictions, but the Assembly delegated the issue to a committee and finally declined to discuss or vote on it.[37]

On 8 January 1865, Efmorfopoulos advanced an appeal for the creation of a "Tax Reform Society." In this appeal, Efmorfopoulos cited Adam Smith and Robert Peel as men who subscribed to the view that the first principle of taxation should be justice. For him, indirect taxation was unjust, because it burdened the working class, not the owners of capital or the usurers. Efmorfopoulos stated that empirical evidence supported the view that the lowering of indirect taxes promoted consumption and production. He concluded, therefore, that a "Tax Reform Society" should be formed with "the aim of promoting the freedom of trade through a just system of taxation."[38] Its main aim would be to advance social awareness that lower taxes are beneficial from an economic point of view. Indirect taxes should be lowered and abolished.

In the process of gathering the 50 signatures needed to create this Society, discussions took place among Syros businessmen with the result that on January 31st, 1865, they agreed to create "The Society for the Freedoms of Trade."[39] On February 27th the juridical form of the Society was sealed (see the local newspaper *Hermoupolis* of that date), and operations started on March 1st. The aim of the Society was to promote the complete freedom of trade and in particular the abolition of customs offices. All the legal means to this end would be exploited through rallies and the press.

The foundation of the Society was greeted with great enthusiasm, and membership grew from 54 in February 1865, to 234 in May, and climbed further to 350 in January 1866 and 428 in February 1867.[40] Membership was open to all sharing the aims of the Society. Diaspora Greeks from cities like Marseille, Liverpool, Amsterdam, Constantia, Beirut, London, Manchester, Odessa, Taigarok, Rostov, Triest, and elsewhere joined. Greeks living in Germany did not become members perhaps because they were influenced by Listian ideas.

Minutes of all the meetings and other relevant material were published in the Journal *Freedom of Trade* (thereafter, cited as FT, followed by issue then by page number). 34 issues were published until December 1867.

The aim of FT was to "educate" members of the Society with fresh arguments. The most outspoken members of the Society[41] used a similar line in their arguments. Abstract analysis and pure theoretical discourse were not present in these articles. Extensive use was made of historical examples among Jews, Phoenicians, ancient Greeks, and the contemporary Dutch and British to show that trade brought affluence, wealth, and high living standards. A typical chain of causal explanations in this line of thought involved the following: The freer the trade is, the lower prices are, because of the competitive element free trade induces in society.[42] Lower prices mean higher consumption on a given income. Usually, however, free trade leads to income growth. A free trade policy benefits not only traders, but also shipowners and sailors. This spillover effect meant a growing accumulation of capital and an accelerated income growth for the future. Through the trading of new products, habits could change and efforts on the part of industry could be made to substitute for imported products. If this could be done without protection, new markets could be conquered for Greece, which meant further income increases. Greece's geographical position, and its relative prosperity in relation to its neighbors, guaranteed this optimistic conclusion.

Furthermore, society would be more prosperous and happier because of the widespread corruption by customs officers, the smuggling of foreign goods, and the spoiling of the national character caused by these activities which would gradually disappear. Last, but not least, Greek agriculture would benefit from free trade. Small peasants would find the cost of living lower, allowing them to accumulate surpluses. The bigger Greek landlords, who heavily influenced politics at that time, should be made to understand these truths, and that free trade was beneficial for them too. This left the role of government as the last castle to be conquered by the free traders.

The government was seen by them as embedded up to 1862, on the rotten ideas of absolutism. The state was absorbing resources, was not granting property rights in agriculture, and was distributing privileges in an arbitrary fashion. For the free traders, the time had come to reform existing institutions or create new ones in accordance with Adam Smith's teachings. The Society hailed politicians, such as Peel, Cobden, and Gladstone, as its heroes, and Greece should imitate what the economically advanced nations did. The Cobden–Chevalier Treaty of 1860 was cited as proof of the validity of the free trade arguments and as the policy that nations seeking to become rich should imitate (FT 18: 131–52).

The Society viewed indirect taxes as disruptive and unjust. It favored a proportional direct tax to be paid by every working person. The policy of the governments to leave big incomes untaxed and to raise indirect taxes instead was, to them, a backward policy that harmed citizens.

One of the most impressive activities of the Society was the effort to link itself with movements, groups, and persons abroad, who had the same ideas and values. It is not clear how these contacts came to be established, but it is more likely that personal acquaintances via export/import activities played a major role. After all, the 1840s and 1850s were very successful decades for the free trade movement. Greek businessmen and economists were aware of the work of the "Anti-Corn Law League" and the "Association pour la Liberté des Echanges," and wished to join an international movement that was growing in importance and recognition in most of Europe (Spall 1988).

The links with Belgium and its free trade movement must be underlined. In the first issues of FT, the outcome of the struggle of the Belgian free traders was seen as a test for the success of the Greek free trade movement (FT 4:86–7, 6:110–15). Alexis Joffroy, a free trade agitator from Antwerp, reported often on the Belgian experiences and became an honorary fellow in the Greek society. When the "Society for the Abolition of custom offices" in Belgium, led by the internationally well-known economist Gustave de Molinari, was inaugurated, Molinari's opening speech was translated into Greek and his reputation used to rebuke protectionists (FT 22:187–99). FT reported developments from Belgium extensively (FT 26:17–27, 27:28–37). Declarations of the Chambers of Commerce in Vervier and Charleroi were translated, and memoranda concerning the advantages of free trade and addressed to King Leopold were cited. An appreciation of Cobden's achievements by Gladstone was also published (FT 21:183–4).

In the UK, correspondence was held with "The Economic Reformer" in Liverpool and its editor McQueen. When Richard Cobden died, the Society sent his widow a touching letter of condolences with the assurance that Cobden's Greek brothers in arms would carry on his struggle for free trade in Europe and the whole world (FT 5:93–6). In the USA, correspondence was held with Charles Bristed from New York, president of a free trade league. The Italian counterpart of the Society was Gaetano Semenza. Semenza's book and recommendations for the abolition of custom offices in Italy were also translated, and Semenza's successful career in local Italian politics was seen as proof of the recognition of the validity of his ideas by Italian society (FT 13:59–61, 16:107–12). The contact in Spain was Alonso de Verazza, editor of the *Gazeta Economista* in Madrid. Verazza furnished the Society with reports on economic conditions in Spain and of efforts there to free trade, an issue his periodical favored (FT 14:78–81). It is worth noting that the Greek society had no contacts with French free trade circles despite the generally close intellectual ties in economics between the two countries. These international contacts served an important function. They diffused arguments and recommendations in the country and especially helped put forward in Greece the idea that free trade was the norm of the economic future.

Of course, not everyone in Greece was convinced that a total laissez-faire policy in trade would be beneficial for the country. For example, Athanassios Koutpas, a Greek merchant from Manchester who claimed to be sympathetic towards free trade, reminded his comrades that in England, the most liberal country of the time, heavy tariffs still existed. For him, a nation could progress "when everyone in his own sphere of action manages to coincide his personal interest with that of his country," meaning that the Society should try to convince the government that its aims were advancing the national interest. In the meantime, Koutpas suggested that merchants should cooperate with each other to increase their capitals. Because of the small-scale activities of lots of merchants, it was for him clear that "without cooperation … it is impossible to achieve the desired outcome," meaning economic importance in society, a prerequisite for political influence and power (FT 6: 125–30). The total abolition of customs offices was for him an inconceivable policy, given the politics of the day.

Aristidis Dosios introduced a pacifist element into the Greek discussion. He cited Bastiat and Cherbouliez as great authors in matters of trade and stressed that protectionism "tends to nourish hatred among nations" and is responsible, among other things, for armed conflicts (FT 13: 63–75). Writing about American commercial policy, he left no doubt that, despite the views of Alexander Hamilton, free trade was the norm in the US. He accepted, however, that the total abolition of customs houses was not relevant in the USA.

Other authors adopted a more hostile stance towards the Society and its aims. Alexandros Rangavis attacked what he called the shortsightedness of the Society's discourse and refused to join as a member (FT 4: 63). For him, the agricultural sector was the main source of the country's wealth. Agriculture badly needed infrastructural works, and despite the immediate need to raise state revenue, the Society advocated a cut in tariff receipts. A drop in government revenue could be no good, he thought, and, in an outburst of irony, he called on the members of the Society to contribute the estimated loss of tariff receipts, which stood at 4 mill drs from their own pockets (FT 3: 50–3).

A similar defense of the need to assist agriculture came from Dimitrios Pappas, a banker living in London. For him, freedom of trade came as a stage after the development of agriculture, and the establishment of industrial enterprises transforming agricultural products into industrial ones. When industry would grow, it would be the time to introduce a policy of free trade (FT 10: 243–4).

Others were very hesitant to espouse such a radical step towards complete freedom of trade. An anonymous author in *Evangelismos* didn't deny the theoretical superiority of the ideal of free trade, but he believed that Greece should not take this step. If big countries, such as the USA, with rich resources, had restrictions on foreign trade, how could Greece, with its poor soil and its small size, take a step like this, he asked? (FT 13: 46–7).

Another anonymous writer in *Ecthinos Tachydromos* lent weight to the fact that tariffs hurt the rich more than the poor, since the latter didn't consume foreign goods. The abolition of custom offices was not therefore in the interest of all members of society. If it were to be implemented, this would mean that "the industrialists and bourgeois would pay less and the whole burden (of the budget) would fall on the peasant" (FT 13: 53–7).

The most outspoken opponent of the aims of the Society was Athanasios Petsalis, a lawyer with landed interests and a parliamentarian. For Petsalis, the Society's aims were class-oriented, to foster the privileges of the merchant class only, regardless of the cost that would be suffered by the rest of society. Petsalis advanced "a stage of economic activities theory." According to him, agriculture is "the first source of the wealth of nations." Greece lacked "native capitals that spring out of agriculture." The accumulation process in agriculture and its advancement should be the prime concern of economic policy. After the development of agriculture, industry should be assisted by the government. Trade should be taken care of in a third and more advanced stage of industrial development (FT 8: 177–97, FT 14: 81–4).

Petsalis rejected that tariffs put obstacles to the circulation of goods. The tariff was an indirect tax and indirect taxes were, according to Adam Smith, the most righteous ones. Smith, Petsalis continued, advocated the Navigation Acts. It was therefore incorrect to portray him as a laissez-faire free trader, as the Society did. An income tax could not be introduced in Greece, according to him. If corruption was encouraged by prohibitions, this was because "of our bad habits." Action against corruption was needed, but not the abolition of customs offices. It was in the interests of merchants, Petsalis argued, to emancipate themselves from the government, by not asking for class-specific legislation. Only without government help could they become strong enough. If they based their hope for personal prosperity on the establishment of a utopian situation, a country without tariffs, no improvement of their situation would occur. The Society countered all these accusations either through collective answers or through articles by individual members (out of many, see FT 13: 61–2).

A foreign policy event associated with the Megali Idea, the uprising in Crete in early 1866, proved fatal for the future of the Society. Greece wanted to supply Cretan revolutionaries with the means to win their independence from the Ottomans, so existing indirect taxes were increased spontaneously to deal with the situation.

A second factor that split the Society came from "within." As soon as the Society was established and started its agitation, it became known that such an act was in fact completely impossible. The revenues of the three larger customs offices in Greece were already serving as collateral for government loans. This applied to the custom house of Syros, too. The customs house of Piraeus was serving as a repayment guarantee for the private financier Vouros-Dikosis, and the custom office of the Ionian Islands was reserved for a loan given by the Ionian Bank (FT 1: 4).

This news surprised everyone, and the Society debated intensively on the course of action. A radical wing prevailed in the voting that took place. The majority thought that, despite this situation, "it is not in the interest of the Society to negotiate a reconciliation with the government" (FT 12: 23). This radical – all or nothing – stance was totally irrational and led the Society to a political deadlock. Efmorfopoulos had voted with the minority. In February 1867, therefore, the Society's general assembly described in its declaration the situation thus: "We confess that we didn't register during the last year the progress that we had hoped for" (FT 24: 222).

The indifference to the implementation of the Society's aims by some prominent politicians who were members of the Society was a further reason for its decline. Quite early, the Journal *New Generation* (Nea Genea), having noted that top-ranked politicians, such as Alexandros Koumoudouros, Efthimios Kehayas, Dimitrios Voulgaris, and others, were members of the Society, stressed that these men "didn't support the Society's aim and won't implement it as a policy" (FT 5, 97). That they paid the fees to become members seemed paradoxical. Professor Ioannis Soutsos, who was also a member, had to write a letter to the newspaper *Ethnophylax* to counter rumors that he would use his authority to recommend new taxes. He supported an administration based on taxes, not on loans, he said. However, he didn't explicitly and openly say that the abolition of tariffs was an urgent, necessary step, as the Society claimed it was (FT 3: 58–9).

Since these celebrities did not support its cause with action, the Society could not count on the support of the press, as it openly admitted (FT 12: 3). The chambers of commerce in Nafplion and Kalamata, two other important centers of economic life in the Peloponnese, in mainland Greece, also refused to support the Society's cause. In this setting, the reform of 1867, which raised tariff rates, gave a final blow to the Society. This happened even though the tariff for the import of goods not produced in Greece was reduced to only 2%. Thus, the effort to make Greece, or at least Syros, a free trade zone, became history.

The publicity created by the Society took a twist with the demand of certain authors to follow Friedrich List's ideas and protect Greek industry from foreign competition, a proposal that provoked exchanges that lasted until the early 20th century (see the original texts in Psalidopoulos 1994).

3.4.1 Skaltsounis and Dosios

Ioannis Skaltsounis, in his *Thoughts on Industry in Greece* (1868), was one of the most openly protectionist authors during these times. The reason for the stagnation of industry in Greece, for him, was the laissez-faire policy of Greek governments. The historical experience of England up until the beginning of the 19th century, and that of France and the USA until the middle was a testament that protection was essential at early stages of nation building. Only Greece was denying this truth and was an exception among European countries. Skaltsounis claimed that even John Stuart Mill showed sympathy for light protection, especially for infant industries. Raising tariffs to protect industry, according to him, paid off as they performed an educational service to the economy.

Greek government policy for industry was tragic for Skaltsounis. He quoted the closing of the Agricultural School in Tyrins, which opened its doors in 1833, as an example. It accumulated a deficit of 211,000 drs in 35 years, serving as proof of the total neglect of the productive sectors of the economy. Protectionism, if introduced, would be temporary and supportive. The new dynasty would cement its authority by assisting industry in becoming a reality in the country, he concluded. Leandros Dosios, a professor of chemistry and brother of Aristidis, echoed the same arguments based on his extensive knowledge of Germany's path to growth (Dosios 1871).

3.4.2 Economos

Judge-turned-economist Aristidis Economos countered with eloquent counter-arguments (Economos 1869). Freedom of trade didn't sacrifice local industry for the sake of foreign industry, he claimed; it guaranteed the optimal distribution of resources on a world scale. Competition was a tremendous and necessary force for social development, and it was not ruled by legislation; it sprang out of the natural harmony of interests in society. In the past, some privileges were given to industrial companies, but these led nowhere. What Greece needed were motives to create larger capitals and cooperation among businesses. If this were to happen, industry would take off. The function of the government was to provide security and technical education to the citizens; economic matters should be left in the hands of private initiative. Ten years later, he reprinted a shortened version of the same arguments in his journal *Economic Review* (OE) (OE 6, 356–70).

3.4.3 Christidis

Kostas Christidis (1870), in his capacity as vice president of Olympia, a committee that prepared the Greek participation in the International Industrial Fairs of 1867 in Paris, and of 1873 in Vienna, stressed that the government should proceed and intervene in the economy without hesitation and dogmatism. If private initiative did not invest in industry, some protection was needed as an incentive.[43] The aim that governments had to fulfill dealt with making the economy strong, and industry was the vehicle for growth. Whoever did not participate in what the signs of the times called for was going to be sidelined – a fate that Greece, according to him, didn't deserve to experience.

3.4.4 Soutsos

Ioannis Soutsos (1870) responded to Christidis by reminding him of what was already happening in the country. Tariffs for raising revenue were sound, but when it came to industrial investments, it was private initiative that needed to take the necessary first steps. Legislation could not bring growth, he stressed, and individuals needed to abandon the notion that government was the instance that led citizens to economic action. Authorities offered the necessary infrastructure and then stepped aside, leaving room for private agents. Protectionism meant higher prices and the curtailment of competition; therefore, it was not the proper way to achieve growth.

Soutsos had the opportunity to repeat the same arguments in the short-lived *Bulletin for the Encouragement of Industry* (1877–80). Industrial strength was undoubtedly a sign of prosperity, but prosperity didn't result from improvisations. Technical education and competition assisted industrial efforts in the country, and industry could perhaps have performed better based on local advantages, if it were not for political reasons. The Megali Idea absorbed resources, and once the question of Greek borders would be settled a new epoch for the economy would start. The *Bulletin* ceased to be published in 1880 and the press was very critical about this outcome.

3.4.5 Aion and Gounarakis

A controversy between the newspaper *Aion* (Century) and Nikolaos Gounarakis erupted in 1881. The editorial in *Aion* argued that all countries used tariffs as instruments in their efforts to promote their economies. What Greece needed was the recognition of the principle that the country needed to assist its enterprises and that it was sad to prefer foreign products instead of local ones, just because the latter's prices were slightly higher. Gounarakis (1881) answered that the best way to grow was the natural one, the one that sprang out of private initiative. Tariffs were not helping industry and neither benefited the working class, he argued. The only beneficiaries were industrialists, incompetent in providing what the market wanted, businessmen who sought to be assisted in their bad decisions that led them to an impasse. His views on the matter would change in the course of time.

3.4.6 Other Authors

The new tariff system of 1884 revived the exchanges about the necessity to protect industry. Athanasios Vernardakis (1884) took a laissez-faire stance and claimed that, if Greece were to become industrialized, it would only happen through competition with the outside world. Similar pro-market opinions were expressed by Panagiotis Psimoulis and others who criticized the new system for not accomplishing what it was supposed to. Ioannis Kalostypis (1885) saw it as an inefficient effort to promote local enterprises, a half-hearted solution to vested demands. The government was not the custodian of society, he argued, it was rather a caretaker of the citizens. Businesses producing equipment and investment goods as well as shipbuilding were activities of national interest and needed maximum protection. Other thinkers, such as Nikolaos Sorokiadis (1887), pointed out the need for credit for industry. The banking sector should be more forthcoming to the demands of the industrialists, who needed more access to capital rather than government protection of their activities.

The 1893 default brought forward the dilemma "agriculture or industry?" instead of the "laissez-faire or protection" arguments. The press, especially the newspaper *Akropolis*, lamented the empirical nature of government policy regardless of which party was in power. The largest economic sector in Greece was agriculture, and its interests had to be defined and defended instead of making exhaustive efforts to promote industry. As Greece went through austerity until 1910, a new mainstream view for an overall inclusive policy promoting all economic sectors gained ground. In this setting, the industrialist Nikolaos Vlagalis (1913) was the one who pointed out that Greek industrial products should be preferred in government sector purchases. This policy was materialized ten years later and made industry a reality in the country during the interwar period.

3.5 Ioannis Soutsos on Economics and Policy

After his 1863 recommendation on the economic future of Greece, Ioannis Soutsos started publishing more theoretical works and rose to superior fame as an economist.

3.5.1 Public Finance

His next theoretical work was published in Athens in 1864, under the title *A Treatise on Public Finance. Theory of the Budget*. He wrote the book after having already served twice at the Bureau of Public Economics. The book started with an extended reference to current political developments at that time. Soutsos criticized these developments with very harsh words, not only the mistakes and the inaction of the royal house, but also of the Greek local and national authorities. These were described as corrupt, inefficient, and equally responsible for not reforming the Greek economy according to well-known principles and for turning the constitution of 1844 into a rug (pp. β-ιστ). In his own words, "the diffusion of economic knowledge can contribute to the betterment of all things wrong" (ζ), and his book aimed in that direction.

The treatise extensively discussed in separate chapters historical experience and accomplished results about total government revenue, the budget, public enterprises (post office, printing office, and others), and extraordinary revenue sources like selling public lands and public lending. Comments about outcomes of the present state of the economy were scattered throughout the text. An extra chapter was about attaining international creditworthiness to gain access to foreign markets. Other chapters were devoted to money and ways to monitor the external value of the drachma, which was inconvertible at that time. The views expressed by the

French expert and academic Michel Chevalier, who offered advice in 1855 to the NBG, were favorably presented.

Turning to state finances, the first thing that Soutsos stressed was the importance of productive versus unproductive expenses (3). His investigation revealed that Greece paid for its army and navy 41% of total revenue, whereas militarily strong France paid only 26% (18). Expenditure for infrastructures ran to a slim 2.5%, a fact more revealing than any other possible evidence. Soutsos discussed budgets and their ex-post results, to conclude that very seldom did the Greek administration evaluate the outcomes of its actions. Reality revealed that revenues did not always reach the treasury, with the money staying in the provinces in the vaults of communities or the pockets of tax collectors. The budget was also undermined by additional laws that passed parliament after the ratification of the budget and made an ex-post control an adventurous procedure. Citing authors such as Smith, Ricardo, Mill, Say, Rossi, Sismondi, Turgot, and others, Soutsos introduced the concept of sound taxation, stressing that it ought to be imposed on net revenue only (46). He also discussed the pros and cons of direct and indirect taxation (67–9) and declared himself a supporter of progressive taxation (73–6).

The attachment of the drachma to the (bimetallic) French franc was approved by Soutsos; he stressed, however, that in this way Greece might become exposed to French decisions and initiatives (100) at times when gold was starting to be considered as a better basis of foreign currencies (102).[44] The role of banks and of credit were also discussed, with Soutsos advocating for rules rather than discretion in monetary management(128). He didn't explicitly demand the extension of the privilege to issue money to all banks operating in Greece but expressed support for possible cooperative/producer banks as proposed by Schultze-Delitzch in Germany (134). Turning to public loans to enlarge the scope of government intervention in the economy, he expressed reservations about this policy tool. He was also against internal loans (162) and speculated, by using expert opinion (Smith, Say, and others) about the most beneficial way of debt repayment for both lender and borrower (192–5). Currency convertibility was seen by him as extremely important in this regard, and using historical examples, he argued that it was necessary for the Greek government to remove excess money from circulation and aim seriously at currency convertibility (203).

In 1890, shortly before his passing, he published a reworked version of this book.

3.5.2 Plutology

The publication of *Plutology* (1868)[45] was a milestone in the development of Greek economics. This was a two-volume book that synthesized existing knowledge and offered advice for citizens and suggestions for policymakers.

There is evidence that Soutsos started working on the topic as early as 1847. A handwritten manuscript titled *Lessons in Social Economics* was followed by another handwritten 708-page-long *Treatise on Government Economy and on the Science of Public Money*.[46] In the course of time, Soutsos must have decided to publish the materials he had assembled in separate books. His *Treatise on Public Finance* came first in 1864 and four years later *Plutology* followed in two volumes. The first volume of *Plutology* saw a second edition in 1882, whereas the second in 1885. Major differences between the two editions were the following: The first volume in 1868 included a chapter on the importance of nature for the economy, which had been substituted in the second by a chapter on exchange and credit. The title of the chapter "Sociology" was renamed in the second volume as "Systems of Socialism." Its content remained almost the same. Part two was renamed from "Political plutology" to "Functions of the state" and the chapter entitled "industrial freedom and limits to it" was renamed to "forms of government."

Soutsos followed Say's analysis on value, stressing utility, and the institutional environment as the key to human actions that create wealth. The same applies for the structure of his book and the basic principles about production and distribution discussed therein. The exposition of Soutsos was close to the one by Say, as it was a custom in the European periphery. (See the contributions in Psalidopoulos & Mata 2002.)

He defined economics as *Plutology*,[47] the science of wealth. According to him, *Plutology* was an experimental science whose test field was society. It was a branch of sociology, the latter conceived as a universal social science, and therefore both induction and deduction had to be used by economists. He stressed that there existed a deep connection between industrial development on the one hand, and cultural and political progress on the other. The creation of wealth was not the end of mankind on earth, but the most effective tool of perfecting humanity (1882, 577). Soutsos recognized the necessity of theoretical generalizations and the importance of approaching economic phenomena while having certain economic principles in mind (1885, 25–6). He rejected, as we saw, the Ricardian theory of rent for not being empirically valid (1861, 376).

As the founders of political economy had shown, the application of the principles of political economy was not singular and uniform for all countries. What the economist had to do was to find the proper way these principles could be better applied for his own country to promote social progress. In this effort, it was essential for the economist to take into consideration national realities as a starting point. Even the "proclaimed principle of 'laissez-faire, laissez aller' must not be admitted as an undeniable truth but is to follow from the widest and most precise induction" (1882, 290), he stressed. Consistent with this methodological approach, Soutsos considered state intervention as harmful for the efficient operation of the economy. He accepted, however, that "the question of a wide government energy, as has been proved, is relative and not susceptible of an absolute solution" (12).

For Soutsos, the role of economic science was not limited to the academic sphere. Economics ought to play a maidservant role for the solution of national economic and political problems the European countries faced. Thus, contrary to the opinion of the French Idéologues who wanted political economy to break away from political issues and from political science more generally (Kaiser 1980, 145–6, 149–51, 158), and Say who believed that the creation of "wealth is [...] essentially independent of political organization" (Say 1828, xxi; cf. Forget 2001:

210–13), Soutsos advocated that a "false" political organization might constitute a major problem for the economic advancement of a less developed country, such as Greece. It was for that very reason that, deviating from his French influences, he opined that political economy needed to propose "the needed reforms with the aim to elevate mentally and materially the majority of the poorest social classes" (Soutsos 1882, 729). Moreover, for Soutsos, political economy was a kind of (Smithian) "science of the legislator." He regarded it as the first task of any economist to study of the conditions of his country. This was the basis to find the proper and suitable tools of economic policy and to recommend the necessary policy measures to the authorities. Soutsos opted, therefore, to concentrate on Greek society and apply a comparative method in his analyses, using historical examples and citing not only economists, but historians, and specialists in administrative law as well. The correct application of conclusions sprung out of an inductive analysis of such an extent would inevitably lead to sound government, he thought.

Despite these reservations on methodological issues, Soutsos shared with Say and Rossi their great concern about the extent of state intervention, their praise of individual liberty, their optimistic view about the socioeconomic evolution of humankind, and the "professed faith that, if left alone, the economy would naturally grow with increasing production, employment, productivity, and consumption" (Sherman 1974, 175).

Soutsos' analysis followed in general the tradition of French liberal economic thought and its policy prescriptions about the legitimate role of government at that time (Arena 2000). This role meant the introduction of institutional reforms and the maximization of social utility (Soutsos 1885, 455–63). This went hand in hand with the freedom of contracts, the abolishment of guilds, and any other barriers on the mobility of people, and the suppression of any privileges that obscured the development of economic forces in favor of certain social strata (371 ff). He also stressed the comparative economic advantage of private over public ownership (195) and expounded an argumentation that had many similarities with the classical statements by Smith (1976, 710) and Bentham (1948, 247–53).

Using this theoretical apparatus, Soutsos dissected the Greek economy and pinpointed the lack of basic infrastructures as the main reason for its backwardness.. The creation of industrial and agricultural banks would assist productive activity and promote industrial activity as well as agriculture (1885, 514). A better education system was important for the creation of human capital (572 ff).

Soutsos devoted an extensive chapter on agriculture as an economic sector (89–312), however, the creation of wealth was dependent, according to him, on industry. It was "through industrial works that the national forces improve themselves and the people's income raises" (561). Grants, import tariffs etc. did not help the improvement of industry, as only competition guaranteed industrial growth. Examples given by Soutsos, international and Greek, underlined that whenever industry was based on privileges, it declined soon (599–613).

Those who called for the intervention of the government, for the purpose of accelerating economic development, were for him wrong. The primary function of the State was to keep public finances sound.[48] Any government aid to industry should be granted with the utmost caution and sparingly and if, and only if, it met the criterion of the advancement of national interests (455–63). Individual liberty was the antidote to authoritarianism and paternalism in all spheres of life. The classical ideal of economic policy was the maximization of economic freedom within a framework of law and order (O' Brien 2004, 125). Soutsos was not blind to the increasing social misery and poverty in industrial nations. The right balance between private activity and social justice was, for him, the most important problem of economics of this time (Soutsos 1885, 720). Poverty and pauperism posed a challenge for an economist The latter should, for Soutsos, stand in the middle between the promotion of the poor and the "sociologists" who demanded changes in private property. At this point, Soutsos discussed authors like Owen, Fourier, and Louis Blanc, without referring to Marx at all. The economist was, for Soutsos, on the right side of the analysis if he would offer practical solutions within the framework that made prosperity a possibility for all. The demand of sociologists/heretics to set limits to private action was, for him, totally wrong.

Soutsos' erudition and liberalism remained unchallenged on a theoretical level during the whole of the 19th century in Greece. However, as we saw, he couldn't influence policymaking. The latter had its own agenda, subordinated as it was throughout the 19th century to the administrative approach and to territorial expansion. For this reason, Soutsos published further works that tried to alert his fellow citizens to the dark sides of policies pursued by Greek statesmen. These were published as *Plutological Studies* in 1874.

3.5.3 On Budget and Taxes, 1876

In the early 1870s, the Eastern Question had been rekindled by the Serbian and Bulgarian uprisings, and an eventual victory by those two Balkan competitors would challenge Ottoman rule and affect Greek territorial claims. Public opinion was alarmed and pushed for closer cooperation of the country with the Great Powers. The Greek government sought a compromise regarding the repayment of its public debt.

It was for this reason that Soutsos felt obliged to speak up and influence decision-making (Soutsos 1876). The Megali Idea was, for Soutsos, a noble pursuit, but Greece had better not be dragged unprepared into "fruitless struggles" (6), he opined. Only a financially strong state could win political wars in the international arena, he reminded. From 1843 onward, those who ruled the country were driven by Machiavellian intentions, governing according to their own interests, rather than for the general good. Therefore, top-priority decisions for the economy were neglected.

The Greek problem of the era was, according to Soutsos, a problem of political economy and of sound finance. The budget of 1876 presented, according to his calculations, accumulated government deficits amounting to approximately 57.5 million drachmas for the period 1861–76. Numbers appearing in annual reports were inaccurate. Public property and state assets in NBG shares totaling 15 million drachmas had been sold to generate state income and expenditure. According to him, the tax system in Greece was incompatible with the one espoused by scientific treatises on Public Finance (14). His thorough examination of the budget demonstrated that a lot needed to change before it was too late (25–50). In summary, he proposed a "yes" to net property income taxation based on a land register/cadaster and on land quality. He also warned against a further rise in taxation of buildings, favored the taxation of profits from shares, demanded the taxation of banks having the privilege to issue banknotes (i.e., the NBG), and proposed the introduction of an inheritance tax. The stamp tax should continue to exist, and tariffs ought not to be protectionist.

The tax on ploughing animals, which was under preparation (and was finally passed in 1880), was a tax on a production tool, a tax existing in economically totally backward countries in Northern Africa. It was a despicable tax, according to Soutsos. Agriculture was the most productive sector of the economy and employed most of the population; it wasn't, however, a sector of government concern. On the contrary, not only did gross income taxation remain in effect, but there was also a tax on grinding which was taking a disproportionate toll on poor farmers. Soutsos accepted that the only fair taxes that served a public purpose were those on tobacco and alcohol. Finally, arrears to the public treasury were viewed as "a moral and political issue" and new loans, under these conditions, would prove "an act of extreme recklessness" (50).

Soutsos understood how the average citizen felt and how faithful to the Megali Idea everyone was. Armed conflict would, however, prove futile without a strong economy, he repeated. An economically vulnerable country would fail to pursue long-term political aspirations. Soutsos proposed the establishment of a National Defense Fund aimed at financing military expenditure. This Fund would have its own resources and would not be dependent on borrowing (1876, 53–4). Its creation would represent a policy breakthrough and it would slow down the country's indebtedness. This Fund was finally created fifteen years after Soutsos' passing, in 1905.

Soutsos was against the then prevailing rhetoric of the Megali Idea, because, in his view, it was not based on an economically and politically powerful Greece. For him, the Megali Idea was the economic and political advancement of the nation: "The moral and material means for the implementation of the Megali Idea consists mainly in the economic and political promotion of the nation and the good opinion of the civilized world about Greece" (1876, 6), he stressed. The irredentist rhetoric was a clear indication of political and national irresponsibility on the part of politicians who looked for temporary political gains. This was the reason, he believed, that Greek governments were thrown into unnecessary struggles that caused great ethical and material damage.

What the Greek state needed was a huge reforming effort of its public finances, which could release resources for the encouragement of productive activities. "We march into a slippery road," he warned, "when we balance our budget through lending and the selling of national property" (1876, 12). The most pressing fiscal problem in 1876 was, for Soutsos, that of the arrears. Their existence reflected the inability of the central government to enforce its will on local interests. These arrears were estimated by him to be as much as 57 million Drachmae in 1863, *viz.* 35% of GDP, and as much as 80 million Drachmae, *viz.* 32.4% of GDP in 1876 (1876, 46). This problem revealed a chronic disease of fiscal management, since the revenues that were registered annually in the budget were fictitious and, consequently, the budget deficits were greater than the official ones.

Soutsos attacked the spending mentality of "a coalition of interests which had been mainly created by the governments" (12) and advocated that public servants had the duty to administer the public sector "as prudent family men" (15). Only productive works, those that created wealth, especially railways, were a *sine qua non* condition for the encouragement of domestic production (9, 12). He repeated his demand that all citizens should pay taxes (49–50). He asked again for the creation of a land register (23). For the same reasons, Soutsos also considered the taxation of mills and of ploughing animals as unfair. The mill-tax affected the price of bread and fell on the "shoulders of the poorest people. Wealthy people eat meat, but meat does not get subjected to a tax," he argued (1876, 33). On the other hand, the tax of ploughing animals was to be estimated not on a revenue basis, but on the number of animals used. It was also an unjust tax because "two farms of different quality and location are taxed according to the numbers of animals used" (1876, 30).

3.5.4 The "Economic Issue"

Three years later, Soutsos returned with an almost identical set of proposals (Soutsos 1879). New frontiers were opened for the Megali Idea. According to the results of the Berlin Congress in the summer of 1878, Greece was allowed to annex the fertile province of Thessaly and a part of Epirus to the Kingdom. The annexation required new expenditures, which could not be afforded through the existing budget. Either new loans would have to be raised to meet these expenses, or public expenditure needed to be rationalized.

Soutsos was not optimistic because, despite Greece's development record in between, not much had happened in the direction he espoused with his reform proposals of 1863 and those of 1876. Except for the distribution of national land in 1871, governments had not undertaken any other essential effort for the encouragement of productive activity. The average annual growth rate of GDP since 1864 was less than 1% (Kostelenos 2003). Soutsos, therefore, could not endorse the foreign lending that restarted in 1879. The public debt had already risen to the amount of 60 million drachmae, which made him think that it could hardly be serviced in the future. Soutsos considered this fiscal anomaly not as a temporary phenomenon, but as "the product of a long-term economic disorder" (1879, 4). The reason for this disorder was the chronic incapability of the State to reduce its expenditures (5). The solution to this situation was a long-term austerity program, the only way for the Greek state to escape from the vicious circle of repetitious lending. A special cause of this situation was the expansion of the "insusceptible reducible expenses" (5). These totally inelastic public expenditures were primarily military expenses

(8). The top priority, however, was the contribution of the "citizens, not paying taxes" to Greek finances. This broadening of the existing very narrow tax base in society, which only included peasants, was unsustainable: "We cannot cover the deficits of the budget … without levying new taxes, particularly on the insufficiently taxed" (15), he stressed. Lightly taxed were, for example, commercial and banking profits, as well as industrial profits (28). The monasteries should also contribute to taxation, according to their property. The inheritance tax should become heavier too (21–35). Moreover, levying indirect taxes on certain consumption goods (such as tobacco and wine) could offer an important alleviation for the budget, without having any gloomy effect on production and the price level (47–52). Last, but not least, new long-term loans were required for the settlement of the loans of the war of independence, which still burdened the budget excessively (53). The government levied taxes without taking into consideration the sources of taxation, and thus prepared its own dead-end (12).

To summarize, Soutsos was an academic and a citizen who tried to influence society with his call for sound fiscal management and inclusive infrastructural works. Stability and efficiency were needed both for economic growth and for the successful fulfillment of the Megali Idea. Sound fiscal foundations were the basis for future welfare for Greece. It was unfortunate that after defaulting in 1893 little was heard about his proposals and ideas for Greece.

3.6 Economos

Aristidis Economos was one of the most prolific Greek economists of the 19th century and a fierce critic of government interventionism. He was born in 1835, the son of a small landowner in Kalavrita in the Peloponnese. He was very well educated privately by his uncle Prokopios, a high-ranking official of the Church. Economos studied Law at the University of Athens from 1851 to 1856 and later taught political economy at the same university. He blended economic liberalism with social responsibility towards weaker members of society, in the tradition developed by the Christian Fathers of the East.

While he was studying, he published a small, short-lived newspaper and translated Guizot's *Discours sur l'histoire de la revolution d'Angleterre* into Greek. His respect for England's growth to an economic power is reflected in his dedication of his translation to Queen Victoria and his introductory statement that "Greece would be happy, if it could borrow from England the seeds of the latter's well-being" (Economos 1950, 94). The Glorious Revolution and the French Revolution had taught the world two different lessons, he wrote, therefore "we should care for and educate ourselves toward true constitutional administration, otherwise blood will be shed" (94). It is evident that he favored the rule of law as opposed to revolution.

He started his career as a judge in 1857 and, after serving in provincial towns, he was promoted to repeal judge, and in 1864 he was transferred to Athens. In March 1867, he was appointed ifigitis for Political Economy at the University of Athens and taught for 12 years. He also lectured at the Society of the Friends of the People, an association committed to the educational betterment of the lower classes. Between May and September 1869, during the year of John Stuart Mill's recantation of the wages fund doctrine, he undertook his only trip abroad and spent five months, mostly in England, where his brother-in-law, Dimitrios Vikelas (or Bikelas), was living. Upon returning to Greece, he took an active part in the establishment of consumer cooperatives and of associations of small businessmen, an activity he pursued until his death. He edited the short-lived *Newspaper of the Prisons,* devoted to the improvement of conditions in Greek jailhouses. In 1873, he founded the *Economic Review*, the only Greek economic journal in the 19th century that can be called scientific, and wrote the book on the importance of free trade, that we already referred to. He also published a study of the city of *Lavrion* (1872), focusing on the foreign company that exploited its mines and was in legal controversy with the Greek government. Economos argued that the license of the company dealt with the exploitation of the underground mines. The existence of precious metals in raw form on the surface nearby was not part of the deal, he opined. Both the public and the government were, in his view, right in pinpointing that the Italian investor had no property rights on findings located on the ground surface.

In 1878, Economos resigned as a judge and started working as a lawyer, preparing for his political career. He was elected MP for Kalavrita in 1879 and distinguished himself in parliament as a speaker on economic issues. In 1881, he failed to be elected as an MP for Attica, but remained politically active by writing in the newspapers *New Ideas* and *The Defender of the People.* He was re-elected to parliament in 1885 but lost his seat in the premature elections of 1886. Judging from his insistence, he would have tried a new comeback, but he died of a heart attack in 1890 at the age of 55.

3.6.1 The Journal

The journal *Economic Review* (Oikonomiki Epitheorisis, OE) appeared in March 1873 as a monthly publication of 48 pages. It stopped after 132 issues, in February 1884 and reappeared in February 1888. In April 1890, one month after the editor's death, its 159th and last issue was published.

The journal's subtitle, "Political economy, public finance, statistics," outlined its contents. Around 1,300 notes and articles were published, with the average article being approximately 5 pages long. Most notes were written by the editor himself, with at least around 50 other authors, businessmen, and intellectuals contributing. Economos' contributions quite often made direct reference to the works of Sismondi, Mill, Bastiat, Droz, Smith, and Ricardo. Economos viewed economic science as a unifying force for people, addressing both poor and rich citizens. "The evils plaguing the Western European society," he said, "have fortunately not yet emerged among us" (OE 7, 303), alluding to miserable working conditions and strikes in Europe, but not in Greece.

Some articles, typically the leading ones, dealt with theoretical issues and included citations that were approximately 50% French, 45% British, and 5% German/other. These introductory articles were followed by informative pieces and comparative statistics. Here, reference was made mainly to British reviews and sources like *The Economist*, *The Bullionist*, *The North British Review*, the *Journal of the Statistical Society*, the *Cobden Club,* etc.

The review's ideological outlook was liberal, inline with mainstream thought in the mid-19th century. As a result, it opposed the interventionism of all Greek governments. Political economy was, according to Economos, the science of the well-being of the nations, the discipline which "enters both the cabin of the poor as well as the mansion of the rich," (1, 155). It taught harmony, which was considered by him as equivalent to love in the Christian tradition. The division of labor was "the greater of the Laws, with which human nature was endowed by Providence" (1, 160).

In accordance with Senior, he distinguished between Political Economy and the Science of Legislation (6, 13–20). The government was invited to interfere to promote welfare, and this was done by introducing the market in place of privilege and government arbitrariness (6, 485). The common people were capable, through work, thrift, and combining forces, to become property owners. He characterized small property as "a school of intellectual, moral, and economic progress of the people" (1, 148).

The fact that he was a very religious person didn't lead him to seek solutions to economic problems in the Bible. "We shouldn't judge usury based on a specific chapter of the Holy Book," he said, "but we should only be based on the law of equity" (8, 506; see also 9, 333–40). He glorified the division of labor and thrift as developmental pathways and favored market-based solutions over legislative interventions, above all in relation to interest rates. He supported the idea of private post offices. He advocated productive labor and industrialization, without endorsing protection. Following Ricardo, he thought that mechanization and industrialization were "definite achievements of humans" (6, 383) and there was no question therefore that capital "as it expands, creates more employment than it destroys" (5, 23). Following Say, he considered excessive production to be a harmless process, just like the air, the abundance of which cannot cause harm (7, 144).

He also argued for producer cooperatives, because he regarded their power to be a multiple of the sum of individual members. By the same token, society was not a mere sum of individuals, but came to life through social groups. He preached the need for municipal banks following the steps of Schulze-Delitzsch in Germany. He also stood for free trade, as already mentioned, but also presented the ideas of List in his journal (3, 524–8). He was in favor of strengthening the agricultural sector before supporting any other productive sector of the economy.

Businessmen should, according to Economos, maintain a close contact with their employees and inform them about business prospects, especially in times of economic distress. Society would progress "if the entrepreneurs distribute what is according to justice harmonious" (8, 242) – meaning a fair share of wages. Absentee ownership and luxurious consumption were evils in society, but shouldn't be combated through legislation, as economic ways could be found to minimize their existence (6, 123–7 and 11, 433–5).

The market mechanism was to be relied upon despite possible fluctuations in prices, especially wages. Economos believed that usury in Greece was a severe social evil and stressed on many occasions the need to bring the interest rate down, by encouraging the creation of cooperative banks that would increase the supply of capital, or by the appropriate monetary policy. Under no circumstances did he accept an administrative setting of the interest rate. Intervention in the market, even if the issue was the pricing of medicine for the poor, was "an economic sin" (5, 493). The government should balance its budget and reduce the tax burden, an issue Economos spoke about many times in parliament.

His view on public finance deserves a more detailed analysis. For Economos, progressive taxation was "a major social truth" (1, 324), and it was a groundbreaking idea. He applauded William Pitt's initiatives in Britain, and while examining the Greek tax system of his day, he stressed: "I do not applaud the grandiose compensation of the bourgeoise paid out of the farmers' pockets" (2, 247). He criticized ever-rising indirect taxes on the necessities of life. Taxation on city dwellers combined with tax cuts for farmers was a "social issue of the first order" (2, 454). He also endorsed the taxation of net, not gross, income. The rich landowners and the holders of stock and joint stock companies should be made to contribute to government revenue.

Overall, Economos was, together with Soutsos, one of the most outspoken critics of the prevalent tax system, as well as of the political system, in general. He testified to abuses in tax collection (11, 257). His assessment of state bureaucracy was explicitly negative. He emphasized the hypocrisy of civil servants, stating that "the public treasury is empty, while the ones stealing from it are eternally speaking of honesty" (5, 255).

With the national income at 320 million drachmas, he calculated taxes at 100 million, that is, at 32% of GDP (12, 51), drawn from a very narrow basis. This indicated that the country was getting closer to collapse. In his words, the country is "treading its bizarre path with slumped shoulders, amidst the peaceful shift of its tax burdens" (12, 104). He also noted that: "Horror is caused by the number of trials between heirs and tax inspectors" (7, 48) to argue for the simplicity of citizen/state relations.

Commenting on Trikoupis' announcements on imminent tax reforms, Economos said that "judging by the many symptoms, the tax plague seems set to start a new tour" (12, 375) and added that: "All these paeans of praise … will not prove enough to anticipate the future. A state, whose existence is based on constant borrowing, cannot forever escape settling its bills" (13, 160). Economos, like Soutsos, considered the fact that the NBG was not yet taxed to be totally irrational.

Finally, Economos believed that "the road of government borrowing entails grave dangers" (2, 290), and that Greece tended to sign loan agreements "without internal provision about their repayment" (6, 519). During the 20-year period between 1858 and 1876, budget deficits were persistent, and 1876, a critical year for the Eastern Question, found state finances vulnerable (4, 385). As he put it, "the country is under the thumb of a dreadful bureaucracy" (4, 389). Someone had to "grip the nation before it fell into the abyss" (5, 527). This was a recurring theme in his later papers (7, 497–8).

In monetary affairs, Economos sided against the agreement with the LMU and stood for monometallism (1, 496). He argued that the depreciation of silver in Europe would confuse transactions and allow for speculation, even by banking institutions (4, 336). Economos referred extensively to the views of Henry Dunning Macleod. He agreed with him that "the idea that the currency is a state-led invention is extremely fossilized" (1, 495). The value of the currency was not legally defined, but instead it was decided by agents in the real economy. The NBG loans to the government demonstrated "how much power was deducted from the industrial sector" (1, 82) and he condemned agreements between the NBG and the Trikoupis government (11, 265–86). Trikoupis, in his view, "rendered the government a puppet of the National Bank" (9, 28–37).

On foreign policy issues, Economos was in favor of the Megali Idea but had arguments similar to the ones by Soutsos. He stressed that "all those thinking that the Megali Idea is only a military issue seem to forget the sort of soldiers the industrial age creates" (1, 573). He was against all those who believed that loans increased the country's wealth and thought they were totally wrong. "The road of government borrowing entails grave dangers," he stressed. "If the people were aware of the terms of these loans, they would control their rulers" (2, 289), he reminded. Greece should wake up and "take care of a dowry with which to endow the future of the East" (3, 560).

As the government was preparing its financial statement for the year 1876, Economos was appalled by the numbers he saw in the draft budget, observing that "their coldness burns like ice" (5, 527). This "terrible situation of persistent deficits" had to change. He considered in 1880 the situation to be the same as before. Financial statements for the last three years showed, for him, a weakened economy. Economos viewed Greece as skating on thin ice. "Our national status has come to a pivotal point," he said. "The East is at risk of getting out of our reach, taking the ideal of Hellenism with it" (8, 322). Greek national claims were perceived by the Great Powers as theft, while Piedmont, thanks to its economic prowess, managed to unify Italy without any objection. Therefore, he did not hesitate to warn: "All these paeans of praise … will not prove enough to anticipate the future. A state, the existence of which is based on constant borrowing, cannot forever escape settling its bills" (13, 160). One can only wish Prime Minister Trikoupis had listened to him.

Economos stood for an active role of the state in furnishing the infrastructure needed for productive activities (4, 325). He advocated, with some reservations, a public railway system both for economic as well as for political reasons (3, 424) and watched very anxiously and with a critical eye the slow efforts of successive Greek governments to accomplish this task (5, 241–5 and 13, 118). Being a paternalistic supporter of the working poor, he also advocated compulsory public education (1, 115) and espoused the adoption of regulations taken out of the British Health and Factory Acts (8, 363–8). Bismark's social policy found Economos' utmost approval (11, 334–9 and 13, 70–5).

Economos advanced a simplistic class analysis according to which 90% of the Greeks were the "working people," who "under the name of a capitalist, – either that of a landowner or that of a worker, are tyrannized" by the "administrating class" (also referred to as "administrative school"), meaning the political elite of the country (177). As he said, "I am disgusted by professional politicians. I don't like those who live and enrich themselves out of public affairs" (225).

He was optimistic that "the best ones of the nation will build on the ruins of the administrative class a new order of ideas," (226) because he saw economic life progressing. According to him, the "working people," being in the majority small landowners, resembled the British Gentry that, thanks to Tudor legislation, came to greatness during the Stuarts. These people would educate their children and claim a share in representing the nation by electing their own in parliament (7, 367).

Once elected under the slogan "everything for the people and through the people" (7, 420), as an independent deputy, Economos declined offers to ally himself with established parties. He spoke in parliament on a very wide range of topics, but was mostly concerned about three: unbalanced budgets, tax policy, and the critique of the NBG. He identified his struggle as one against absolutism (1, 143) and anticipated a trend among the ruling class "to share the power to appoint employees with the central authority" (1, 53–4). It was a huge misfortune that the Greek political system was unable to "integrate social life … within the limits of its resources" (3, 192). Bavarian rule in Greece represented a "genus of locusts that drained tens of millions out of the country's treasury" (8, 534). This situation remained unchanged in the decades that followed. Whereas, in every country, there were two political parties, the conservatives and the progressives, in Greece "a third genus of humans emerged, which could be called the cultivators of power" (362). Due to bureaucracy, the country was flooded with bills and administrative measures and then "the art of interpretation comes to assemble what cannot be assembled" (365). In his reports to his voters, which he published in sequels in his journal, Economos called the then political elite a "governing school" and a "governing class" (7, 358–70), defining it as "a gang of people assuming politics as their vocation and Greece as their feud" (10, 34).

The year when Economos was first elected coincided with the resumption of debt repayments and access to new foreign borrowing. This meant, for him, that loans would be used to cover the budget deficit, and all reforms for modernizing Greece would be postponed. He was therefore one of the most outspoken critics of this policy. "The road of foreign loans disguises severe dangers" (2, 290), he claimed and condemned the continuing budget deficits as a policy that not only crowded out the private sector (4, 196), not only postponed the convertibility of paper money to specie (4, 256), but also led Greek national claims to a dead end (3, 560 and 8, 322).

The long-awaited reform of the tax system was implemented in 1881 with the burden falling upon peasants owning animals used in agriculture. Economos' reaction in parliament was harsh. He said to Prime Minister Trikoupis:

> Through this form of taxation you tax the means of production, which, by the way, has not the same productive power in every case, and you don't tax the revenue. You violate thus the principle of equity and that of science as well.
> (Economos 1950, 291)

The tax on ploughing animals was unjust because it was not based on net income. Ownership of a ploughing animal revealed nothing about the peasant's income. "One day," he said ironically, "you will tax the scissors of the tailor and the hammer of the laborer."[49] Predictably, this new legislation aroused considerable controversy and sharp debate. Nevertheless, when put to the ballot, the law was successfully voted in the parliament and constituted a major victory for Trikoupis.[50]

Economos also opposed the government's tendency to increase indirect taxes on the necessities of life (2, 451). In many articles he tried to be constructive (7, 48; 11, 5; 11, 481), by pointing out tax increases that could be sustained. What he demanded in return was the elimination of corruption (11, 258) and the taxation of the rich that Trikoupis avoided for political reasons. "What we demand," Economos said, "is justice and equity, … a taxation … proportional to each man's ability to pay" (13, 53), and added: "Do you want to see fire from the sky to believe the word of truth?" (55).

Another target of criticism for Economos was the privilege of note issue that the NBG possessed since its foundation. It was extended in 1861 and was being discussed for renewal in parliament in 1880. The double role of the National Bank, a profit-seeking private enterprise on the one hand, while performing the duties of a central bank on the other, found Economos' utmost disapproval. The NBG didn't function as it should and didn't furnish Greek agriculture, the country's most important economic sector, with the loans needed (2, 406). An Agricultural Bank should be called into life (1, 412).

His argumentation was twofold: On the one side, the NBG had become a part of the state apparatus and was unashamedly exchanging favors with the ruling elite. This explained the low taxes it paid and the fact that the monopoly on issuing banknotes was awarded to the NBG for free. On the other hand, he argued, a monopoly normally raised prices – in this case, interest rates. Greater competition in the banking sector would lead to a better allocation of resources, especially the much-needed financing of agricultural improvements.

He returned many times to the issue of the close ties between the government and the NBG's board of directors. According to him, the privilege to issue banknotes was based "on rotten ideas from the times of absolutism" (1, 231). He demanded the introduction of a free banking system in Greece, as in the USA (5, 337). In the case, however, that the privilege of the NBG would be retained, he demanded a compensation with at least 1/6 of total bank profits (3, 172; see also Economos 1950, 305–13). Registering that in Japan the right to issue banknotes was awarded to 4 banks in 1875 and 103 in 1879, he ironically remarked: "Free banking has acclimatized itself in the land of despotism! What can one say about the places of freedom that sigh under the banking privilege?" (9, 267). As the bonds between the NBG and the state remained very tight and Economos failed to be re-elected, he openly admitted that this failure was the outcome of an uneven battle between the interests of the NBG that fought against his re-election (10, –130–44).

To conclude, Aristidis Economos was a liberal, a supporter of free trade, and an opponent of every kind of government privilege that spoiled competition. He was also in favor of the gold standard and rejected bimetallism. Through his scientific journal, he had the opportunity to diffuse his liberal views and thus create an important forum for the absorption of economic ideas into Greek society. As a politician, Economos didn't succeed in building up an alternative block of political forces, and the "working people" continued in their majority to vote for the two bigger political parties. He was, however, an original thinker, who combined political economy creatively with his entirely Greek, religiously inspired, education. He was a man who passionately got involved in current affairs, one of the most astute critics of Greek political and economic life of the 19th century.

3.7 Other Academics

Next to Soutsos and Economos, there were other economists who left their mark on Greek economic thought in the 19th century, with various contributions of a theoretical nature or through teaching.

3.7.1 A. Dosios

Aristidis Dosios was the first Greek economist who published a book in a foreign language. His *Les Limites d' Economie Politique*, a small popularizing book of 92 pages, came out in Paris in 1867. In his treatise, he synthesized the views of German and French economists on the scope, nature, and importance of economics as a science (10–18). The aim of economics was to make society rich and enable citizens to be happy. He discussed the nature of capital and labor as factors of production and the creation of wealth (55–73). These two factors combined forces to create, through exchange future growth and were therefore equally important for the economy's future.

The book, through its simple language, informed readers about the economy, avoiding complicated ideas and theories. French and German contemporary authors were cited, with John Stuart Mill being the only Briton in the references. The book didn't create a public sensation, but reflected the state of the art at the time when classical economics was being challenged by Marx and the Historical School, while the neoclassical approach was still in the making.

3.7.2 Trikaliotis

Based on his publications in the 1860s, Stamos Trikaliotis became an ifigitis at the University of Athens, where he taught for five years. In his inaugural lecture (1866), he agreed with Sismondi that the right answer to the question of whether wealth was of supreme importance and the individual a secondary agent was "no" (28).

His textbook *Manual of Political Economy* appeared in 1871. In it, he defended political equality and attacked state intervention beyond some basic institutional settings. Following Sismondi, he attacked classical political economy in his lectures for being dogmatic and too focused on the British experience (386). His combination of individualism and liberalism didn't result in concrete suggestions for reforms in Greece. He rather believed that the new dynasty would opt for a different path than that of its predecessors. His liberalism was not unconditional. He could see ideological uses of economic doctrines and would warn his students about their consequences.

3.7.3 Adamopoulos

Timoleon Adamopoulos was an ifigitis at the University of Athens and was voted MP for Thessaly. His only publication, and probably the topic of his lectures, was a pamphlet on *The Human Being as a Subject of Economics* (1874). As the title suggests, Adamopoulos adopted a humanist approach glorifying all forms of human work, manual and mental. He stressed that economics should play a more unifying role in its analysis of mankind and should offer an inclusive, not a radical view about human efforts to achieve prosperity.

3.7.4 Zografos

Ioannis Zografos studied in Germany and received his PhD in Heidelberg in 1868, supervised by Karl Heinrich Rau. This was probably the first dissertation of a Greek citizen in Economics in Germany. His *Essay on Money* was prefaced in 1876 by another prominent German public finance specialist, Lorenz von Stein. He was an early follower of the currency school in Greece, an advocate of the protection of infant industries, and a critical observer of Greek economic policy in the late nineteenth and early twentieth centuries. He served for a brief period (1885–6) as a professor of Public Finance at the University of Athens and later became the general secretary of the University of Athens. In parallel, he followed a political career with the Party of Theodoros Deliyiannis. His collected works were included in three volumes in Zografos 1925.

He initially devoted himself to monetary theory. In the *Essay on Money,* he explained in broad strokes what money was, the use of metal money in ancient times, the use of gold and silver in modern times, and the appearance of paper money. The banknote had substituted the metallic circulation of the past, posing challenges for authorities (34). Paper money was, for Zografos, "a machine" (37). The basis of value of paper money was the security transactors felt until they needed to be reimbursed in specie, if needed (36). Securing confidence was therefore of paramount importance for policymakers. Profits derived from the circulation of paper money should be cashed by the government. On this point, and in agreement with Henry Dunning Mc Leod, he stressed that credit was capital. Therefore, in his view, the monopoly of the NBG to issue money without returning a part of its profits to the government was questionable (45). He criticized legislation enacted due to NBG pressure that allowed the bank to keep in its vaults specie only up to 1/3 of total circulation as an extreme privilege that allowed the bank to shamelessly speculate in the economy.

Discussing in detail monetary developments in Greece, Zografos blamed those who rather endured "the imperfection of ordinary things rather than innovation toward real progress" (64). Times had passed since the drachma was defined in relation to gold and silver. Changing the value that was set when Greece became a kingdom would not be an offense or something negative. On the contrary, and due to different growth paths between Greece and the rest of Europe, a new parity was necessary. Development in relation to the signing of the agreement of the LMU and the inability of Greece to abide by that proved the accuracy of his position, he stressed. Otherwise, the LMU would not be in accordance with the needs of the state (71). One must either apply a treaty or not enter it and then remain outside, he concluded.

In his follow-up study, *The Value of Paper Money in Greece* (1878), he underlined that, up to then, Greek governments "were not children of social needs and healthy national beliefs, but expressions of one-sided clans … not real governments" (93–4). They simply neglected the national interest, in his view. Zografos renewed his critique against the NBG (98, 109), because it provoked panic in the market with its decisions (125). He wondered why no state officials sat on its board (169) and why the bank financed only 100% secure activities and not Greek agriculture. In this regard, he attacked those who disregarded economic science, equating it with metaphysics, and remarked that they favored their own empiricism (142).

In the same year, he defended his ifigessia about *Tariffs and Tariff Quotas on Currants* and demonstrated a wide knowledge of external economic relations, both historical and theoretical. He referred not only to French and German authors but to British authors as well, as he comparatively explored tariff systems in the developed world. He concluded by referring to the main Greek export commodity, currants. He proposed offering lower tariffs for their products in the Greek market to countries importing currants. His inaugural lecture as Professor for Public Finance in 1881 testified once more to his wide knowledge of theory and history. It was devoted to the topic of the evolution of taxes and of public finance from ancient times to that day, as did his textbook that appeared shortly thereafter.

Zografos was also a keen observer of contemporary developments. Starting in 1893 and every three years, he published a pamphlet on economic developments during this time (1925, vol. 3). He criticized the Trikoupian law of 1880 on taxing ploughing animals, as Soutsos and Economos had done, and thought that the 1882 return to convertibility with the backing of a loan was a mistake (71). He criticized the raising of taxes and then the spending of the revenues for the mobilization of the armed forces by Trikoupis (11) but admitted that Deligiannis followed the same path three years later (129). He discussed the tariff system of 1884, criticized the lack of sufficient protection for industry and clearly used protectionist arguments (121). "In the battle you don't send infants to fight giants" (121), he stressed. After 1901, his reviews of economic policy became less affiliated with party politics, but provoked discussions in newspapers and the wider public.

In short, Zografos criticized both monetary and fiscal policy of successive governments, which led to huge external deficits (1925, 175–230). With his work and the work of Nikolaos Gounarakis, economic thought in Greece transitioned to an era when the GHS set foot and slowly developed into a new conventional wisdom.

3.7.5 Gounarakis

Nikolaos Gounarakis studied in Greece and after the death of Ioannis Soutsos, he was elected professor of economics at the University of Athens. However, being a MP with the Deligiannis Party, he was mostly on leave from his academic duties. He even served as the Minister of Finance for six months between 1904 and 1905.

He became an ifigitis with his *On Metallic Legal Money, in Particular on Bimetallism* (1882). Gounarakis tried to explain international monetary developments (on these see Willis 1901) and at the same time to contribute to policy discussions. From the beginning, he put power politics at the center of his analysis. Protection was, for Gounarakis, discussed in the past for economic reasons only, but lately it was discussed due to political ones, to make a country stronger in the international political arena (17). Monetary discussions in developed economies reflected this, in his view. The LMU changed, according to him, after Germany took a different monetary route in 1876. Silver coins were not printed in France anymore (27). Fixed weight and denomination of national currencies were extremely important (33), but this was not enough for small nations participating in world trade.

Gounarakis believed that bimetallism provided them with flexibility and that short-term fluctuations between gold and silver didn't really matter (42). The existence of just one standard had, for Gounarakis, a minor effect on the stability of the value of money in the short term, but a bigger one in long term (45). Legislation about the exchange value between gold and silver was therefore very important (55). Gounarakis conceded that a fixed permanent legal exchange value for gold and silver was against economic nature (74), but, on the other hand, he admitted that precious metals, due to their nature, didn't obey the law of supply and demand (88). In a rather axiomatic form, he argued that gold was in short supply in relation to the needs of trade (117) and that fluctuations in the value of money caused economic crises (140). Between monetary expansion and contraction, it was better to endure a crisis of oversupply of money than to deflate the economy (143).

Another factor that demanded Gounarakis' attention was the role of the exchange premium (157–8). Greece, due to its importation of foodstuffs, was dependent on developments abroad and needed to adjust to what its main trade partners decided (171). In a country like Greece, paper money facilitated transactions but also kept metallic money relatively stable, he argued (173). Paper money was "splendid" (175), he stressed, for it circulated among transactors and metallic reserves as its backup gained in value (177). Different exchange standards for gold and silver were negative for the global economy. Greece should favor bimetallism, because its needs in global trade needed an open door to fluctuations in the relative value of gold and silver (183).

Gounarakis supported current government policy in Greece and set the needs of the state and the NBG on a higher level than the demand of transactors to immediately convert their drachmas to specie. For him, paper money gave government authorities the opportunity to save on specie and control the price level and external trade without the fear of a constant negative exchange premium on the currency.

In his inaugural lecture as a full professor, Gounarakis accepted the State as the instrument for maximum production and equitable distribution of income (1890, 13). He praised Smith for his achievements but referred without elaboration to "theoretical deficiencies" in his work (7). Free enterprise undoubtedly brought prosperity, but this occurred not as a rule, but "according to conditions" (8). At the same time, repeatedly occurring crises challenged policymakers. The remedy for this situation was legal action to stabilize the economy for the benefit of all. Socialism was a false doctrine, but on the other hand government action could support weak private initiative and thus provide the basis for a better economic future. In other words, if the citizens could not fulfilll their targets and if there was a social need, then the government ought to interfere in the economy and lead it to maximum results (16).

In his *Elements of Political Economy* (1st ed. 1891, 3rd ed. 1918) he provided a less liberal approach to economics than Soutsos. He suggested that there was no sound theoretical reason to limit the role and scope of state-action in the Greek economy (13). The main reason was that Greece was a country where "obstacles to a maximum full production are still existing and measures to facilitate economic activity were not still at place" (23). Markets were not enlarged, a full division of labor was non-existent, machinery was scarce, large-scale production was absent, and there were no large cities to sustain labor supply for industry. Greece "was a large farm" (23) divided into two parts without linkages between them. One part, the most fertile, was in touch, through external trade, to the world economy and was thriving. The second was oriented toward self-consumption, didn't exploit natural resources, and didn't aim at diversification of production and market exchanges. Due to this situation, Greece was not, according to him, an "equal part of the great homeland of capitals" (24). This negative situation had a positive collateral: the harmonious co-existence of labor and capital up to that period. Gounarakis didn't think that immediate reform in this setting was urgent, for the main goal of Greece was "the fulfilment of our national aim," meaning the Great Idea (24). Once the country would have reached its justified borders, then this would "act as a unit toward more development and civilization" (25).

In the meantime, small steps should be undertaken. Gounarakis praised Friedrich List's protectionist views and the economic policies pursued by Chancellor Bismarck in Prussia and advocated for Greece an economic policy that would give priority to the encouragement of industry. The tariff reform by Trikoupis in 1882 was not supportive enough for domestic industrial activities. Gounarakis stressed the need for policies that paid respect to national necessities and needs, and praised the historical investigation of economic phenomena, since a sound and solid foundation of economic theory could only be based on historical terms.

On a theoretical level, he accepted the possibility of an economic crisis in a capitalist system. Production and consumption could not coincide "with mathematical precision" (201). Therefore, there were times of overproduction or of underconsumption. These phenomena occurred, but they were the price "society paid for economic progress" (203) In other words, he thought crises were inevitable parts of a business cycle leading to more growth. He rejected deflation as a means of curing economic crises and favored flexibility in monetary policy. He recommended the creation of a monetary buffer to be used during crises to smooth the situation in the market and assist the self-correction of the market mechanism. It was for this reason that he also accepted bimetallism in international economic relations.

3.7.6 Kazazis

Neoklis Kazazis, a professor of the "Encyclopedia of Law" at the University of Athens, was the interim professor for political economy when Gounarakis was on leave due to his parliamentary duties.

Trained in Germany and France, he published the *General Principles of Political Economy* (1894), a 500-page treatise in which he displayed erudition, synthesis, and knowledge of the literature in French, English, German, and Italian. The textbook was divided into five sections: Fundamental concepts, production of wealth, circulation of wealth, distribution of wealth, and consumption of wealth. After the introduction, he offered 120 pages on methodology and history of economic thought, explaining the differences between deduction and induction, the analytical and the synthetic method, and focusing on the current state of economics. His history of economic thought in France, England, Germany, and Italy showed an acquaintance with primary sources and followed major thinkers and their work. He discussed Smith extensively, as well as the work of authors belonging to the GHS.[51] He declared, however, the analysis of the French Liberal School, especially Jean-Baptiste Say, Frederic Bastiat, and others, as superior. He proposed a synthesis of objective and subjective explanations on the theory of value (138–44) and covered both monetary and fiscal theory with practical information and recommendations. He also discussed economic crises, citing Clément Juglar and the sunspot theory of Stanley Jevons (362–7) to explain the phenomenon.

In contrast with other authors, Kazazis made no attempt to take Greek reality into account in his lectures. He praised the entrepreneur and the general manager, whereas he was against trade unions and non-market determination of wages. He was supportive of free trade, and the introduction of new machinery in production processes without referring to any counterarguments. He attacked socialists and their ideas. He examined the infant industry argument and condemned it, even if he acknowledged that if tariffs were in place, it would be wrong to lift protection suddenly. He distinguished between fair and catastrophic competition and accepted government interference if action were temporary. Laissez-faire could lead to extremes as well, but on the other hand government should not attempt to solve the so-called social issue to alleviate poverty (21). State intervention created moral hazard problems and reliance of individuals on government assistance was for Kazazis catastrophic.

From this review, it is evident that Kazazis, as a non-specialist who was called to fill a vacancy, synthesized existing doctrines to a middle-of-the-road liberal approach, quite distant from his politics that were extremely conservative and nationalistic (Kokkinos 1996).

3.7.7 Zygouras

Another author with great influence was Xenophon Zygouras, an instructor of economics at the prestigious (Greek) Commercial School of Halki in Constantinople, and later a teacher at Arsakeion, another famous high school for girls in Athens. A student of Ioannis Soutsos, he wrote two textbooks about the business of trade: *Greek Commercial Correspondence* (1870) and *History of Commerce in General* (1874), where he praised Colbert (1874, 231). He concentrated on primary education for the 8th and 10th grades and wrote textbooks including ones on embroidery and the duties of the housewife.

His 1876 book, *Elements of Plutology*, published in Constantinople, was liberal in its outlook and demonstrated a good knowledge of French and English literature. His greatest contribution to the popularization of economics, however, lies in his *Compendium of Home Economics* (1878), a book recommended for schools by the Greek Ministry of Education. In it, Zygouras stressed the importance of a national approach to political economy. For him, Europeans who emptied the national element from economics and put in the front of their investigations an internationalist political economy made a big mistake. He argued that many such textbooks had been translated in Greece, even though their teachings "have spread throughout Europe poverty and viciousness and have loosened the holy bonds of family life everywhere" (z). According to Zygouras, acquiring wealth was easy, but keeping and multiplying it was very difficult without the guiding hand of religion (27). He continued to state that a heavy burden in this respect fell on the shoulders of women (e), as they kept track of home finances. He concluded that they could rise to "holiness," if they performed their house duties by restricting themselves to the absolute necessary expenses.

The economics of the "oikos" should be managed as if every household were governed as an economic unit striving for autarky (50–60). For example, if the family possessed animals, it could organize a meat conserving unit. The household should possess its own tools and equipment and in general avoid the market for services that could be produced by their own means at home. The division of labor was not discussed in this context. Economizing and saving were values of the utmost importance.

On the other hand, Zygouras demonstrated realism. For example, insurance contracts were sound (68), especially when compared with the evils of luxurious consumption (88–9). According to him, poverty was a situation of misuse of talents by the poor, especially because "they are sick in theirsould," meaning they lacked Christian values like the willingness to work (72).

To conclude, for Zygouras, the household was a big economic unit that practiced within its limits, but not broadly, the division of labor. It kept books, and it even practiced medicine. Zygouras believed that the ideal of early Christian communities was what home economics was about, and this kind of economic organization was better than the one espoused by the economists of his time.

In his *On General Industry* (1877) he stressed that the import of machines in the Orient would help this region to overcome economic backwardness. For the same reason, he pleaded for free trade and against protectionism (97). Patience was of utmost importance in this process and individuals ought to be energetic and not expect the government to initiate growth in the economy (98).

3.8 The Popularization of Economics

3.8.1 Economics in Theater

In 1866, retired civil servant Konstantinos Ramfos, wrote, using the pseudonym Fouram, a short stage comedy in four scenes and two acts: "The Duck of the Economist." The play was also published as a pamphlet, circulated in the country in the same year, and was performed in salons and theaters. Research in the history of 19th century economics has revealed that the process of dissemination of classical political economy was gradual and it involved different actors and groups in society. Henderson (1995), Sockwell (1994), Tribe and Kadish (1993), and others have analyzed the importance of popularizers, minor figures, and institutional behavior as important parameters in this process. The role of literature has also been important, as the case of Charles Dickens' "Hard Times" reveals.

The "Duck of the Economist" is a farce that makes fun of the economist who is from the very start negatively presented (Psalidopoulos & Theocarakis 2015). His Greek name is Agyrtion, vagabond, "Frauderick" in English. The play opens with him being ridiculed, for he is standing upside down so that his brain is adequately filled with blood to advance sound ideas. A servant provides him the opportunity for a monologue where Frauderick confesses that he would be happy serving an absolute ruler without any scruples, an indication that political economists are opportunists. He confesses that he doesn't even understand the theories he advocates.

The play ridicules the concept of saving. The economist has become famous because he gives his duck 130 pieces of corn every eight days and, according to rumors, the duck is alive and well – we only learn later in the play that the duck starved to death. The purpose of the nutrition experiment was, according to the economist, for the duck to consume only 1/8 of its income (food), so that it could export the rest. This would serve as an example for a country to save enough, thus repay its total debt and even become a borrower in the future.

Groups of students and of retired working men visit Frauderick to learn how someone can survive by eating so little. In the scene with the students, the concept "to economize" is made fun of. The students speak as a chorus in order not to waste time, a caricature of the division of labor. Smith and Say are two names identified with the economist and his teachings. The retired old men have regretted working as civil servants, because they feel like beggars in their retirement. They accuse the government of paying pensions exclusively to political friends, while the economist defends government policies. Politics is, as the economist admits, a system of fraud, hypocrisy, and self-interest. People exist to work and suffer. Economics is dismal, not because of its analysis but because it is being exercised by corrupt men, who impose or propose nonsensical ideas on people. In the end, Frauderick proves to also be irrational, for he wholeheartedly believes a fortuneteller who predicts that he will become rich, and a young woman is going to fall in love with him. His servant despises him and quits his job.

The play is a farce meant to make people laugh and identifies the economist as a person of negative qualities. It shows impatience toward unrealistic assumptions made by economists, and concurs that economics is dismal but not for the reasons the classical school assumed.

3.8.2 Society of the Friends of the People

In 1869, the *Précis for the Working People, or Advice for Manual Labourers,* a tract based on Théodore-Henri Barrau's *Conseils aux Ouvriers* (1850), was translated into Greek by the Society of the Friends of the People. The original was written with an eye for social unrest that threatened French political order after the 1848 revolution. It was "crowned" by the French Academy the next year and went through many editions, the last one in 1884. The pamphlet was distributed gratis to workers in major industrial centers in Greece (Kordatos 1932).

The tract started with the causes hindering the workers from improving their status in society. Bad behavior, vicious living, drinking, and in general moral degradation were the main reasons for falling into poverty and for being unable to look after oneself. Early marriage, unsettled private finances, and political passions were cited as possible reasons for pauperism. The luck of the unskilled worker could be improved through good behavior, if he was religious, and if he could select good friends to socialize with. Knowledge, dexterity, and a positive disposition toward his occupation helped the worker learn how to economize. Economizing had two dimensions, according to the précis. First, learning how to save even from a low wage, and second, learning how to make good use of time. It is worth noting that it was advised that Sunday's rest should not be followed by laziness on Monday, for this might be a handicap for the continuation of the work contract.

A large part of the précis was devoted to relations within the working trades and how the trainee must obey his master and what the latter's obligations towards the young workers ought to be. Advice was given to the workers on the proper selection of a bride, on how to proceed in case of illness (treatment at home is considered better than going to a hospital), on their proper diet (where limited wine consumption is considered good for the health), and finally on personal finances (how to record expenses and how to avoid taking loans).

The book advised workers to be obedient, churchgoing, not to strike, turn a deaf ear to socialist theories, and not to become "an instrument of dreamers, schemers, and troublemakers" (1869, 28). This popularizing book closed with reflections on labor conditions and on the importance of employment for the wealth of society. The use of machines was applauded, and an optimal evolution of the economy was foreseen, if the workers adjusted and behaved according to the laws of the economic system and not the contrary. At a time when industry and mining were gaining momentum in the country, publications like this added to bridging the gap between liberalism and proto-socialist ideas.

3.8.3 Translations

The popular attitude toward economics was also shaped by translations of foreign treatises into Greek. A look at them reveals that only 10 books in all were translated from 1865 to 1903. With one exception (Fawcett), all translations were of French or francophone authors.

The contents of the translated books reveal a close resemblance to certain ideas. For example, in every translation, the benefits of the division of labor are discussed (Fawcett 1881, 31ff; Block 1882, 19–24; Beaulieu 1902, 82–94), and so is competition in a market economy (Garnier 1869, 41ff; Block 1882, 72–5). The use of machines in the productive process has a positive effect on the economy (Rapet 1865, 243–52; Block 1882, 68–72; Laveleye 1894, 88–97; Garnier 1869, 27–32; Beaulieu 1902, 95–108, and mostly 98–101). Beaulieu's text is the only one in which opposing views are mentioned as regards the use of machines (Beaulieu 1902, 96–8). Almost all the authors extol the virtues of frugality to create capital for future productive activities (Rapet 1865, 252–61; Fawcett 1881, 69–70; Block 1882, 79–80; Laveleye 1894a, 260; Franklin, cited in Garnier 1869, 165–6).

All translated authors advocated the abstention of the state from intervening in the economy. According to Beaulieu, the state was not a determining factor in the improvement of human societies (Beaulieu 1902, 406–7). For Say, public consumption had no positive implication for economic activity. The reasoning behind this view was that public consumption was financed by resources extracted from the private sector (Say 1828, 112). Laveleye had a differing view as regards the economic role of the state; to a certain extent, states could take on activities in infrastructure, building roads and providing transport, in case of an unwillingness of the private sector to undertake such work (Laveleye 1894a, 119–21).

Therefore, except for Laveleye, all authors shared the view that the economy should be free from state interference in the tradition set forth with the translations of Droz (1833, 102) and Say (1828, 117) in the past.

As expected, all translations extolled the benefits of the freedom of trade (Rapet 1865, 226ff; Laveleye 1894, 242; Beaulieu 1902, 339). According to Rapet, free trade was able to ensure low and stable prices of food (Ibid). On the other side, protectionism could have catastrophic consequences (Fawcett 1881, 311; Garnier 1869, 91–4; Laveleye 1894, 245). Laveleye was again the only one who analyzed List's opposing views at this point.

Regarding the distribution of income, only Fawcett pointed out the notion of a wages fund, which, in the last analysis, determined daily wages (Fawcett 1881, 221). For Rapet, work was a commodity, and its price was not determined arbitrarily but based on rational calculations. For Block, if the economy progresses, wages rise; otherwise, they fall (Block 1882, 65). Strikes because of falling wages could not have any success, but merely provided the pretext for laziness (Ibid). On this topic, Rapet stressed that the poor shared similar economic interests with the rich, and property was the result of working; thus, each worker had the potential to climb the socio-economic ladder on his or her own (Rapet 1865, 126).

At the end of the 19th century, the translation of Laveleye's work brought to the fore of Greek society topics and views, which departed from the tradition of classical liberalism.[52] Apart from his already mentioned views, he was the only one amongst the other translated authors who discussed the problems of monetary, commercial, and industrial crises, and acknowledged that these problems were a major drawback of the economic system. He also suggested ways in which governments should act to face the consequences of crises (Laveleye 1894, 234–41). Even though his textbook followed a common path, with other translated economic texts of the time (production, circulation, distribution, and consumption of wealth), it differs while discussing the matter of the living standard of salaried workers (158–71). Furthermore, although he acknowledged the need to set limits on state interference in the economic sector, he regarded public consumption as being beneficial in principle (267–8). Finally, his perception of state interference in the economic process deserves consideration. He examined the natural laws in contradistinction to "positive laws"; the latter derived from legislation, which was a key factor in social development (5–15, especially 9–11). A positive opinion about trade unions was also expressed by Fawcett.

To conclude, the popularization process through translations does not reveal at first glance a specific particularity. Most ideas disseminated were liberal in the sense of 19th-century French economic thought (Breton & Lutfalla 1991). The translation of Laveleye marked the transition to more interventionist ideas in the tradition developed by German economic thought.

3.9 Early Heterodox Thought

Even though industrial capitalism wasn't a reality in 19th-century Greece, the economic misery felt by peasants and the low living standards of manual workers provoked the reaction of intellectuals, who envisaged different social conditions. As we have already seen, the fear of the establishment about strikes, and the working class possibly undermining the social order led to popularizing books that preached the benefits of free markets. As economic conditions towards the end of the century did not improve significantly, heterodox thinkers grew in number.

The teachings of French and German socialists, and of the Fabian Society at the end of the century, were absorbed and disseminated in Greece. With the passing of time, utopian socialist/anarchist thought gained a critical mass. Relevant newspapers were printed, and anarchist uprisings followed in Patras, Pyrgos, and other Greek cities in the 1890s. Efforts to explain what went on in Greek society from a heterodox point of view, and where society should better head, multiplied.

There exists a major anthology of Greek socialist thought (Noutsos 1992) that includes names, newspapers, and periodicals where heterodox thinkers expressed their discontent about current Greek society and articulated a different future as visionaries. Despite the at times polemic attitude, most of these intellectuals did not favor a revolution, but rather a transition to a more equal society, where labor would get the wage and respect it deserved. As it often happens, these intellectuals changed their minds in the course of time, according to circumstances and events. It is to the work of some of these thinkers that we will turn our attention in the following.

3.9.1 Pylarinos

Fragiskos Pylarinos was an activist against British rule in the Ionian Islands and a Professor of Philosophy at the University of Athens. He combined Saint-Simonian ideas with national independence and was suspended many times from his duties due to supposed anti-Church and anti-social-order agitation during his classes. In his *Political Lectures* (1833) he defined in Saint-Simonian terms law as an expression of the will of the "workers of society" (82). The human mind was progressive, and so was the need for "liberty, equality, and socialism (koinonismos)." The workers of society were the sovereigns of the state, and once they could control power, they would use legislation to change the existing order and create a different one where everybody would have a job and would be the master of their own products. Future laws would secure a life without conflicts and wars, would be "precautious, organic, philanthropic, and caring about the natural and moral obligations of the citizens." Harmony in society, as opposed to exploitation, would thus become a reality.

3.9.2 Sofianopoulos

Panagiotis Sofianopoulos studied Medicine in Italy and defined himself as one of the working fathers of "the scientific progress of the Greeks." The Greek Church considered him an enemy and denounced his teachings. With reference to Charles Fourier, he coined the term *cooperative life* (sympraktorikos vios) to articulate what he envisaged as an ideal form of society. The concept of the worker included everyone from emperor to king, to tailor, to teacher, to builder. Fourier and Sofianopoulos developed rules of cooperation that made labor perfect. Cooperation meant socialism in practice, the unification of capital with intellect and manual work. Shares obtained from cooperative work were to be split according to the contribution of everyone in the common effort. The capital owner would get a bigger share due to his cleverness and devotion. An over-proportional share, however, would make a tyrant out of him, and this should not be allowed. Otherwise, injustice would prevail, and uprising and revolution would follow.

Sofianopoulos claimed that cooperative life was becoming a reality in France, Italy, and Germany, where the workers were transforming into perfect brothers by creating mass movements. The Greeks needed to follow that path.

3.9.3 Argyriadis

Pavlos Argyriadis studied Law at the University of Paris, actively participated in the Paris Commune, and became a French citizen in 1880. He was a co-contributor to the Journal *Bibliotheque Socialiste* that brought him closer to Paul Lafargue and also wrote editorials for *Crie du Peuple*. In 1883 he was among those who orchestrated protests about the (liberal) teaching of Paul Leroy Beulieu at the College de France. In 1885 he became a founding member of the "Partie Socialiste Revolutionnaire." His works frequently referred to Marx. In his "Contemporary Socialism" (1892–3, 3) he analyzed the division of labor according to Smith and arrived at the conclusion that production expanded through it, and that overproduction and crisis might be the outcome of the capitalist process. Crisis destroyed the workers' ability to work, but, on the other hand, the division of labor was welcomed as it made the work process more humane for the laborer.

Argyriadis offered a short sketch of the transition of modes of production from slavery, through feudalism to capitalism and declared the arrival of socialism as a natural outcome of the development of productive forces. The workers ought to be ready for the upcoming change and should not allow sentiments to distract them, otherwise the revolution to create a new society would fail (1893, 2). On the other hand, he didn't plead for the formation of a worker's party, as party discipline was alien to him. He favored individual action in the steps of anarchist authors who felt hostility toward the capitalist state. He envisaged a possible Balkan federation of workers and tried to coordinate with individuals from Southeast European states to make common action possible.

3.9.4 Drakoulis

Platon Drakoulis was born on the Ionian Island of Zakynthos (Zante). He taught Modern Greek Literature at the University of Oxford from 1984 to 1899 and was acquainted with the work of Alfred Marshall. His mixture of socialism was peculiar, incorporating antiliberal, anarchist, theosophical, and utopian ideas. Thus, as a participant in the plenary conference of the second international, he remained a centrist and didn't join either the "possibilistes" or the Marxists. He also published the first Greek Socialist magazine *Ardin* (Upend) in 1887. He translated texts of Kropotkin in 1887 and wrote pamphlets and books, such as *What Is Socialism*? (1886), *The Worker's Manual, i.e., the Foundations of Socialism* (1893), and *Results of the French Revolution* (1890). He continued writing until the second decade of the 20th century, transmitting in his writings a positivist humanism and transcending from his former views to more moderate ones, incorporating ecological maxims and healthy food into his plans for a better life for the workers.

In an editorial of *Ardin*, Drakoulis defined his basic principle as the effort of the individual to get rid of the need to take care of his next day in life, for it destroyed both his spirit and its heart. Society needed a change of realities and facts. Socialism meant saving one's life. For Drakoulis, this change could be gradual, based on progress and solidarity, but it would happen. Inequality should cease to exist, and money should stop being so important in society, for its existence made the moral betterment of individuals impossible.

Labor was defined to include productive and unproductive human activities, and these brought humans closer, thus preparing for common action. Revolutions without preparation were not the key to societal change. What was needed was education, acquaintance with modern ideas, and organization.

Drakoulis published the philosophical journal *Research* (Erevna) in 1899 and based on his observation of developments in England, predicted that socialism would arrive and alter the way people lived. Cities would be created that would be ecologically friendly and combine town and countryside so that people would not have to work in polluted factory towns. The government ought to adapt the "positive agenda" to fulfill these reforms. His influence among Greek intellectuals was substantial until the second decade of the 20th century.

3.9.5 Kallergis

Stavros Kallergis abandoned his studies to devote himself to political activism on the side of the labor class. He initially cooperated with Drakoulis and edited the periodical *The Socialist* from 1890, which appeared irregularly. The crisis after default in 1893 multiplied those who followed both Drakoulis and Kallergis, but they split about the right way forward and as of 1892 they followed different political paths.

The fundamental principles and final aims of socialism were defined by Kallergis in *The Socialist* as follows: "A life free of caring about everyday life, regular food and hygiene for everyone, enough and clean clothing for everyone, a home safe from a hygienic point of view for everyone, existence of work for everyone, enough means of education according to the capabilities of everyone" (Socialist, v. 1, 1). A socialist was, for Kallergis, someone "who works to benefit all" (v. 12, 2) and not an egoist.

The political platform of his journal pleaded for liberty, equality, and tolerance, and distinguished between short- and long-term goals of the socialist movement. In the short term, demands included 8 hours of work, Sunday rest, a wage that satisfied worker's needs, the payment of pensions to the elderly, the abolition of privileges, free education for the children of the workers, and, finally, constraints on private property and abolition of excessive luxury. In the long run, property and inheritance rights had to be abolished and working people should have secured food, clothing, a place to stay, and live. Education should be free for all, freedom of speech and of conscience was necessary, and all nations would be united and fraternized (v. 13, 1). This platform was instrumental in the organization of the strike on May 1st, 1893, that introduced Labor Day in the Greek calendar and is considered a milestone for the further development of pro-workers legislation in Greece. In the course of time, Kallergis became, like Drakoulis, more of an evolutionary socialist and he developed a thorough plan to develop his native Crete.

As the 19th century was ending, socialist thought was making its presence felt in the country, even if the Marxist analysis of capitalism was still rudimentary. Equality and better conditions of living were becoming more and more demands of a wider group of citizens. This group grew bigger during the "rethinking" process of Greek intellectuals after 1897.

Notes

1 See Svolos (1998, 83).
2 This topic is discussed in Karanikolas (1963).
3 See Koliopoulos and Veremis (2002, 51).
4 On Italian economic thought, see Faucci (2000), and on Greek students in Pisa, see Sideri (1994).
5 See the *Official Journal of Parliamentary Debates* (henceforth OJPD), session 50, 14.2.1863, 637.
6 Ibid., 637–40.
7 Equity was a major theme in the session 333, 3.10.1864. For the discussion that took place in Britain, see the massive volumes edited by O'Brien (1999). See also Sabine (1966) and Shehab (1953). For the Greek case, see Dertilis (1993).
8 OJPD, session 73, 23.3.1863, 340.
9 Ibid., 341.
10 OJPD, session 103, 17.5.1863, p. 733. On Rontiris, see also Psalidopoulos (1994).
11 See the "Report on State Budget for the Financial Year of 1865."
12 See the "Parliamentary Speech on State Budget for the Financial Year of 1865."
13 OJPD, session 93, 3.5.1863, 585.
14 See the "Report on State Budget for the Financial Year of 1857."
15 See the "Parliamentary Speech on State Budget for the Financial Year of 1873."
16 Ibid.
17 OJPD, session 128, 1.7.1863, 331.
18 OJPD, session 172, 8.11.1863.
19 OJPD, session 192, 16.12.1863.
20 For details, see McGrew (1985).
21 OJPD, session 266, 16.5.1864, 101.
22 The outcome was that the experiment of the creation of a land bank failed. For a discussion of a renewed, failed attempt to create a new bank some years later, see Dertilis (1980).
23 OJPD, session 72, 24.11.1865, 471.
24 Ibid.
25 OJPD, session 75, 27.3.1867, 326.
26 OJPD, session 37, 22.2.1871, 23.
27 Ibid., 26.
28 OJPD, session 18, 27.10.1876, 87.
29 OJPD, session 19, 28.10.1876, 102.
30 In that connection, see also the speeches by Zochios and Petimezas in OJPD, session 20, 29.10.1876, and session 24, 3.11.1876, respectively.
31 OJPD, session 24, 3.11.1876.
32 See, for example his report on railways and his arguments in favor of a cooperative bank (OJPD on January 20th, 1880). Valassopoulos also wrote also *Bank of Land Workers* (1877) where, following Schultze Delitzsch, he argued in favor of a cooperative bank that would provide capital to farmers
33 OJPD, session 93, 22.3.1880.
34 See the "Parliamentary Speech on State Budget for the Financial Year of 1884."
35 See the "Parliamentary Speech on State Budget for the Financial Year of 1885."
36 It is a sad fact that this period, when Greeks were ruled by Greeks without a foreign sovereign dictating everyday politics, hasn't been deeply studied as far as local political and economic power structures and interests are concerned.
37 See the Official Gazette of the Assembly, vol. 6, session No. 316, September 10th, 1864, Athens: National Printing Office, pp. 374–5.
38 The chronicle of events is cited in the Journal of the Society, Freedom of Trade, No. 15, pp. 94–8.

39 The use of the plural word "Freedoms" underlines the fact that the Society's founding fathers viewed their activities as an attack on several fronts. They spoke against tariffs as obstacles to trade and industry and were against indirect taxes. Unfortunately, we have no evidence suggesting why this semantic distinction between freedom and freedoms was made. In his inaugural speech in 1865, Efmorfopoulos used the singular form.
40 These numbers have been compiled from names given by the Society in its journal. Possible withdrawals from the Society are not accounted for.
41 These included, besides Efmorfopoulos, Stylianos Kassimatis, Kosmas Sigalos, Stamatis Proios, and Petros Rallis.
42 This reconstruction is based on Efmorfopoulos (1865), Sigalos (1865), and Kassimatis (1865). Starting from issue 23 up to 34 of the Society's journal, translations of documents from Belgium took central stage.
43 Greece had participated in the international fairs in London in 1851 and 1862 too.
44 For the LMU, see Willis 1901, and for an analysis of international conferences dealing with bimetallism, see Russel 1898.
45 2nd edition 1882. Here we quote the second.
46 Both manuscripts that were never published were made available to the present author by the staff of the Popular Library of Kalamata, to which I extend my gratitude.
47 The term *plutology* was coined by J.G. Courcell-Seneuil, by which he labeled the pure theory of economics, juxtaposing it to applied economics, *ergonomy*. Surprisingly enough, the same title was given by the Irish-born scholar William Edward Hearn to his textbook of political economy (*Plutology or the Theory of the Efforts to Satisfy Human Wants*, Melbourne 1863), which was highly praised by Jevons, Marshall, Edgeworth, and other eminent economists. Hearn was a pupil of Mountifort Longfield and professor of history and political economy at the University of Melbourne (La Nauze 1972; Goodwin 1968, 569–71). Hearn shared some common theoretical and biographical features with Soutsos; he was an exponent of French political economy and cautious about state intervention in economic affairs, but not rigidly opposed to it; he held the first *ex officio* professorship of political economy; he occupied public office, and he was widely recognized as the most celebrated economist in Australia. However, there is no evidence that Soutsos had been acquainted with the work of his Australian colleague.
48 On this topic, see Giouras (2000, 157–69).
49 OJPD, session 100, 1.4.1880, 1012.
50 It is worth noticing that during these sessions in parliament, the economist most widely cited was Paul Leroy-Beaulieu.
51 Wilhelm Roscher was often quoted by him in support of liberal arguments. Kazazis was methodologically against the GHS, especially the Socialists of the Chair, due to his own political views.
52 According to Schumpeter, Laveleye belonged to a non-existent, i.e. French historical-institutionalist school (Schumpeter 1954, 820).

4 The Age of the German Historical School (1897–1944)

4.1 Overview of Economic and Social Developments (1897–1920)

Despite defaulting in 1893, Greece provoked a war with Turkey in 1897, in which it suffered a humiliating defeat. The Great Powers mediated the peace treaty between Greece and the Ottoman Empire and imposed an International Financial Control (IFC) on Greece, with the aim of monitoring Greek state finances to secure their debt repayments. Therefore, a new period started after 1897, a period of austerity lasting until at least 1910, and of introspection for the Greeks regarding what had gone wrong and what could be done to bring the country back to growth and glory.

1897 can also be seen as a starting point for a shift in economic thought that brought the country closer to German economic ideas, even if French influences remained. As we have already seen, there were some Greeks, such as Zografos, who went to Germany for graduate studies. Those who chose economics ("Staatswissenschaften") led the transition to the new economic paradigm after their return to Greece. The process was gradual, but clearly a new generation of economists emerged that synthesized German economic thought for the benefit of the economic development of Greece. This generation dominated the academic and the social scene for quite a long time. It merged Anglo-Saxon economic thought with its discourse after 1944 and remained active until the late 1960s, when another generation of economists took the lead.

Returning to the early 1900s, the "peaceful" co-existence between the IFC and the Greek authorities was an everyday reality. An institutional framework was imposed on Greece, which included the following: Monetary policy had to be restrictive with an annual withdrawal of 2 million drachmas from circulation, to allow the return of the drachma to convertibility. Fiscal policy had to accumulate surpluses so that debt could be repaid. Expenditure was fixed at around 60 million drachmas annually and revenues at around 90 million per year. The "Company for the Administration of Public Debt" was tasked with collecting revenue from indirect taxes on necessities of life, channeling them to debt repayments. Past foreign loans were split into three categories and their repayment was directly associated with receipts from specific taxes (tobacco, the stamp tax, certain tariffs, etc.). All these payments had priority over the needs of the Greek authorities.

The IFC enjoyed veto power over all fiscal and monetary actions of the Greek government. The control was tight at first but became moderate after a decade of

DOI: 10.4324/9781315413419-5

strict adherence to repayments. Its results were twofold: On the one hand, it produced deflation for a decade. Massive emigration to the USA started in 1901 due to economic stagnation and austerity. Supply in the labor market declined in a country short of population. On the other hand, the exchange rate of the drachma slowly but steadily regained parity with the French Franc, reaching 1 to 1 in 1909 (from a 1.8 to 1 rate in 1897). More importantly, it made public administration more efficient and delivery and helped thus the country modernize. Things that did not materialize because of lack of political will in the past now became a reality.

The tax system was under constant scrutiny. In 1903, the parliament debated the possibility of tax reform. The tax on ploughing animals was recognized to have been a failure both from an economic point of view, since its revenues were low, as well as from a scientific point of view.[1] Nevertheless, parliament decided not to cancel it because of the government's inability to promote a new tax agenda at that time. The manipulation of existing taxation, especially indirect taxation, was therefore continued, combined with an effort to control expenditure and the creation of lotteries and special funds for the benefit of the army and navy. As the exchange value of the currency steadily improved, the necessity of an overall tax reform became unanimous. Athanasios Eftaxias was the main speaker in parliament on fiscal issues. He wanted to introduce a modern tax system (Syrmaloglou 2007, 180). In 1909, he brought before parliament a law on net revenue imposed on all Greek citizens, an income tax, opening thus a new era in Greek taxation.[2] Despite problems of implementation, this tax was reintroduced in 1918, together with an inheritance and a tax on business profits.

The inertia of the old political guard was also attacked by the group of the "Japanese,"[3] a small team of parliamentarians, headed by Dimitrios Gounaris and Petros Protopapadakis, who argued with eloquence, persuasion, determination, and numbers in the direction of reforms (on them, see Syrmaloglou 2015).

On the monetary side, in 1910 the governor of the National Bank of Greece, Ioannis Valaoritis, obtained the approval of the IFC to issue banknotes covered with emigrant remittances sent to relatives in Greece from the USA. Law ΓΧΜΒ, or the Valaoritis Law, named after its inspirator, allowed monetary circulation to increase and provided capital to civilian and government activities during the Balkan Wars (1912–14) and World War I. However, monetary instability rebounded after 1917 due to NBG policies and a schism between the King and statesman Eleftherios Venizelos. Venizelos wanted Greece to enter World War I on the side of the Allies, while the King wanted a neutral Greece. The country was split with two governments in power. Allied Credits opened to the Venizelos government to enter the war were monetized by the NBG, but only one out of three payments was actually disbursed. The NBG, however, under pressure, circulated drachmas for the full amount of the credits. The drachma started to devalue. Then, due to Venizelos losing the 1920 election, the allies wouldn't disburse the remaining two installments. Monetary circulation was recognized by everyone to be uncovered, and the drachma devalued further. Finally, monetary chaos emerged in 1922, when Minister Petros Protopapadakis, eager to finance the Asia Minor expedition, forced a compulsory internal loan, halving all circulating banknotes and transforming the other half into a bond. The full monetary catastrophe occurred when the expedition failed and 1.2 million refugees entered mainland Greece, a country of approximately 5 million inhabitants until then (Psalidopoulos 1989).

The economic progress of the country until 1897 was, as we mentioned, questioned by many authors. New plans started brewing during times of contractionary monetary policy, recession, and large-scale emigration. Voices that demanded a restart of the economy, this time by following a path like that of Germany multiplied. As Milward and Saul ascertained, the "failure of the attempt to develop, along liberal lines in mid-century, inevitably strengthened the protectionist movement, but until the 1890s the manufacturing industry was too weak to exert any effective pressure on the government" (Milward & Saul 1977, 251). Protection and the stages of economic development taught by the GHS acted as a lighthouse for economists in Southeastern Europe.

In the following paragraphs, we will investigate developments in academia and in society, turning first our attention to Andreas Andreadis. We will see how liberal thought merged with the historical approach to economics and how the community of economists started becoming an autonomous group with their periodicals and ideas. Important steps toward the institutionalization of economics were introduced. An important catalyst in this process was Eleftherios Venizelos and his economic agenda, new liberalism, that brought liberalism in line with British social thinking. We will offer an overview of the intellectual ties in economics between Greece and Germany. We will also refer to Alexandros Papanastasiou and underscore his importance as a state socialist, intellectual, and politician for the whole process. The chapter will close with a look at the popularization of economics and at heterodox thought.

4.2 Andreas Andreadis

The dominant figure of economic science from the beginning of the 20th century until his passing in 1935 was Andreas Andreadis. In his international publications, he spelled his name as Andréadès. Born in Corfu, he studied in France and obtained two doctorates, one in Law and the second in Economics with a thesis on *The History of the Bank of England* (English edition in 1909). This book was praised as a milestone in financial history and made him the first internationally renowned Greek economist. His obituary was written by none other than John Maynard Keynes (Keynes 1935).

After completing his second PhD in 1901, Andreadis traveled to England, where he met major economists, most notably Francis Y. Edgeworth. He was also in close contact with Italian public finance specialists. Upon his return to Greece, he was appointed in 1902 as ifigitis and one year later as professor of public finance at the University of Athens. Andreadis was a conservative aristocrat, a liberal economist, a true scholar, and a man of letters, devoted to teaching and research. In the interwar years, he constantly and bitterly opposed the involvement of governments in the free market, both in Greece and in Europe. He also mistrusted universal suffrage, as he thought it might lead to excessive public spending.[4] He engaged his students in research and inaugurated a series of twenty books written by them. He was the first to introduce the writing of essays to pass the exams, and his archive is full of these original excursions of his students into science.[5] There are three editions of his lectures (1906, 1920, and 1925) that were widely read by subsequent generations of students.

His research interests were concentrated on the *History of Greek Public Finance*, a titanic project on the evolution of state finances from ancient times to the present (translated into German in 1931, and into English in 1933). Andreadis was a staunch liberal, a precursor of modern public choice theory yet he strongly believed in the national character of economic science and followed the lead of the GHS in his research. He insisted that combining economic theory with economic history was at the heart of every modern systematic analysis, especially for less developed countries. The historical approach could provide useful evidence for both theorists and policymakers. According to him, historical explanation provided just backing and didn't substitute for theory. Pure economic analysis was indispensable for the scientific explanation of the economic process.

Although he served as a delegate of the Greek government at major international meetings, such as the Danube Conference in Paris in 1920–1, the Assemblies of the League of Nations in 1923, 1924, and 1929, and the World Economic Conference in London in 1933, his influence on the conduct of economic policy in interwar Greece was marginal. His fiscal conservatism was at odds with the political priorities of Greek governments after 1922.

Andreadis wrote extensively on current problems of the Greek economy (see the 3-volume edition of his collected works edited by Varvaresos, Petropoulos, and Pintos in 1938). He also edited a Carnegie Endowment of International Peace-sponsored volume on the economic and social effects of World War I on the Greek economy (Andréadès 1928). He gave lectures at the Academy of International Law in The Hague on International Financial Controls in 1925 and participated in edited volumes in French, German, and English. Despite his aversion to those who supported interventionist policies and dissenting economic theories in general, he showed scientific integrity by helping many young economists believing in strong government action to be appointed to academic positions, thus imposing thus plurality as *the* guiding principle in the Greek economics profession.

Andreadis's dissertation was the first ever effort to write the history of a central bank. In addition to providing a history of the Bank of England, it offered a complete history of the commercial and financial evolution of the English nation since 1694 (Andreadis 1909). The creation of the bank was a commercial and political necessity to support British claims to global hegemony. The difficulties during subsequent restriction periods, the ensuing debates, and the overall national and global developments were thoroughly and precisely discussed. Of particular interest was the discussion of the Banking and the Currency Principle (vol. 2, 269–77).

According to Andreadis, neither school was theoretically or practically perfect (272–3). The Banking school was in favor of discretion. It saw banknotes as a form of credit needed by businesses and objected to the efforts of authorities to impose restrictions on the quantity of money or loans. Bankers knew better than politicians how to assist business transactions without jeopardizing monetary stability. Unused loans to businesses would return to the banks. The Currency school favored rules and aimed for a policy restricted by the existence of reserves, which had been seen as extremely important since David Ricardo. Despite its shortcomings, Andreadis modestly suggested it was a better approach of monetary management, as financial crises of the 19th century had demonstrated (275).

He made it clear in his lectures that Public Finance was a discipline bearing national characteristics (1925, 177). Every economy had its own shape and structure according to political, social, and historical circumstances. Colonial powers didn't apply their own fiscal systems to their colonies as they respected the ways in which these countries collected their taxes. Andreadis compared the fiscal systems of England and Germany and concluded that even industrial nations had different tax structures due to peculiarities in their development. The same applied to independent Greece that continued Ottoman taxation because both authorities and citizens were accustomed to this practice.

The continuous expansion of the scope of government action since the end of the 19th century was for Andreadis a negative development. He admitted that it all started with the efforts to correct certain failures of the market, but this intervention didn't stop there. Individuals, however, knew better, and their rights were more important than anything else. The priorities of the nation as put forward by the GHS and by state socialists found his disapproval because they led to government overspending (1925, 142). On the other hand, the GHS was right in criticizing the Ricardian deductive method, which was, for Andreadis, a brain teaser. However, most German economists were, for him, just empiricists and avoided theoretical conclusions, thus doing a disservice to economics. The best way to proceed was, for Andreadis, the eclectic approach: studying events, collecting facts by observation, drawing theoretical conclusions, and providing policy advice. Approval would be given if the advice proved fertile, and disapproval if the results were negative. Comparing the GHS and the classical/neoclassical approaches, he underlined that "we should not accept unconditionally the teachings of either school. Economic schools belong in the environment they were born and developed" (1925, 150).

Andreadis discussed Greek finances and public debt in his lectures in a non-polemic style, combining numerical facts with statements made by officials. He condemned the tendency of successive governments to borrow rather than to tax. He criticized both Trikoupis (119, 128) and Deligiannis (132) and pleaded for government restraint and economies. He was against progressive taxation (313) and, as always, cautious about everything involved with more government spending, like the introduction of the minimum wage (325).

The approach used by Andreadis in his research allowed him to defend his positions as they sprang out of historical inquiry. He didn't teach "theory"; therefore, he could stand above all matters, state the pros and cons of every possible solution to economic problems, and appeal to his students to remain neutral and unbiased in the face of issues seeking solutions. His approach to the currant/raisin crisis in Greece of the 1890s was characteristic. After the bubble of the early 1890s, a company had been created with the aim of stabilizing prices by controlling supply. Andreadis underlined that "for my part, I continue to think that the true solution to the question of the dry raisins lies in the free play of the law of supply and demand" (176). On the other hand, he admitted that the country, despite its other problems, had created a company that was "successfully completing operations of a very large scale from a commercial, industrial, and financial point of view, and for coping with difficulties which, at first glance, seemed insurmountable" (177). By opting for the middle way and by not being partisan (except to his own central idea, the balanced budget) he stayed distanced from party politics and was able to act as Kassandra did in the Trojan war in the face of the problems Greece faced in the 1920s.

4.3 Developments in Academia until 1920

As already mentioned, Professor Gounarakis was involved in politics from 1893 to 1911, and Neoklis Kazazis took on the task of teaching Political Economy as a non-expert to fill the void. At the same time, from 1890 and up to 1910, lots of ifigites were appointed to cover topics and areas in economics. Their work mostly followed the historical method and was influenced by German economic thought. In addition to Andreas Andreadis, others named included Athanassios Bassias-Typaldos, Konstantinos Zografos, Ilias Zeggelis, Sotirios Vezanis, Konstantinos Vournazos, and Thalis Koutoupis. They all aspired to becoming full professors, but, apart from Andreadis, they didn't make it. They held, however, prestigious positions and their views didn't go unnoticed among students and society. In 1911, a new law governing tertiary education was passed, and the teaching assignments of the ifigites were terminated. Due to the turbulent political years that followed, the new university law was implemented in 1917, and the authors we are about to explore were not reinstated in their former positions.

4.3.1 Bassias-Typaldos

Athanasios Bassias was the author of *La Protection Industrielle et le Nouveau Regime Douanier* (1893) and a supporter of protection. According to him, economic policy in Greece had been empirical and this needed to change. Industry was welcome, but the country was agricultural and policy measures should be tailored according to the needs of the primary sector. Wherever Greece possessed raw materials or manufactures, the government was called to imitate what the rest of European countries were doing and protect industrial initiatives. Focusing only on metrics like revenue from tariffs was, for him misleading. The times called for an all-inclusive approach to economic policy.

4.3.2 Vesanis

Sotirios Vesanis studied in Berlin and was influenced by Adolph Wagner. He wrote a monograph in German (Vesanis 1895), in which he argued that empirical findings suggested that interest rates and income from borrowing grew faster than capital invested in industry. Therefore, in current conditions, productive capital was steadily losing power to finance and banking capital. His conclusion was that the government as mediator needed to intervene and smooth things out between these two fractions of capital. According to him, productive uses of capital should be given priority over financial speculation.

In 1897 he was named ifigitis, with a study that dealt with the varying positions of the businessman and the worker in the closing of the labor contract (Vesanis 1897). The position of the former was stronger because the latter faced the specter of hunger; therefore, the deal between supply and demand in the labor market was not neutral but biased. Society had, for Vesanis, the duty to secure the means to the necessities of life "not on reasons of philanthropy but on the basis of the right that people possessed, the entitlement to live" (5). Poor people were, for Vesanis, not lazy by nature, as some liberals suggested (24). Their condition was the result of the distribution of income. Workhouses, as those existing before capitalism, should be reopened so that laborers could turn there for a job and subsistence. The cost of these workhouses, for Vesanis, wouldn't be very high and, in all cases, it was the only means to counter the privileged position of the employer in relation to the worker. Workhouses could provide an outlet for those in need who found the terms imposed by the employer to be exploitative.

4.3.3 Zografos

Konstantinos Zografos, the son of Ioannis, was a supporter of the Historical approach and argued in favor of government intervention to assist private initiative in his book *The Development of National Production* (1895). His ifigessia was *On Land Rent* (1896), and he used it as a vehicle to attack Ricardian theory on the basis that it was a theoretical construct based on British experience. He made explicit reference to Carl Menger as an individualist theorist whose work needed to be studied further and referred to the work of Cournot and those working in mathematical economics who were opening new avenues in the study of economic phenomena. He didn't publish any other books.

4.3.4 Zeggelis

Ilias Zeggelis studied in Paris, Heidelberg, Munich, and Leipzig before returning to Greece. He specialized in Public Finance and wrote *On Progressive Taxation* in 1894 and *On Usury and Measures to Combat It* in 1895. Progressive taxation allowed, in his view, important revenue for the treasury, while leaving very low incomes totally untaxed. It was a far better way to finance expenditure than loans, he stressed (1894, 13). He condemned usury and suggested that the government set interest rates by law, as it could do with the price of bread (1895, 37).

He suggested, like so many others before him, the creation of a land register and an Agricultural Bank as vehicles for the improvement of Greek agriculture. In his *Current Political Affairs* (1901), Zeggelis was more partisan. He demanded the election of deputies from larger areas than the smaller ones existing at the time, so that parliamentarians would concentrate on national, instead of regional, issues. He also demanded a better allocation of existing financial resources so that infrastructures could be improved.

4.3.5 Vournazos

Konstantinos Vournazos submitted an ifigessia in 1897 *On the Freedom of Activity*. The book was dedicated to the "laboring class" and defended the position that "bad things can happen when individual power is abused" (11). This extraordinary power of some people in the past was the reason for discrimination in the present, claimed Vournazos. Therefore, he pleaded for solidarity both within the borders of the national economy and in international trade. Quoting Sismondi, he was critical of the extreme division of labor societies were witnessing, but he was also critical of the "reformers," as he labeled the socialists.

His lectures appeared as a book in 1904 entitled *System of Political Economy*. They included five parts: Production of Wealth, Distribution, Circulation, Consumption, and the Role of the State and Money. The exposition was encyclopedic and erudite with references to French and German authors. One of the most quoted authors was Emile de Laveleye, whom Vournazos praised as a great synthesizer. He also wrote *Une Position Particuliere du Change en Grece* (1910), where he explained the workings of the Valaoritis law.

4.3.6 Koutoupis

Thalis Koutoupis was a Law graduate who, after his first degree, found temporary employment in London. From there he moved to Berlin, where he became close to state socialist ideas and befriended Alexandros Papanastasiou, with whom he founded the Sociological Society in 1909.

He wrote a book entitled *Economics of the Greeks* (1908), which was accepted as an ifigessia at the University of Athens. His study analyzed ancient Greek economic thought, based on primary sources and on secondary, mostly German, contemporary interpreters of ancient Greek contributions to economic life.

He taught topics in political economy for two years and went on to a career in politics. In the mid-1930s, he became a professor at the Panteios School of Political Sciences. For his students, he wrote *Political Economy* (2 vols., 1933–4) and *Public Finance* (2 vols., 1935–6), which were compendia of useful knowledge with applications to Greek economic life.

The conclusion drawn is that protectionism and progressive taxation prevailed as themes in Greek academic life since the imposition of the IFC until 1920. Still, having a legal training and broadly following the GHS, they represented various positions with an emphasis on social issues, while at the same time not challenging the fundamentals of the capitalist economy, except for Vesanis.

4.4 The Continuous Rise of the German Historical School

The number of graduate Greek students in German universities grew steadily since the 1880s, peaked in the interwar period, and continued rising until the mid-1930s. After the *Methodenstreit*, the GHS started losing appeal internationally, but remained quite influential among students and policymakers.

German economic thought emphasized history as a methodological tool to approach economic problems The social classes approach, as well as the value and distribution theory of Classical Political Economy leading to universal laws, were rejected. In the German tradition, economics was thought to be culture-specific and historical analysis provided clues for future policies. All countries were moving from different development stages to industrialization, and what was needed was a strong state to set the framework for achieving the best results. State needs, therefore, had priority over individual business plans, and social considerations played a major role in the works of academics who belonged to the older and younger GHS (Brandt 1992/3; Winkel 1997).

These ideas sounded reasonable in Southeastern Europe, and the German path to industrialization and political power acted as a beacon for young Greek students. Fifty-five doctorates were awarded to Greeks in "Staatswissenschaften" between 1918 and 1938, 23 between 1939 and 1945, and 25 more between 1946 and 1960 (Scherer 1968), a total of 104. The universities that particularly attracted young Greek economists were Berlin, with 21 doctorates between 1918 and 1950, and Munich with 31, followed by Leipzig with 16, Vienna with 14, and Hamburg with 10. Economists such as Karl Bücher and Werner Sombart supervised the doctoral theses of several Greek students. Adolph Wagner also attracted the attention of graduates. Other notable professors of economics that were preferred by Greeks were, in Berlin, Heinrich Herkner, who supervised four doctorates, and Herman Schumacher, who was responsible for three, while in Leipzig, Alexander von Hoffman supervised three. These findings underline the strong scientific link between the two countries during that period.

The doctorates of Greek economists dealt with sectoral aspects of the Greek economy, such as tobacco, currants, banking, and shipping. They used a historical method and sought to explain the growth lag in Greece. They concluded with a plea for social engineering through state intervention combined with social protection.

Another issue worth mentioning is that many Greek Law graduates after obtaining their PhD in Germany pursued political careers in Greece and were able to influence the policy decisions of both major political parties in post-World War I Greece (and later): the liberal Venezelists and the popular pro-king right-wingers. Important names among these students (with university and year of obtaining the PhD title) include Georgios Papandreou (Berlin, 1909), Panagiotis Pipinelis (Freiburg, 1921), Panagiotis Kanellopoulos (Heidelberg, 1923), Alexandros Demertzis (Leipzig, 1929), Georgios Kartalis (Leipzig, 1929), and Spiros Thiveos (Leipzig, 1933).

4.5 Venizelos and New Liberalism

The gradual abandonment of French liberal optimism and the trend toward historical economic research in Greece were intensified by the tectonic political and economic changes that took place before and after World War I. In 1910, Venizelos assumed the duties of the Prime Minister. He immediately created, next to the Ministry of Finance, a special Ministry for the Economy, and a little later another one for Transport, responsible for infrastructures. A Ministry of Agriculture, Trade and Industry followed in 1917, and another one for Social Affairs in 1924.

The victorious participation in the Balkan Wars and along the Entente forces in World War I provided the historical chance for territorial expansion and the long-sought realization of the Megali Idea. What seemed within reach in 1920 led to Venizelos losing the election and concluded in events that led to the Asia Minor catastrophe in 1922. Venizelos remained active until the mid-1930s and introduced sweeping political and economic changes during his tenure, according to the principles of new liberalism (Psalidopoulos 2014; see also Agriantoni in: Kitromilidis 2006).

As is known, new liberalism emerged in Britain as a synthesis of classical liberalism with contemporary demands for a more interventionist state that would ensure, through proactive measures, freedom and equality for all. Basing themselves on John Stuart Mill, authors such as Thomas H. Green, Leonard Hobhouse, John Hobson, and others proposed ways to create favorable social and economic conditions that would give true and deeper meaning to individual freedom and action (Freeden 1978). Progressive taxation was a useful tool for this purpose and didn't violate equality in society. Even neoclassical marginal utility theory concluded that the marginal gain of the poor was bigger than the marginal loss suffered by the rich, therefore tax progressivity did not violate citizens' rights. Venizelos framed his Liberal Party's policies in the footsteps of the British paradigm, following Asquith and Lloyd George, and attracted intellectuals and activists who strove for reform after a decade of austerity and stagnation.

Creating conditions of positive freedom in Greece required the regulation of labor issues. Between 1912 and 1923, 29 laws and 35 law decrees were issued to shape industrial relations on a totally modern basis (Malamatianos 1931). Politicians, such as Alexandros Papanastasiou, and academics, such as Dimitrios Kalitsounakis, offered their advice and support, even if they didn't always agree with Venizelos.

A prominent topic for Venizelos was just taxation. In 1910 he promised to bring prosperity to most citizens who were taxed "brutally and in an unjust manner" (Venizelos 1969, vol. 1, 204). Taxes were "colorful, and rich people didn't pay any" (vol. 2, 88), he said. He put Lambros Koromilas in charge "so that some light should penetrate the mysterious agglomeration of figures in the past" (Kerofilas 1915, 72). He asked for patience in view of the need to fulfill the obligations imposed by the IFC and, through thick and thin, the introduction of the income tax was passed in 1919.

Industry was also a recurring topic for Venizelos. He thought that high tariffs benefited few industrialists, and this needed to change. He accepted, however, that wages should be low and wanted emigration to stop, so that labor supply could grow (vol. 1, 205–6). Speaking about agriculture, Venizelos admitted that, next to property rights already in place since 1917, many other things needed to be done. The public interest, or "public utility" (vol. 1, 269) in agriculture needed to be identified and a balance between small and big land property should be aimed at (264). His government compensated, where necessary, big landowners, demonstrating thus respect for property. A distinction was made between landowners, who were farmers, and absentee property holders (vol. 2, 690–2). A law prohibiting usury, the first of its kind in Greece, was also passed in 1911.

This activity was done with a plan to create conditions of solidarity and cooperation between social classes. The present status of society was not perfect, as many claimed, Venizelos emphasized (vol. 2, 100). It was "full of injustices" (vol. 2, 101) and his legislation aimed to silence the propaganda of the "exploiters of the workers, the Bolsheviks" (vol. 2, 100). When in 1914 social tensions were running high, he stressed that "the duty and the mission of the state was neutrality" (vol. 2, 264). Arbitration had helped resolve at least 200 possible strikes in 3 years (vol. 2, 79) and there were limits to assisting workers in their demands. The introduction of machinery in the tobacco industry was welcomed "for it was a step toward progress" (vol. 2, 80) and the workers should not object to such a step despite possible layoffs.

Venizelos couldn't help getting into conflict with the NBG. In 1914, the government demanded a loan, and the NBG asked in return for the extension of the issue privilege it possessed, something close to blackmail for Venizelos. The NBG was "a power within the state, against the state" (vol. 1, 598) and should learn that "the present Greek state doesn't bend before anybody" (vol. 1, 599). In an act of power demonstration, Venizelos proceeded to the creation of the position of a co-governor of the NBG, who would be appointed by the government, and to a law that required board members of the NBG to be approved by the government. The same law foresaw the special status of the government as a borrower in relation to the NBG. Alexandros Diomidis, his former Minister of Finance, became Vice Governor of the NBG thanks to this intervention. However, the NBG could secure the extension of its privilege in 1917, during the time when Dimitrios Gounaris was Prime Minister. Venizelos was furious about the actions of the NBG and warned that once back in office he would "restrict the bank to a central bank" (vol. 2, 324). Developments on that front would have to wait until 1928.

Other important steps of the governments of Venizelos included the population and employment censuses that were initiated during his tenure. The general statistical service was inaugurated in 1917 and conducted many investigations in the 1920s, thus basing policy on real situations and needs. Finally, a decision was taken to inaugurate schools of professionals and technicians. In this context, and imitating the Grandes Ecoles scheme of the French, a special School of Economic and Commerce studies, ASOEE, assigned to award degrees in economics and in accounting was pronounced, staffed, and started operating in the early 1920s. This decision led to the institutionalization of economics in Greece.

New liberalism in Britain withered after the end of World War I, with the Conservatives regaining power. In Greece, in the aftermath of 1922, the institutional edifice that was built upon new liberal ideas remained in place. It was supplemented by state socialist-inspired legislation of German origin and contributed to the stabilization of the political system despite social turbulence after 1922.

4.6 Papanastasiou and State Socialism

Alexandros Papanastasiou was an intellectual who sought to combine science with political activity. He became a major politician for the center-left, serving twice for short periods as Prime Minister (in 1924 and 1932, respectively). At other times, he supported Venizelos as his Minister or as a coalition partner. An ardent democrat and social reformer, he was involved in the (temporary) expulsion of the monarchy in 1923 and personified the ideals of social democracy in Greece. He was the promoter of the social insurance organization in Greece, which was introduced as a law after his passing.

Papanastasiou studied law in Greece and then moved to Heidelberg and to Berlin, where he attended courses for the full undergraduate degree of Staatswissenschaften. He heard courses by both Gustav Schmoller and Adolph Wagner and kept extensive notes, as archival work has demonstrated (Psalidopoulos 1999). Interestingly, he heard Schmoller teaching "Theory," then "Policy," and in the following semester he went to similar classes offered by Wagner, an indication that he wanted to hear both these masters of German economics to form his own opinion about their theories. He also followed the sociology courses by Georg Simmel and heard lectures by Ignaz Jastrow on the Social Question.

In 1908, upon returning to Greece, he published the article "Methodological Issues in Economics" (reprinted in Papanastasiou 1972, 4–21), the first Greek publication to deal with the *Methodenstreit*. In it, and while trying to keep his distance from dogmatism, he sided with Adolph Wagner and those who believed that alongside reliance on historical facts, the existence of economic laws and of the need for theoretical abstraction were equally important and necessary. He criticized neoclassical economics because self-interest alone was not sufficient to build up a theory. This narrow basis needed to expand to include other motives of human behavior, such as altruism and moral considerations. In a future economic system, all these criteria would form the basis of a synthetic theory of human economic action (20). The inclusion of morals in government and political action was, for him, a top-ranked issue that he repeated continuously (74, 306, 333, 746). By advocating this position, Papanastasiou again followed Adolph Wagner (Wagner 1892, 122) and Immanuel Kant's "categorical imperative." Self-criticism, a clear conscience, and an internal drive to do the right thing played an important role in human action for him. These motives were sometimes dormant in human agents, he said, as survival made them selfish and profit-seeking. However, society aimed at moralizing economic life and achieving higher levels of social cohesion and development. State socialism as practiced in Germany, was, for Papanastasiou, the best way to promote both the individual interest and the economy. Greece, aiming for higher levels of income and growth, should follow the same path.

The influence of Wagner is evident in the statutes of the Sociological Society founded by Papanastasiou and other learned intellectuals in Athens in 1910, the year when Venizelos became Prime Minister. This was a club in the tradition of the Fabian Society (Papanastasiou 1972, 54, 96, 184). It was the first of its kind in Greece and exerted considerable influence on labor reform and legislation throughout the 1910s and 1920s. Many progressive and modernizing scientists, who became high-ranking civil servants sided with him.

The statutes of the society aimed to fight for the government to acknowledge that the state ought to give equal opportunities to its citizens. The means of production should serve the common purpose, the distribution of income ought to be regulated, and the economic system should constantly adjust to higher standards (3). Private property was not a natural right, but a historical outcome of certain processes. It was welcomed and should be sustained if the national economy improved.

The same ideas were articulated as the basic positions of Papanastasiou's political party. According to them, the capitalist system had not fulfilled all the hopes it initially nourished (73). Reference was made to the exploitation of the worker, but this was identified with long working hours rather than a reference to surplus value. Whatever reforms were needed, these should materialize peacefully and through gradual reforms (75). The material means for these reforms could be found in a just, progressive taxation system. The scope of government intervention included extending land ownership to peasants, encouraging cooperatives, and framing institutions accordingly so that they support production. Necessities of trade and the overall national interest of the moment were also factors under consideration since, as already mentioned, these reforms would be introduced by consensus, gradually, and not in a revolutionary manner. Papanastasiou defined his party as "conservative socialist" (557), and his aim was to break down the "party oligarchy" (743) that had governed Greece since its independence. Whenever his party stood alone in elections, it won less than 10% of the votes.

To conclude, Papanastasiou advocated the national character of economic policy and reassessed the role of the State, especially on social issues such as the regulation of wages and working hours. Economic efficiency and adherence to moral law and national interests had great importance. Ethical issues in economic theorizing, argued Papanastasiou, were not of secondary nature and should be respected in the formation of economic policy. This main idea came directly from Gustav Schmoller and the GHS (Shionoya 1997, 71). This normative dichotomy served for Papanastasiou to enlarge the scope of state action. Moreover, a gradual reform program, the political inclusion of the working class in society, and income redistribution towards more economic and social equity were the only ways of keeping social unrest at bay and averting a violent overthrow of modern democracies. It was along these principles that Papanastasiou got involved in politics, providing all his energy for the official establishment of workers' and peasants' rights, until his passing in 1935.

4.7 The Spread and Popularization of Economics

While Greece was under the supervision of the IFC and until the second decade of the 20th century, economics in Greece started showing signs of maturity. New approaches started now from theoretical analysis before arriving at policy conclusions. Methodologically, they always used the historical approach, but their references were pluralist, an indication that they were informed about current developments and important advances in economic literature. In this section, we will refer to the first efforts to join forces and analyze economic problems, as well as to some major books that were influential during the time the country experienced the deep crisis of 1922.

On the front of common efforts, the Sociological Society was quite active since its inauguration with meetings, speeches, and conferences not only in Athens, but in the provinces as well. It captured the attention of many enlightened citizens. It also capitalized on the eagerness of the public to discuss and digest what had happened to the country in the past 15 years.

In 1916, the Hellenic Society for Political Economy and Statistics (Elliniki Etaireia Politikis Oikonomias kai Statistikis, EEPOS) was called into life. Its foundation was an illustration of the existence of a critical mass of citizens and scholars who identified themselves as economists. Its members, academics, businessmen, and politicians initially envisioned contributing to the economic development of Greece and to promoting research and dialogue about pressing socio-economic problems.

The society was very active in 1916, and the minutes of its first four meetings between 6 February and 7 May 1916 reveal that the war-like conditions that Greece was experiencing since 1912 were a cause of concern for all. Whereas the first meeting was an introductory welcome by banker and landlord Giorgos Christaki-Zografos and included many speakers, the other three had one central speaker each.

In the inaugural meeting, the Society's president admitted on behalf of all that the descriptive historical method and applied propositions of theoretical systems were now used by Greek scholars. "Rational mind and imitation as well as adjustment of applied economic policies in France were in the past the leading forces of policy," he said (EEPOS 1917, 4). Social policy was until recently unknown, protection existed, but was not the norm, and indirect taxes were dominating the tax system. All this needed to change, because laissez-faire principles were "no longer capable of fulfilling the aims of modern society" (11).

Participants broadly agreed, and there was a unanimous acceptance that the political economy of the 20th century endorsed state intervention (24). The level of state activity was a topic of concern. Government intervention was not automatic, but a "product of historical development" (12). It was for this reason that the Society of Political Economy needed to define the stage at which the Greek economy found itself and to propose the right course of action.

The tax system was discussed, and the reason why citizens despised direct taxes was sought. Tax revenues had grown due to territorial expansion from 98 million drs in 1898 to 137 million drs in 1916, and the mindset of the Greeks needed to change toward the acceptance of a direct tax. Other speakers noted that warlike conditions prevailing since 1912 had led to higher prices for all goods, including necessities of life. This led them to the conclusion that national production should diversify and aim at the satisfaction of basic needs through increased national production (18).

There was also discussion about the aims of the Society with most speakers agreeing that it ought to avoid influencing policy directly and just serve as a consultant to any government. They agreed that different economic approaches and sympathies to political parties were present among them. What they agreed to do was to provide an analysis and make it public for the benefit and use of everyone interested. The Society proclaimed itself a free forum for interested parties to speak up (26). It wanted to provide sound advice to public opinion (95).

Spiros Loverdos spoke on "War and the Economic Intervention of the State," and he declared himself in his presentation a pupil and follower of Adolph Wagner (30). He clearly saw the moral need for more solidarity in Greek society but envisaged a gradual transition to more social cohesion after the end of the war (47). On the question of extra war profits – a topic treated by Georgios Kofinas – all participants agreed that the government ought to have a share to expand its sphere of action. They were, however, skeptical about the capability of government authorities to identify extra profits since the organization of the state apparatus was still deficient. The extra profits should provide material means to repay debt accumulated to finance the war. Greece had not financed the war through taxation and needed to find the right balance between revenue, spending, and public debt in the post-war era, they concluded (90). Some speakers were afraid that the only source where extra profits could be identified was shipping (105). Shipping was the most promising sector of the Greek economy, and its further development shouldn't be jeopardized by greedy state needs.

Industrialist Leontios Oikonomidis pleaded in his presentation for the encouragement and protection of Greek industry. He criticized the labor laws that had passed parliament as premature and demanded care for industry. Greek businessmen were short of capital and needed to cooperate and be awarded tax breaks and benefits (129). Trademark laws and tariffs needed to be used as vehicles for industrial improvement. Protection in Greece aimed at more state revenue and not at supporting existing industries. Tariffs were dictated by circumstances, not rational decisions (162). This needed to change for a better economic future. Participants agreed with the general thrust of these arguments, with only one of them, Alexandros Diomidis, pointing out the real fact that currants, olive oil, and tobacco were the main Greek exports that covered around 70% of the Greek balance of payments. This spoke in favor of taking greater care of agriculture for quick positive results. Industry needed government care but would unravel its potential in the mid- to long term (153), he stressed. It was therefore agriculture that ought to be taken primary care of, he concluded.

These four meetings were quite promising for the advancement of economics as an applied science in Greece. The tense political climate, however, between Venizelos and the King led to a political impasse in 1917. The country was split into two, and the Society, after its initial steps, went through an eclipse and fell into oblivion. After 1922, it was renamed the "Society of Political and Economic Sciences" and became a forum of intellectuals and public servants only. Bankers and industrialists abstained from these meetings. Papers and minutes of this Society were published in the *Archives of Economic and Social Sciences,* edited by Dimitrios Kalitsounakis.

Next to these associations, lots of books by very well-read authors appeared, intellectuals who were working in the judiciary, the press, or the public administration. It is impossible to review this activity in detail, but mention should be made of some economists.

4.7.1 Koromilas

Lambros Koromilas studied Physics in Tübingen, Germany, and Political Science, with a heavy dose of Economics, in Paris. Back in Greece, he worked in the private sector as a freelancer, and one year after the Greek default, he published "Revenues and Taxes" (1894, reproduced in Syrmaloglou 2021) as a series of articles in two newspapers. He won acclaim for his erudition and deep knowledge of the theory and practice of public finance and was appointed general secretary of the Ministry of Finance in 1897–8. After holding other government positions, he became an MP and then Minister of Finance in the first Venizelos government. After two years in this position, he moved to other ministries and later became Ambassador of Greece to the USA.

According to Koromilas, the Greek governments after 1882 lacked a theory behind their economic policy and proved to be bad administrators. Statistics given to foreign analysts Charles Roux and Edward Law in 1892 were misleading, and announcements about future surpluses were used to temporarily ease market pressure on Greek bonds. Policymakers relied on the existing tax system as it had evolved, instead of trying to introduce a new one that would fulfill the needs of the treasury and serve the economy. Tax authorities were "infant and barbarous" at the same time. The government still relied on tax collectors for many indirect taxes, indicating that it was not yet in control of its own destiny.

Theory indicated that every government ought first to bring order to its own budget and organize its tax-controlling agency accordingly before any other action. The rhetorical use made by politicians of positive developments was a policy based on sentiment rather than reality. Introducing new taxes instead of efficiently running the existing ones was also a negative feature of Greek reality. The same applied to payments of foreign experts and to military supplies, under the excuse that these expenditures were for a noble cause. Internal loans from the NBG and external loans were used as additional resources without any attention to theories that emphasized that loans were to be used only for extraordinary expenditures in abnormal times. In light of default, the top priority was to start from scratch with the following agenda: first, agreeing on the level of existing revenue needed, and then setting the exact level of yearly debt repayments. The next step should be an agreement with creditors about yearly repayments. Then, with a better organized tax administration, a reform should be introduced, a reform that wouldn't harm the real economy. Parallel to these efforts, a statistical service should assist the whole endeavour. Policy should be based on numbers and not on wishful thinking.

Koromilas went to great lengths to document that all governments before default had short-sighted policies and were equally to blame. In addition to not administering the present properly, they didn't care about arrears. When confronted with this, the citizens were accused of tax evasion. Koromilas started examining in detail one by one all existing taxes and all spending categories of the budget. He showed the inefficiency of the tax on ploughing animals and advocated for an income tax for all. He distinguished between indirect taxes on export goods, such as raisins, and those on basic goods, and calculated tax receipts from various regions of the country to determine why certain taxes and regions fared better than others.

In short, Koromilas presented the most exhaustive and data-filled analysis of the Greek tax system, which left little to be criticized. It was a pity that instead of sticking to the position of Minister of Finance, he moved to other governmental posts and did not oversee the tax reforms he helped initiate with his work. What he recommended was implemented later, thanks to his eloquence and persuasion.

4.7.2 Diomidis

Alexandros Diomidis held a PhD from Leipzig in Law and became ifigitis of administrative law at the University of Athens. In 1905 he wrote *The Budget*, the first book of its kind in the Greek language. His emphasis was on legal and constitutional questions, but he also touched upon the economic fundamentals of the budget and its implementation. The study was based on German and French literature and started with a detailed analysis of laws and procedures of the budgeting process in Germany, France, and Britain. The book discussed the uniform nature and the distinction between an ordinary and an extraordinary budget, as well as the monitoring and its execution. The book did not include references to Greece, but it was clear that the author was contributing toward filling a void and setting standards that the country, which was in dire straits at the time, should follow.

Diomidis went on to become a politician close to Venizelos, a Minister, and later a banker. He served as governor of the NBG and later of the Bank of Greece. He became Prime Minister in 1949 (for more on his life and works see Pantelakis 2018).

4.7.3 Katselidis

Georgios Katselidis was the editor of the journal *Economic Greece* (Oikonomiki Ellas), which ran from 1902 to 1910 and monitored economic life in the country. He wrote *The Currency* (1902), because he wanted, as he put it, to analyze money without stubborn theoretical assumptions followed by other writers (1902, i). Indeed, Katselidis started with definitions and by explaining the transition from metallic to paper money. He touched upon the role of banks and of credit and discussed the pros and cons of bimetallism and monometallism. He was a supporter of the gold standard, admitting that he became one once silver was downgraded on the international arena (93). He went on to inform the reader about monetary developments in the USA, in India, and in Russia, before turning to countries where forced circulation was in place. He tried to analyze the advantages and disadvantages of non-convertibility.

Finally, he devoted his last chapter to Greece. He admitted that in the 1880s monetary circulation was inflationary and accepted the directives imposed on Greece by the IFC. On the other hand, and based on an analysis of the Greek market, he thought that monetary contraction had gone too far and needed to cease, as it was choking off private initiative (326). The economic development of the country had started late. The government had to create infrastructures and, simultaneously, to build national defense and military capacity. Overborrowing became a habit, an easy solution to finance various activities. Then, because the attraction of foreign capital was seen as beneficial, the country joined the LMU, first on paper, then in practice and for short periods of time. It was, however, for Katselidis, a mistake to do so, because Greece would be obliged to exchange drachmas for gold to aspiring drachma holders (337). The conclusion he drew was that Greece needed to opt for "the natural way" (327). It had to first stabilize the external value of the drachma and then enact convertibility. The stabilization level indicated the level of competitiveness and there was no need to return to an old parity simply to demonstrate economic strength to third parties. With this argument he was clearly criticizing the agreement with the IFC. Stabilization also meant patience on the side of monetary authorities and no rush to let other countries know you are doing fine. In other words, Katselidis accepted a possible devaluation (340) and recommended that Greece should seek an agreement with the IFC so that deflation would be terminated, a new drachma enacted, and then convertibility introduced. All other plans would hurt the Greek economy. His proposal had an impact, and eight years later the Valaoritis Law modified the agreement with the IFC in a positive direction for Greece.

4.7.4 Simantiras

Ioannis Simantiras studied in Athens, Paris, and Berlin. He dedicated his book *The Issue of Forced Circulation* (1905) to his mentor, Adolph Wagner. His study was an exhaustive documentation of monetary developments and the exchange rate of the drachma from 1885 to 1905, full of charts, figures, and a long statistical annex that provided food for thought for all readers. Simantiras declared the deductive method to be the best approach to studying monetary phenomena (1905, 39) and tried to interpret fluctuations in the Greek currency by referencing internal political problems as well as foreign developments on a year-by-year basis. He reviewed the six-month period in 1885 when the drachma was convertible, and again based himself on the theoretical foundations provided by Wagner's theoretical treatise (126). He emphasized that the return to convertibility needed to be based on certain premises (109–45). A quick solution could be found if the drachma were to devalue. This, however, was impossible, because the IFC didn't espouse it. The IFC expected profits from the re-evaluation of Greek bonds that was taking place instead. Having, however, caused austerity, the constant contraction of money from circulation might lead to negative results, he thought. On the other hand, what was agreed with the IFC needed to be respected. There existed "a general interest" (147) of the country, based on a reconciliation between the producers' and the exporters' interests, and the government ought to define it and do its part to help national production raise. This would provide revenue for the repayment of bondholders and the financing of state activities. The interests of the IFC and the government would thus converge.

Simantiras was appointed ifigitis, and in 1911 he became a full Professor of Procedural Law at the University of Athens. He passed away in 1916 due to cancer.

4.7.5 Damiris

Christodoulos Damiris studied in Athens and Paris and wrote a monumental 715-page dissertation on "Le Systeme Monetaire Greque et le change" (1920) that appeared in three volumes. He investigated the Greek monetary system from the year 1910 onward when the NBG enacted the Valaoritis Law and used emigrants' remittances as backing of the money supply. By following developments in the global economy on a practically day-by-day basis, Damiris put the policy of the NBG in context with both local and international developments. He underscored the success of keeping parity with the French Franc on a 1-to-1 level until 1917 and investigated the possibility that the world was moving away from gold to a gold-exchange-standard. He quoted Keynes (vol. 3, 155) and his *Indian Currency and Finance*, and concluded that times after the end of World War I demanded flexibility and adoption of new rules, instead of staying fixed to old ones. The Valaoritis Law was a perfect example of using circumstances as they evolved and formulating sound monetary policies with win–win results.

Andreas Andreadis applauded him as a very promising monetary economist (1927, 238), but some years later Damiris passed away and could not pursue the academic career that his mentor envisaged for him.

4.7.6 Bakopoulos

Nikolaos Bakopoulos was a lawyer with an interest in monetary matters. In his work *On Banks of Issue* (1920), Bakopoulos first offered a theoretical introduction on banks, specie, banknotes, and paper money, and then proceeded to analyze how paper money was covered over time in countries such as Britain, Germany, and the USA, before arriving at Greece (171–90). He admitted that the question of whether the bank of issue should be private or state-owned could not be answered easily. Free banking was welcome, but entailed disadvantages, as did state ownership of the issue privilege (230–45). The partnership that was introduced in 1880 with the state participating in the profits of the bank was seen as a way to have the best solution in this contested field (239). Especially in the complicated situation after the end of World War I with inflation, overissue of money, debt, and monetary turbulence, the bank of issue and the government ought to cooperate as partners for the benefit of the currency and the country.

4.7.7 Other Authors

Among other authors attesting to the drive to contribute to a better economic future for the Greek economy was future banker and politician Spiros Loverdos with his informative work *The National Wealth* (1901–2). Loverdos started with population trends and supply of labor, set out cultivated soil and primary production in detail, described which raw materials and other metals were to be found in Greece, and named all this as the wealth of the country. His treatise, an update of the work done by Friedrich Thiersch, was full of numbers on all agricultural and handcrafted products for internal consumption and for exports, informing prospective investors and state authorities about productive potential and prospects of development.

A similar target was set by Vlasis Gavriilidis, editor of the newspaper *Akropolis*, with his edited book series on *Laboring Greece* (1918). These volumes were written by practitioners and included detailed information about start-up industries in Greece, the merchant marine, commerce, and banking.

Many authors dealt with problems of Greek agriculture. Panagiotis Decasos (1904), while in Germany, wrote his thesis on the topic. Sofoklis Triantafyllidis (1906) followed with a plea for land distribution. Authors close to landowning interests included Dimitrios Tsopotos (1912). All authors agreed that the primary sector of the economy ought to be reformed, gave descriptions of its status and future potential, and analyzed property issues that needed to be settled for the sector to provide a greater share of GDP.

4.7.8 Translations

Translations of foreign economic bestsellers in Greek continued but were limited during this period. The liberal tradition was represented by Paul Leroy-Beaulieu and Jean-Jacques Rapet, whose books were re-translated from their latest editions. Charles Gide's famous treatise was re-published too. Despite Gide's scientific objectivity, his partiality for the principle of solidarity was evident and conformed with sentiments in Greece at that time (Gide 1923, 44–6). The same message was disseminated in his *Cours d' économie politique* (Gide 1923, 238) translated in the interwar years. For Gide, the self-seeking competitive spirit generated "waste of strengths and riches" (Ibid., 147), and was not as beneficial as the classical economists assumed. Under the new circumstances of the 20th century, social interests could be protected, and liberal goals accomplished better than ever through free cooperation and collaboration between the forces of production (Gide 1911, 149ff, especially 243–71).

Kostas Hatzopoulos, a socialist, translated the *Communist Manifesto* in 1913 (sections thereof were translated as early as 1908), disseminating for the first time in the Greek language the views of Marx (and Engels) on the future of capitalism.

The book by Richard Cooper, *The Claims of Labor and of Capital* (1919), was a plea for collaboration between workers and capitalists. Any differences of opinion between the two parties, Cooper thought, could be mediated at Joint Industrial Councils, that could discuss and distribute earned profits in a justifiable manner. He was against the minimum wage (8) and believed that the only way for a worker to get better pay from his employer was by raising his own productivity (34). Strikes were to be avoided (111), and working hours limited to 48 per week (85). Cooperation instead of conflict ensured happiness in society and the advancement of the common interest, making the nation prosperous. An incentive-based policy which included workers' participation in profits was required (66).

Cooper's ideas were like those of Gaston Richard (1920). The latter attempted to prove that scientific socialism "does not really deserve the name" (169) and proposed that the notion of "class conflict" should be replaced by "the tendency of social forces to cooperate" (172). Richard espoused a Saint-Simonian plea for "the subordination of the economic forces that have gotten out of control to the demands of human education" (173).

Another important translation was Heinrich Herkner's *The Labor Issue (*Die Arbeiterfrage 1919–20). The book was translated and adapted for the Greek reader by Dimitrios Kalitsounakis, who wrote special chapters on the cooperative movement and on trade unionism in Greece, focusing on the efforts of workers to enforce legislation aimed at sustaining their daily lives. There is no evidence that this book was the reason that attracted so many Greek students to do their doctorates with Herkner in the interwar period.

4.8 Heterodox Thought

In 1894, on 1 May, Labor Day, was celebrated for the first time in Greece. The working class made its presence as a social force visible in Greek society. Better working conditions and demands for higher living standards were supported by their action and by intellectuals. The latter wrote articles in newspapers and periodicals, trying thus to coordinate action among different groups and to find solutions to the problem of poverty. The demands of the laboring class found an echo and went hand in hand during that period with the demands to have the *demotiki* language recognized as equal to the purist *katharevousa*, the one that was officially recognized by the state.

4.8.1 Skliros

Next to Drakoulis and Kallergis, who continued their activities, a new major figure of heterodox thinking emerged: Georgios Konstantinidis, better known under the alias Georgios Skliros. As a student of medicine in Moscow, he came under the influence of Georgii Plekhanov, participated in the 1905 revolution in Russia, was forced to leave the country for Estonia and Germany, and arrived in Greece at the time of Venizelos becoming Prime Minister. In 1907, he wrote *Our Social Question*, a book that was discussed continuously for two years through the pages of the periodical Noumas, which supported the use of the *demotiki*.

Skliros started with the statement that class struggle was a necessary factor for social progress (85). Human history had demonstrated that societies went through three levels of development, associated with the existence of three distinct classes and the exercise of power by them. In the first level, nobility and aristocrats were dominant, in the second one the civil/bourgeois class, and in the third level workers/

proletarians. He proceeded to discuss what had happened in Europe since the dissolution of feudalism and used a chart to depict the psychological inclination of social classes toward forms of governance, the church, reforms, military expenditure, and parliament (105), before turning to Greece.

In that chapter, he started with a negative assessment of both the Byzantine and the Ottoman Empires and concluded that Greece was deprived of a possible aristocracy (111). Commerce, however, gave the material means to question despotism in times of Enlightenment in Europe; the Greeks revolted, and their uprising had anti-feudal and bourgeois roots, and not only national liberation as a goal.

Skliros saw two possible future avenues for Greece: one of the existing realities and a second of the great historical traditions (115). Reality meant that, due to prevailing internal and external conditions, Greece should be satisfied to at best become "the Switzerland of the East" (115). Historical traditions demanded that Greece should reinstall something like a smaller Byzantine Empire and let its aristocracy lead the country toward capitalism. Indeed, Skliros remarked, the Greek bourgeoisie, small in number and relatively rich, got rid of the imposed Bavarian king and imposed its rule on all poor Greeks (119). Intellectuals and the press supported this rule through "fanatical conservatism" (120) and led the situation of the country to a junction: either follow "great historical traditions" (121) or practice "ruthless critical analysis (and) reform" (121). Greece had a small number but very wealthy bourgeoisie, many bourgeois with a small capital basis and a small number of proletariat. Political representation was important for the workers because they could also impose the demotic language they spoke (126). Demotiki supporters who believed that they could prevail by reason and not by intense political struggle, by not seeing things like sociologists did, were for Skliros losers. The proletarians could, by growing in number and by organizing themselves politically become the class of the future. Students and educated people were possible allies in this fight. Skliros concluded with another chart indicating how this alliance would break the veil of lies of the upper classes, prevail, and win the struggle against them to install a perfect social future for Greece (137).

The book used for the first time a Marxian rudimentary scheme to explain aspects of Greek society. It was normal that it would cause an uproar and lots of controversies. After a short stay in Greece, Skliros moved to Cairo, Egypt, where he worked as a doctor. He wrote a pamphlet on war and peace (1917) and supported Venizelos in his drive to stand by the Allies during World War I. Shortly before his passing, he reworked his 1907 study that was published as *Contemporary Problems of Hellenism* in 1920.

4.8.2 Giannios

Nikos Giannios, who studied languages in Paris, came to Greece in 1911 and created the Socialist Center of Athens, which gave him the opportunity to become a public figure among Greek Leftists. In his *Socialism of the State* (1914) he downgraded the labor legislation passed by Venizelos as measures that profited the employers in the last instance. For him, this kind of socialism had nothing in common with the socialism of the Marxists. The latter didn't sponsor a compromise between capital and labor. The real socialist ought to consider a state socialist as an enemy, and state socialism would wither rather soon.

Political developments, however, pushed Giannios to side with Venizelos in 1917 and to follow a path that alienated him from his early comrades. He stuck to the Socialist Party he had inaugurated and tried to influence public opinion after 1917, as socialist groups were moving toward unification in the direction of a revolutionary party. His anti-Jewish rhetoric in this context led him to the margins of left-wing politics. His endorsement of the German SPD's 1918 policy agenda was not supportive of his cause either. He lost appeal and influence, but remained however active politically until after World War II.

4.8.3 Chatzopoulos

A similar political path was followed by Kostas Chatzopoulos, translator of the *Communist Manifesto*. A vocal supporter of *demotiki* and a verbal believer in revolutionary socialism in 1910, he later sided later with Venizelos, seeing in the latter's program the chance to accelerate politics in Greece to more reforms and economic growth.

During this period, heterodox thought was more political than economic and too involved with the language question. Marxian notions and historical materialism were known, and efforts were made to understand developments in Greece within the broad spectrum of Marxian analysis.

Notes

1 OJPD, Supplement, 2.5.1903, pp. 443–4.
2 For the history of income taxation, see Sabine (1966) and the discussions about tax progressivity Shehab (1953).
3 The nickname "Japanese" was given to these parliamentarians as they demonstrated a dynamic and combative spirit similar to the one that led the Japanese to a military victory against the Russian Empire in 1905, an event that stunned the international community.
4 For a recent evaluation of his thought, see Stassinopoulos (2021).
5 The archive is accessible and is the property of the University of Athens.

5 Economics Takes Off

The Institutionalization of Economics (1920–71)

5.1 Overview of Economic Developments (1920–40)

After ten years of a war economy and internal political strife, Greece experienced the dissolution of the Megali Idea with the Asia Minor catastrophe in 1922. The influx of refugees provided industrialization with cheap labor power, but also posed great problems for government authorities (Freris 1986, 38–102). The public sector grew in numbers, with its employees jumping from 37,000 in 1915 to 72,000 in 1924 (Anastasopoulos 1947, vol. three, 1126). Challenges were overcome through financial aid from the League of Nations and other donors. The settlement of the refugees was the major policy concern of the period and up to the mid-1930s. An international committee that included Henry Morgenthau and John Campbell managed the whole enterprise. It remained active until December 1930, and handled, among others, the compensation of the refugees for their abandoned properties in Asia Minor. It also provided loans to assist the activities of the settlers that later were overtaken by the Agricultural Bank of Greece created in 1928. Approximately 50% of the refugees were settled in big cities and the rest in rural areas mostly in Northern Greece. Government expenditure rose to provide for infrastructure and some minimum social services. This was done under conditions of monetary instability until 1928, when a Central Bank was called into life. High rates of inflation and the gradual devaluation of the currency (from 25 drachmas to one pound sterling in 1918 to 375 in 1928) gave rise to numerous debates among economists, whose number in turn grew to unknown dimensions (Psalidopoulos 1989).

Eleftherios Venizelos returned to power for a brief period in 1924 and then for four years in 1928–32. He declared the economic development of Greece as a new Megali Idea. He tried through so-called "productive works" to improve infrastructure and the state of agriculture, made the currency convertible, and emphatically expected foreign capital to invest in Greece. His efforts were halted in 1932 when, in the wake of the Wall Street Crash, Greece declared bankruptcy and its economic policy became more regulative and protective. Foreign trade began to be exhaustively controlled, and the country made use of clearing arrangements mostly with Germany to save its currency reserves and combat shortages. Self-sufficiency in wheat was declared a prime goal. Negotiations with foreign bondholders were settled by 1935, and the economy started improving slowly until the outbreak of World War II.

DOI: 10.4324/9781315413419-6

In the following paragraphs, we will see how economics was institutionalized and who were the major figures of the period in academia and in political life. We will focus on the work and influence of certain professors and other academics before turning to economics in the public arena and debates about monetary issues and the scope of state intervention. This will help us distinguish two major, distinct camps of economic thought in interwar Greece. We will then investigate the influences in economic thought through translations and turn our attention to heterodox thinkers and activists. In a separate chapter, we will reconstruct the reception of John Maynard Keynes's *General Theory of Employment, Interest and Money* in the country.

5.2 Institutionalization Kicks Off

During the interwar period, economic science in Greece made a qualitative step forward, reflecting the changing structure of the Greek economy after the first tenure of Venizelos in power. Economists started being in demand as specialists, and this trend was depicted in the evolving academic landscape. The expanding institutionalization of economics was manifest in the creation of new universities and commercial schools and the increased numbers of academic chairs for economists, while degrees in economics started being awarded from the mid-1920s.

With the launch of the Highest School for Economic and Commercial Studies in Athens (ASOEE) in the early 1920s, economic education in Greece was boosted and this was supported by the hiring of more economists at the Law School of the University of Athens and the University of Thessaloniki. In addition to these developments, two important events were registered in 1929. The Association of Greek banks was inaugurated and started publishing an Economic Yearbook with much analysis of the Greek economy. The Supreme Economic Council (Anotaton Oikonomikon Symvoylion, AOS) – a group of 15 economists – was also called into life for government authorities to consult on whatever problems Ministers might feel tempted to seek expert opinion on. AOS published 30 studies on problems of the Greek economy before 1940. These developments gave institutional recognition to and societal acceptance for economics and were in step with developments in other European countries.

Andreas Andreadis played an important role in this process while advancing the diversity of economic ideas in the country. He was appointed as a senior academic in all selection committees, the role of which was the filling of university positions. Through his recommendation, a handful of promising young scholars came to occupy university chairs. Andreadis expressed his approach about economics in Greece in an article in German on the state of economic science in different European countries (Andreadis 1927). As he explained, both the classical/neoclassical school and the German Historical School (GHS) were products of certain political and philosophical ideas which sprang out of concrete historical and economic facts. The theories suggested by these schools were therefore valid for a limited time and for countries sharing similar characteristics. "The Greek scientist should not belong exclusively to any one (of these schools). He should inquire how far these teachings could be applied in his country" (1927, 237), he thought.

He believed that after a time of intense historical research and debate among different schools of thought, there could follow a time of more theoretical work and of a synthetic effort to produce an economic theory best suited for Greece. For this reason, he helped various economists of the most different world views and theoretical viewpoints to advance their civil/academic careers. One can therefore conclude that, despite his liberal views, Andreadis was very distant from what Alfred Marshall pursued in Britain (Maloney 1985) regarding the search for the "right" economic theory.

The economists hired on his recommendation were Kyriakos Varvaressos Xenophon Zolotas, Demosthenis Stephanidis, Dimitrios Kalitsounakis, Ioannis Tournakis, and Spiros Koronis. Zolotas and Kalitsounakis became the editors of two scientific economic journals: the *Review* (EKDO) since 1932 and the *Archive* (AOKE) since 1921. Whereas the *Archive* defined economics in a broader social science setting and its editor espoused interventionism, the *Review* put emphasis on theoretical and empirical economics, and the bulk of the contributions therein followed the prevailing neoclassical paradigm of those times.

Seven of the many contributors to the *Review* who already had a PhD submitted monographs to the University of Athens during the 1930s to become ifigites. Zolotas and Varvaressos assumed the role played by Andreadis a decade earlier. These readers in economics at the University of Athens proceeded then in the 1940s and 1950s to occupy existing or newly created chairs at other Greek universities.

Andreadis's goal at a university level was thus fulfilled. No Greek School of Economics emerged, but pluralism of views prevailed. Greek economists multiplied in number, economic monographs and articles were published in growing numbers, and all schools of thought flourished. Marxism was disseminated among intellectuals and the working class; it remained, however, outside academia.

As far as Greek students and places of study are concerned, Germany remained until 1933 the most attractive country for them to do a PhD, with France coming distantly second. This was in line with international developments at that time (for the American case see Dorfman 1955; Herbst 1965). This trend slowed down after the Nazis came to power.

5.3 Developments in Academia: The First Generation

5.3.1 Varvaressos

The claim for a new place for government action in the economy found a powerful and eloquent exponent in the writings of Kyriakos Varvaressos (Kakridis 2017). He was devoted throughout his career, in parallel to his academic duties, to policymaking, and his contributions during the 1930s testify that he favored an ethical approach to economic reasoning, like the one espoused by members of the GHS.

After getting his PhD in Athens, Varvaressos moved to Munich and then to Berlin for advanced studies (1908–11). In Berlin, he worked in the Prussian Statistical Office, and upon his return to Greece, he was appointed to the Statistical Service of Greece and oversaw the censuses enacted after 1915.

His *Theory of Population* (1912) was the first treatise in Greece that addressed demographics, trying to evaluate Malthusian theory in the light of statistical evidence. Varvaressos presented the theory of population and the Malthusian assumptions about the wage level and poverty. He juxtaposed real population growth in 32 regions and countries, to arrive at the conclusion that it took between 40 and 100 years for populations to double (73–4). Places where population growth was delayed included rich regions such as Bavaria, Spain, and France, meaning that institutional and structural changes relativized Malthusian theory for industrialized nations. Findings by authors such as Lujo Brentano and Franz Oppenheimer supported Varvaressos, who went on to investigate wage levels in various countries. He again concluded that labor wages depended on many factors and that only unskilled workers received a wage close to the subsistence level (125). Using statistics of production of primary goods (133–140), he was able to conclude that scarcity was being overcome and that nutrition levels were secure despite population growth. He also discussed birth and mortality rates (164–71) and underlined the increasing trend in average life expectancy. Varvaressos did not reject Malthusian theory in general. He accepted that Malthus was an original thinker, and his views had a certain validity (173). What he objected to was the deterministic element of population theory as suggested by the great Briton. Society had entered an atomistic stage of human life (175), he thought, that had psychological implications for all individuals, men and women. In advanced countries it seemed, for Varvaressos, that married couples distinguished childbearing from sexual intercourse and were thus able to plan their lives accordingly. In less developed countries, this process was still under formation but would follow the same pattern if material conditions improved. Malthus was right at the time to argue as he did and alert his contemporaries, but over the course of time, he was proven wrong and his arguments were very ideological due to his theological training (179). Varvaressos understood that the lower classes were only marginally profiting from industrialization and was against efforts to accuse/sideline them for creating pressures in the economy by their willingness to have children (180).

Varvaressos was a member of the Greek delegation in Versailles and in his inaugural lecture at the University of Athens in early 1920, shortly after the publication of J. M. Keynes' *Economic Consequences of the Peace*, held a lecture about *The Meaning of the Economic Clauses of the Peace Accord* (1920). In this lecture he didn't quote Keynes, and, in fact, the written version of the lecture does not include any references. He compared the clauses of Versailles with those of the treaty between Prussia and France in 1871 and concluded that Versailles was a regression. It included clauses impossible for Germany to fulfilll, to the disadvantage of post-war global economic cooperation. Future economic progress involved the participation of all countries in international economic exchanges and Varvaressos interpreted the harsh treatment of Germany by the allies as a bad omen for the future. Political leaders ought to stand above the psychology of the masses that demanded revenge, and Varvaressos was sad to underline that European leadership was lacking a sober and straightforward approach.

In his *Trade Agreements and the Clause of the Most Favored Nation* (1923), he dealt with the evolution of international trade before 1914. He analyzed the tendency of many nations to avoid economic cooperation and to seek international exchanges only under mutually beneficial circumstances. This was an outcome of protectionist ideas which were understandable to a certain point but threatened peace and cooperation on a global scale. Varvaressos understood that humanity had entered a difficult path after World War I but argued in favor of setting war experiences aside and adopting a multinational way of addressing commercial exchanges between nations like the one existing before 1914. He didn't use comparative advantage or free trade rhetoric and opted to stress the need for elites to stand above emotions so that international economic life might continue contributing to economic growth.

Varvaressos was from 1923 onward heavily involved in monetary policy matters, as a consultant to the National Bank of Greece (NBG). He was the only Greek economist after September 1931 to advise, when Britain left the Gold Standard, that Greece should abandon convertibility, but he was ignored. After the default in 1932, he was called by Venizelos to manage the new situation as a Finance Minister, which he did with success.

In 1937 he became a member of the Academy of Athens. His inaugural lecture was *On the Problem of Economic Organization* (1937) and is quite revealing of his overall beliefs. The global economy was experiencing, according to him, the results of the failure of the World Economic Conference in London in 1933. National solutions such as the New Deal, Nazi economic policy, Soviet economic planning, and Swedish countercyclical policy were evolving. In view of these developments, Varvaressos questioned the capacity of the classical liberal system "to adapt according to modern social views and claims" (406). He started from Robbins' definition of economics and the expectation that the market would provide solutions to the problem of scarcity. He argued that times had proven that the social economy was not the mere addition of individual actors. Society had its own life and aims that were either identical to or diverging from private goals. Competition might be ruinous and destroy social structures, he claimed. The monolithic and abstract treatment of society by orthodox theory found its limits in massive unemployment created by the depression. Despite its formalistic perfection, it was clear that society could not rely on neoclassical theory to achieve its goals.

On the other hand, socialism as a theory of society had its own deficiencies, and by all standards was not a system that would combine individual and societal goals. The best solution for the current economic order could be a combination of private initiative with state policies aimed at an inclusive society. These policies dictated that the government should intervene to solve market failures and ensure economic welfare and opportunities for all. Government activity was the main instrument "for the domination of social ends over the private ones" (410). Varvaressos insisted that the economic system he favored went beyond capitalism and socialism. Societies needed to define their interests and aim for their satisfaction. Private interests should follow them and deliver to society what they were seemingly unable to deliver after 1929.

A similar line of analysis was provided in his *Some Thoughts About the Problem of Value* (1939). The labor and the subjective theory of value were presented, and the question posed was whether they were able to offer a sound basis for the determination of prices. Taken alone, neither approach, for Varvaressos, provided satisfactory explanations. Value had a social dimension and reflected, besides scarcity and production cost, society's values. These were changing over time. Economics needed theory, and abstraction was important for its construction. Theory needed to investigate causal relationships, but economists should not forget that their theoretical assumptions were intellectual constructs, and that society might not benefit from a narrow base of principles that ran contrary to the interests of the state. The organic conception of the state was, as we see, at the heart of his analysis. The problem of value was important for Varvaressos, and economists should try to enrich their investigations by taking social considerations into account and finding the right theoretical balance.

In his *History and Problems of the Greek Monetary System* (1939), he attacked speculation as responsible for fluctuations of the external value of the Greek currency since its inauguration. Policies to regulate the financial market and tame speculation were essential for Varvaressos. Money was a medium of exchange; society depended on it, and its value ought to remain outside egoistic individual plans. The public should enjoy priority over the private benefit.

Varvaressos became governor of the Bank of Greece in 1939 and shortly before the Nazi occupation he left the country for Egypt, South Africa, and then London, with a cargo full of the gold reserves of the Bank. Next to his governorship of the Central Bank, he was Minister of Finance of the Greek government in exile. In a speech entitled "The Greek Battle: Economic interests and moral factors" at the Royal Institute of International Affairs in December 1941, he defended the position of Greece next to the Allies. He admitted that during the 1930s Greece had developed close economic ties with Germany due to the clearing system that made foreign transactions for countries short of reserves easier. These ties, however, could not compensate for ideals such as freedom, dignity, and respect for the other. In a remarkable closing of his speech, Varvaressos anticipated the Beveridge Report and declared the common fight against the Nazis as an effort to create a political and social system after the war that would guarantee the full satisfaction of social interests. In this system, all individual forces would combine to create full use of productive resources and produce maximum individual as well as social utility.

In three radio speeches for the BBC between October 1941 and February 1942, he articulated hopes that international cooperation and the creation of global economic institutions would promote the goal of human welfare after the end of the war. Tired of internal Greek political machinations concerning the return of the monarchy in Greece, he resigned as a Minister and assumed the representation of Greece in international economic affairs. He was present at Bretton Woods and was elected by his peers to the committee of interpretation of the articles of agreement. He sided with Keynes on the issue of bancor, the proposed new global currency, thus earning his sympathy (Steil 2013, 231).

He returned to Greece after liberation at a time of political tensions that were to lead to civil war. His colleague Zolotas was named Deputy Governor of the Bank of Greece, and the two men clashed over the correct way to stabilize the drachma. Zolotas favored the determination of its value based on market reactions, and Varvaressos proposed the setting of its value through a government decision. Political inertia followed. Six months later, Varvaressos was called to coordinate, as Deputy Prime Minister, the return of the economy to normalcy. The issue of stabilizing the economy had top priority, but the Varvaressos plan, a politically centrist solution to the actual situation, was opposed by both right and left, who fought his plans and accused him of dictatorial predispositions. He resigned after three months and returned to the States, where he worked for the World Bank, at first as an executive director and later as an advisor to President Eugene Black. In that capacity, he wrote 39 reports on various issues of interest to the Bank. Consequently, he resigned from his professorial position in Athens.

Varvaressos was very embittered by developments in Greece. In 1947, he exchanged accusations with Alexandros Diomidis and Stefanos Stefanopoulos on the causes of his inability in 1945 to contribute to Greek stability, accusing vested interests and Greek petty politics for his failure. When asked, however, by PM Plastiras to submit a plan for the reconstruction of Greece in 1952, he did so. His "Report on the Economic Problem of Greece" was a detailed, impressive, and visionary report that aroused controversy. As Plastiras lost the 1952 election, the recommendations of Varvaressos were not followed.

In his report, Varvaressos cautioned against visionary proposals that expected a quick industrialization of Greece mainly based on foreign resources. Being an experienced realist, he approached the Greek economy through a pragmatist lens. He recommended the restoration and support of Greek agriculture, which would raise income and nutrition standards. Next, assistance to the construction sector should be given. Infrastructural projects on a nation scale should improve transport and communications, and last, but not least, the administration of the country needed to upgrade to modern standards of economic monitoring and provide rational use of foreign assistance. This well-documented report found the disapproval of Zolotas and a group of economists around the EOPE, with the main thrust of criticism being the possibility to industrialize Greece using foreign assistance, since the country was the only one under the Western sphere of influence in the Balkan region.

Varvaressos continued opining about the Greek and the global economy in interviews and short papers. In an interview for the Greek newspaper *Ethnos*, published in Washington DC, he expressed his views about post-World War II tendencies in economics as a science (Varvaressos 1954). He admitted that the scientific paradigm introduced by the neoclassical school was continuing to describe economic phenomena with the use of mathematics in a satisfactory manner. This explained the tendency of the economy to equilibrium, but it was just an intellectual exercise. The assumptions of the marginalist approach were simplistic and could not be used for understanding the real world. John Maynard Keynes had provided a synthetic and realist way of analyzing economic problems, in his view. For Varvaressos, Keynes had combined production and the creation of value with the study of money and had created a far more realistic model to study the economy. This had led economists to see monetary expansion in times of non-utilized productive sources in a relaxed way, whereas in older times any monetary expansion would be called inflationary.

The world economy was still in a reconstruction phase, with the USA aiding the rest of the Western World. An economic slowdown in the USA would impact global recovery. It was essential for Varvaressos not to return to times of cutting expenditures for the sake of supposedly keeping a sound currency through a balanced budget. Economic progress and welfare rested upon a theoretical approach in economics that was realistic and earned credit by advancing well-being for society.

5.3.2 Kalitsounakis

Dimitrios Kalitsounakis received his PhD in Greece in 1909 and moved in 1914 to Berlin, where his brother Ioannis was a professor of Oriental languages. He lived there until 1918, attended university lectures, and wrote informative articles on the economic importance of Greek and German trade agreements, and on the cooperative movement in Greece. He translated and adapted Heinrich Herkner's *Die Arbeiterfrage* (the labor question), adding chapters on Greece (1919–20). In 1920 he was named ifigitis with a contribution about Gustav Schmoller. He started lecturing at the University of Athens, teaching History of Political Economy for the first time at a Greek University. (These lectures were published in 1929.)

He became a professor of economics at ASOEE and taught Applied Political Economy, and as well as fiscal and monetary policy, he introduced social, agrarian, and transport policy in his courses. His textbook was full of historical developments that had led to present conditions. He also edited, as already mentioned, the *Archive* for 50 years (1920–71) and wrote extensively on almost all fields of economics (economic methodology, business cycle theory, tobacco, cooperatives, etc.). However, his main research interests were labour and social legislation, unemployment, and the alleviation of poverty. He was a prolific author, and his works were easily accessible to the average citizen.

From the very start of his career, Kalitsounakis sided politically with Venizelos, as the second part of his *Political Science* (1925) revealed (see also his 1936). He shared with Venizelos the vision of a new society, where the fruits of capitalism would be shared by all citizens. He stressed that Venizelos was implementing social policies and had introduced up-to-date legislation and welfare programs, thus helping Greek society avoid "violent social riots, by improving the condition of the vast masses of the working people to the point that is demanded by our modern civilization" (1925, 170).

The location of Kalitsounakis in science and in politics is clearly depicted in his inaugural lecture, "*The present tendencies toward nationalization*" (1921). He presented himself in between two extreme positions: those who defended a laissez-faire capitalism, ignoring John Stuart Mill's analysis, on the one hand, and ignorant people who misinterpreted Marx and opted for revolution on the other. Kalitsounakis sided with economists like Karl Buecher and politicians like Karl Kautsky, who believed that "the economic world moves toward socialism" anyhow (50). What was needed in society was an organized private initiative and a conscious and disciplined working class. Both sides, with the state as a coordinator, would take decisions about better organizing the production process and about choosing which industries could be run by government authorities to the benefit of society. The German plans for a *Gemeinwitschaft*, a supplementary economic sector run by the government in parallel with the one run by private agents, was a good example of the way forward. Turning his attention to Greece, Kalitsounakis didn't see an industrial sector in need of nationalization but demanded state planning for agriculture. He warned that "progress doesn't happen immediately, but through twists and turns" (59). The dominant trend in society would materialize through evolution and not through voluntarism. Neither "Russian fanatism nor Hungarian despair" provided good examples for Greece, he stressed (72), referring to political events in these countries. Preparation for a better Greek future included collective action and creation of material prerequisites for future growth. Labor legislation was a step in the right direction.

Addressing the failure of post-World War I economic conferences on a new global financial system, Kalitsounakis opined that monetary stability was not a supreme goal, but came second after the restoration of internal production. The negative balance of payments of Greece reflected structural weaknesses. The exchange value of the drachma was not the reason for low exports, he stressed. The economy had gone through dire straits and the production structure needed to become policy issue number one. Views that espoused the stabilization of the currency and suggested that this policy would solve all problems were based on "magical laws and untested theories" (360).

In his *Theory of Money* (1926) Kalitsounakis elaborated on monetary theory and policy more fully. He distinguished two theories about the external value of money, the Purchasing Power Parity theory, and the Balance of Payments theory, without taking sides as to their validity. The social cost of inflation was discussed in relation to its consequences for financiers, businessmen, and workers. Whereas inflation was an "injustice" mostly for workers, depression was "stagnation" and was felt by all members of society (40). To arrive at a stabilized external value of money, three possible ways existed: Revaluation, devaluation, and stabilization at the current level. Kalitsounakis welcomed the return of the pound to the gold standard in its pre-World War I parity through a revaluation (73), but for a small economy such as the Greek one, he recommended a stabilization at the current drachma value as a better way. He underlined the need for a smooth transition to a stable currency as important but stressed that insufficient production and an unjust distribution of income were far worse economic phenomena than inflation. Stabilizing the value of money didn't solve these two major policy issues that were of higher importance for society.

After the Wall Street Crash, Kalitsounakis published *Economic Forecast: The Rhythm of the Economy*, a book that went through four editions (1930, 1943, 1952,

1958).[1] He declared the principle of natural harmony in the economy as non-existent. Following mostly Arthur Spiethoff, he put emphasis on the evolution process of a capitalist economy that constantly moved toward a higher quality standard (26–30). He discussed the theories of Say, Marx and Juglar, the policy proposals of Fisher and Hawtrey, and the work of newly created institutes worldwide on the study of business cycles (59–97). Overproduction, income inequality, expansionary monetary policy, and sunspot theories were analyzed, and the conclusion was reached that the normal in the current phase of capitalist development was the change of phases as the economy grew. These changes led to concentration of capital and technological improvements, whereas economies that didn't experience these ups and downs remained stagnant. Until a higher level of collective human understanding was reached, Kalitsounakis concluded, crises would occur, and they would only turn out milder or be tamed if society would be ready to move to the correct policy choices that would have the common interest of all citizens as a goal (100–15).

In two other publications, "Sombart and the Systematization of Political Economy" (1930) and *Tobacco* (1932), he demonstrated his ability to deal with both theoretical and practical economic problems. The first was an effort to interpret Sombart's *Der Moderne Kapitalismus* from a methodological and history of economic ideas perspective and combine sociological and economic thought. The GHS' contribution in offering an alternative to both classical political economy and Marxism was praised, and its roots in both positivism and romantic thought were analyzed. The second dealt with Greece's most valuable export commodity, and the problems faced by the producers after the fall in international prices due to the Wall Street Crash.

In the early 1930s, Kalitsounakis wrote many textbooks for his students on applied economics, public finance, and other classes he was assigned to teach. Then, he turned his attention to classical political economy. In 1938, he published in his periodical an extended translation of John Stuart Mill's *Principles* and wrote a study on Ricardo, followed by the translation of Ricardo's magnum opus into Greek. Then, in 1940, he wrote a paper on Malthus and edited and wrote the introduction to the *Works* of François Quesnay. In these studies, he praised the economists he dealt with and presented their views thoroughly, trying to introduce them to an audience not much exposed to classical economic thinking. Indeed, besides some praise for Adam Smith, little had been written in depth about the British tradition in economics until then. This activity coincided with translations of works by neoclassical economists like Irving Fisher undertaken by other economists.

In 1946 he wrote a short paper about the future of the world economy after World War II. He declared freedom as the main goal of human existence and underlined that freedom could not exist "if there was economic injustice in society" (1946, 52). Private initiative had to become more collective, and competition ought to give way to solidarity and cooperation. This would solve the contradiction between labor and capital, he thought. Franklin D. Roosevelt was praised for his policies and efforts to stand in the middle between social classes and aim at the general good. Another factor showing the way forward was, in his opinion, the creation of greater national economic units, in Europe and elsewhere. Their function would be to coordinate global economic activity, smooth out any possible conflicts, and make sure that economic growth would remain stable and incomes would be sufficient to buy production (53).

Kalitsounakis earned extra credit from the academic community by initiating and editing the first translation of Adam Smith's *Wealth of Nations* into Greek in 1948. Parallel to that, in the new edition of his textbook, he included the views of Walter Eucken and Ordoliberalism, and praised Eucken's thesis that economic theories that articulated hypotheses of general validity were doomed to failure (1954, 757–811). He kept a certain distance from Ordoliberalism (815) but was keen to make this strand of thought familiar to his students. He also wrote on Keynes and remained faithful to his historical-evolutionary approach until he retired and ceased editing the *Archive.*

To sum up, Kalitsounakis was deeply convinced that a new era had arrived in the 20th century in economic policy, which called for close cooperation between society and state, a collective action that would "tend to substitute the private with the social economy" (1943, 107) and to deal effectively with business cycles and economic instability. He remained distanced from neoclassical theory and revolutionary Marxism, and faithful to his efforts to contribute to a new economic theory that aspired to social unity, a collective economy, and a government that would accelerate development with its actions. He was equally distanced from Keynesian economics.

5.3.3 Stefanidis

Dimosthenis Stefanidis was a professor at the Universities of Thessaloniki (1928–42) and Athens (1950–65). His tenure in Thessaloniki was terminated by the Quisling government during occupation because he didn't show up for his classes for two consecutive years. He was initially a follower of the methodology of the GHS, a pioneer in unequal exchange theory and therefore a protectionist, who moved gradually to totalitarian political beliefs.

He studied in Athens, where he earned his first degree in Law, and then spent five years in Jena and Frankfurt, where he studied economics under Franz Oppenheimer. It was in Germany where, according to his autobiography (1944), he started distancing himself from liberal ideas. He wrote many shorter essays, published as *Economic Studies*, and then a book on *Chambers of Commerce, in Particular in Greece* (both in 1926). In parallel, he prepared an ifigessia under the supervision of Andreas Andreadis on *Imperialism*, which was submitted at the University of Athens and defended in 1927. With his publications in the 1930s, he moved toward a more authoritarian scientific outlook, blended with economic romanticism. He regarded liberalism as an economic doctrine not suited for less developed countries and went on to praise the Greek dictator Ioannis Metaxas and German National Socialism. After World War II, he remained silent about the politically extreme part of his views. He successfully fought the effort to keep him out of the University of Athens, where he was elected in 1950, and kept to politically conservative approaches in Greek post-World War II economic issues.

The ifigessia of Stefanidis was inspired by an article of the German universalist Othmar Spann and was divided into two parts: imperialism in science and politics, and imperialism as a driving force in history. He claimed humans possessed two motives: a material one to survive and a moral one for recognition (1927, 49). Group motives were more powerful than individual ones, and the state was the instrument they used to articulate their desire for distinction internationally, even at the expense of other nations. These two motives collided at both a national and a supranational level, and a fight of the stronger against the weaker was taking place within society and among societies (79). Stefanidis used and applied arguments put forth by social biology and Herbert Spencer in his analysis. He presented the socialist view critically (26–32) and explained the bourgeois approach (32–45). At times, imperialisms of different nations co-existed beside one another, he claimed.

In the 20th century, a renegotiation of global dominance was taking place. Economic power had become a new factor that led nations up and down the scale of political and military strength. This factor changed the attitude of governments in relation to economic evolution, making the state the prime vehicle of growth and a driver of individuals. The countries that were better equipped economically dominated the others. Foreign trade was nothing but a substitute vehicle to suppress other nations and impose the will of the imperialist power on a global scale (93).

Stefanidis wrote extensively about economic crises, demonstrating an exhaustive detail of information about actual situations in various countries, but lacking a particular theoretical instrument to explain either the post-World War I developments or the post 1929 conditions. He surprised the community of Greek economists when he argued that it would be better to slow down the transformation of capital from circulating to fixed in order not to promote overproduction, and thus an inability to sell total output (1926, 16). It was clear that he was not conceiving capitalism as a dynamic system with its own rules but believed that a government authority could manipulate the economy, keeping it traditional for the sake of not exposing it to crises. He named speculation "a satellite of trade" (30) and stressed that the value of the currency should be managed by the government authorities without letting the free flow of goods and services determine the country's exchange rate.

His study on the *Inflow of Foreign Capital in Greece* (1930) was an original and exhaustive stocktaking of all foreign investment in Greece since its independence. He started with an analysis of international capital flows and divided countries into either capital exporters or capital importers. This distinction originated with the amount of saving in a country, the productivity of labor, and "international economic exploitation" (129). Importers of foreign capitals could use the money for productive or unproductive purposes, and repayment of loans/export of profits to the exporting capital country could lead to international crises as in China or in Egypt (151–65). Stefanidis then turned his attention to Greece. He started with the Loans of Independence, moved to the Trikoupis period, and then investigated the foreign loans/capital inflows in Greece after 1893. He devoted extreme thoroughness to the loans after 1922 (233–99) and arrived at the conclusion that, despite improvements in handling foreign capital flows, the Greek authorities needed to revise their lending policies. In his view, Greece should aim to become self-sufficient in its capital needs. The economic exploitation of Greece by other countries needed to end (312–13). Greek saving and the productivity of labor needed to rise. Foreign capital should be used for productive purposes only, and national authorities needed to oversee and make sure that the means of repayment or any export of foreign profits would not harm the terms of production. Before turning to foreign capital, the Greek government needed to attract Greek savings from abroad.

After default, he wrote *The World Economic Crisis and Greece* (1932), and he repeated the arguments he had put forward in the past. Deliberate industrialization entailed the danger of crisis whereas a balanced, slower growth path, with emphasis on primary production and self-sufficiency in basic foodstuffs, might have been an alternative that would not have led to crisis (16–17). Greece had over-borrowed money from abroad in the past. The introduction of convertibility in 1928 was based on a small pool of reserves and was doomed to fail. In general, Greek policy relied on foreign economic investment decisions and was not paying the attention required to Greek realities. "Abstract and outdated principles" (27) propagated by liberal theorists had been proven totally wrong. For Greece to quickly recover, he rhetorically wished "an economic dictatorship for some years" (33–4) that would prepare a different framework for the economy, one based on a balanced exploitation of the country's economic resources.

In his *The New Tendencies in Foreign Commercial Policy* (1935), he applauded the regulated and introverted economic policy that had been practiced in Greece since the default. He admitted that total self-sufficiency was impossible (13), but, in his opinion, equally wrong was a policy of specialization and of growth through external trade. Industrialization had made certain countries extremely rich, and these countries were flooding others with cheap products, not allowing them to develop. Exchanges between rich and poor countries were not favorable for the latter, and the theory of free trade and of comparative advantage had led to economic discrepancies among nations. He asked rhetorically: "Where should the balance be restored?" (14). The cosmopolitans, he continued, defended the status quo. Those however who "witness with disgust the contemporary exploitation of poor and underdeveloped countries" (15) wanted a different kind of development. The crisis of 1929 shattered the basis of the global economy and poor countries ought to exploit circumstances and start gradually putting national development on their agenda. If this new national policy "leaves certain delicate needs of our aristocracy unsatisfied, or makes traders unhappy, or liberal economic circles sorry because their principles are being overlooked" (21), the better for society, he concluded. Trade should mediate between production and consumption, and not aim at importing foreign goods, because no additional wealth is thus created. Any claim to the contrary is "an error, a grave error" (25), he stressed.

In 1937 Stefanidis published *The Position of Industry in our Social Economy*. In line with German national socialist authors such as Walther Darré, he admitted that agriculture provided society with "elements of higher moral and conservative standards" (5). However, industry was essential for any economy and should be a part of serious government planning. The production of services should be brought down, and secondary production should be assisted. For Greece, this meant that emigration should stop, and industrialists should be reminded that any profits they made should be reinvested to provide more and cheaper goods to citizens (39). Liberal views associated with specialization and freedom of choice should not be supported for the sake of the national economy (42).

In the same year, 1937, Stefanidis published his lectures on *Applied Social Economics*. Economics had no relation with physics, he stressed, but had ties with law (13). In theoretical economics, different schools and approaches existed, but, despite this reality, in applied economics, the consensus was to blend political and cultural principles in policy decisions (34). Applied economics was the ultimate judge of economic developments and supplied policymakers with the right choices for the future. Stefanidis repeated arguments from his book on *Imperialism* to argue that some countries could be governed democratically and provide for all citizens, but others were governed badly, awarding privileges to certain wealthy social strata (57). This had led to the appearance of governments led by a "higher ideology, and a real wish to raise all classes in society" (59). These regimes were very close to the psyche of popular strata, transforming class competition to cooperation, thus synthesizing the individual with the social. Examples of the "higher level of this category are today fascist Italy and national socialist Germany" (60), he concluded. These two countries were setting the best example for others to follow (86–99). Turning to Greece, he concluded that the Metaxas dictatorship had a similar goal (139–41). The lectures ended with an assurance to students that parliamentarism was losing ground and a New Order was being imposed, leading the economy to higher income levels (141). These passages were deleted from postwar reprints of the lectures. In 1939, he repeated these arguments in his article "The Social Question Under the Light of National Socialism."

5.3.4 Tournakis

Ioannis Tournakis got his Law degree in 1914 and continued his studies in France at the Universities of Montpellier and Paris. From there, he moved to Switzerland for another four years, hearing lectures in Zurich, Geneva, and Bern, and writing short essays and papers. Upon his return to Greece, he submitted a thesis on "The Concentration of Wealth and its Economic and Social Outcomes" (1924). He was elected professor in ASOEE in 1925 and continued serving in various civil service positions during the 1920s, setting the foundations of the Greek Tourist Organization. With time, he started hailing fascist Italy and the guild economy, and was disappointed to see that the Metaxas dictatorship didn't take this economic model seriously into consideration. He passed away in 1941.

His thesis was quite original. Tournakis did not approach the issue from the point of view of economic theory, but rather synthesized the existing literature and events surrounding market conditions and the emergence of trusts and cartels as capitalism evolved. Legislation enacted in the USA and in Europe to restrain the influence of monopolies in the economy was also detailed. In his view, the results of these developments were a natural outcome of the workings of the global economy and had positive effects even for the working class (99). There were, however, dangers involved, the most important being the corruption of duties and of political consciousness, as well as the degradation of morals due to big business aspiring for extra power and profits (120). Tournakis closed his investigation with an exhaustive presentation of anti-trust and pro-competition policies in various countries.

The same thoroughness is to be found in his lectures on applied economics, on external commercial policy, on currency and currency policy, and on emigration and immigration policy in Greece. These lectures were based on exhaustive literature surveys and led to his *International Emigration Movements and Emigration Policy* (1930).

Having been a member of the Greek delegation in post-war monetary conferences, Tournakis didn't espouse the neoclassical belief that markets, and the value of money, could rebound, if the economic system would return to its pre-World War I work mode (1923, 104). The economy was, for him, "not an individual business anymore, but a case for the community" (105). Therefore, state intervention and the concentration of business were new phenomena destined to change the economic landscape and lead societies to a new civilization.

Tournakis also wrote sociological essays for the periodical *New Policy* (Nea Politiki), edited by his brother. Titles included "Nationalism and Racialism," "The Biological Differences of Sexes," "The Spirit of the Greek Race," and others and define him as a social scientist seeking sociological interpretations of human development, as these were discussed in the interwar period by nationalist and racist authors. The periodical was discontinued and was republished by Tournakis personally in 1937, with the aim of pushing the Metaxas dictatorship to the adoption of the Italian fascist model. Italian economic management was hailed in many articles written by students of Tournakis. He personally wrote *Study on the Greek Problem* (1937–9), a series of essays on the topic. There he vehemently attacked liberal principles and democratic solutions to economic problems. The formation of an elite was needed, according to him, to enable the transformation of Greece into "a Prussia of the East" (928). Based on Nazi ideas, he wanted the capital city of Greece to be transferred to a "Hinterland" and the introduction of a "dynamically regulated economy" (906). This economy should be mostly based on agriculture, a traditional sector that stuck to traditions and morals of the Greeks and was not "a victim of machines" (160). Industry was welcome but had to be controlled and mostly focus on exporting its products to countries to the east of Greece, for the benefit of the balance of payments. It would also prepare the country for the "technical total war of the future" (132).

The views expressed in the articles in *New Policy* were slightly modified after 1940. The journal marginally influenced the economic policy of the Greek dictatorship, and Tournakis claimed in his last editorials in 1941 that he was equally distanced to all existing approaches in economic policy. Shortly thereafter, he passed away.

5.3.5 Koronis

Spiros Koronis graduated with a Doctorate from the Law School of the University of Athens in 1904 and studied economics in Berlin, where he completed his studies in 1910. His return to Greece coincided with the first premiership of Eleftherios Venizelos. He served at the Ministry of National Economy and became a member of the circle of intellectuals around Alexandros Papanastasiou. He also belonged to the group of intellectuals that prepared and enacted the labor legislation during that decade. In 1917, he was elected professor of political economy at the National Technical University of Athens.

He wrote *Greek Railways and Railway Policy* in 1914, where he pointed out the importance of Greek rail connections to neighboring countries and the rest of Europe. The railway route to Europe would expand the market and benefit the economy of Northern Greece in particular. He discussed the pricing of commodity transport by rail and concluded that only a public/nationalized enterprise would introduce a price policy favorable to the economy (13). Price policy for rail transport ought to have, for Koronis, a similar target to tariffs: to expand national production and encourage exports. Private interests would hardly invest in railways, and if they did, their interest in profits would run contrary to the interest of the economy.

Koronis was appointed as head of the railways authority in 1926. In 1932, he became a Minister of Transport and then a Minister of National Economy in two short-lived governments. In 1936, he was called by dictator Ioannis Metaxas to head the Social Security Agency, which Papanastasiou and himself had worked so hard in the past to see materialize. Despite his declared social democratic beliefs, he accepted and remained in office until 1941, thus drawing the ire of the communist resistance movement during the occupation. When armed clashes took place after the liberation in December 1944, he was arrested by a communist militia together with other public servants. His body was never recovered.

Koronis' inaugural lecture *Technique and Economy* (1920) dealt with the importance of engineers in economic life. There was a reference to Taylorism and its implications for production, and in general the belief was expressed that technocracy would benefit society. His lectures circulated from 1920 and were published as a book in 1934. There was little economic theory included; instead, there was much information about the location of enterprises, their legal form, and the role of engineers in private business and public works.

His political views and his motivations are clearly depicted in his translations and introductions of two books by Edward Bernstein and Werner Sombart. These books dealt with the phenomena of strikes and the living standards of the proletariat, respectively. He also translated the well-read book by French solidarist Charles Gide, *Principles of Political Economy* (1921).

In the introduction of Sombart's book, *The Proletariat*, Koronis underlined that "the economy, also in the case of Greece, is directed by the needs of capital" (1921, 17–18), and the economic system needed reforms to balance these needs and bring them in tune with the rest of society. Social policy was a reform that ensured consensus and a rebalancing of interests in the economy. According to

Koronis, Sombart provided a rounded understanding of society that included the study of the psychology and the living standards of the proletarians. Sombart gave "a warning and at the same time a wise advice" (18). The main aim of this book was to demonstrate the gradual change and development of the working class from the 18th to the 20th century. There was an obvious need for the government to include the workers in society in order not to make them its enemies, he stressed.

In the introduction of Bernstein's *The Strike* (1921), Koronis noted that the "Greek economy would benefit greatly, if the two sides, employees and employers, would manage to enter into each other's soul" (35). Bernstein attempted to analyze workers' strikes from their primary causes to strategies and tactics, including political strikes. Trying to fulfill this aim, he used primary sources based upon the experiences of the labor movement in Great Britain and Germany. Koronis did not provide similar material for Greece but was keen to alert readers to the possibility of revolutionary uprisings in the country, in the absence of care for workers' needs and standards of living.

In an article written after the Wall Street Crash, entitled "International Commercial Policy Can't Save Europe" (1931), he argued that liberal theory could not come to grips with developments after 1918. Protectionism and nationalist policies prevailed. The democratic state was the vehicle that could provide unity and good prospects for all. The destruction of supply chains around the world to avert the falling prices of goods amid global poverty was, for Koronis, unbelievable and a sign that changes needed to be introduced.

Shortly before his death in 1944, he published *The Labor Policy of 1909–1918*, a full history of the conception and enactment of the measures passed by the Venizelos governments. He stressed that this policy was not the result of pressure from labor organizations but an outcome of forward-looking politicians and civil servants. Despite implementation delays, it materialized and brought Greece in line with more developed countries.

The teaching of Koronis was oriented toward making clear to his students that engineers needed to accept their role in society as guarantors of economic efficiency and social cohesion. His assassination in 1944 was a totally unjustified, brutal result of political polarization.

5.3.6 Zolotas

Xenophon Zolotas' work encompassed the whole 20th century. He started his academic career at an extremely young age, survived all his contemporaries, and can be regarded as one of the most important Greek economists (Psalidopoulos 2008).

He started his law studies in 1920 in Greece, but before completion he moved to the Commercial School in Leipzig, where he graduated in May 1924. He moved to the University of Leipzig, where he received his PhD in 1926. His dissertation was on "Greece in the Stage of Industrialization" and was supervised by Ludwig Pohle, an economist known for his distance from the GHS and state socialism. Pohle was closely collaborating and wrote textbooks together with

Swedish monetary expert Gustav Cassel. In 1927 Zolotas was named ifigitis and a year later, in 1928, aged only 24, he was appointed as full professor of economics at the University of Thessaloniki. In 1930 he was elected associate and, in 1933, full professor at the University of Athens. He devoted himself to teaching and publishing throughout the next 15 years and was heavily involved in the reproduction of economics in Greece through dissertations he supervised and ifigitis titles he endorsed.

In 1944, he served briefly as Vice Governor of the Bank of Greece. Later, in 1953, he became a member of the Academy of Athens, and from 1955 to 1967 and from 1974 to 1981, he was Governor of the Bank of Greece. He continued commenting on the international and the Greek economy and became Prime Minister in a National Unity government in 1989. As an editor of *Social and Public Economics Review* (EKDO) from 1932 to 1944 and of *Review of Political and Economic Sciences* (EPOE) from 1944 to 1967, he hosted publications of subsequent generations of young economists. He also served on committees of the Organization for European Economic Co-operation (OEEC) and the EU which aimed at contributing to global economic understanding and governance.

In his 1926 dissertation, Zolotas argued that Greece met the criteria for industrialization set by Bruno Hildebrandt and Karl Buecher in their studies about the stages of capitalist development. He identified a certain scarcity and a small size of Greek capital due to them having been accumulated through trade, but numbers showed that as of the early 1920s industry was gaining ground. Raw materials were not abundant, but were enough for that moment the transport conditions were improving, shipping was gaining access to foreign markets, and the institutional setting was changing for the better (98). Zolotas proceeded to analyze data and developments in different industrial branches, from food to chemical products and from clothing to metals. He stressed that the encouragement of industry through tariffs would not contribute to long-term industrial growth (136).

In his *Quantity Theory of Money and the Fluctuation in Prices* (1927), he demonstrated the validity of the quantity theory of money under Greek circumstances and included in his considerations empirical and psychological elements, which he derived from discussions with Greek merchants. In *Currency Theories* (1927), he supported the view that the Purchasing Power Parity Theory was the main determinant of the exchange rate of a national currency, but he underlined that, at times of speculation or global disturbance, psychological factors entered the stage and the fluctuations of the external value of money were not easily explained by any theory.

These two articles formed the basis of his book on *Monetary and Currency Phaenomena in Greece, 1910–27* (1928). Zolotas applied the Fisher equation of the quantity theory in Greek data and claimed that it explained the observed fluctuations of the value of money. At the same time, he criticized government intervention in the 1920s, which was for him responsible for the gradual devaluation of the currency. Credit expansion, speculation, and government borrowing needs led the drachma to lower exchange parities. Only the return to sound finance would help the country to overcome the impasse it found itself in.

In *Monetary Stabilization* (1930), he undertook the task of comparing monetary developments since 1918 in twelve European countries. He concluded that, because of gold shortages, and, despite theoretical objections, the view expressed by John Maynard Keynes for Britain in 1923, to stabilize the pound at the current rate of the market, and then respect this new reality with market-friendly policies, was correct. Despite creating a central bank and introducing convertibility, Greece was in a vulnerable position because of expanded state activities since the 1910s. Their continuation would not be a good omen for Zolotas. The NBG was until 1928 a subsidiary of the Ministry of Finance, and the Bank of Greece ought to avoid being tied to government priorities in its actions (199). Emphasis should be given to "the scarcity of capital" (235) in Greece and how to overcome it, instead of expanding state activities in the hope that they would benefit industry.

In his early academic lectures and speeches, Zolotas defined economics as both an abstract and an empirical science assisted by mathematics and statistics. Following Gustav Cassel, whom he explicitly praised throughout his inaugural lecture (1929, 18, 35, 38, 40, 43), he declared the theory of value as of little importance in economics. Prices were determined by supply and demand. He also hinted at Alfred Marshall's view that prices included both subjective and objective factors (1929, 9), therefore debates about the origin of value were not fruitful in his view. He praised American institutionalists such as Wesley Mitchell but blamed them at the same time for exhausting their efforts in mathematical/statistical works and avoiding dealing with theory (19). Zolotas concluded that after a time of historical studies and another one devoted to psychological explanations of human behavior, economics was currently turning to causal theoretical explanations of economic events (54).

With other books, he turned his attention to fiscal issues, Greek foreign borrowing, and agrarian policy. His conclusions were always critical of government intervention. Using statistics, he demonstrated that in the past 20 years, the fiscal burden had increased in Greece by almost 80%, and that 34% of total revenue went to the repayment of foreign loans (1930, 37–9). Transfer payments were financed through higher taxes for business, which meant that the optimal distribution of resources was violated, and economic growth delayed (41). A distinction should be made in his view between quantitative and qualitative economic growth, the latter being based on innovation and technological improvements. Authorities should aim to assist these processes instead of focusing on current consumption, he opined (14). The right distinction of foreign borrowing was not between productive and consumptive uses, he proposed, but between yielding and non-yielding, meaning the service of the loan should be paid out of revenue created by the use of the loan (21). Using this criterion, Zolotas went on to argue that only the 1914 loan to modernize railways was yielding, and none of the others had added any value to total national income (72).

In 1934 he addressed the question "Is theoretical economics in a crisis?" and he answered the question with a clear "No." The wider public should be aware, he underlined, that economists were value-laden individuals with very subjective opinions and unable to experiment with their theoretical views. The use of the mathematical method and the reliance on facts was a promising way forward. Therefore, no crisis in theory existed. The existing plurality of views alienated citizens from the study of economics. The crisis of 1929 contributed additionally to the loss of respect for economists. This was unfortunately a fact; however, economics, remaining oriented in the study of free markets and their outcomes, was steadily being enriched, and even economic history could contribute to innovations in theory. Therefore, economic theory was alive and well.

As all economies were, however, implementing interventionist policies after the collapse of the World Economic Conference in London in 1933, Zolotas accepted, despite his declared liberal views, this new reality. In his *The Orientations of our Economic Policy* (1936) he admitted that regulatory interventions of successive governments since 1932 had allowed the global economy to modestly rebound. He indirectly noticed that even Walter Eucken with his writings was suggesting a strong state in the economy as a prerequisite of a competitive market (113). However, Zolotas questioned whether this return to economic normalcy would be permanent, and he proceeded to analyze the proper way for economic policy. A prime target ought to be, in his opinion, the preservation of the current value of fixed investment. He noted that capital was scarce in Greece and therefore any loss of its value would hurt entrepreneurs and the economy severely (22). Authorities needed to prevent "false" investment decisions and even restrict market entrance to newcomers if existing investments needed to mature (74). The Supreme Economic Council (set in place since 1930 in Greece) could function as a mediator and assist businesses and government to make the right decisions about the economic future. parliament unfortunately didn't include economically literate deputies, and leaving economic decisions to parliament (which was suspended at that time due to Metaxas dictatorship) was not an ideal solution. This idealization of technocracy by Zolotas didn't lead to an endorsement of Keynes' proposals.

During the occupation, Zolotas finished his magnum opus of 719 pages, *Theoretical Economics* (1942). This was followed by another book on *Economic Fluctuations* (1944) and, shortly before liberation, by *Creative Socialism* (1944).

His 1942 teaching manual started with the definition of economics by Lionel Robbins. Scarcity and restrictions in the satisfaction of human wants led to the division of labor and to production processes, productivity gains, and exchange in markets that solved distribution issues. The theory of value was not discussed, with demand and supply simply setting prices that reflected, through scarcity, a certain value/price. Zolotas presented in much detail and by extended references to foreign bibliography basic concepts, the factors of production, market equilibrium, and money. General economic equilibrium was defined following Gustav Cassel's paradigm (423–7), and indifference curve analysis as pioneered by John Hicks was also extensively referred to. Finally, money and equilibrium in non-competitive markets were also analyzed, even if not diagrammatically. The determination of the interest rate according to Keynes was refuted (538), and in general Keynes was credited for offering a theory valid only during an economic downturn and not for normal times (317–19).

In his *Economic Fluctuations* he surveyed existing empirical works and proceeded to analyze the explanations put forward by Nikolay Kondratieff, Friedrich von Hayek, and John Maynard Keynes. Gottfried Haberler's *Prosperity and Depression* was also used as a primary source (28–9). Two factors were closely intertwined in the business cycle, he stressed: profits and wages. During the upswing, both were rising, but wages only at a reduced tempo. At some point, profits stagnated, but wages kept rising, and then profits declined, and so did wages. Thus, workers were laid off, and the economy was in depression. The best policy under these circumstances was for an authority to better coordinate the whole production process and avoid the worst. Special attention should be given to the accelerator, as suggested by Haberler. Any quick upswing with lots of investment in a short period of time could become fatal at a later stage, he noted. Underconsumption was not a reason for an economic downturn, he opined (32). Zolotas provided long descriptions of all phases of the production process, distinguishing between smooth and sudden upswings and downturns. He concluded that statistics of the International Labour Office and material provided by Gustav Cassel confirmed his analysis, and the policy recommendation he offered was an eclectic mix of oversight and government corrections of "excess" activity.

In his book on *Creative Socialism*, Zolotas acknowledged that the introduction of a new economic system not resembling the pre-war one "was a moral demand of absolute value" (ε). Nineteenth-century capitalism was extremely old and "had lost its hair and teeth" (73), he eloquently declared. After the end of the war, it would be replaced by a new system based on economic freedom, maximum production, economic growth, and a just income distribution. He proceeded to analyze communism, the regulated economy, and neoliberalism as ideal types in Max Weber's sense to extract their advantages and incorporate these in the envisaged new system. He repeated that both moral and economic reasons were leading to creative socialism, a system that would make all citizens satisfied and happy. Happiness would be secured through the working of the market system in tandem with the existence of large nationalized public enterprises that would provide their services at an affordable price to the community. Pricing their services was not an easy task, but it was possible through trial and error, and at this point, Zolotas declared that in the socialist calculation debate, Oskar Lange had better arguments than Ludwig von Mises and Friedrich von Hayek. Computed prices for these products would be corrected based on analysis undertaken by an independent economic supervision board. This board would draft a plan according to democratic procedures and see that the average cost of the products produced under socialized conditions would approach the required minimum, and marginal cost would be close if not identical to the market price. If there were discrepancies, then the board would aim through a tâtonnement process to reach full economic efficiency.

Zolotas believed that the post-war economic policy ought to combine market and planning in this optimal way. He accepted and used socialism as a concept but insisted on market-friendly basics. His endnotes confirm that he was aware of the socialist calculation debate; however, there is no reference to the 1942 first report by Lord Beveridge. During times when democratic and egalitarian ideas combined to defeat Nazism, he commented that private property and the price mechanism were indispensable for the creation of a just society in the future.

Some months later, Greece was liberated, hyperinflation ran high, and Zolotas was named Deputy Governor of the Bank of Greece for three months. During this time, he opined that the ideal value of the currency should be set by the free market and not by a government decision due to the drachma having lost all its value. Political developments left the stabilization effort in limbo.

Summarizing his pre-World War II contributions, we can say that Zolotas, even if he wove historical insights into his works, was highly critical of the GHS approach. Using neoclassical theory, he defended the soundness of theoretical assumptions. His discourse, despite its lack of clear demarcation lines, gradually gained authority among the young generation of economists and policymakers. After World War II, he would adopt the Anglo-Saxon paradigm, enrich his work, and continue influencing economics in Greece.

5.4 Academics of the 1930s: A Second Generation

Since economics had been institutionalized, new appointments were needed, and a second generation of academics entered the teaching and scientific scene in the 1930s. With different fields of expertise and research interests, they added to the bibliography and introduced new insights with their publications. They also had different political views and could thus contribute to a pluralism of approaches and opinions in economic matters. Due to their age, they remained active until the late 1960s/early 1970s and were involved in the reproduction of academic economics in the country in a variety of ways.

5.4.1 Charitakis

Georgios Charitakis was the editor of the *Economic Yearbook of Greece* (1929–38) and a professor of political economy at ASOEE from 1933. He had a doctoral degree in law from Hamburg in 1918 and rose to prominence through his book in German on *Contemporary Greek Industry* (1927). Before joining academia, he served as a Minister in the short-lived dictatorship of General Pangalos in 1926. His studies and his voluminous university lectures were of historical orientation and focused on aspects of Greek political and economic organization. In his *State and Economy* (1928) he claimed that until the interwar period a consistent government policy in Greece had been either weak or imperfect (25). He emphatically raised the issue of an enlarged activity of government in the economic process. The State was not standing above society, but was "part of society, an advanced and sophisticated form of society governed by certain rules […] regulating the relations of individuals that constitute a state" (21). The state as an economic actor was for him necessary, and the scope of its intervention could not be determined in advance. It should be defined according to historical studies that would shed light on the way modern national states were formed. Following Adolf Wagner, he justified the increasing role of the state on economic and moral grounds. State action would balance individual and collective interests. The principles of collectiveness and inclusiveness had, for him, paramount importance for the organization and regulation of the economy, as they incorporated "the principle of symbiosis and of natural order" (18). Charitakis believed that the economic system should be based on cooperation and solidarity, and not on competition only. On the other hand, he stressed the importance of the neoclassical theory of price determination and the Austrian approach to economic methodology. He provided to his students a very eclectic menu on economic crises by seeing all theoretical explanations as compatible. In his own words he was following authors such as Eugen von Philippovich, Friedrich von Wieser, Adolph Wagner, Alfred Marshall and Othmar Spann, a quite contradictory mix of economists (1930, 8). He also wrote extensively on banking and addressed issues of interest to the Association of Greek Banks that he served.

5.4.2 Santis

Dimitrios Santis completed his thesis on "The State Budget and the Fiscal System of Greece" in Berlin in 1924 and, having returned to Greece, he wrote *The Concept of Taxable Income: A Theoretical and Comparative Study* (1928). He then proceeded to do an ifigessia at the University of Thessaloniki about *Tax Exemptions: A Contribution to Greek Tax Policy* (1932). He was elected as a full professor in Thessaloniki in 1933 and became a specialist in tax law. He wrote a manual on tax policy (1936) and investigated tariff law and the implementation of tax legislation by the Greek administration and the decisions of courts that dealt with tax disputes. His complete teaching manual entitled *General Principles of Fiscal Law* was published in 1959.

During Nazi occupation, he was appointed a member of the board of the Bank of Greece by the Quisling government, and his professorial position was moved to Athens. After liberation, these acts were voided, and Santis returned to Thessaloniki. He represented a law-oriented version of tax policy with scant references to the theory of taxation. He also lectured on the History of Economic Thought.

5.4.3 Christodoulopoulos

Pindaros Christodoulopoulos got a first degree in law in 1919 and, after having worked as a lawyer, he moved to Munich and Berlin from 1927 to 1930 to study economics. There he published two articles in *Jahrbuecher fuer Nationaloekonomie und Statistik* (1930a) and in *Allgemeines Statistisches Archiv* (1930b). Back in Greece, he was named ifigitis at the University of Thessaloniki in 1932 and, in 1936, he was elected a full professor there. In 1940, he was elected in ASOEE, from where he retired in 1967. With full knowledge of both German and English bibliography, he distinguished himself as a consequent neoclassical economist and it was unfortunate that he wrote very little after World War II.

His initial interests lay in business cycle theory and monetary policy, and this led him to intervene in an exchange between Arthur Spiethoff and Walter Eucken about the origin of capitals that accompanied the passing of the cycle from recession to upswing. Christodoulopoulos argued that the answer depended on where the theoretical search would start from. If one was looking at the business cycle in its entirety, as Spiethoff was doing, it was clear that money not spent during depression would find its way to the banking system and be transformed to investment when the downturn ended. If one would look only at the time slot between depression and the start of an upswing, as Eucken did, then the question was to what extent the interest rate influenced new investment and what policy central banks should pursue (1930a, 221). Christodoulopoulos insisted that two factors were at play: first, individuals who saved and took existing interest rates into consideration; and second, central bank authorities who set interest rates while considering multiple economic factors, above all the level of supply and demand of capitals. A private issue, saving, became a socioeconomic one, when investment materialized after a downturn. There was no need for an investment push by banks supported by low interest rates. Offering credit practically for free for the economy to enter an upward phase was useless. Agents knew better than government authorities (223–4).

The second article dealt with the pricing of shares in the stock exchange and was incorporated in his book *Credit Policy and Reoccurring Crises* (1930c). Christodoulopoulos presented all statistical investigations about the fluctuations of the value of shares and proceeded to investigate the policy of the Bank of Greece that controlled money supply in the country after 1928. He declared from the start that economics should concentrate in "the quantitative-statistical analysis of the causal relations of economic life without losing touch with theory" (ι). Statics were dominant, he argued, until the interwar period, then dynamics were taking over. Economic fluctuations were a dynamic expression of the evolution of the economy. The commodity market and the value of stocks both influenced individual behavior. It was true that during depression stocks were sold and during the upswing they were in demand, but new issuance of capital shares also played a role in the whole process. Christodoulopoulos agreed with Ludwig von Mises that the overexpansion of credit during crises would be a wrong policy, as it would intrude into agents' decisions, distracting them from proper behavior. The only thing central banks should care about was the respect of the currency principle and the sound backing of monetary circulation with reserves. In this connection, Christodoulopoulos introduced Knut Wicksell's distinction between the natural and the nominal interest rate and assigned to any central bank the task to watch for their coincidence.

Business cycles were, for him, the result of "false" central bank policy and this critique applied to the Bank of Greece too. The drop in the interest rate from 10% to 9% in November 1928 was seen by Christodoulopoulos as a bad sign, as an effort to insert Silvio Gesell's naïve ideas into the economy. The Greek economy was faring well at that time, and the overexpansion of credit became in the course of time a nightmare when the Wall Street Crash erupted. He provided his own statistical and diagrammatic explanations and concluded that the Bank of Greece ought to better monitor economic indicators and act according to numbers and not instructions from the government. He accepted that the Greek economy was still struggling to absorb the population influx after 1922 and that incomes were very low, but rejected the opinion that prosperity could be enforced through cheap credit.

In his article "Savings at the Bank of Issue" (1930d) Christodoulopoulos expressed, like Charitakis, reservations about the introduction of minimum reserve deposits by the commercial banks to secure the stability of the banking system. Greece lacked payments by cheque, and the working of its banking system, he argued, guaranteed in his view a certain stability. Government intervention ought to exist on a case-by-case basis and not introduce permanent restrictions on banking activity.

In his "Elasticity of Demand for Greek Tobacco" (1931), Christodoulopoulos introduced for the first time in Greek literature Alfred Marshall's demand and supply diagram, as well as the concept of elasticity of demand. He spoke about the "mathematical school of economics" (466). By gathering lots of statistical information, he focused on parameters that affected demand for Greek tobacco and concluded that its quality was the most important factor explaining demand fluctuations when prices changed.

Christodoulopoulos cemented his status as the most consequential neoclassical economist with his *The Rebalancing of International Payments* (1935). The economic crash of 1929 affected the balance of payments of all countries and the existing disequilibrium in these accounts led international trade to shrink. Christodoulopoulos insisted that one had to start from theory to be able to contribute to policy solutions. "Any economy based on free exchange possesses automatic mechanisms that are independent of regulatory interventions, and they bring the economy back to equilibrium" (309), he stressed.

The balance of payments might lose equilibrium due to shocks like a sudden withdrawal of foreign capitals, a false internal monetary and credit policy, if the interest rate didn't adjust to the natural one, and for other reasons. The consequences differed according to whether a country had a positive or a negative position before any imbalance, and if it found itself in a state of expanding its productive sector or not. The economic condition in countries with which an economy mostly dealt in trade was also an important factor in the re-equilibrizing process. An international initiative to bring cooperating economies back to normal was welcome, but any government decisions should respect results that the working of the free-market mechanism would offer. The central idea therefore that Christodoulopoulos suggested was in line with the free market and not based on regulation. Christodoulopoulos was not shy of controversy. He criticized the work of other colleagues, defending his positions and thus encouraging debate among economists. He was also critical of Keynes' *General Theory*.

As already stated, he didn't publish much after World War II and neither did he serve in a public position. His *Theoretical Political Economy: Introductory Lessons* from 1945 was reprinted until his retirement with marginal changes. His lessons started with human needs and a discussion of the factors of production. Then, a general economic axiom was introduced, a synthesis of utilitarianism with Lionel Robbins' definition of economics (1945, 41–4). The next chapter dealt with the price mechanism under perfect competition without mentioning other market forms, followed by a discussion of the business unit and its technical and practical problems. Another, longer part of the lectures was devoted to the pricing of factors of production, and the lectures concluded with two chapters on money and its functions.

Christodoulopoulos was a consequent neoclassical economist who remained faithful to his view that economics needed to be grounded on theory and tested by statistics and empirical evidence. It was a great pity that he didn't publish any works after 1948, and his academic silence is indeed hard to interpret.

5.4.4 Angelopoulos

Angelos Angelopoulos started his distinguished career as a Public Finance expert with two doctorates, one from his alma mater, ASOEE in 1928, and a second one from the University of Leipzig in 1931. The topics were "Societes Anonymes in Greece from an Economic and a Fiscal Point of View" and "The Taxation of Personal Income in the Light of Statistics on Taxation," respectively. He wrote papers on fiscal issues and in 1932 published "*Charges Fiscales and Depenses Publiques*" in French. In the same year he was elected as ifigitis at the University of Athens, an associate in 1937, and a full professor of public finance in 1939. He co-edited with Zolotas EKDO and was a member of the AOS. Having been a member of the left-leaning "government of the mountains" during Nazi occupation, he was dismissed from the university in 1946 and went on to live in Switzerland for the next 10 years. He edited the journal *New Economy* (Nea Oikonomia) from 1946 to 1967, a forum that became a platform for critical contributions relating to Greek economic performance and policy. In 1959 he returned to Greece, and in 1961 was elected professor of public finance at Panteios Highest School for Political Sciences. He resigned in 1967 because of the dictatorship and left the country for a second time. After 1974 he returned to become governor of the NBG, and in 1976 he joined the Academy of Athens. He remained active in writing and commenting on the Greek economy, especially in the 1980s. During the National Unity government in 1989, he presided over the Committee for the Stabilization and Development of the Greek Economy, whose aim was to offer suggestions toward the desired path of economic integration with the EU. He passed away in 1995.

Angelopoulos started as a believer in government intervention, aiming cautiously at sociopolitical objectives. He moved during the occupation period to socialism and planning, thus keeping a distance from Keynesian analysis. In the 1950s, he pleaded for indicative planning in Greece and for an active role of the public sector in economic development. After 1974, he demanded the application of a Keynesian economic plan for the development of all Third World countries and supported government action to alleviate poverty.

From his early academic works, Angelopoulos supported an active government role in the economy not because of any dogma, but because of statistical data about tax revenues and the tax burden he investigated. He supported Adolph Wagner's social-political agenda and saw government action as the necessary outcome of existing realities in society that made a holistic interventionist agenda necessary (Giouras 2000, 99).

His *The Public Debt of Greece* (1937) was the first effort to analyze the evolution of public debt in relation to the economic development of Greece. For Angelopoulos, the state "is not the addition of individuals. It is a long-term sum of subsequent generations" (9). Government borrowing was a necessary step if needed, but of course terms of borrowing and use of funds were very important issues. Economic effectiveness was, for Angelopoulos, a key to assessing the results of government spending in the economy and these results could not be measured only quantitatively. The productive works of Venizelos would have positive long-term consequences for the Greek economy. Trying to estimate their impact by comparing returns with sacrifices only was not the best method (128). In this relation, he referred to Keynes and the latter's positive views on public works aiming at reducing unemployment and smoothing the business cycle (129). He didn't elaborate further but proceeded to express reservations about the extent and time frame of the speed to pursue so many different projects simultaneously. The productive works ought to be embedded in a thorough plan and not be done without considering short-term consequences for the taxpayer, as was happening. Therefore, one can conclude that although positive, Angelopoulos was at the same time skeptical about the volume and timing of state activity in the Greek economy and would opt for checks and balances in government activity. If the tax burden would be high and the results of public works very long-term ones, then the economy might enter a dangerous zone (132), he repeated.

In his *Fiscal Policy and Economic Fluctuations* (1939 in French and 1940 in Greek) he used the same line of arguments. Keynes' General Theory was not included in his extensive bibliography. The government "could and should" (1940, 292) intervene and this reality "was now generally accepted" (292), he stressed. But again, limits were set by falling tax revenue in the downturn and by long-term consequences of interventions. Government activity should not aim to abolish business cycles but just to soften the downturn. Fiscal measures in the downturn should aim at improving productivity, he stressed (298). During the upswing, taxes should be lowered and households allowed to create "tax reserves" (302). In general, public works ought to be independent of the business cycle and serve a higher purpose than just the amelioration of the ups and downs of economic activity (310). They should rather be financed by the central bank, if possible, and if not, with loans, and attention should be paid to factors such as future export revenue and the rate of inflation in the country.

Special reference was made to the Swedish experiment with a four-year budget and reservations were articulated in relation to this innovative state planning. Angelopoulos agreed with Gustav Cassel that the increase of savings ought to be the goal of all actions in the economy. He didn't object to government intervention but found state activity to be sometimes hasty and short-term oriented (318).

In his lectures "Public Finance" (1942), he repeated that the government sector in the economy was not an independent actor in society. It should be rather an instrument. The arguments of all schools of thought about state intervention were clearly defined and discussed, but Angelopoulos avoided taking sides and left the question open for his students to adopt any side they thought best. We will refer to his post-World War II ideas in the following chapter.

5.4.5 Paraskevopoulos

Ioannis Paraskevopoulos earned his PhD in Jena in 1929, with a thesis on the Greek monetary system. He submitted an ifigessia in 1936 entitled *Economic Credit* at the University of Athens. In this work, after having dealt with definitions and concepts, he proceeded to analyze whether banks expanded the volume of monetary circulation through credit creation. His answer was positive. Banks financed business investment through cheques or transfer orders, and the means of payment in the economy depended on whether these means would become liquid or not. Central banks could use the discount rate or investment quotas forcing commercial banks to a particular credit path. Paraskevopoulos addressed the question of whether credit expansion led to productivity growth or to inflationary pressures, and his opinion on the matter was eclectic (82–93). Wicksell's natural rate of interest was "a phantasy concept" (94), he opined, and Hayek's neutral money could be disastrous if applied. He was in favor of discretionary policy that would approach economic problems with a trial-and-error attitude (92). Experience had shown that at any time there were unused resources in the economy, and investment opportunities needed to be offered through credit to businessmen (102). However, certain barriers to the unlimited extension of credit existed, and these were determined by actual circumstances and not through theory. The introduction of minimum reserves for commercial banks enacted by the Bank of Greece in 1931 was an act imitating similar measures abroad but was obstructing Greek banks.

When Paraskevopoulos came to discuss theories of credit in relation to fluctuations, he demonstrated a distance to theoretical explanations of the cycle. Overproduction was supported "by those who approach economics from an amateur viewpoint" (179), he claimed. Underconsumption was refuted, in his view, by reality (184), and overcapitalisation seemed "true at first glance, but false in its fundamentals" (195). According to him, all these theories lacked the element of time and were therefore not dynamic and real. In real life, there was a delay between the birth of money and its use, and this had to be incorporated in a future theory of credit.

Paraskevopoulos became a Professor of Political Economy at Panteios in 1942 and served up to 1967. He also served as a governor of the NBG and as a Prime Minister in a caretaker government in 1963. He did not publish anything after his 1936 book except for notes for students.

5.4.6 Delivanis

Dimitrios Delivanis defended his dissertation "On Short Term Credit Policy of German Banks" in 1934 in Paris. He became an ifigitis at the University of Athens in 1938 and held the chair of political economy at the University of Thessaloniki from 1944 to 1974.

He published *The Relationship Between the Internal and the External Value of the Currency* in 1935, trying to identify which theory explained economic reality best. Monetary developments in five countries, including Greece, were analyzed, with the French Franc being the currency of reference, as it entertained a constant parity to gold until 1934. Monetary theories were also presented. Next to the quantity theory, purchasing power parity, and balance of payments explanations, Austrian School explanations and the psychological theory of Albert Aftalion were extensively dealt with. The conclusion of his analysis was that only purchasing power parity theory was able to explain international developments after 1931, when in the wake of the Great Depression many currencies devalued.

His 1938 ifigessia was on "International Economic Relations and the Influence of Direct Government Measures on Them." This study was of a theoretical nature and included three parts. The first was about the classical theory of the gold standard, the second about measures taken by governments after 1929, and the third was devoted to the consequences of these measures for future international economic relations. Delivanis concluded that the great crash had worsened economic cooperation among nations, global income was falling, and the international division of labor was challenged. Despite these negative developments, Delivanis stressed in his final remarks that the regulated economy had become a reality of the 1930s, and it was not expected that a reversal of this new state in global economic affairs would occur anytime soon (193). National economies needed to adjust to this new normal, he argued.

In *The Bank of Issue Under the Regime of Direct Economic Measures* (1940), he defended Greek economic policy and the effective action of the Bank of Greece. The country was not losing reserves as it had before, and the coordinated national effort for a self-sufficient economy promoted full employment and economic welfare.

The mix between conformity with mainstream theory and acceptance of the regulated economy by Delivanis can be interpreted by his political views. He served as Secretary General of the Ministry of Social Welfare in the government of dictator Ioannis Metaxas. In two papers written for non-academic outlets as *Neon Kratos* (New State) entitled "Economic Policy before and after August 4th" (1939) and "The Instruments of Modern Economic Policy" (1940), Delivanis demonstrated a fine tuning with the dictatorship he was serving. He explained that governments didn't wait anymore for market results. These would rather be achieved in a speedier way through government intervention (1940, 299). The hierarchy installed by the dictator and the reliance on expert opinion guaranteed the avoidance of delays and other negative sides of parliamentarism, as the need to legislate for the pleasure of voters (1939, 270).

In a third paper called "The Economic and Fiscal Policy of Ioannis Metaxas" (1941), he eulogized the dictator who had just passed away. He painted a portrait of Metaxas as somebody who was in favor of limited government spending and followed best practices applied abroad. Continuity was said to have been the basic principle in economic policy during the dictatorship, and this had benefited the economy greatly.

His publication record after World War II was impressive, but except for becoming scientific director of KEPE in the late years of the dictatorship of 1967–74, he was not involved in policymaking.

5.4.7 Pintos

Ieronimos Pintos earned his PhD in Munich in 1934, with a dissertation on "Price Determination in Imperfect Monopoly", and two years later he became an ifigitis at the University of Athens with his "The Theoretical Analysis of Price Changes in the Modern Economy." His intention was to contribute to a dynamic analysis of price determination that would include the behavior of cartels and of dominant enterprises in the market. Thus, an abstract approach in the form of general equilibrium analysis was not the appropriate methodology in his view. Alfred Marshall and Wesley Mitchell were quoted by Pintos as economists who didn't lose sight of economic reality and were not totally lost in abstract reasoning. Special mention was made to the Marshallian concept of the elasticity of demand and its importance for explaining price fluctuations of products as results of demand desirability (46). The existence of different elasticities explained the relative stability of demand for certain products despite price increases, the result being that the freedom of the consumer as an axiom was not valid in the modern world (59). Another factor not considered in price theory was, for Pintos, the reality of self-sufficiency in the 1930s, when prices were determined by internal factors and not by international exchanges. This trend in policy was destroying price competition and was creating market forms not discussed in economic theories until then.

The existence of substitutes for a certain good and speculation also played an important role in price fluctuations. They forced consumers to rearrange their expenditure, making price interventions necessary. Next to supply-side supremacy in certain markets, prices behaved differently from what orthodox theory suggested, due to depressions and recessions in the economy. Prices, demand, and production didn't go together during an economic downturn; their oscillations varied, and economic theory needed a temporal approach to explain price behavior. Without a reference to a specific source, Pintos claimed that during an economic boom, production was not led by demand; producers were led by hypothetical prices they considered probable in the future. In a dynamic economy, this reality should be seriously considered. The conclusion of Pintos was that government interference in the market mechanism, the setting of price ceilings, and other ex-post interventions were legitimate.

Pintos served as a professor of public finance at Panteios from 1947 to 1961. He moved to the Chair of Economic Geography from 1961 to his retirement in 1978, and in this capacity, he introduced the study of regional economics in Greek academia. He belonged to the group of academics who didn't publish much after they secured their final appointment.

5.4.8 Katiforis

Spyros Katiforis earned his PhD in Paris in 1933 on "The Crisis of English Money" and proceeded to become an ifigitis in 1938 with a study on "The Theory of Monetary Policy."

He admitted that he followed the Cambridge School in monetary theory (1938, ζ). After a thorough treatment of the workings of the gold and the gold-exchange standard, he focused on the mechanics of the global economic system. Overinvestment and underconsumption theories of the business cycle could not offer adequate explanations of the business cycle without taking money into deeper consideration, he stressed (119). He agreed with Keynes that interest rate policy could not lead to more investment after interest had reached a certain low level. Wicksell's "ideal interest rate" (179) could not serve as a policy tool either. For this reason, Katiforis endorsed fiscal policy as a vehicle to promote investment and growth (178). He also pointed out that fiscal activity needed to stop if prices started rising (188).

Discussing pros and cons of high interest rates, Katiforis distinguished between the interests of productive capital as opposed to those of rentiers. He wanted to see only the interests of the former served. The latter were "parasites that drain society without offering anything" (210). The capital owner had certain social duties to perform, namely, invest and take risks. Idle capitals were not permitted, in Katiforis' view. His conclusion was that credit policy ought to be adjusted to the needs of economic activity and the interest rate should be managed by the government accordingly. A slight rising level of prices was a welcome long-term consequence, and here Katiforis quoted Ramsey McCulloch to support the soundness of this policy. It would combat "the endogenous tendency of a progressing economy to consume a smaller part of an ever-increasing income" (230), he continued. Central banks had to follow a policy based on the "intensity of economic activity" (228) rather than relying on their gold reserves. Between thrift and entrepreneurship, societies and politicians ought to favor the latter, not the former.

In his *Retrospect and Additions to the Theory of Distribution* (1939), Katiforis started with a Ricardian analysis and proceeded to analyze contemporary trends in income distribution. He underlined that classical value theory was no longer followed, with the concept of value having been abandoned. Price was the central concept in current theory and it covered profit, the cost of production, and the marginal utility of demanded goods (11). Price in that sense was not equal to the natural price advocated by Smith (12). If the normal/market price determined the pricing of the factors of production, then classical value theory was obsolete and marginal productivity theory was better at explaining distribution in an economy. Katiforis concluded that economic fluctuations constantly changed the prices of factors of production. Capital needed to be seen as credit capital and as productive capital. To sum up, distribution theory was for Katiforis an expanding field with new insights constantly being included in economic analysis.

In his follow-up *Reward of Capital and the Interest Rate* (1941), he started with Eugen von Böhm-Bawerk's theory of capital and investigated later developments by Alfred Marshall, the Austrian School, and the mathematical school. He tried to synthesize what he believed were the most valuable insights of these theories and arrived at the conclusion that capital needed to be distinguished into money and real capital (49), with saving being directly related to money capital only. Katiforis went on to investigate the reward of capital and stressed that contrary to the demand/

supply scheme, the reward of capital was not the outcome of demand/supply of capitals in the economy. The reward was the consequence of entrepreneurial action, an ex-post determined award. As far as the interest rate in the economy was concerned, Katiforis analyzed exhaustively all known contributions to arrive at Keynes and his liquidity preference theory (107–16). Reward of capital and interest rate would be identical if there wasn't any speculation taking place in the economy. Speculation brought innovation and progress but could also lead the economy to unpleasant circumstances. Close monitoring of economic developments and an active monetary policy were needed to keep the economy on a steady path of progress (129–30).

The above analysis makes clear that Katiforis was very original, well-read, and possessed an erudition not found in other Greek authors. He had a thorough knowledge of English economic literature and was aware and approving of J. M. Keynes' works. Katiforis would have contributed a lot to economic discourse in the country, but, unfortunately, he died at a very young age during the German occupation, leaving a gap not easily to fill in Greek academia.

5.4.9 Dertilis

Panagiotis Dertilis earned his PhD in Paris in 1929 with "*La Reconstruction Financiere de la Grece et la Societe des Nations*" and became an ifigitis at the University of Athens just one year later, in 1930, with "The Economics of Local Administration." He taught as an ifigitis Public Finance and published many books and articles with a historical and fiscal character both in Greek and in foreign languages. His *State Budget* (1936) revisited a topic of great importance in view of a growing literature and the discussions about the scope of government financing in the economy. Having not been elected at the University of Athens, he moved to the University of Thessaloniki where he served from 1944 to 1970. He also taught at the Highest School of Industrial Studies in Thessaloniki from 1957 to 1965. His post-World War II publications shifted to fiscal law, public finance, and to numerous textbooks. He also published *Lessons in Sociology* in 1950 and *History of Economic Life* in 1953, a sign of his broad interests and his readiness to support the needs of curricula of studies.

5.4.10 Saounatsos

Andreas Saounatsos became known with an article on the stabilization of the drachma (1928). There he defended the purchasing parity theory of money against the quantity theory because it included psychological factors and was not mechanistic. He proceeded to earn a PhD from the University of Athens in 1935 with a study on "The Long-Term Economic Fluctuations." He followed Nikolay Kontradieff in his analysis and Gustav Cassel's principle of action and response in the economy. The dissertation had a bibliography, but no quotes in the text.

The first part of the thesis was full of statistical material concerning all aspects of economic life, followed by a second devoted to the reasons behind big waves in economic activity. The most important one was, for Saounatsos, population growth, followed by technical progress and the development of food prices. As a result, industrial production started to decline, leading to a downturn. For Saounatsos, the median/average price level, despite fluctuations, remained stable for 25 years. Gold discoveries might change monetary circulation and the price level; however, a cyclicality of prices in the economy was, according to him, proven by statistical facts.

Saounatsos worked at the Bank of Greece from 1933 to 1959, rising to become director of the Economic Research department. He also worked in other positions in the public sector as an experienced technocrat. From 1959 to 1973, he was professor at the Highest School of Industrial Studies in Pireaus, where he taught Applied Economics.

5.4.11 Kokkalis

Alexandros Kokkalis did a Doctorate in Tuebingen and published two books in German about *The Business Profit* (1930) and *The Problem of Unemployment* (1932). He taught as ifigitis in Thessaloniki until 1940, and after 1945 he moved to ASOEE in Athens.

In Greece he published *The Factors of Production and their Interrelationship* in 1931 and *The Economic Crisis: Reasons and Treatment* in 1934. The aim of this last book was to analytically compare the German and the Greek economies before and after the crisis. Economic science was unique, he opined, and its laws were valid in every country, making comparisons necessary. The belief that theory had no relevance in practice was false, he stressed, but on the other hand he didn't offer any theoretical clues. He didn't espouse overproduction or under-consumption as the most accurate theory. He rather focused on economic policy measures. The crisis of 1929 was, for example, the outcome of an "unfavourable combination of the global production process" (1934, 6). The comparison he attempted was interesting from the point of view of data gathered, but the book lacked theory completely. It discussed policy measures taken, and judgements were passed about their success or failure. Kokkalis expressed a negative view about economic liberalism and its policy proposals to overcome a crisis (102 and 104). Liberalism was dominant "in those developed countries that knew how to exploit it delicately" (106) but was not the major provider of economic recipes for countries like Greece. What was needed for Kokkalis was structural changes through government investment that would raise production and income, so that public debt would be repaid and foreign intervention to secure repayments would diminish.

5.4.12 Agapitidis

Sotirios Agapitidis wrote a thesis in Paris in 1935 about "Corporatism in Italy." He had already published a study about his native island of Symi in 1930. After his PhD, he returned to Greece and continued publishing in EKDO and other periodicals. He was named an ifigitis in 1942, and from 1949 to 1977 he was professor of political economy at the National Technical University of Athens. He also taught at the School for Industrial Studies in Piraeus from 1950 to 1965.

In his *Policy of Economic Autarchy* (1940), he investigated the tendency of governments in the 1930s to pursue policies of self-sufficiency. Autarchy could be distinguished as absolute, relative, and partial, and the historical record confirmed that empires, states, and regions initially strived for self-sufficiency. Mercantilism opened the door to trade and later led to the classical doctrine of free trade and the abandonment of ideas about autarchy. These were attacked at a later stage by protectionists and economic nationalists, he commented. Agapitidis then proceeded to discuss the advantages and disadvantages of economic autarchy from the point of view of economic, political, and war-like situations. An economic policy striving for the autarchy of a country necessarily had to be based on a strong, totalitarian government (39). Private property and individual economic freedom were thus tamed, as was the case for Germany and Italy at that time. Greece had benefited in the 1930s from the plan to reduce its dependence on imports of agricultural products, confirming thus the advantages of a protectionist policy. This policy might show disadvantages in the future, and according to Agapitidis, everything depended on existing alternative policies and evolving circumstances.

After World War II, Agapitidis wrote on monetary developments and turned his interest to the economic development of Greece.

5.5 Translations after 1920

The 1920s saw a new epoch of translations of foreign economic books into Greek. Ideas expressed therein were diverse. In many cases, only a few chapters of the books were translated. Socialist literature was abundant and could be divided into two categories: reformist, inspired by the principles of state-socialism, and "pure" Marxist, involving texts of e Karl Marx himself. Obviously, these texts reflected the gradual rise of a conscious working class and the creation of many socialist parties, including a communist party.

Among the most widely circulated translations were, as already mentioned, the two volumes by Heinrich Herkner on the labor question. The message by Herkner was that social policy could maintain cohesion in society, improving productive efficiency at the same time. State intervention as practiced by Prussia was depicted as the way forward in policymaking.

An abridged version of Marx's *Das Kapital,* edited by Marx's son-in-law Paul Lafargue, appeared in 1921. In this edition, emphasis was given to the distinction between capital and money, that is, in the conversion of money into capital and then the creation of surplus. The book was prefaced by Vilfredo Pareto, who, as expected, rejected the Marxian labor theory of value (71), and even raised strong objections to the historical evidence presented in the book. According to Pareto, workers were poor in all hitherto existing societies. Thus, pauperization was not an essential defining characteristic of capitalism (73).

Books by Karl Radek and Karl Kautsky about Marxian theory were also published in separate booklets in 1927–8 Rudolf Hilferding's *Finance Capital* was translated in 1937. French authors were also translated. Charles Gide's *Principes d'économie politique* was republished in a new translation twice in the interwar years, one in 1923 and a second in 1943. So did his co-authored book with Charles Rist on the *History of Economic Ideas* (1930). Edgard Allix's book on *Public Finance* (1931) was also part of the continued influence of French economic discourse in Greece.

Conrad's and Hesse's *Grundriss zum Studium der politischen Ökonomie* (1924) was one important German textbook of the time that was in favor of the intervention of the state in economic activity. According to the authors, their views derived from the social need to protect "the public interest and those who were in a weak position economically" (17). During the same period, monetary economics in the form of contributions by Gustav Cassel and Irving Fisher were translated, and so was John Maynard Keynes' *Tract on Monetary Reform* in 1937.

Due to the efforts of Dimitrios Kalitsounakis, works by François Quesnay and David Ricardo appeared in Greek, as did the first chapters of Smith's *Wealth of Nations* (1935) and the Cannan summaries of Smith's magnum opus in 1948. Other books that appeared in shortened versions were by Joseph Schumpeter, Thomas R. Malthus, and Alfred Marshall. Finally, during Nazi occupation, in 1942, Lionel Robbins' *Essay* was translated into Greek.

In all, one can argue that the institutionalization of economics during this period and the creation of a distinct community of economists and interested citizens nourished this pluralism of translated texts.

5.6 Controversies in Economics before and after the Great Depression

During the interwar years, as economics as a science was expanding at a university level, so was economic literacy among the public. Next to the two academic journals edited by Kalitsounakis and Zolotas, several weekly and monthly magazines with an economic context circulated. Opinions were expressed, authorities were cited to support arguments, and consensus was sought in a country quite used to political dogfights and controversies. A consensus materialized in an all-party government in 1927–8 that prepared monetary stabilization and continued monitoring the refugee settlement.

Names of administrators and commentators who, with word and action, participated in these exchanges included politicians (such as Georgios Kafandaris and Stefanos Stefanopoulos), bankers (such as Emmanuil Tsouderos and Alexandros Diomidis), and public intellectuals and men of affairs (such as Georgios Kofinas and Spyros Loverdos).

Monetary economics was a topic of great interest among academics and practitioners, especially until 1928. The views expressed in public discussion could be classified into three categories: there was a group that suggested the return of the exchange rate of the drachma to its prewar parity (in the lines of the British return to the gold standard in 1923), those who favored stabilization at the current (devalued in comparison to 1918) exchange rate, and those who proposed a further devaluation before stabilization to promote exports and boost competitiveness.

These proposals entailed a reasoning that touched upon bigger issues discussed internationally during those times. There were men such as Evangelos Farmakidis,

Ioannis Koutsogiannis, and Spiros Chatzikyriakos who supported the validity of the quantity theory of money. In their many articles, they promoted the idea that the overexpanded monetary circulation after 1922 had to be curtailed to tame inflation. Other economists, such as Konstantinos Vournazos, Andreas Saounatsos, and Stefanos Stefanopoulos, opposed these conclusions. They were pointing to the extreme situation the economy was in after 1922. Refugees had to be settled, production needed loans, and social policy had to be a priority, they argued. Foreign assistance was doing its part, but government action was also needed, and this action could not be curtailed by theories that suggested low expenditures. Waiting for monetary stability to be implemented and then start supporting the economy meant for them time loss at periods demanding immediate action.

The monetary question was discussed with foreign experts from the League of Nations, the Bank of England, and other interlocutors that were advising Greek politicians. Post-war international economic conferences promoted the idea that European countries should create central banks if they had not already done so. In Greece, the NBG was performing the duties of a central bank while being at the same time a commercial bank too. Its shareholders were businessmen well-connected in politics and they were hesitant to accept the rationale for a central bank.

At this juncture, the *London Times* attacked the NBG and its governor, Alexandros Diomidis. He was accused of defending the arguments of the Banking School in monetary matters, a theory dismissed in Britain since Ricardo. According to Diomidis, the NBG could not be blamed for the monetary mess, as it had always supplied investors with the capital they wanted. If the money was not used, it would return to the vaults of the Bank in the same form or in another. The law of reflux was clearly articulated by him. The *Times* pointed out that this theoretical position had been declared wrong for a modern economy and that in Britain the Currency School's idea prevailed that a Central Bank needed to monitor the economic and commercial banks as well as adjust monetary circulation to the country's reserves.

Heated discussions followed. The Central Bank was inaugurated by Venizelos in 1928 with financial backing from the League of Nations. An interesting matter that provoked new exchanges concerned the ownership of any surplus value created by the revaluation of reserves that the NBG kept in its vaults. There was a group that argued that the NBG should keep all surplus value the reserves had accumulated until then, a second one that claimed that they all ought to go to the new bank of issue, and a third group that recommended splitting the surplus into two, with each bank getting equal shares. Venizelos, as Prime Minister, opted for the third group, and asked Diomidis to switch positions, becoming the first governor of the Bank of Greece. The drachma was stabilized around its current (devalued) exchange rate, and convertibility was introduced.

After 1928, public discussion moved to the need and the extent of a program of "productive works," a huge program of public infrastructure mostly in Northern Greece, connected with irrigation projects and agricultural improvements (Psalidopoulos 1989, 361–9). Liberal-minded neoclassical economists argued against them. Their arguments started from the already heavy tax burden carried by the private sector and the crowding out of private activity as the companies involved in these works would raise credit from the banking system. Academics such as Andreadis and Zolotas argued, as we saw, that these works, despite sounding positive, would lead to more intervention and to higher future taxes. Thus, state finances would always be negative, and the goal of a balanced budget would remain elusive. Comparing Greece with other Southeast European states, they found the tax burden in Greece to be higher and discouraging foreign investment. Other authors criticized different aspects of this project. They thought that starting the works without having secured the whole amount of money required to accomplish them was a mistake, because the state was going to interfere in the credit market in the future. They also criticized the lack of studies explaining the overall value of the works for the Greek economy and the speed of the government to close deals with private contractors, without pressing them on the terms of the contracts. The issue of properties around the places where the works were implemented was not discussed either, they underlined (see more extensively Angelopoulos 1932, 118–27).

Support for the implementation of the works included the rising class of engineers in the economy. They argued that half of the refugees had settled in Northern Greece and needed to be assisted in finding property and fertile lands to cultivate. Floods would be averted, and marsh regions made fertile. Unemployment would drop, and last but not least, public interest would be shown in an economically promising region that had been integrated in the country during the Balkan Wars. It was also argued that any increase in production would substitute for imports ae the pressure on the Greek balance of payments. A temporary budget deficit could be excused if better economic conditions could thus be achieved in the mid-term. It should be noted that the arguments concerning deficit spending were not embedded in any sort of economic analysis. Arguments in favor of public works such as those used (later) by Keynes in the Macmillan committee (Clarke 1988, 133) were not used at all.

What really happened was that the works started and yielded initial results, but due to the world economic depression that followed and the Greek default in 1932, they were discontinued and took long years to be fully implemented. However, in front of these new unforeseen difficult economic times, economists softened their tone and accepted a middle-of-the-road government activity, as this was happening in the rest of Europe.

We can therefore conclude that, according to evidence from public opinion and academic publications, economic thought in Greece during this time was characterized by two dominant and rival schools of thought: an eclectic liberalism based on the teachings of the then rising variants of neoclassicism and an interventionism with a historicist or a state-socialist flavor (Psalidopoulos 1989).

Common to all neoclassical economists of the interwar years were certain policy proposals all stemming from their liberal points of view. The government should refrain from all social expenditure for the relief of the refugees and balance its budget. Taxes should be lowered, and private initiative allowed to lead the economy. The currency should be stabilized, and a liberal external policy should be introduced to encourage foreign investment. The Greek economy should be "outwardly oriented" and seek complementarity with the economies of the industrially advanced countries with which it held close ties in trade.

The second school of thought based its power on the remarkable number of Greeks who had followed postgraduate studies in Germany. These economists and politicians, who had closely witnessed Germany's industrialization and growth, envisaged a similar path for Greece. The government should intervene to promote economic growth. Industry should be protected and helped to substitute imports. Taxes should be raised to make possible the building of the infrastructure which is necessary for the economy. A deficit in the budget should be tolerated if economic growth could be thus accelerated. The currency should be stabilized, and although foreign investment was welcome, external economic policy shouldn't be so liberal as to adversely affect internal economic activity.

The culmination of the world economic depression, Greek default in 1932, led to a de facto acceptance of interventionism by liberal and interventionist economists alike. Whereas in the 1920s debates and controversies centered around a sound monetary policy and the limits to social policy, now the argument was about the proper government functions to restore and maintain economic equilibrium. Whereas liberal economists tried to work out a theory which could incorporate interventionism, interventionists, happy with their recommendations being implemented, did not try to formulate a theory of government interventionism. They were even hostile to Keynesian economics when it became known.

5.7 The Reception of J.M. Keynes in Greece

J.M. Keynes was very well known in Greece as an authority on international economic policy issues. His opinions on monetary developments were reported in economic periodicals throughout the interwar years and his "Tract on Monetary Reform" and "The End of Laissez-Faire" had been translated into Greek (Psalidopoulos 1988, 454–6). His views on the Versailles Treaty, the British return to gold, and his proposals for a managed currency had been heeded.

However, the absence of a British tradition among Greek economists didn't allow them to understand Keynes as an economist who was gradually sliding away from the Marshallian synthesis of classical with neoclassical economics, adding a new edifice to the existing mainstream approach. His views on monetary matters were used by Greek interventionists to support their objections to anti-deflationist policies as a means out of economic depression, and to plead for more government responsibilities in the development process (Psalidopoulos 1989 and 1996).

It was in this context that the publication of the *General Theory* in 1936 became known in Greece. When it came out, it was, as in most places in the world, received critically, if not negatively, by Greek liberal and interventionist economists alike. Neoclassical economists articulated their dissonance quite early, while interventionists rejected Keynesian thinking explicitly in the 1950s. Keynesian *Theory*, being a theory of state interventionism of a very specific nature, didn't conform with Greek interventionist priorities of the day.

Of the neoclassical economists' reaction to the *General Theory*, the most prominent one was that of Xenophon Zolotas. In a review, Zolotas focused on Keynes' negative stance towards saving and his policy proposals to encourage consumption, to tax inheritance, etc. (Zolotas 1939, 260–2). Economic progress depended, for Zolotas, who referred to G. Cassels' theory of insufficient capitals (*Kapitalmangeltheorie*), on the volume of savings. Today's savings were tomorrow's investment, he commented. Plans to reduce saving in the economy were, according to him, dangerous, and could lead to economic decline. Zolotas accepted that Keynes was trying to interpret the seriousness of the world economic crisis, but he believed that Keynes had failed in generalizing out of a very special situation for the economy (1939, 269).

For Zolotas, the Wall Street Crash was an extreme case due to instabilities dating back to World War I, most notably the abandonment of the classical gold standard. The world economy offered indefinite opportunities to make profits on a global scale. Governments should focus on psychological elements in the economy and try to incentivize individuals to pursue their plans. State expenditure could be productive, he agreed, but should not be seen as a substitute for the accomplishments of private saving. Especially if increased government spending were financed by higher taxes, this would be disastrous for the economy. In this connection, Keynes' underlining of insufficient demand in the economy was rejected. The introduction of concepts like marginal propensity to consume, marginal efficiency of investment, and others by Keynes were confusing. An optimistic outlook of the world economy was foretold by Zolotas if the capitalist system was left to its own devices. It should be noted that Zolotas, 15 years later, praised Keynes in his inaugural speech at the Academy of Athens for having saved capitalism from its enemies (Zolotas 1954).

Professor Pindaros Christodoulopoulos was also very negative in his extensive, two-part, survey of the *General Theory* (1939). In the first part, he presented Keynes' ideas, and in the following, he concentrated his critique on the way Keynes treated consumption and the interest rate. He admitted a high standard of analysis in the *General Theory* (310–14), but immediately proceeded to attack the concept of unemployment as seen by Keynes. It was a big mistake, and contrary to accepted theory, he argued, that Keynes accepted involuntary unemployment as intrinsic in capitalist society. To demonstrate weaknesses in the Keynesian argumentation, Christodoulopoulos viewed society as a large majority of low-income earners, whose marginal propensity to consume was close to or equal to one, and a slim minority where the psychological law of consuming less and saving more materialized. Savings of wealthy people could not remain idle, for Christodoulopoulos, therefore the fear of savings not being transformed into investment was totally out of the question. On the determination of the interest rate, Keynes' focus on liquidity totally ignored Knut Wicksell's explanation of economic fluctuations, and this was, in Christodoulopoulos' opinion, wrong. The demand for money for speculation was another novelty in terminology, and Keynes was criticized for not following existing wisdom. Neoclassical theory of interest rate determination might be deficient, he rhetorically agreed, but what was needed were new developments "within" this theory, not a search for a different one. Keynes, by overthrowing the classical system and introducing a new vocabulary, was accused of practically throwing the baby out with the bathwater. His hypotheses were not convincing, and his theoretical proposal was deficient, he concluded. The *General Theory* was generally based on unsolid ground, and was to be rejected (1939, 95).

For other younger economists serving as ifigites during the 1930s, the validity of the *General Theory* was also a matter of controversy. For Ieronimos Pintos, the determination of the rate of interest, as suggested by Keynes, was restrictive and unacceptable, especially for the study of the dynamics of the economic system (Pintos 1939). These dynamics were, for him, better explained through Walrasian assumptions and Wicksell's natural rate of interest. For Dimitrios Delivanis, a full employment policy could be effective only when "the whole economic life of a nation is being totally coordinated from above on the grounds of a specific plan" (Delivanis 1939). In other words, what Keynes suggested could hardly be implemented into policy under a democratic regime. Therefore, his theory led to a dead end.[2]

A welcome exception to these negative treatments of the *General Theory* was, as already mentioned, Spyros Katiforis who, as we saw above, after a thorough presentation of the monetary theory of the Cambridge School (Katiforis 1938), proceeded to approach Keynes through the prism of his views about money. He agreed with Keynes on his analysis of the liquidity trap and accepted fiscal policy as a tool to promote investment and growth (178), and his overall stance to avert stagnation due to ineffective demand. The early passing of Katiforis was very unfortunate for the acceptance of Keynesian economics in Greece. Evangelos Bitsaxis summarized what he called "the international critique" (1943, 78) against Keynesian analysis at times when the General Theory was not yet academically accepted.

Upon Keynes' passing, EOPE published a special issue (1946, 129–223) introduced by an obituary by Roy Harrod, and followed by articles by Marina Goudi, Rena Christoula, Andreas Saounatsos, Andreas Kyrkilitsis, Vassilios Damalas, and Dimitrios Delivanis. The articles threw light on theoretical issues such as the business cycle and the rate of interest, and policy recommendations such as the financing of the war effort and the Keynes' Plan at Bretton Woods. According to Damalas, "the analysis and comprehension of this (i.e., the Keynesian) theory is very difficult" (1943, 191), and this explains the slow path of intrusion of this novel approach into economics in a setting where other economic paradigms prevailed.

Economists known to belong to the interventionist camp made explicit statements about Keynes' work after World War II and the Greek Civil War. For Dimitrios Kalitsounakis, Keynes' theory, with its focus on the aim to achieve full employment in a capitalist system, completely neglected the battle against the primary causes of unemployment. It prescribed a cure without a diagnosis of the illness (Kalitsounakis 1952). According to Kalitsounakis, two economic systems existed, the liberal and the Marxist. Keynesianism, as an in-between system, incorporated, for him, their disadvantages and not their advantages. The gradual transition to a more just human society would follow the spread of growth in the world economy, and the economic uprising of the Third World countries, he opined (see also Kalitsounakis 1957).

Similar views were expressed by Angelos Angelopoulos, who had moved during the occupation period to more radical ideas. In his *The Planned Economy in the Face of Liberalism* (1953, here cited from *Oikonomika* 1974, vol. two, 535–53) he argued that "the liberal system is outdated and can't guarantee economic and social progress" (538). He advocated a theory that would support the ever-changing functions of the state in the economy, for it was this axiom that would make theory into the "commanding principle in history" (538). Angelopoulos proposed a different scheme than the Marxian one between productive forces and relations of production. His scheme was about ideas and legal order. Under certain conditions and developments in society, ideas clashed with the existing order and a new order was thus created, taking a legal form in conformity with the new ideas. Social consciousness about the surrounding world changed, and so did human mentality.

Like what Thomas Kuhn was to suggest ten years later, Angelopoulos referred to the demise of the Classical School and the dominance of the German Historical Approach that was then followed by the rise of Neoclassicism. Keynesian economics was modern, in the sense that it reflected social necessities of the post-World War II era, both in the developed world and in less developed countries. But when he posed the question to himself if he were a Keynesian, he responded "I don't think so" (547). Authors such as Harold Laski and George D.H. Cole were closer to his views, he confessed.

He accepted certain Keynesian insights but believed that times needed nationalizations of heavy industries and economic planning on a large scale. This planning presupposed international economic cooperation which did not exist during that time. However, small steps on a national scale could be introduced, and they would mature when the global political divide between the USA and the Soviet Union ceased to exist. The most important issues therefore were the overcoming of the division of the world into two separate blocs and the advancing of the convergence of the opposing economic systems. Keynes' theory was, for Angelopoulos, too much directed towards rectifying capitalism rather than aiming at its transformation by democratic means (Angelopoulos 1953).

In conclusion, we see that the reaction of Greek economists to Keynes' *General Theory* was mostly negative. The absence of academic economists in favor of a "New Liberalism," in Keynes' terms, or of a "Social Democratic" contract for full employment in a free society, had been very crucial in this respect. This is especially so, because the generation of economists following the arguments outlined above remained, as we repeatedly stated, dominant in and out of Greek universities until the restoration of democracy in 1974.

To most of the Greek economists who had followed postgraduate studies in the UK and the USA after World War II and started their professional careers in Greece after 1965, Keynesianism meant discretionary policies for fine-tuning, as explicated by the neoclassical synthesis. This policy was practiced by American economists active in Greece after 1947, and a neoclassical synthesis Keynesianism was finally introduced in the country in the mid-1960s with the translation of Samuelson's *Economics*.

5.8 Heterodox Thought and Interwar Marxism

Heterodox thinkers from the late 19th century to the mid-1910s were preoccupied with the living standards of workers and with the language question. Labor centres in the main cities were created, and ideas associated with the improvement of living and working conditions of the poor were circulated. After 1917, some of them sided with Venizelos, his pro-labor legislation, and his vision of a more developed Greece. Others followed other routes. Socialist activists, united under a group called "Federation," after the name of a trade union in Thessaloniki, entered parliament and distanced themselves from Venizelos.

Before going into detail about the ideas articulated by economists influenced by Marxism, it is necessary to clarify the evolution of socialist politics in Greece, as it provides clues about how individual economists belonging to this tradition developed their ideas. Due to financial turmoil and military mobilization after 1917, an anti-war political front gained ground, supported by Lenin's criticism of social democracy and his condemnation of the willingness of German social democrats to side with "their" bourgeoisie in World War I. In 1918 SEKE (Socialist Labor Party of Greece) was inaugurated in the wake of the communist takeover in Russia of 1917 with the aim of representing the revolutionary tradition in Greece. Various groups and smaller parties advocating workers' rights united. After 1920 SEKE opposed the Asia Minor arrangements of Venizelos on an anti-war platform, and after continuous internal fighting about the "best" political platform, the revolutionary faction in the party prevailed. In 1924 SEKE was renamed as KKE (Communist Party of Greece), and, having accepted the 21 points suggested by the Third International, it joined the latter.

The Third International played a big role in KKE's internal affairs. In 1925, it led KKE to espouse the autonomy of Macedonia and Thrace, a policy declaration that KKE paid for politically, and recanted in 1935. It was also involved in the party's bolshevization, a process that was completed in 1931 when Nikos Zachariadis became the general secretary. It also provided economic arguments to the Greek communists mostly through the publications of Eugen Varga (on him, see Mommen 2011). The Third International was constantly debating "the crisis of capitalism" and disseminated an analysis of global economic development in a way that suited the evolving political interests of the Soviet Union.

From 1918 to 1923, and up to 1931, there was a big turnover of SEKE/KKE members at the high level of the apparatus. Three fractions initially existed within the party. A right-wing one, with Aristotelis Sideris as its main advocate, that supported cooperation with "bourgeois" parties. For this reason, this group was expelled from KKE in 1923. A second one, with Giannis Kordatos, Giorgos Georgiadis, and Avraam Benaroya, that advocated a "long legal existence" before any revolutionary aspiration. They were also side-lined and either left KKE or were expelled as well. The third, revolutionary and majority one, elected Pantelis Pouliopoulos as party secretary in 1924. Pouliopoulos, however, started distancing himself from KKE, resigned from his position, and in 1927 was expelled from the party as a Trotskyist. He then joined Spartakos, a group that published a periodical with that name. Serafim

Maximos, who sat in parliament for KKE for two years, was also expelled in 1928 and joined Spartakos too, until 1934, when he opted to distance himself from Trotskyism.

The names referred to were important not only for their participation in politics, but for their theoretical contributions, their translations of socialist literature, and their educational duties within the party. It is these Marxists that we will now focus on.

5.8.1 Georgiadis

Giorgos Georgiadis quit his job as a deputy district attorney in 1919 to pursue a political career. He joined SEKE, was very well-read and competent, and started writing and influencing public opinion. At first, he had radical views and sided with the necessity to join the Third International, but during 1922–3 he turned to more centrist positions and influenced decisions concerning a long and legal political activity that would help the workers first develop class consciousness and then follow more radical steps. He wrote extensively, was responsible for the education of party members, and was the editor of *Communist Review* (*KOMEP*). In many articles, he stressed that the Greek plutocracy had risen due to state privileges and profits reaped from World War I and was still strong (vol. 2, 16). The Asia Minor expedition was "a satisfactory sideroad for (nourishing) its hunger," he opined (vol. 1, 192–6). Those talking about a crisis should distinguish between a temporary, fiscal, and a long-term, universal capitalist crisis. The former was for Georgiadis a reality for Greece, but the latter had not entered the scene yet. The creation of SEKE gave, according to Georgiadis, the opportunity for workers to come together, educate themselves, and become politically active. The October Revolution in Russia was a signal that the times when workers gave the upper hand to bourgeois political parties were over. It was, however, a fact that "the transition from one period to the next can't be radical and mathematically determined" (as cited in Noutsos 1992, 194). Dogmatism should give way to the dialectical method of analyzing current politics, he declared. The workers had to assemble, turn their backs to the other parties, and fight for their rights together. The bourgeois order in Greece was regaining lost ground, and 1922 was only a partial setback for its aspirations (vol. 1, 22). The workers needed first to cement their autonomy from the other political parties and then demand changes in society. Having articulated the need for a well-prepared transition to socialism, Georgiadis left SEKE/KKE. He remained active in politics until the early 1950s, as a reformist supporter of the working class.

5.8.2 Kordatos

Giannis Kordatos was a self-educated, prolific historian and writer of more than 30 books. He was active in SEKE/KKE for five years, contributing to the socialist education of the workers with his articles in *Rizospastis*, the party's newspaper. He contributed immensely to the application of Marxian dialectics with the works he wrote after he left SEKE/KKE. He started with *Social History of the Greek Revolution of 1821* (1924). It was later followed by *Introduction to the History of*

Greek Capitalism (1930) and his *History of the Greek Labor Movement* (1932). These were highly informative works, accessible to the average reader and applying historical materialism in the study of the evolution of Greek society. They were very popular, even if in some instances they lacked historical accuracy, and provoked responses from both the establishment and from KKE. This publicity kept them circulating until the 1970s, long after Kordatos' passing.

5.8.3 Sideris

Aristotelis Sideris held a PhD in Law from the University of Athens since 1910 and was a socialist parliamentarian (in 1915 and between 1917 and 1920). He was active in regional and international efforts of European socialists to coordinate their action during and after World War II. He joined SEKE in 1919 as a supporter of the October Revolution but expressed simultaneously reservations about the possibility to apply immediately the Russian experience in Greece. He published many opinion articles and scholarly articles. In his *The Paris Commune* (in KOMEP 1921) he applauded workers seeking to establish their rule in society in 1871 and explored the reasons that could have led the Commune to success. In his *On the Crisis* (1924) he criticized the opinion expressed by KKE that the Greek economy was in a crisis. KKE was blindly following, in his view, what was expressed by Eugen Varga about capitalism being in a permanent crisis. There were organic and functional crises in capitalism, Sideris argued, and the most affluent part of Europe, having just exited an organic crisis, was experiencing functional problems that were in the process of being solved. For Sideris, Greece, not being a part of developed Europe, was not in a crisis. It was facing the problem of settling the refugees, but on the other hand shipping was doing well and industry was taking off. Therefore, no objective situation to overthrow bourgeois order existed in Greece. What was needed was a long fight to improve living standards and to create a real massive workers' movement.

In his *Reconsideration of Economic Ideas of Karl Marx* (in AOKE 1926), he reviewed the book by Italian communist leader and academic Antonio Graziadei on Karl Marx's labor theory of value. Graziadei held the view that the labor theory of value could not serve anymore as a practical tool to explain interwar economic conditions. Sideris applauded this idea and drew the conclusion that more time was needed to develop an analysis of modern capitalism on a realistic basis.

Sideris went on to associate himself with Alexandros Papanastasiou and served as his Minister in 1932. He became a Professor of Political Economy at the Highest School of Agricultural Studies in 1925 and moved from there to ASOEE, where he occupied the Chair for Economic History and History of Economic Thought from 1943 to 1960. The books based on his lectures were widely read.

5.8.4 Maximos

Seraphim Maximos sided until 1928 with the leadership of KKE. He espoused the view of the Third International that both Europe and Greece were in a crisis. In his words, the Greek working class had been, until recently, following and voting for either the Popular or the Liberal (Venizelist) party. Having been disappointed by their policies, workers turned their backs on them, seeking new political housing. Fiscal derailment in Greece led the economy to disintegration, and persisting European antagonisms proved that international capitalism was standing on weak feet. Therefore, Greece would not withstand the existing shock, and the time had arrived to overthrow the dominance of capital in Greek society. (On his trade union activities during those years and before he became an MP, see Noutsos 1992, 317–25.)

In 1930, after the Wall Street Crash and before Greek default, in his monograph *Parliament or Dictatorship?* he equated dictatorial and democratic rule in Greece to demonstrate that parliamentarianism was not delivering on its promises for the working class. The proletariat could not see its interests accommodated, regardless of the right to vote it possessed. According to Maximos, Greece should not have participated in World War I, because the war was about imperialist European Empires trying to outplay one another (10). Labor legislation introduced by Venizelos was a bait to lure the working class into supporting the war, he underlined, but he failed. The workers sided with the pre-1910 "household economy," the pre-capitalist administration of the populists on economic matters (14). The effort to impose the Treaty of Sevres and secure Asia Minor as Greek territory was adventurous (16) and not a progressive policy that would have benefited the workers.

Maximos went on to observe that after the Asia Minor Catastrophe in 1922, General Plastiras briefly imposed dictatorial rule, and so did General Pangalos in 1926. The transition from one to the other form of governance led him to claim that "a democracy can be called democracy and be nothing else than dictatorship of the worst kind… This is what contemporary bourgeois democracy is" (28). Parliament and dictatorship were, for him, "synonymous" (30), and this fact explained police brutality in the massive August 1923 workers' strikes and demonstrations. Maximos compared the pro-workers' coverage of the press in 1909 to what it reported in the interwar period to conclude that the bourgeois class had turned its back on the laborers. The latter should unite in a party of their own to claim their rights. A dictatorship was not unwelcome if it led people to overthrow their tyrants, he stressed. "A proletarian dictatorship is the healthiest way for a new social situation" (112). The stabilization of the economy pursued by the national unity government of 1927 was "a stabilization of surplus value created" (135), with a slim capitalist class and the NBG exploiting the rest of the citizens (136). Greek workers should understand that parliament could not represent them politically. They should rather fight to overthrow it. In his own words, "parliament and dictatorship, democracy and fascism, are a brotherhood in the service of capital" (153).

Having been disappointed by Greek political developments, Maximos devoted himself to economics and economic history. Having understood the importance of the textbook published by Xenophon Zolotas in 1942, he criticized the contents of this neoclassical treatise. Maximos (using the pseudonym "Vorios") started his *Theoretical Economics and Economic Lack of Judgment* (1943) with the thesis that political economy had not set roots in Greece and was, until then, the privilege of a small clan of state administrators and bankers (11). He then compared the views of Ioannis Soutsos with those of Xenophon Zolotas, finding the latter reducing economics to the study of empirical, rhythmical ever-returning phenomena. However, studying just the determination of prices was like "a butterfly flying close to light" (33). The study of causality in place of the laws governing production and distribution was a regression, in his view.

Maximos attacked the concept of scarcity (45–62) and the ideal type of homo economicus in Zolotas. Humans lived in societies and were not to be approached as isolated individuals, he opined. He then compared the Marxian labor theory of value with the value theory of the neoclassical school (65–86). In general, he argued, it was fatal for economists to just focus on and analyze exchange and totally avoid discussing laws governing production. It was in production that surplus value, the source of capital, was created, he concluded. Classical political economy should not be stamped as outdated, and David Ricardo was a superior analyst to Gustav Cassel, whom Zolotas followed, he insisted (77).

He moved to discuss the determination of prices (87–104), criticizing the insistence of Zolotas to associate them not only with the cost of production, but with predictions made by traders concerning their future trend (97). Maximos thought that Zolotas' readiness to apply human psychology to market equilibrium might sound like a plea to introduce elements of reality in the abstract frame of economic subjectivism. He criticized, however, this attitude, as one that concealed the importance of labor cost in the determination of prices and contributed to a vulgar interpretation of market outcomes.

His critique led to a riposte. Sotirios Agapitidis and Stylianos Poulopoulos (who went on to become university professors after World War II) defended Zolotas in separate publications. Thus, a first public debate concerning the nature and significance of economics in Greece took place. Maximos was accused of misunderstandings and ignorance. For Poulopoulos, he demonstrated "arteriosclerotic insistence in the economic theories of scientific socialism" (1943, 45). With quotations from modern works and the classics themselves, he argued that Maximos was not fully educated as an economist, therefore his critique was weak and out of order. Agapitidis followed the same line of arguments.

Around the same period, two other books by Maximos were published. He had traveled in the past to Paris and Marseille, where he unearthed archival material documenting the rise of Greek shipping capital. Out of this research, he published *The Greek Merchant Marine in the 18th Century* in 1940 and the *Dawn of Greek Capitalism: Turkish Rule 1685–1789* in 1945. Both investigated the rise of a capital-owning business class in Greek society that contributed to the financing of the War of Independence. Quantities, prices of goods, estimated profits, as well as routes of trade were disclosed. Thus, future generations of Greek economic historians were assisted in similar research activities.

Maximos left Greece during the civil war and was not allowed to return to his home country. From Prague, and later Vienna, he continued writing in *New Economy* and in AOKE until his death in 1962.

5.8.5 Pouliopoulos

Pantelis Pouliopoulos had a degree in law and was active as an anti-war activist until 1922. Having joined SEKE/KKE, he represented the revolutionary line and fully supported the analyses of the Third International. In his article "Greek Mensheviks" (Pouliopoulos 1924, 129) he attacked those who claimed that Greece was not in a crisis. There were two views concerning crises, he claimed, a reformist-counter revolutionary and a communist-revolutionary one. The second was founded on the revolutionary will of workers who wanted to see their standard of living improve, whereas the first didn't want capitalism to end, therefore propagating economic improvement under capitalism. Despite occasional upswings, capitalism was doomed to failure and this was also supported by analyses of the Third International, he commented. Greece faced unsurpassable economic problems and a crisis was already evolving. Above all, what mattered to him more was the willingness of the proletariat to move toward socialism. According to Pouliopoulos, a distinction should be made between objective economic conditions preparing a socialist breakthrough and the ripeness of the proletariat seeking the takeover of power. Subjective issues played the most important role in the struggle for socialism, he believed. If somebody, like the opponents of KKE, negated the possibility of a strong revolutionary movement, then a defeat would follow. In all cases, the current crisis in Greece should be exploited by KKE to mobilize workers and keep them on a revolutionary course.

Having been expelled from KKE, Pouliopoulos transitioned to a more realist analysis of current circumstances. It was now KKE believing that a crisis was imminent, and he was arguing that a breakdown of capitalism was not on the agenda. KKE expressed in an article in KOMEP in 1932 the view that Greece was in a semi-colonial condition. Any recovery was based "in the breakdown of partial stabilization," undertaken by bourgeois governments (as cited in KKE 1975, vol. 2, 205–257, 573). Whatever development there was in the Greek economy since 1912, the KKE analysis continued, it was artificial, and economic policy measures adopted by successive governments were short-term and ineffective. Left-wing opponents of KKE were underconsumptionists, didn't attack Greek capitalism, and believed that a possible rise in incomes and consumption would dampen the willingness of the proletariat to fight against their oppressors.

Pouliopoulos (1932) responded that the crisis of 1929 was unique, not only because of very high rates of unemployment, but also because of misery and a total breakdown of the banking system. However, no automatic collapse of capitalism would occur without active masses of workers participating in the political process and leading society at a different level. What was needed was the unity of the proletariat despite diverging views. KKE divided, in his opinion, the proletarian front with these attacks and was caught in an "abstract kind of a revolutionary looking theory of crises" (19).

After the Nazis rose to power in Germany, the Third International changed its attitude about capitalist crises and suggested the creation of party coalitions on an anti-fascist basis in European countries. KKE changed its discourse accordingly.

It defined Greece as a country of average level of development in its sixth plenary meeting, and in need of first completing civil-democratic reforms before proclaiming the transition to socialism. In essence, the platform of the 1923 right-wing fraction advocating a long legal existence of the party was resurrected.

To this, Pouliopoulos answered with *Democratic or Socialist Revolution in Greece?* (1934). The book was a harsh polemic against the Stalinist bureaucracy dominating KKE (21) and included an analysis of Greek capitalism and its peculiarities and contradictions (38–86), a lengthy discussion of revolutionary socialism from Marx through Lenin to Trotsky (115–59), and a plea for proletarian action in Greece under the existing circumstances (171–88).

Pouliopoulos admitted that he and his comrades had sacrificed time exchanging accusations with other left factions of the working-class movement and had not spent time objectively analyzing the circumstances in Greece (20). Setting aside the fact that protectionism and economic isolationism were the norm in international economic relations (27), Pouliopoulos spoke of a unified global capitalist market and of Greece being a part of it. There existed many capitalist models and each country possessed one. It was not necessary to wait for full industrial development in a country to accept that capitalism was the dominant mode of production. Greece transitioned to a full bourgeois democratic economy in 1910 with reforms in agriculture, labor laws, and industrial promotion (41). Foreign capital assisted the whole process (80–6) despite anachronisms such as the monarchy and the role of the church. The economy was fully capitalist as numbers from all censuses revealed (55–7). The proletariat was becoming an important factor in the economy (57–71) and despite a primitive accumulation taking place and exploitation reaching high levels, it was conscious of its mission, contrary to what reformists of all sorts believed (70). For Pouliopoulos, the future path of Greek capitalism would be the "repeal of every democratic luxury for the benefit of the supremacy of capital" (77). KKE was, for him, to blame for having sidelined activists and thinkers loyal to the proletariat, because of Stalinist fixations imposed by the Third International (107). Revolutionary Marxism as analyzed and practiced in various countries testified to the need to remain on track with the moment, but never forget its primary goal (115–159). After discussing the international situation, Pouliopoulos turned again to Greece. He polemically denounced all "enemies" of the proletarians, such as Georgiadis, Sideris, and others who had turned their backs on the workers' cause (180). He also accused the Stalinist KKE of having adjourned the immediate interests of Greek workers for the sake of a supposedly more thorough development of capitalism in the country, following Stalin's orders. His conclusion was that Greece was in line with Trotsky's analysis, ready for a socialist revolution, and that arguing the contrary was defeatist and harmful for the labor class.

As we saw, Pouliopoulos transitioned from a crisis believer and propagator to a sober analyst of concrete economic conditions, without abandoning, his belief that a socialist revolution in Greece was possible. He was arrested and imprisoned during the Metaxas dictatorship. He remained a prisoner under Nazi occupation and was executed by the fascists without trial in 1943.

Notes

1 All subsequent editions don't include Keynes' General Theory in the bibliography. The third and fourth include Gottfried Haberler's *Prosperity and Depression.*

2 It should be noted that in 1955 Delivanis translated the General Theory as part of the efforts of the Association of Greek Economists to acquaint the interested public with seminal works in economics.

6 The (Subtle) Anglo-Saxonization of Greek Economics (1944–71)

6.1 Overview of Economic and Social Developments

The Greek economy emerged from German occupation with its productive basis destroyed and its currency in shambles after the hyperinflation of the years 1940–4. Its economic reconstruction was further delayed by the Civil War (1946–9). Economic policy was run up to 1953 on an adhoc basis and was oriented toward relief and monetary stability. Through the generous support of the United Nations Relief and Rehabilitation Administration (UNRRA), as well as British and US funds, the economy steadily improved (Freris 1986, 120–54). The USA supported the economy until 1961 with financial assistance reaching at times 20% of GDP, first with the Truman Doctrine in 1947, then through the Marshall Plan, followed by the Economic Cooperation Administration, and later the Mutual Security Agency.

At first, government finances were impossible to balance, and inflation was high. A Monetary Committee was established in 1946 to monitor monetary policy. The banking system was vulnerable, and ways were sought to assist it in assuming its role in the economy. Complicated trade restrictions obstructed transactions. After the outbreak of the war in Korea, the US government made it clear to the Greek authorities that the continuation of US aid would start to diminish. Georgios Kartalis, the responsible Minister in 1951–2, aimed to balance the budget through deflation and to restore equilibrium in the balance of payments. He increased taxes and pressed for the integration of the Greek economy in the international division of labor (Candilis 1968, 67–85).

After four failed attempts, the drachma was finally successfully devalued in April 1953 and stabilized at a parity of 30 drs = 1 US $. As a result, from then on and for the next 20 years, monetary stability was the major goal of economic policy. Development through industry was the clear target, but came second after the priority of a stable currency, which would serve to attract foreign capital. Xenophon Zolotas was the most outspoken supporter of this view. This policy was followed consistently until 1967 and held the inflation rate (until 1973) to a modest 2.3% per year. The average rate of growth of GDP was 6.8% per year during the same period, a performance that gained worldwide respect and approval by authorities and economists alike. Milton Friedman among others was very positively impressed (Friedman 1967, 41). It was hoped that the problem of

DOI: 10.4324/9781315413419-7

widespread unemployment (12.1% in 1960) would be overcome in the future through increased private investment. A new income tax was introduced in 1955. From the late 1950s, emigration to Belgium, Germany, and other countries, as well as economic growth, brought the unemployment rate down to 3% in 1971 and kept it at low levels until 1978.

Agriculture was the most important sector of economic activity, accounting for 30% of GDP, 50% of total employment, and 80% of exports in 1960. Its importance started to decline over the following two decades to the benefit of industry, which reached 30% of GDP in 1970. Services accounted for 50% of GDP until 1980. Shipping, tourism, and remittances from workers abroad covered, on average 70% of the deficit of the balance of trade and contributed, on average 20% of GDP in 1970 (Psalidopoulos 2014). A major factor in these developments was the association agreement of Greece with the EEC, which went into effect in 1962. Trade liberalization with the EEC countries was agreed upon, coupled with Greek access to European Investment Bank financing. This agreement was subject to heated discussions and worries by the opposition that more government intervention was needed to enact necessary structural changes. The imposition of a military dictatorship in 1967 met the disapproval from the EEC, and the development financing of the Greek economy froze until 1974. However, the lowering of tariffs on both sides continued. Indicative economic planning for structural changes was a common theme discussed by economists.

To legitimize the dictatorial regime in the eyes of the public, the colonels explicitly declared their intention to shift the emphasis from monetary stability to economic development. Faced with a recession in 1967–8, the military government expanded the volume of public investment and stimulated economic activity. A policy of cheap money, the suppression of trade union activity as well as price and income controls, accelerated rates of growth, but perpetuated structural weaknesses. Faced with the collapse of the Bretton Woods system in 1971, economic policy reached its limits when the dollar went off gold and currencies started fluctuating. This caught the dictatorial regime totally unprepared, politically isolated, and confused. Despite price controls, prices soared with inflation reaching 35% in 1974. The economic turbulence was followed by quarrels within the dictatorial hierarchy, a change of guards, and a decision to overthrow the president of Cyprus. This led to a Turkish invasion in Cyprus and the breakdown of the dictatorship in July 1974. The restoration of democracy was unanimously applauded. The economy, however, struggled, like all Western countries, to fight stagflation in an international environment of floating exchange rates.

The military dictatorship proved to be a catalyst for the internationalization of Greek economics in a twofold sense. First, to strengthen its ideological influence, it pushed for an educational reform through which separate Departments of Economics were created within the Law Schools from the academic year 1970–1 onward. The university degree in economics after a full four-year study of the field became a reality in 1971. New academic positions were filled, thus helping a young generation of economists to become academics. This started the internationalization of economics in Greece.

Second, because of the emphasis placed by the military on economic development, there grew a bigger need for the economist-specialist capable of analyzing problems and issues in the context of the structural change of the country. This led the ratio of students preferring an economics rather than a business degree to go from 1:6 in 1966 to 2:5 in 1974 (Psalidopoulos 1997). This trend continued in the following decade.

In the following sections, we explore the influence of Anglo-Saxon economics in Greece during the period 1945–70. We present some women economists who entered the profession during the same period, and then move to developments in academia that occurred in the post-war period. We devote extra space to Xenophon Zolotas, Panagis Papaligouras, and Andreas Papandreou, who were very influential in terms of writing and action. We also discuss camps of thought and their priorities as well as issues of importance among Greek economists, in particular attitudes toward Keynesian economics. We focus on important translations of economic textbooks into Greek and close with a reference to heterodox thought and Marxism in particular.

6.2 Origins of Anglo-Saxon Influences

Economics was institutionalized during the interwar period and reached a level of unprecedented pluralism. Economic thought was exposed, not only to German and French influences, but also to British thought through translations in the 1930s. This process was slow and persistent and reached a new quality after the end of World War II.

Anglo-Saxon thought during that period was essentially Marshallian, empirical, and applied mathematical techniques in solving economic problems. The New Deal experience and a mix of neoclassical and Keynesian insights were the starting point when discussing economic policy issues.

Greece became subject to British and American foreign policy interests after its liberation. British economists were active as members of the United Nations Relief and Rehabilitation Administration in Greece, or as consultants to the British embassy in Athens before and after 1947. They advocated for the creation of the Monetary Committee at the Bank of Greece, which included seats for a British and an American expert until 1955. The Committee, together with three high-ranking Greek officials, determined monetary and banking policy. Another body, the Foreign Trade Administration, was also introduced to centrally monitor external trade, with a foreign expert as its head until the mid-1960s. American economists were very active after 1947 and disseminated American economics, influencing economic thinking in the country. International organizations such as the OEEC coordinated economic cooperation, the FAO commissioned surveys of Greek agriculture, and, in general, specialists of all kinds were interacting with their Greek counterparts. Economic development as a special field in economics was established, and there was a demand for special knowledge related to growth and higher income (Arndt 1987). During these years, American interest in foreign economic development as a collateral to diplomacy became evident (Simpson 1976, 641).

This multiple Greek–US/British interaction led to major changes in attitude towards analyzing economic policy problems by Greek economists. To start with, American-trained economists during that period had been brought up in the tradition of the Roosevelt New Deal administration (Nelson 1987, 52–4). Economists in the British civil service were also familiar with planning for war and its aftermath, even though not in a collectivist sense. They also apparently knew "Full Employment in a Free Society" by William Beveridge. The situation of the Greek economy in the immediate post-war years, with hyperinflation, an infrastructure destroyed by occupation, the private sector unable or incapable of satisfying basic needs of consumers and the government facing the above, plus a civil war, became a testing ground for new ideas and approaches to economic policy. Agreement was unanimously reached from the beginning on basics: balancing the budget, seeking currency stabilization through sound monetary policy, relieving the poor, and liberalizing the economy. Differences in method, extent, and timing of course existed, and political battles were fought over them, but at the end the Greek public administration benefited from this timely extended exposure to new styles in economic thought.

The most important innovation that the Americans introduced was "the inflationary/deflationary balance sheet" to keep track of inflows and outflows in the economy. Full employment equilibrium was not an issue, just the need to monitor what was happening and where the trend of economic activity was headed. It was the invention Frank Mahon, a member of the American Mission for Aid to Greece (AMAG), who was apparently aware of the "Keynesian cross" that was incorporated in American economics textbooks through Lorie Tarshis' (1947) and Paul Samuelson's (1948) textbooks.

The description of the inflationary/deflationary gap around full employment equilibrium was something that Mahon used to monitor the Greek economy. Inflationary factors were the budget deficit, supply account, credit expansion, export earnings, and invisible receipts. Deflationary factors were imports, invisible payments, increased legal entity deposits, collection of principal and interest, increase in banking deposits, and non-inflationary increases in currency circulation. Defense support, imports of capital goods, and creation of reserves were separately monitored. The balance sheet was based on the quantity theory of money. What was supposed to be held in check was the volume of monetary circulation in a distressed economy with a high degree of uncertain actions and outcomes. This account was explicitly used by the Americans until the stabilization of the drachma with IMF support in 1953 (Psalidopoulos 2013).

Another significant contribution of the Americans was the initiation to create an Association of Greek Economists that was formed in 1950 and served as the overarching institution for all Greek economists. Individuals with postgraduate degrees were automatically part of the group, while those without could become members if supported by three individuals who were already accepted. The Society held conferences every three years and was active until the dissolution of the dictatorship in 1974, when it disintegrated. Its most important contribution, next to conferences, was the 1953 decision to encourage its members to translate important foreign economics textbooks into Greek. These books included works by John Hicks, Eric Roll, J.M. Keynes, Simon Kuznets, Alvin Hansen, and others.

Following the end of the Civil War, American interest in the Greek economy gradually lost ground and withered to a minimum, particularly when Greece became associated with the EEC. However, during this time, the Fulbright foundation gave scholarships to young Greek students and civil servants to study, among other disciplines, economics in the USA It also encouraged American scholars to visit and conduct research in Greece. According to a 1995 manual of the association of Fulbright Scholars of Greece, between 1950 and 1975, 52 students went to the USA to study economics and pursue graduate degrees, and 16 American economists arrived for longer or shorter stays in Greece.

There were exceptions to transatlantic exchanges though. When in the late 1950s, the Greek government was interested in foreign assistance to accomplish its first indicative five-year development plan, it officially invited Professor Pascuale Saraceno, University of Rome, to assist in these effots. Reasons for this choice were the government's desire to avoid demonstrating continuous reliance on US help for internal political reasons and the similarity of Greek underdevelopment and economic conditions in Southern Italy that the Italian expert had long studied.

The most important new institution for the internationalization of economics in Greece was the creation of the Center of Economic Research in 1961, which in 1964 was renamed the Center of Planning and Economic Research (KEPE). It was established by Professor Andreas Papandreou, who came to Greece at the request of the Karamanlis government. The Ford Foundation and the Rockefeller Foundation played significant parts in the activities of KEPE through their generous financing.

KEPE hired young researchers and some PhD holders and invited many American and British economists in the following years to conduct research and give seminars to the staff of the center. These scientists brought mathematical techniques, a policy-oriented economic analysis, and a Keynesianism of the then mainstream neoclassical synthesis type into Greece. The names of economists that visited KEPE included George C. Archibald, Kenneth Arrow, George Break, Martin Bronfenbrenner, Howard Ellis, Robert Eisner, Milton Friedman, Arthur Goldberger, Robert Gordon, Laurence Klein, Roy Radner, Peter O. Steiner, Daniel Suits, Ralph Turvey, Jan Tinbergen, Benjamin Ward, and Pan A. Yotopoulos. The lecture seminars included topics such as fundamentals of model construction in macroeconomics, theory and application of econometric models, theory of multiple regression analysis, advanced calculus, linear algebra, location theory, regional economics and planning, and others.

KEPE corresponded with American Universities sponsoring graduate studies for its staff. About 25 scholarships were awarded between 1963–5 to young economists, who went mainly to the UK. One big group of five preferred the University of Manchester and did PhDs in Economic Planning. Others went to the USA with the Universities of Rochester, North Carolina/Raleigh, and Wayne State attracting small groups of students. Some of these KEPE economists returned eventually to Greece and came to hold academic appointments in the 1970s. The names of this group include, among others, Georgios Agapitos, Michalis Chatziprokopiou, Emmanuel Drandakis, Kostas Glezakos, Theodoros Gamaletsos, Theodoros Georgakopoulos, Zoe Georganta, Stavros Theofanidis, Sakis Karagiorgas, Theodoros Lianos, Kyprianos Prodromidis, Panagiotis Pavlopoulos, Andreas Kintis, Theofanis Benos, Diomidis Psilos, Georgios Christou, Georgios Chiotis, Triantafyllos Eleftheriou, and Ilias Balopoulos. Without doubt, KEPE was a catalyst for the internationalization of economics in Greece.

Next to working toward a five- and a ten-year indicative plan for the economic development of Greece, KEPE published monographs, seminar series, lectures on important topics of the Greek economy, and lots of reports. A new style of economic argumentation was introduced, one that put emphasis on numbers, models, and analysis based on thorough empirical investigation.

The Bank of Greece followed a similar pattern during the 1960s. At first, it created the Institute of Banking Studies, offering specialized courses for its staff. It also encouraged its staff working at the Department of Economic Research to follow postgraduate studies abroad as well. Its policy allowed every single economist to choose a scientific field and a university completely freely, keeping only in mind the broad needs of the service and the development process in the country. Many economists exploited this opportunity. One group preferred Yale University, which offered a special PhD course in "International Foreign Economic Administration," while others went mostly to Britain.

During the military dictatorship, the Ford Foundation came to sponsor democratic artists and intellectuals in Greece to pursue activities and research that would not have been possible otherwise. This activity benefited economics, too. One Ford Foundation project was the financing of translations of seminal articles from US economic periodicals. These were distributed in classes taught by Professor Ioannis Pesmazoglou shortly before he was expelled from the University and exiled by the junta. These articles circulated among students for many years and brought Greek students closer to Anglo-Saxon economic literature. Economists imprisoned by the junta also received research awards.

In all, economics in Greece gradually shifted toward the Anglo-Saxon paradigm after 1944. At first, the generation that dominated Greek academia remained loyal to their early beliefs in historical/institutional approaches. However, as they were eager to learn from their international counterparts, they assimilated the new international consensus in economics. By 1970, the stage changed totally.

6.3 Women Economists

In 1934, the right to vote in Greece, which had been reserved for males only until then, was extended to women as well, thus culminating a process that had started at the end of the 19th century. The education of women accelerated, and they started devoting energy and resolve to enter professions and positions held by males. In this section, we discuss four pioneering women economists: the first Greek woman to ever earn a PhD in economics, the first woman to earn a PhD in

Greece, the first woman who did an ifigessia, the first female economist to pursue a career abroad, and the first woman economist to become a rector at a Greek university.

6.3.1 Zafiriou

Irini (Rena) Zafiriou was a graduate of the University of Athens with degrees in Law and in Economics and a civil servant at the Ministry of Finance. In 1938, she won a scholarship to study abroad. The jury interpreted the letter of the law that a scholarship was to be awarded to a "fititis" (male student) broadly, so that it could be applied to a "fititria" (female student) as well.

Zafiriou went to the LSE for a master's degree and then started working toward a PhD, initially under the supervision of Lionel Robbins and later Friedrich von Hayek. When the LSE moved to Cambridge, she attended classes by Cambridge faculty and came under the influence of Keynesian ideas. While in England, she published "The Contemporary Status of the Theory of Monopolistic Competition" in 1942. In this article, she introduced the contributions by Edward Chamberlin and Joan Robinson and their incorporation in microeconomic theory to a Greek audience. The defense of her thesis was delayed because of the ongoing war and differences in methodology and approach between her and Hayek. She finally successfully submitted her PhD on "The Concept of Capital in Economic Theory" in 1945. Her external examiner was Paul Rosenstein Rodan, the development economist.

Zafiriou's dissertation was an extremely well-supported attack against neoclassical theoretical contributions. Orthodox theory was, for her, refusing to face "uncongenial realities" (10b). Neoclassical economists assumed an ideal world in their models, and this was particularly true for the concept of capital, whose definition repeatedly changed its form and content according to circumstances. Zafiriou discussed the concept of capital in economic thought. There was the means of production concept of capital of the classical school (11), the socialist critique to this concept (105–44), orthodox approaches (144-77), the German historical-legal approach (178–84), the services of goods considered as the revenue from capital (185–220) and modern interpretations based on the means of production concept (221–87). Finally, she discussed the period of production analysis and its significance for capital theory (288–305). Relying on Maurice Dobb, she recommended a return to Marx and his realist analysis of the capitalist process as opposed to staying on the surface of harmonies and free contracts agreed by agents (323). Modern economics needed, according to Zafiriou, to get rid of abstract theorizing and multiple definitions of the term "capital" according to circumstances and argumentation.

Unfortunately, this thesis, which preceded in a certain sense what was to be called 25 years later "The Cambridge controversies in the theory of capital," didn't attract the attention it deserved. Zafiriou didn't show any interest in following it up. Since the outbreak of World War II, she had contacted the Greek government in exile and her former mentor Kyriakos Varvaressos, who hired her as an assistant.

She wrote papers and memoranda dealing with Greece's finances and needs in foreign aid and interacted with high-ranking British civil servants. As a member of the Greek delegation, she participated in allied economic conferences in the USA and worked closely with UNRRA.

In October 1944, she returned to liberated Athens. The economic situation of the country deteriorated, however, because of political instability and clashes of opinion about the "correct" new exchange rate of the drachma between the two great men of Greek economics at that time, Professors Varvaressos and Zolotas. In this clash, Zafiriou stood next to Governor Varvaressos and reached high echelons of policymaking when Varvaressos became Deputy Prime Minister in June 1945. She assisted him in the so-called "Varvaressos Experiment," an effort to put a strong government in charge of the reconstruction of the country. The plan foresaw the immediate distribution of UNRRA supplies and raw materials to firms, the taxation of wartime profits, and the provision of basics to the people through government authorities. The plan, a comprehensive, well-argued solution to attack the economic misery of the country, was abandoned in September 1945 because of lack of political support from both the right and the left. The net result was that the Greek currency was stabilized only seven years later.

In June 1946, Zafiriou resigned from her post at the Bank of Greece and left for the USA, where she worked for the World Bank until her retirement. Had she opted to stay in Greece, she might have become an academic. However, as she chose to emigrate to the USA, this did not materialize.

6.3.2 Christoula

Rena Christoula was the first woman economist to obtain a PhD in Economics in Greece. She received her degree in Politics and Economics from the Law School of the University of Athens in 1938 and started working as an assistant to Professor Zolotas. She submitted her thesis on "Modern Theories of Interest" in 1945. In her monograph, she investigated the views expressed since Adam Smith about the determination of the interest rate, trying to distinguish between different definitions and approaches.

One year later, she published *The Labor Theory of Value and Marxism*, attempting to reassess the importance of Marxism in economics, as Joan Robinson had done in her *An Essay on Marxian Economics* from 1942. In Christoula's opinion, Marx, to his credit, had understood the deeper meaning of capitalism as an economic system and had revealed the origin of private property and the exploitation of workers under capitalism. His theory of value, however, had been rightly criticized (115) for having neglected subjective factors. Economists ought to study and supplement the labor theory of value, instead of abandoning it because they disagreed with the political interpretations of Marx (138). Having been identified as a follower of Marx, even at a scientific level only, Christoula faced difficulties in pursuing an academic career at times when left-leaning ideas were persecuted. She worked at the Bank of Greece and later as a journalist. A university career was not possible for her due to Greek politics of the times.

6.3.3 Goudi

Marina Goudi obtained her degrees in Politics and in Economics from the University of Athens in 1939 and a second in Law in 1940. She obtained her PhD in Economics under the supervision of Xenofon Zolotas in 1947.

In 1946, before submitting her dissertation, she wrote *The General Theory as an Explanation of the Business Cycle* (1946). She focused on chapter 22 of the *General Theory*, seeking to better understand the position of Keynes on the reason behind economic fluctuations. She discussed comparatively the views of the classics, of Wicksell and of the Austrian School to see if they fit with the analysis of Keynes. She arrived at the marginal efficiency of capital as a new theoretical tool and tried to analyze how a changing attitude from business optimism to pessimism led to variations of investment and total income with effects on effective demand (216). She included in her analysis the possibility that the Central Bank would assist business activity through a falling interest rate policy. Goudi also discussed whether Keynes could be classified as a follower of overinvestment, of underconsumption or of Marxism. She concluded that Keynes was very original and couldn't be considered a follower of any existing school (220). Citing Maurice Dobb and Joan Robinson, she pictured Keynes as a theorist above other approaches to business cycles even if certain of his ideas resembled those of other schools. The socialization of investment was an idea that brought Keynes close to left-leaning policies, but again, as he was defending the capitalist system, he was a reformer, not a revolutionary, she underlined (222).

The topic of her thesis was "Equilibrium in a Static Economy According to J. R. Hicks." Based on it, she wrote *Indifference Curve Analysis According to J. R. Hicks* (1947). In these two studies, she discussed extensively Hicks' *Value and Capital*, trying to associate the views of Alfred Marshall and Vilfredo Pareto with those of the neoclassical school. She credited Hicks for trying to make subjective value theory more convincing, introduced his indifference curve approach (321), but reminded that, despite its formal superiority, the Hicksian approach was too abstract and distant from a dynamic perspective of consumer behavior (324). In all, Goudi demonstrated familiarity with cutting-edge economic research and enhanced the ideas of the neoclassical school.

During the academic year 1948–9, she enrolled at Harvard as a Rockefeller scholar and obtained a MA in Economics. Her thesis was supervised by Alvin Hansen. Before returning to Greece, she spent a semester at the University of Chicago and attended classes with Lloyd Metzler and Frank Knight. It is worth noting that immediately after her return, she wrote a review of *Theory of Games and Economic Behavior* by John von Neumann and Oskar Morgenstern, a sign that she had absorbed discussions taking place in American academia.

Her next monograph was *Observations on the Problem of Exports after the Readjustment* (1950), an empirical investigation of the major issue of the Greek balance of payments under an unsettled monetary regime. She expanded this study to an "ifigessia" on "The Readjustment of Exchange Rate Parity" that she defended in 1954. She emphasized, for the first time in Greek literature, the deficit of the balance of payments as the permanent economic problem for economic policymakers. Her empirical investigation concluded that the cost of production in Greece was a push factor that obstructed exports (8–9). The result was the drain of reserves and the need to devalue. This outcome seemed, for Goudi, very short-term. A new start for Greek exports should not only be based on a new exchange rate, but on a market-driven approach to the balance of payments problem, as well. She criticized the existing system of subventions given to Greek exporting companies to allow them to sell their products cheaper abroad. Her recommendation was that these interventions were distorting the market. She computed the effect of currency devaluation on the export performance of individual products, while dismantling exports from all existing interventions. She concluded that the exchange rate introduced in April 1953 was very close to accomplishing the goal of a restart of the export effort.

As already evident, Goudi dealt mostly with monetary issues in her works. This was the result of her preoccupation with business cycle theory and economic dynamics in general. From 1955 onward, she taught at the University of Athens. She became an adjunct professor in 1968 and a full professor only in 1978. This was proof of discrimination against women in Greek universities during these times. She was a democrat, and her colleague, Ioannis Koulis, objected to her promotion during the dictatorship.

In 1962, she published the work *How General Is Contemporary Theory of Economic Development?* Starting with the distinction between development and growth as concepts used in economic literature, she turned to Roy Harrod and Evsey Domar, crediting them with the effort to introduce Keynesian-type thinking into the problems of less developed countries to which Keynes himself had not contributed. Goudi found, however, that developing countries didn't face effective demand shortages, as might have been the case in developed countries. In economically lagging countries, according to Goudi, disproportionalities existed in the labor and the commodities markets, and monetary developments played an important role in the economic process, especially if they were distorting market outcomes. What was needed, for her, was more emphasis on the supply side if one wanted to assist growth and development and alleviate poverty.

In her *On Money*, part of her lectures on money and banking, published in 1967, Goudi combined theoretical competence with practical experience, offering in a condensed form a tour de force in monetary economics. She defended the monetarist approach, but allowed however in her analysis of inflation psychological and behavioral explanations, especially for less developed countries.

Goudi was intensively involved from 1945 to 1970 as a high-ranking official at the Bank of Greece, writing memos and recommending action. Her published record demonstrated the post-World War II turn of Greek economics to the Anglo-Saxon mainstream. From 1950 to 1967, she also managed EPOE and wrote editorials and book reviews for the journal.

6.3.4 Koutsoyiannis

Anna Koutsoyiannis started working as a young academic researcher in Greece and succeeded in continuing her remarkable academic career in England and Canada.

She obtained a degree in Economics at ASOEE in 1954 and proceeded to earn a PhD at the University of Manchester in 1962 on "An Econometric Study of the Leaf Tobacco Market of Greece." Upon returning to Greece, she taught Economic Analysis as a lecturer at the Highest School of Industrial Studies in Piraeus. The title of the course she taught indicated modern micro and macro theory with the use of algebra and mathematics in economic analysis. She collaborated with *Studies* (Spoudai), the peer-reviewed journal of the school, and worked as a project director at the newly founded KEPE.

She was named ifigitria with a study on *Production Functions in Greek Industry* and started teaching at the University of Thessaloniki from 1964 onward. Together with economist Anastasia Gana from KEPE, she published *Input-Output Table for the Greek Economy for 1960* in 1967. Facing, however, difficulties as a democrat to pursue an academic career because of the dictatorship, she decided to emigrate to England. There, she taught Economics at the University of Lancaster from 1968 to 1975, and later moved to Canada, first at the University of Waterloo (1975–83), and then at the University of Ottawa, until her passing in 1986.

Koutsoyiannis rose to superior fame among economists and was included by Mark Blaug in his *Who's Who in Economics* (1986), with two textbooks she published: the first in 1973, *Theory of Econometrics,* and the second in 1979, *Modern Microeconomics*. Both books avoided mathematization for its own sake and the teaching of economics based on abstract foundations. Koutsoyiannis opted for an experimental approach to estimating economic models, one where observation would lead to modelling (1973, 23). She was critical of those who were supporting models without any relevance in empirical reality as the mainstream was doing according to her.

In her 1979 textbook, she provided the basics for a critical microeconomics focusing on oligopoly theory as the dominant market form in modern economies rather than perfect competition. According to her, the main assumptions of neoclassical microeconomic theory could not explain the real world in its complexity and needed to be amended. She also wrote articles in industrial organization and oligopoly theory. Using empirical data, she showed that in modern markets, firms preserved their status by creating barriers to entry to other firms (Koutsoyiannis 1984). Her loss at a young age was a blow to critical microeconomics and to economics in general.

6.3.5 Negreponti-Delivani

Maria Negreponti-Delivani obtained her first degree from the University of Thessaloniki with distinction and went with a scholarship from the French government to the University of Paris-Sorbonne, where, in 1959, she obtained a state PhD (Doctorat d' Etat) in Economics with a thesis on "L' Influence du Développement Économique sur la Repartition du Revenu National." In the same year she married Professor Dimitrios Delivanis, her mentor.

After returning to Thessaloniki, she became an ifigitria in 1961 with *The Economic Development of Northern Greece since 1912* and started teaching at the

University of Thessaloniki and at the Graduate School for Industrial Studies of Thessaloniki. In 1970, she was elected full professor there and became rector of the same institution in 1984 and in 1985–8, the first woman economist in Greece to rise to this prestigious position.

Her many honors include consulting posts in the Greek government and in the Organization for Economic Co-operation and Development (OECD). She has been a visiting professor at the University of California at Berkeley and the European University in Florence. She was also very active in the association of French-speaking economists, as well as in Greek politics, both local and national. She was, and still is, a prolific author of numerous books and articles in Greek, French, and English.

Negreponti-Delivani was one of the economists of the new generation who started teaching "Economic Analysis," meaning micro- and macro-economic theory. Her first textbooks, published between 1969–72, used mathematical analysis and helped Greek students cope with recent developments in economic theory, when older textbooks were descriptive and of a historical-encyclopedic nature. She developed an interest not only in economic theory, but in applied economics, too. At the beginning of her career, she taught and researched in the history of economic thought. Her ifigessia on the economic development of Northern Greece was a chance for her to explore regional development and public finance. In more recent books, she analyzed the structure of the Greek industry, small and medium enterprises in Greece, the shadow economy, the Greek public debt, and unemployment in the country. She also published on international political economy. In these publications, she focused on structural weaknesses of the Greek economy and rejected monetarist and neoclassical policies to reduce Greek inflation in the 1980s and early 1990s. More recently, she became one of the most outspoken commentators of developments in Greece after 2010, defending the return to the drachma and an autonomous path of growth for Greece.

6.4 Developments in Academia

Academic life in Greece did not change much during the 25 years after World War II. After the first appointments initiated by Andreas Andreadis, a second generation of economists followed during the 1930s and up to 1942. Some younger economists entered the scene in the 1950s, and a few in the 1960s. Perhaps the biggest breakthrough of this period occurred with the appearance of women in Greek economics.

Existing numbers dating from 1967 reveal that out of 33 economists who occupied a university post from the 1920s to the late 1960s in all Greek universities, 20 had done their PhDs in Greece, 9 in Germany, 4 in France, 2 in the UK, 1 in the USA, and 1 in Switzerland. Four professors held two PhDs, one from Athens and a second from a foreign university. Twenty-two out of the 33 had done an ifigessia and 16 out of them submitted it at the Law school in Athens – 4 did so in Thessaloniki and 2 at ASOEE. Three out of the 33 professors had obtained their positions in the 1920s, 3 in the 1930s, 13 in the 1940s, 10 in the 1950s, and only 4 in the 1960s (Psalidopoulos 1997). In short, economics in Greece remained decisively introverted and, despite the work and influence of foreign-trained economists, the reproduction of economics in Greece was the work of those who, having worked close to important academics, had succeeded them and kept economics a nationally determined science. German/French influences were dominant, and the University of Athens remained, through the ifigessia process, the primary channel to enter Greek academia. The qualification for getting a university chair remained, until 1982, very low: what was needed according to the law was a PhD, possibly an ifigessia, and just one publication. Any new position was filled through a majority vote of the members of the specific faculty. The voting body usually followed the recommendation of a select committee consisting of those three members of the faculty who were more closely associated with the subject advertised with the new position. The Ministry of Education was obliged to appoint the person elected.

The university system remained very closely modeled after the German one, as it had also been in the past. From the academic year 1955–6 onward, the minimum time required to obtain a first degree was expanded from three years of study to four. Lecturing needs were frequently covered by assistants (without a PhD), epimelites/caretakers of the chair (with a PhD), by ifigites, and by the existing ordinary professors themselves.

Postgraduate training in economics was completely absent and remained so until the 1990s. PhD candidates were encouraged to travel abroad. If they opted to write their thesis in Greece, they had to follow courses of their supervisors, a practice that was not institutionally required by the university for the degree. In the late 1960s, there were a lot of MAs and PhDs from the UK and the USA familiar with the then mainstream ideas and techniques in economics, thinking of themselves as bearers of a new spirit, eager to enter the prestigious university jobs but unable to do so due to scarce openings. This was going to change in the 1970s.

6.4.1 University of Athens

Developments at the University of Athens were set in motion due to two departures from staff. Kyriakos Varvaressos resigned from his position in 1949, and Angelos Angelopoulos was dismissed from his in 1946.

These two chairs were occupied by Demosthenis Stefanidis in 1951 and Ioannis Koulis in 1949. Ioannis Pesmazoglou became an ifigitis in 1950, and so did Marina Goudi in 1954. Nikolaos Giannakopoulos and Panagiotis Pavlopoulos followed in the mid-1960s. These academics undertook the task, together with a group of assistants, to educate economics students at the University of Athens until the early 1970s.

6.4.1.1 Stefanidis

Stefanidis was elected at the University of Athens to fill the void of Varvaressos in 1951. The election process took a long time, as Zolotas did not favor his appointment, but his opinion did not prevail.

Stefanidis continued to be a very conservative thinker. He had, however, set aside his glorification of totalitarianism of the past. From 1945 to 1951, he published five books. First came his lectures on Agricultural Policy and on Trade Policy from his early career, and then a book on *Greeks and Bulgarians*, a geopolitical treatise (1945). His next opus was the three-volume *Social Economics in its Historical Evolution* (1948–50), a valuable and exhaustive history of economic thought from ancient times to that day. All these works were very detailed analyses, full of references, abundant in historical material, and in proposals for government action. Legal arrangements were also present in his writings.

Four years before his retirement, in 1961, Stefanidis published his *National Economic Policy*. This was a volume of 15 essays, some of them abbreviations of interwar books he had written, others original and touching upon contemporary economic policy issues. As he confessed in his introduction, he chose the title deliberately to express his commitment to "nationalism and socialism in the sense of the worldview that relegates in an inferior position the interests of the individuals against the interests of the society that houses them" (1961, 6). His older essays were full of new updated references, and it was clear that Stefanidis stuck to his critique against global capitalism. He was in favor of the industrialization of the country (1961, 49) but pointed out the weaknesses of Greek businessmen who sought security of profits before any investment decision (89). The inflow of foreign capital in Greece was not a panacea and the government needed to transform the country into a creditor one, instead of allowing companies from abroad to exploit existing resources (25).

He pleaded for a psychological unification of the Greek people around a development agenda that would restructure productive activities on a new basis (121). Foreign assistance and reparation payments were welcome, but Greece needed to rely on its own resources and not expect equal treatment in world trade (120). The emigration of unemployed or underemployed citizens to other European countries would prove disastrous for the Greek economy. Stefanidis compared the economic performance of the interwar period with other epochs and concluded that the Greek economy would take off only if it relied on a numerous and robust labor force (147). Coming to the discussion taking place in the late 1950s/early 1960s about the association of Greece with the EEC, Stefanidis declared bluntly that "what Germany could not enforce through the strength of arms, it was trying to achieve peacefully" (176) by co-creating the EEC. An immediate accession of Greece to the EEC would be "a national suicide" (191), he opined. Recalling his past ideas about winners and losers in world trade, he was critical of what was brewing at a European level and afraid that the Greek economy would lose any chances it had to become economically independent (198–9). The history of international commercial relations since the dawn of capitalism led him to the conclusion that Greek economic policy needed to aim at the extension of the national market and not focus on abandoning protection (215–38).

We conclude that Stefanidis remained a nationalist, faithful to the ideas he inherited from his early studies in Germany. His views about foreign trade not being supportive of growth in less developed countries echoed arguments articulated by the Economic Commission for Latin America of the UN. He had identified the dictatorship of Metaxas in Greece as a possible vehicle to a new development path for the country and remained throughout his life a believer in strong state involvement in the economy. His approach, dormant over many decades, resurfaced in a new guise after the crisis of 2010.

6.4.1.2 Koulis

Ioannis Koulis took a law degree at the University of Athens and worked in the 1930s as a general secretary for the AOS (1934–40). His thesis in 1939 was "On Fiscal Monopolies" and was supervised by Angelos Angelopoulos. During the occupation period, he studied in Munich where he took a second doctorate with "Basic Questions on Public Credit" supervised by Fritz Terhalle in 1943. He became an ifigitis in 1949 with a monograph on *Public Expenditure from an Economic Perspective* (also published in German in 1948), an associate professor in 1955, and a full professor for public finance and fiscal law in 1959. During the dictatorship, between 1971 and 1973, he was Minister of Finance and, therefore, after the restoration of democracy, he was dismissed from public service. He passed away in 1977.

Koulis' approach to public finance departed from the interwar German mainstream and the views of his supervisor Angelopoulos. In his *Social Arrangement of Taxation or Economic Tax Policy?* (1948), he advocated the abandonment of a taxation aimed at social goals. He also dismissed a tax system aimed at economic development goals. What was needed, for him, was just a tax policy that would ensure revenue for the government without burdening the private economy. Nothing more. Social aims advocated by political parties should not be achieved through a strong tax-state. This was, for Koulis, perhaps popular in the late 19th century, when social cohesion was a government priority, but not anymore. In times of antagonism, of opposing economic systems, and of the need to promote a strong private economic sector, capitalism needed low taxes, he stressed.

The same conservative attitude in public finance was articulated by Koulis in his *The Tax Burden in Greece* (1950), where he argued, as Zolotas had almost 20 years before, that the tax burden was quite heavy on households and businesses and that economic growth was dependent on lighter tax rates for businesses. In another monograph, he kept his distance from countercyclical policy (*Public Finance and Fiscal Policy*, 1954), arguing that government activity should be restrained and cautious when it came to interventions in the economy. From the mid-1950s, he turned his attention to the reform of the Greek tax system, providing insights at times when the reform of the income tax was passing parliament (*On a Unified Tax System*, 1955). He wrote on *Public Creditworthiness* (1956) and on the best possible tax incentives so that the private sector could invest more (*Tax Incentives, in Greece in Particular,* 1957).

After becoming a full professor, he wrote teaching manuals and remained faithful to fiscal restraint and a conservative approach to the role of the state in the economy. Government could shape the economy by demonstrating necessities but should not interfere if there were no resources to support any involvement. His conservatism led him to accept serving the military dictatorship as a Minister of Finance with dire consequences for his academic career.

6.4.1.3 Pesmazoglou

Ioannis Pesmazoglou was one of the most prominent economists of his generation. He obtained two degrees: one in Law and a second in Political and Economic Sciences, both from the University of Athens in 1939 and in 1940 respectively. He submitted a PhD at the University of Athens on "Labor Market and Labor Employment" in 1945. His supervisor was Xenophon Zolotas. He proceeded with a scholarship from the British Council to study at the University of Cambridge in the UK, where he submitted a thesis on "Certain Aspects of the International Transmission of Cyclical Fluctuations, 1870–1913," in 1949. His supervisor was Dennis Robertson.

After his return to Greece, he became an ifigitis at the University of Athens in 1950. He worked at the Ministry of Economic Coordination and from there he moved in 1955 to the Bank of Greece, first as an advisor to Governor Zolotas, then as its Vice Governor in 1960. He was the chief negotiator of the association agreement with the EEC in 1961. After 15 years of teaching as an ifigitis, he was elected associate professor in March 1967 for an initial term of three years. The imposition of the dictatorship affected his tenure. Being an outspoken democrat, he clashed with the junta and was persecuted. After the restoration of democracy, instead of returning to academia, he opted to enter politics. He served in the Greek and in the European parliament for the next 20 years. He also became a member of the Academy of Athens.

In 1939, still a student, he had written *The Subjective Theory of Value* (1939), a comparative study that sought to identify similarities and differences between the Austrian, the Walrasian, and the Cambridge approaches in value theory. Gustav Cassel's definition of value, which was accepted by his mentor, Zolotas, was also discussed by Pesmazoglou.

His thesis in Greece was based on an extensive study of German and English literature, with the approach of the Stockholm School being also part of the analysis. He identified his contribution in line with the Keynesian effort to scrutinize weak aspects of classical theory. Starting from a methodologically individualist angle, Pesmazoglou was led to conclude that the neoclassical approach couldn't explain the determination of the wage level in a satisfactory way. Labor supply possessed a negative elasticity when the real wage fell under a socially accepted minimum and classical theory didn't consider this reality. The preference Pesmazoglou showed for empirical relevance brought him closer to the approach of Paul Douglas, rather than John Hicks, and certain Keynesian arguments about the peculiarities of the labor market were also visible in his study.

In the same year he wrote *On Transports in General and Especially in Greece* (1945), where he addressed the issue of infrastructures and their importance for the extension of the Greek market under existing circumstances then. Their significance for future development and growth was more than apparent in his view.

His UK thesis concentrated on economic fluctuations in the USA, Britain, France, and Germany over a period of 40 years before World War I and submitted existing material to econometric testing. The period from 1870 to 1914 associated with industrial expansion and relative stability was a period worth investigating at times of a complex institutional world and of government interventions.

Pesmazoglou applied macrodynamic correlation analysis, aiming to grasp the movements and interrelations of economic aggregates in the four industrialized countries he investigated. He initially discussed theoretical explanations of the business cycle by Jan Tinbergen and Mihal Kalecki, and then approached statistical data and variables, specified his analysis, and discussed these data in tandem with historical developments in the countries under investigation. The relation of business cycles with the evolution of interest rates was also part of the analysis, as were expectations of investors. Pesmazoglou offered calculations that confirmed the importance of the marginal propensity to consume as the most important factor for industrial expansion in the countries under investigation. He discussed the acceleration of investment in relation to exports and consumption. Despite differences in structure and industrial potential in the countries under investigation, he emphasized that the empirical evidence suggested income levels and demand were the crucial factors of industrial fluctuations in a tranquil, liberal global environment.

Shortly after the defense of this thesis, Pesmazoglou published his results split into six articles in prominent English, German, and French periodicals such as *Oxford Economic Papers*, *Weltwirtschaftliches Archiv,* and *Revue d' Economie Politique*. He thus set a high standard for other Greek economists and won recognition for his laborious study. His contribution was recognized as an ifigessia from the University of Athens, and he started his teaching career first with classes in money and banking and later with courses in macroeconomics and in the theory and policy of economic development.

Pesmazoglou was, as mentioned, both an academic and a high-ranking civil servant. He witnessed and co-organized the transition of the Greek administration from post-war reconstruction to negotiations with EFTA and later with the EEC before joining the central bank. During these years, he wrote *Developments and Prospects for the Greek Economy* (1957) and *Greece in Face of Tendencies of European Economic Unification* (1958), where he combined economic theory with applied policy questions, theorizing and suggesting paths to growth for the Greek economy. He later wrote *The Association of Greece with the EEC* (1962), explaining the importance of the historical step the Greek economy made toward multilateral economic cooperation that would promote exports and adjust the economy to modern standards. He repeated and enriched his arguments in favor of international economic cooperation in French and German publications during the mid-1960s.

In 1965, he turned his attention to *The Relation Between Monetary and Fiscal Policy*. This monograph was not oriented toward the dilemma posed between Keynesians and Monetarists. It was a treatise on applied economics and economic developments in Portugal, Spain, Greece, and Turkey from the mid-1950s to the present. Empirical evidence suggested that the growth of consumption led to housing bubbles and high inflation in these countries, instead of functioning as an incentive for investment in industry. His analysis led him to suggest that what was desirable was the control of total liquidity and the channeling of home savings and foreign investment toward productive investment and export-oriented activities. Fiscal policy, according to his view, needed to be tailored toward this goal and instead of promoting the use of idle resources and aiming at full employment it needed to assist the overcoming of structural obstacles for productive investment.

Pesmazoglou cited material that suggested that in Spain and in Turkey, in particular, investment promoted by public corporations was nurturing inflation and not growth. Inflation and high interest rates in Southern European countries were, for him responsible for short-term, speculative decisions by businesses, and for this reason, the taming of inflation was an indispensable variable in the development process. In other words, and using the Greek experience as a guide, Pesmazoglou suggested a path to growth based on stability rather than excessive spending.

His decision after 1974 to devote himself entirely to politics was not in line with the interests of students of Economics, as they lost a gifted teacher. It was, however, favorable for the Greek political arena that could profit from his wide experience as a policy planner and his solid theoretical and empirical approach to economics.

6.4.1.4 Giannakopoulos

Nikolaos Giannakopoulos received his first degree from the University of Athens and proceeded to do a PhD at the University of St. Andrews in Scotland. He worked at the Bank of Greece and as an epimelitis to the Chair of Professor Zolotas from 1964 to 1969. In 1969 he was named an ifigitis with a monograph on *The Application of Solutions of Neumann, Morgenstern, and Nash on Bilateral Monopoly*. In this capacity, he taught courses in Economic Analysis, Theory and Policy of Economic Development, Monetary Theory and Policy, and Trade Theory, and co-edited and wrote textbooks and articles until 1975, when he became a professor at the Highest School of Industrial Studies in Pireaus. He remained active in teaching and research until his retirement.

6.4.1.5 Pavlopoulos

Panagiotis Pavlopoulos obtained his first degree from ASOEE in 1956 and a PhD from the University of Manchester in 1963 with a thesis on “A Statistical Model for the Greek Economy.” He submitted an ifigessia at the University of Athens on “Supply Functions of Agricultural Products” in 1968 and was elected first as an extraordinary professor in 1970 and then as a full professor in 1973. He retired in 1997.

Before assuming academic duties, he served as an economist at the Ministry of Economic Coordination. He was deputy director at KEPE (1971–3) and ran the

Foundation of Economic and Industrial Research (IOBE) from 1985 to 1990. His research focused initially on microeconomics and later on applied issues as the shadow economy, privatizations, Greek–EU economic relations, and the tourist sector.

6.4.2 ASOEE

In ASOEE, vacancies emerged due to the passing of Professors Charitakis and Tournakis during Nazi occupation. Professor Pindaros Christodoulopoulos from Thessaloniki partly filled this void. Dimitrios Kalitsounakis continued his teaching, writing, and publishing his journal, *AOKE*, until 1960. Aristotelis Sideris was elected in 1943 to teach Economic History and the History of Economic Thought, whereas Athanassios Sbarounis was elected as professor of public finance one year later. Other economists were appointed to cover business economics, accounting, and the private economy. As was the custom of the day, all ASOEE professors usually published lengthy textbooks in their fields of expertise to assist students in their individual study after a few years in office.

6.4.2.1 Sbarounis

Athanassios Sbarounis held a PhD from ASOEE on "The Taxation on Net Income" and a second one from Lausanne in Law. He worked during the 1930s at the Ministry of Finance and left the country secretly during the occupation to join the Greek government in exile. He was a member of the Greek delegation at Bretton Woods and wrote *Thoughts on a Post-War Viable Greece* in 1945 and *Studies and Reminiscences from the Second World War* in 1950. These studies included a full description of the Greek economy under the Axis occupation, the post-war negotiations between the allies and Greek authorities, and the need for economic policy to secure the best possible policy mix to accelerate growth in the country through government monitoring and initiatives for private sector activity. After his appointment, he published only textbooks.

6.4.2.2 Chalkiopoulos

Giorgos Chalkiopoulos was elected professor of political economy in 1959. He held both a Law and an Economics degree from the University of Athens since 1936 and proceeded to defend his thesis "On the Theory of Wage Policy" in 1943. He submitted his ifigessia in 1945 on *The Price Mechanism in a Socialist Society* and taught at the University of Athens until 1950 and from then, until his election in ASOEE, at the Highest School of Industrial Studies in Pireaus.

Chalkiopoulos investigated the determination of wages based on the contributions of John Hicks and Paul Douglas in the first part of his thesis. He followed the standard interpretation that wages were determined by the marginal productivity of labor, admitting however that the supply of labor was inelastic and therefore oscillations of the wage from its competitive level could occur. He further investigated the influence of the inflation rate on wages and distinguished between nominal and real wages, trying to sort out any causal relations between the two. The second part of the thesis was devoted to an investigation of effects of higher wages on labor productivity and on the reorganization of the production process through the substitution of factors of production. Keynesian themes, such as the higher propensity to save among rich consumers and the higher one to spend among wage earners, were leading to imbalances in the real economy. Arthur C. Pigou's insights from his *Theory of Wages* were also incorporated into the analysis, as was the case with effects of economic upswings and downturns in the economy. Chalkiopoulos admitted that a theory of wages incorporating all parameters influencing its level was difficult to propose and get accepted, but he was however optimistic that current contributions would offer a satisfactory solution to the problem posed by economic theory.

The eclectic and open-ended approach adopted by Chalkiopoulos in his thesis was also applied in his ifigessia. The arguments in favor of the possibility of applying the price system in a socialist economy as propagated by Enrico Barone and Oscar Lange were discussed, as were the counterarguments of Ludwig von Mises, Lionel Robbins, and Friedrich von Hayek. Although he kept a distance from purely ideological positions, Chalkiopoulos found merit in the possibility of determining prices in a socialist economy and distinguished between temporary and final prices in this process. From consumer prices, he moved to the determination of prices of capital goods and to distribution. Here, he incorporated insights from Keynesian theory, finding the determination of full employment equilibrium a similar problem to the determination of "right" prices in a socialist system.

Chalkiopoulos continued to publish on employment theory and wage developments, but also started writing on monetary issues and Greek external economic relations. Economic development and growth were also preferred topics of research for him in the mid to end 1960s. In 1967, he edited *Long Term Trends of the Greek Economy*, a volume co-written by 25 young economists for the (Greek) Royal Institute of Research. This was a stocktaking investigation that aimed at depicting what had happened in the past 15 years in the Greek economy and suggesting measures for improvement. Chalkiopoulos was suspended during the dictatorship for six months for disobeying orders by the junta. He served until his passing in 1980.

6.4.2.3 Kokkalis

After having served at the University of Athens as an extraordinary professor without a chair from 1939 to the early 1950s, Kokkalis received the same status in 1963 at ASOEE, where he taught until his retirement in 1970. In the period after World War II, he wrote *Introduction to the Total Theory of Labour* in 1950, in which he suggested that value was based on a combination of both manual and mental labor.

6.4.2.4 Coutsoumaris

Georgios Coutsoumaris was elected as professor in 1964. He had a PhD from the University of Chicago, experience as an economic advisor in Venezuela, and was one of the team that accompanied Andreas Papandreou back to Greece. He succeeded Papandreou at KEPE, commanded research and activities there until 1968, and wrote important books such as *The Morphology of Greek Industry*, a detailed depiction of the industrial sector in the country, its accomplishments, and weaknesses. He also co-authored other books with KEPE economists. His textbook *Economic Analysis,* published in 1967, was a "Samuelson in Greek" kind of manual, totally different from the ones used by older professors. It included micro and macro analysis, equations, and diagrams, thus exposing students to a new kind of approach to economics as a discipline. Coutsoumaris served briefly as a Minister during the dictatorship and was suspended from his duties for one year after 1974. Later, he became the first scientific director of the IOBE, which was established by the Federation of Greek Industries and promoted research related to the needs of Greek businesses (for its history see Politis 2011).

6.4.3 Highest School for Agricultural Studies

Chrysos Evelpidis became a professor at the Highest School of Agricultural Studies in 1954. The school created a chair for economic theory during that time. He studied agronomy and engineering in Montpellier, France, and served in the Greek civil service before becoming a MP and a Minister for the Liberal Party. He started publishing on Greek agriculture as early as 1923, and in 1931 he wrote *The Agricultural Crisis in Greece*, a detailed study on the state of the primary sector with lots of statistical information and policy recommendations. He also wrote *The Balkan States* (1930), a treatise aiming at advancing economic cooperation in the Balkan peninsula at times of global crisis and regional tensions. In 1935 he wrote *The National Income*, a pioneering effort to calculate Greek GDP. With his *Agriculture in Greece* (1944), he was named an ifigitis at the University of Athens, where he taught until he received the appointment at the Agricultural School. In 1948 he wrote *An Introduction to the Social Sciences and to Economics in Particular,* followed by *Utopias and Realities* (1949) and *Economic and Social History of Greece (*1950) following. He also wrote textbooks and manuals on agricultural economics and the interrelation of the primary sector to the whole economy.

6.4.4 Technical University of Athens

Sotirios Agapitidis was appointed at the Technical University of Athens in 1949 and taught Economics to prospective engineers and technocrats. He wrote books and articles on post-war Greek economy, regional economics, social policy, economic development, the effects of land redistribution for Greek agriculture, and on the relationship between technology and economics. He became a Minister during the dictatorship and was suspended from his position for three years after 1974. His collected works were published in five volumes after his passing.

6.4.5 Panteios Highest School for Political Sciences

At "Panteios," Ioannis Paraskevopoulos was a professor of economics until 1961, with Ieronimos Pintos teaching Public Finance until 1961 and regional economics thereafter and up to 1978. In 1961 Angelos Angelopoulos was elected to teach Public Finance but served only up to 1967.

In 1964, Dionisios (Sakis) Karagiorgas started teaching Public Finance as an ifigitis. He held a PhD from the LSE, worked at the Bank of Greece, and modernized the teaching of Public Finance in Greece by following Richard Musgrave's analysis. Early during the dictatorship, he was arrested as a member of a resistance group, sentenced to life in prison, and expelled from the university. He returned to his position in 1974 and reached superior fame as an academic, researcher, and commentator on the Greek economy until his early passing in 1985.

6.4.6 Highest School of Industrial Studies in Piraeus

At the Highest School of Industrial Studies in Piraeus, the lecturing needs were at first covered by freelance lecturers, who held appointments at other institutions. Theoretical and Applied Economics and Public Finance were taught by Georgios Chalkiopoulos (1948–59), Sotirios Agapitidis (1948–64), Andreas Kyrkilitsis (1950–73), Andreas Saounatsos (1959–73), Dimitrios Kollias (1941–65), and Apostolos Lazaris (1962–7 and 1974–81). Kyrkilitsis had been named ifigitis at ASOEE in 1942.

Lazaris belonged to the new generation of post-war economists. He graduated from ASOEE, followed postgraduate studies in Manchester and Rome, and obtained his PhD from the University of Thessaloniki in 1960, with a thesis on "Investment Planning for the Development of Less Developed Countries." In 1961 he was named ifigitis at the University of Athens, with a treatise on "Econometric Investigation of the Optimal Rate of Savings," and in 1962 he was elected professor in Pireaus for economic analysis. He introduced input-output analysis in his lectures. He wrote *Introduction in Economic Analysis* (1964), *Theory of Employment and National Income* (1965), and *Economic Planning* (1967). During the dictatorship, he left Greece, worked for the UN as an economic expert, and after the restoration of democracy, he became active in politics with the socialist party of Andreas Papandreou. During his involvement in politics, he wrote *The Mechanics of Control in the Construction of a Development Plan* (1977), *What Socialism?* (1989), and *At the Dawn of the New Millennium* (2001).

6.4.7 University of Thessaloniki

At the University of Thessaloniki, Dimitrios Delivanis had been elected professor in 1944 and continued tirelessly until his retirement in 1974 to publish books in Greek, French, and German. Dimitrios Santis and Panagiotis Dertilis taught Public Finance until 1962 and from 1944 to 1970, respectively. Antonios Damaskinidis, ifigitis since 1943, taught as a professor of business economics. A further appointment in Political Economy was enacted with Vasilios Vogiatzis. Vogiatzis had studied Pharmacy in Athens and Economics in Munich, where in 1938 he submitted a thesis on "The Structure of Society and the Ideals of Its Ingredients" (*Gesellschaftsstruktur und die Ideale ihrer Zusammmensetzung*). He worked for the Social Security Agency (IKA), and in 1946 he wrote *People without Space*, a study that was published by the Society of Macedonian Studies.

This study opened with the elaboration of the concept of nutritional space. The Greek economy was agricultural and there was a "choking density" of Greek nutrition due to a high population density, monoculture in production, and low income. Monoculture in Greece was not the outcome of an international division of labor. In Latin America, Vogiatzis argued, through monoculture and exports this continent could finance imports of food, but this could not happen in Greece. Industry couldn't solve the problem due to its size and the lack of raw materials. Greece therefore had a "poverty of space" (94) and needed "nutritional space" (99) to be able to feed the entire population. This suggestion a couple of years after the demise of Nazism was supportive of irredentist claims but led to no results due to the politics of the day. In 1948 Vogiatzis was named ifigitis, with *Free Competition and Private Initiative*. He also wrote *Theory and Meaning of Social Policy* (1949), *Some Problems of Theoretical Economics from the Perspective of Social Policy* (1949), and *The Importance of the Human Factor in Economic Development* (1970).

6.4.8 Highest School of Industrial Studies in Thessaloniki

As was the practice in the respective school in Piraeus, initially professors from the neighboring department of the University of Thessaloniki taught classes in economics. Vogiatzis taught from 1958 to 1970, Damaskinidis from 1950 to 1968, and Panagiotis Dertilis from 1951 to 1970. In the course of time, the School started becoming autonomous and elected its own staff. The first chairs in economics were filled by Maria Negreponti-Delivani, Diomidis Psilos, and Charalambos Sepentzis. Psilos was a graduate from Panteios, who did his PhD with Howard Ellis at Berkeley in 1963 at the time of Papandreou's transition to Greece. He worked for KEPE and wrote *Capital Markets in Greece* (1964) and co-authored *Public International Development Planning in Greece* (1964). Sepentzis held a PhD from ASOEE in 1967 and was considered a specialist in development economics and monetary policy. These three economists were in charge when the internationalization of economics knocked on the door of their institution.

6.5 Xenophon Zolotas and Monetary Stability

The first contribution by Zolotas after liberation was a book on the long-run viability of the Greek economy, *Greece Ought to Become Viable* (1945). He opined that after 1922 and due to the influx of the refugees from Asia Minor, the economy had not rebounded due to an asymmetry between land, resources, and population. Interwar economic assistance had blurred the picture, but the Wall Street Crash and Greek default had brought these asymmetries to new levels. The government ought to find ways to reach an optimum path to growth based on the country's resources. In his quite radical *Distribution of Income and Social Exploitation* (1947), he also demanded income redistribution so that society could avoid social injustice.

However, after the proclamation of the Marshall plan, his position shifted. Now Greece could move through industry "from misery … to prosperity" (1948, 14). It was for this reason that he dismissed the Varvaressos report of 1952, as we saw above. Economic policy should, according to Zolotas, aim to absorb funds from abroad, attract foreign investment, invest in industry, and take off economically. Post-war capitalism had transformed itself and the government was not simply monitoring the economy, but intervening actively, thanks to insights of "the great Keynes" (Zolotas 1953, 23). Capitalism was no longer a system of insecurity and mass unemployment, but a system where liberal ideas had merged with socially democratic demands that raised efficiency and market outcomes.

Zolotas was a highly influential academic and an eclectic liberal. His speeches at the IMF meetings in 1957 and 1958 distinguished him internationally, and he was one of the four "wise men" who recommended the transformation of the OEEC to the OECD in 1961. He was a man of action who sought refuge in theory whenever he wanted to support his policies, and not a theorist wanting to implement abstract models into practice. Since his early career, he advocated, as we saw, a "flexible" liberalism. He did not have a high regard for abstract theories, such as those advanced by Austrian economists. He was also not in favor of Keynesian economics and the socialization of investment, despite his courtesy reference to him. He was a moderate monetarist and a believer in sound regulation and oversight of the economy, and this is what he repeated in his various books (Psalidopoulos 2008). He was not a strong supporter of the subjective theory of value but held strongly to the quantity theory of money.

From his long list of books during this period, one stands out, for it encapsulates his economic thought better. The book was published in 1964 and was entitled *Monetary Equilibrium and Economic Development*. There he considered the policy proposals recommended by monetarists and structuralists as one-sided and of little importance for developing countries such as Greece, a country in need of both low inflation and structural changes (11). Historical experience also played a role, and if a country had experienced high inflation in the past that left its mark on citizens and businesses, this should not be underestimated, he stressed (18–19).

Therefore, monetary stability was the start and endpoint for evaluating economic performance. The devaluation of the drachma and the stabilization of the Greek currency in 1953 had to be defended, according to him, at all costs because it was very important for the economy to have a sound monetary base. Individuals would know that their savings would be worth their price, businesses would make sound investment plans, and foreign capital would be thus attracted to invest in the country. Next to monetary stability, and possibly zero inflation, in a country that had witnessed a horrendous inflation between 1940 and 1953, the budget of the central government had to be balanced. Of course, the country was poor, and the need for public investment was high. But the rationale for Zolotas was to keep the current budget balanced; he recommended, therefore, the introduction of a new account, the budget of public investment. This could eventually run a deficit, but it could be covered by loans from abroad, foreign assistance, and/or through public savings.

This is what the central bank practiced during his tenure. The economic/monetary system of Greece was highly regulated. The Currency Committee at the Central Bank oversaw business activity and instructed commercial banks to impose quotas on loans and particular interest rates, according to the size of the applying firm and the nature of its activity. Industrial investments and big companies offering collateral received preferential treatment in this process. This policy ensured positive results in output and employment for Zolotas, and there was no justification to experiment differently in the economy.

In 1959 Zolotas admitted that unemployment was "the gravest problem of our economy" (15) and saw emigration to Belgium and Germany as an unwelcome, but economically sound solution. At the same time, he dismissed the idea of deficit-financed expenditures as "inadmissible under the Greek circumstances" (22) and warned about the increase of imports that could threaten the stability of the balance of payments. As the economy was progressing, Zolotas declared himself open for expenditures in education and public health if the financing was secured and limited. Greece didn't need deficit spending, he opined; it needed more investments (1967, 15).

He supported the association agreement of Greece with the EEC and lamented the freezing of the agreement during the dictatorship as highly disadvantageous for the economy (1973, 5). Despite this freezing, the subsequent delay in the adjustment of the Greek economy to the EU framework and the stagflation of the mid-1970s, he favored the full accession to the EU (1976).

As already mentioned, Zolotas contributed to international political economy at times when the Bretton Woods system was providing cooperation to overcome possible global imbalances (see his 1977). As early as 1957, he suggested that surplus countries should deposit their surpluses as savings at the IMF, so that deficit countries could lend and circumvent their external imbalance. In the 1960s, he suggested that certain currencies as the yen, the pound, and the deutschmark, which were important in international trade, should be accepted, next to the dollar, from the IMF, be backed by gold, and form a part of global liquidity. His proposal was criticized as an indirect attack against the gold-dollar-standard, and he countered with an argument about the need to accommodate the real problem of international monetary stability rather than adhere to the letter of what had been agreed 20 years before (Psalidopoulos 2008, 157–61). In a follow-up intervention, he argued that many investors turned their dollars into gold and proposed that the price of gold should be left to float to avoid speculation due to the weakening of the dollar as an international currency. He thought that speculation was unavoidable and that central banks ought to limit its influence. When the IMF introduced the Special Drawing Rights expressed through an algorithm of currency prices and not in gold,

Zolotas endorsed this step. This didn't prove enough, and Zolotas, going back to Keynes' proposal about the "bancor" in 1944, proposed the "metron," a new international currency to assist global stability. This was not, however, included in the international agenda, and the IMF went on to find other financial tools to assist its members in need.

6.6 Panagis Papaligouras and "Applied" Liberalism

Zolotas found in prominent politician Panagis Papaligouras, the right-hand of Prime Minister Constantine Karamanlis in his successive governments from the 1950s to the 1970s, a counterpart in economic thought and a disciple in policy implementation. Papaligouras was a politician with a liberal, but not ideologically stubborn, credo. The two men shared the same core values and Papaligouras transformed these values into practical everyday policy measures calling his economic philosophy "realist liberalism" in the 1950s and "radical liberalism" in the 1970s (Papaligouras 1996; Psalidopoulos 2023).

Papaligouras started with degrees in Law and in Economics from the University of Athens and in 1937 moved to the Graduate School of International Studies in Geneva, where he obtained a PhD in 1941. During his undergraduate years he developed an interest in Philosophy and started publishing essays on Ancient Greek authors, contributing to the ongoing discussion among Greek intellectuals on what constituted "the Greek spirit." He also investigated the intellectual transformations that were set in motion once Alexander the Great disseminated Greek Thought to the East.

His graduate studies, however, were in International Relations and his thesis was on "The Theory of International Society" (1941). There he discussed international politics of the day, the problems faced by the League of Nations and suggested, among others, a distinction between homogenous societies, democracies that had gone from slavery through feudalism to industrial capitalism, and heterogenous societies that had blurred economic systems and mostly autocratic forms of rule. These two blocks were said to be in continuous geopolitical strife, leading to armed conflicts and economic warfare. This distinction was followed up in research by post-war theorists of international relations such as Raymond Aron and others.

Papaligouras studied economics under Andreadis, Zolotas, and Varvaressos in Greece, and had William Rappard and Wilhelm Roepke as teachers in Geneva. Rappard was a follower of the Austrian School and Roepke a disciple of Walter Eucken, ordoliberalism, and the post-war German "social market economy." All these economists led Papaligouras to his own blend of liberal thought with an emphasis on international economic cooperation. In fact, the Graduate School in Geneva was the birthplace of Globalism (Slobodian 2018), the effort to impose liberal economic principles on a world scale through international institutions, where national economic policies seemed to lead to intervention and disrespect of market outcomes.

Papaligouras was, during his entire political career, a liberal and an advocate of European Integration and global economic governance. He explained early in his career that it was better to enter compromises in politics, so that things could be driven toward the right direction instead of opting for a stubborn ideological position leading to an "all or nothing" situation and abstinence from politics (Psalidopoulos 2023, 116).

After completing his thesis, Papaligouras offered his services to the Greek government in exile and after liberation he assisted the relief and rehabilitation process in Greece from various administrative positions. He became an MP in 1946 and eventually joined the right-wing Papagos government as a Minister of Commerce and later of (economic) coordination. In the latter capacity, he explained in 1954 that the government had opted for a middle way between "inflationary paranoia and deflationary reaction" (Psalidopoulos 2023, 120), and stressed that "we are not liberals in the sense of 19th century classical liberalism. We believe in a realist liberalism adapted to modern theories about the mission of governments and toward international technological developments" (120). This realism involved the recognition of the achievements of the New Deal, and the need for a well-defined social policy, a topic that he frequently touched upon in his speeches. The goals of economic policy after the devaluation of 1953 were, for him, economic growth and monetary stability, and the most difficult issue for policymakers to handle was "the balance of payments problem." To develop industry and aspire for a better economic future, Greece needed to import technological equipment, but on the other hand exports were not high as to guarantee its constant financing. Foreign private investment and government assistance were therefore necessary to ensure industrial growth, and it was for this reason that he personally lobbied in the USA for foreign aid.

Papaligouras continued his efforts to explain the dilemma of Greek economic policy to voters and used his eloquence to support the idea of a Greek association with the EEC. This step involved, according to him, a risk for the Greek economy, but if the prospective partners could be convinced to a fair and balanced agreement with Greece, any negative side effects could be dealt with. The factor that could help the Greek economy grow and maintain monetary stability was the inflow of foreign capital. The negotiations with the EEC foresaw Greek access to European Investment Bank loans for various infrastructural works. Out of government due to disagreements with the Prime Minister between 1958 and 1960, Papaligouras supported the negotiations with the EEC, referring to the economic miracle for Germany after the Zollverein and for Italy after its Unification. In a relevant speech in parliament, he referred however to risks involved that could create regional discrepancies and growth gaps in economic cooperation among nations. In this connection he referred to Keynes and credited his theory with transforming the morally neutral liberal doctrine of the 19th century "to the better system that could assist working people to raise their income" (Psalidopoulos 2023, 135).

Back in government in 1960 as the Minister of Coordination, he was extremely active in fulfilling the task of promoting growth and monetary stability combined with a moderate social policy. Greek agriculture had, in his view, a low productivity due to the average small size of properties, and the cost of Greek primary products was relatively high, meaning low export capability. Industry was raising its contribution to GDP, and the association agreement with the EEC would act as an incentive for more investment. At the same time, the balance of payments would not be posing a grave problem for the economy if the Greek administration would be planning the use of resources and monitoring macroeconomic aggregates. He was therefore supporting the creation of KEPE and all its activities.

All these ideas were present in his speech in parliament on the day of the ratification of the agreement with the EEC. The ratification would be the start of constant negotiations for a better economic future of Greece toward something that history had already proved right: that economic cooperation was an open-ended game. Papaligouras used the scheme that Walt W. Rostow had suggested in his *Stages of Economic Growth*. Greece was at a takeoff stage. A new liberalism and a new socialism had mixed into a new pragmatist approach that his government supported.

In close collaboration with the German government and its vice chancellor, Ludwig Erhardt, he negotiated loans to Greece, as Germany was a surplus country and capable of financing the expansion of its companies abroad. He also opposed the plans of the opposition for an expansionary fiscal policy and for measures to absorb the unemployed instead of leaving them to emigrate. When his party went to opposition, he referred to the "consumption oriented" budget of 1964 (149). The governing Center Union was, for him, "the prophet of consumption" (149). Effective demand could not, however, for Papaligouras, grow the economy "technically" through a government push. Any negative effects on savings would destroy, according to his analysis, what had been achieved until then. Demand was one of the many parameters of economic stability. Believing that through government spending one could keep savings stable, and inflation subdued, was a mistake, according to his view. He repeated these arguments during the dictatorship, when the junta was raising public expenditure to promote growth and, indirectly, to win the approval of society. He also criticized the dictators because of their distance to Europe and for the freezing of the association agreement.

It is therefore clear that Papaligouras believed in a strong, monitoring government that set rules, promoted competition, ensured monetary stability, and practiced limited social policy. This was in line with Walter Eucken's ordoliberalism and the German social market economy. Papaligouras knew Keynes, endorsed his courage and views, but at the same time he interpreted Keynesianism in a conservative way. "Any wage increase has limits in increases in productivity" (202), he opined.

Returning to political power in 1974 as governor of the central bank and as Minister of Coordination, he promoted these ideas further and sought in a full membership with the EEC a solution to Greece's economic dilemmas in times of stagflation.

6.7 Papandreou and Structural Change

Andreas Papandreou was the son of Georgios Papandreou, a popular politician and Prime Minister in 1944 and in 1963–5. After completing his primary education in 1937, Andreas was admitted to the Law School at the University of Athens. His opposition to the dictatorship of Ioannis Metaxas drove him to collaborate with a

Trotskyist group (Papandreou 1973, 68), which caught the eye of Greek security forces. In July 1939, he was arrested and tortured. Being the son of an exiled, yet prominent politician, he was freed after two months without charges. Friends of the family arranged for him to leave in May 1940 for the USA, where he enrolled at the Department of Economics at Harvard. He was awarded a MA in May 1942 and a PhD in October 1943, defending a thesis on "The Location and Scope of the Entrepreneurial Function."

After serving in the US navy and earning American citizenship, Papandreou returned to Harvard as an instructor. His research interests laid in economic methodology, the theory of the firm, and public policy. In 1947 he accepted the position of an associate professor at the University of Minnesota. His first articles started appearing in prestigious journals (Papandreou 1949, 1950). He assisted in the edition of an undergraduate textbook (Naphtalin 1953), headed the Laboratory for Research in Social Relations of the University of Minnesota, and wrote a book on *Competition and Its Regulation* (1954), as well as a survey article of contributions to the theory of the firm (1952). In 1950, after a brief stint at Northwestern, where he stayed for less than a year, he returned to Minnesota as a full professor. In 1955 he moved to the University of California at Berkeley where, in 1956, he assumed the duties of the chairman of the department. Papandreou recruited for the department such economists as Abba Lerner, Howard Ellis, Dale Jorgensen, Hyman Minsky, Irma Adelman, Benjamin Ward, and others, and led the department to a very high reputation in economic education. Beside his administrative duties, he continued working on methodology and experimental economics (Papandreou 1957, 1958).

In 1959, after 20 years abroad, he revisited Greece as a Fulbright scholar to study the Greek economy. His reunion with his father, who was on his way to becoming a Prime Minister, played an important role in his future decisions. From 1960 to 1964, he divided his time between Athens and California. In Greece, he was hired by Constantine Karamanlis, his father's opponent, to build up KEPE. During the same time, he continued publishing in his areas of academic interest and on various aspects of the Greek economy (Papandreou 1962, 1963, 1964, and 1965).

In 1964, he resigned his post at Berkeley and started his second career as a member of parliament in Greece, serving as a Deputy Minister of (Economic) Coordination. He also became the spokesman (of the left-wing) of his father's party, the Center Union. After 15 months in power, the party was dismissed from office in July 1965, by the king, under circumstances bordering on constitutional violation. One month before the general elections of May 1967, which would have resolved the issue and would presumably have brought a triumphant Center Union back into power, a military coup took place. Papandreou was arrested and remained imprisoned for eight months. Torn between his prosecution and a world-wide solidarity movement on his behalf, the military dictatorship released Papandreou on the condition that he would leave the country – which he did. As we will investigate his contributions to economic theory and policy after 1970 in the next chapter, we will turn our attention to his contributions from the times of his studies at Harvard until the imposition of the dictatorship (Psalidopoulos 2010; Zoumboulakis 2023).

During the late 1930s and early 1940s, economics at Harvard flourished and the department hosted such eminent figures as Joseph Schumpeter, Edward Chamberlin, Alvin Hansen, Wassily Leontief, Gottfried Haberler, and Seymour Slichter among its staff (Mason 1982). Harvard's Department of Economics maintained a critical attitude toward the New Deal, and its members became involved in public policymaking only after 1938 (Mason 1982, 423). The department's strengths lay in monetary, fiscal, and agricultural policy, as well as labor relations and anti-trust regulation.

Papandreou enrolled directly at the MA program based on his three-year enrollment at the Law School of the University of Athens. He therefore had a tremendous amount of reading to catch up with to pass the general examination for the PhD in Economics. Papandreou's record shows that he attended the following courses at Harvard (Macrakis 2000, 76–7) during the academic years 1940–1 and 1941–2.

1 Economic Theory (Professors Chamberlin and Haberler)
2 Economic History (Professor Usher)
3 Money and Banking (Professors Williams and Hansen)
4 Fiscal Policy (Professors Williams and Hansen)
5 Industrial Organization and Control (Professors Crum and Mason)
6 Modern Economic Theory and Its Critics (Dr O. H. Taylor)
7 Statistics (Professor Frickey)

Papandreou's dissertation was a 350-page monograph, written in a single year's time – an astonishing achievement. His supervisor was William Leonard Crum, professor of economic statistics. The second reader of the thesis was Dr Hans Staehle, an émigré economist-statistician from Germany, who had been hired at Harvard as a visiting lecturer.

As the academic expertise of the supervisors reveal and as Papandreou himself admitted, the dissertation studied the function of the entrepreneur, not from the perspective of economic theory, but from that of the organization and the structure of the economy during its historical evolution (Papandreou 1943, 1). In its six chapters, economic history played a prominent role. It furnished the historical record, leading from the profit-maximizing individual-entrepreneur to the then-dominant modern corporation that Adolf Berle and Gardiner Means had studied. It was argued that, as the economy passed through different historical stages, the entrepreneurial function underwent fundamental changes. It moved from the competitive stage of the industrial revolution to a monopolistic-competitive one of the early 20th century. At the time of the writing of the thesis, Papandreou argued that the economy was dominated by state entrepreneurial activity.

A central part of the thesis was devoted to the study of the modern corporation as a "concrete social force" (1943, 12). The main entrepreneurial innovations associated with the modern corporation were, first, that decisions became collective rather than personal, and second, that the decision-making process was gradually becoming indirect, in the sense that decisions had to be submitted to technical personnel with specialized knowledge and skills, who advised owners and managers on how to reach decisions.

A further chapter was devoted to problems faced in the "quasi-public" corporations, whose stocks were owned by individuals, the government, and/or semi-public authorities. The next, empirical, chapter, which formed the core of Papandreou's contribution, examined patterns of ownership and entrepreneurship in the 200 largest US corporations. He devised a new classification system that took account of different empirical situations in these enterprises. He developed a statistical technique and a coefficient indicating the type of enterprise according to the form of entrepreneurship. His empirical study indicated that in only 1/8th of cases did entrepreneurship and ownership in the USA coincide. This confirmed his hypothesis that a new phase of entrepreneurial activity, centered more on collective decision-making, was already taking shape in the USA.

The last chapter was devoted to state entrepreneurship. State economic activity was predicted by Papandreou to increase significantly in the future, with the entrepreneurial function moving closer to the public sphere. In his words "the owner of productive wealth will have been reduced to a rentier" (325) and the government would have to "keep up the profitability of investment (and) to guarantee relatively full employment" (229). State actors would have to consider potentially adverse effects of their actions on the economy. Private initiative and decision-making would still constitute pillars of the economic system in the future, but the locus of the entrepreneurial function would move "from the private to the public sphere" (350).

Papandreou's study of the entrepreneurial function was an original contribution that emphasized the structure of power and decision-making in large modern corporations. It was a mainstream study that capitalized on all previous discussions about big enterprises and economic activity, many of which had been produced while the New Deal was progressing. It was also a study that approached business activity from an evolutionary perspective, trying to draw a distinction between the private and the collective, at a crucial historical junction: the aftermath of World War II.

Although Papandreou had a solid mathematical training in Economics and was very capable of using it, he was, from the very start of his career, suspicious of pure theory, and, reflecting perhaps the intellectual climate of his Harvard years, viewed Economics as a social science that should maintain its contact with other disciplines, such as sociology and psychology. Methodologically, he accepted human rationality and the maximization postulate as assumptions in economic reasoning but was opposed to deductively formulated theory. To him, pure theory was tautological. He was convinced, however, that by manipulating the maximization postulate, inspired by the works of Samuelson (1947) and Duesenberry (1949), economists could turn pure theory into a source of operationally meaningful theorems (Papandreou 1950).

According to him, contemporary economics was divided into two parts: a back room where a conceptual scheme was designed to impose restrictions upon economic analysis, and a front room, where a system of equations or a list of given variables was tested by applied economists.

Papandreou called for a widening of the back room of economics and, following Talcott Parsons (1949, 43), believed that the value system of the society in which human behavior was studied must find somehow a place in the action framework employed in the analysis. If economics was to base itself only on the rationality postulate, he argued, it could build a theory of universal validity by avoiding all psychological and sociological commitments – but at too high a cost. The universality of the propositions of pure theory, if the back room of economics were to become bigger, would have to be reduced, but its range of meaningfulness would be broadened.

Papandreou did not provide concrete enrichments of the back room of economics. He just stressed the need to experiment with less general, but more useful, realistic constructions, while remaining open-minded and aware of achievements in other sub-disciplines of the social sciences.

In his *Economics as a Science* (1958), Papandreou set out to investigate the methodological nature of comparative statics, by using the arsenal of symbolic logic and set theory. He put forward the proposition that economists devoted too little attention in their research to the identification of the "social space" of their theories.

According to Papandreou, if an economist constructed a theory, but failed to characterize the social space in which it was applicable, then he hadn't really put forward a theory, only a model. A theory possessed the additional attribute of falsifiability. If it was applied and predicted badly, it was rejected. A model, however, had only the criterion of acceptance in that, if it was applied to a given instance and it provided the correct result, it was accepted for that instance. Models, and thus, in other words, most of economics, had at best *ex-post facto* explanatory power. It was therefore natural for Papandreou that public policy authorities would act based on models selected for their *ex-post facto* explanatory power, rather than their predictive power. For Papandreou, this meant that economics had limited value as a science, and this was something that economists should admit openly. On the other hand, he conceded that if the applied economist used mathematics with a full understanding of its limits, he could avoid sterile formalism and contribute to the progress of economics.

In a follow-up publication in 1963, Papandreou insisted that the practice of economists centered around the construction of taxonomic models, which, when anchored to some space-time segment, became descriptions of that segment, and could be tested with reference to data from that segment. If tested and confirmed, they constituted a prediction.

To distill reality into existing theory, Papandreou pioneered experimental economics. He conducted two different experiments (1953 and 1957) to show how economic theory was related to reality. In the first, the objective was to test the hypothesis that individual preference systems satisfied the axiom of transitivity. The axiom was formulated in stochastic terms, and the experiment strongly supported the hypothesis. However, the sample of subjects and choices was randomly selected and not representative of any known population, rendering any generalizations out of these results quite problematic. In his second experiment, Papandreou tested the theory of choice both in a stochastic and in a probabilistic form. These papers confirmed that Papandreou was a pioneer in experimental economics, an accomplishment still not fully acknowledged.

In his first contribution to microeconomics (1949), Papandreou based himself on Nicholas Kaldor's suggestion (1934, 1935) that types of market organization could be determined by reference to elasticities and cross elasticities of demand – an approach that had found its best exposition in Robert Triffin's *Monopolistic Competition and General Equilibrium Theory* (1940). However, Papandreou felt that the Kaldor and Triffin approach was incomplete because it only used demand phenomena to classify markets and wanted to enrich it by incorporating aspects of the supply side.

Papandreou was particularly critical of Triffin's statement that under perfect competition, cross elasticity of demand was infinite, and showed that on the contrary, it became zero in terms of actual or realizable changes in the volume of sales. To prove his claim, Papandreou introduced a coefficient he defined as the "coefficient of penetration," indicating a rise in the market share. His coefficient considered the capacity of the firm which attracted additional demand by cutting its price, to match them with additional units of supply. If a firm had constant or declining average costs over a wide range of output, one could assume that the coefficient exceeded zero. If a firm experienced rapidly rising unit costs, the coefficient equaled or approached zero. In the former case, the firm fell within the oligopoly/monopoly form; in the second, it was competitive. Using a combination of cross elasticities and penetration coefficients, Papandreou suggested that market forms should be defined by a combination of both criteria. According to him, five possible market forms existed: atomistic homeopoly, atomistic heteropoly, circular homeopoly, circular heteropoly, and pure monopoly. Atomistic competition meant that neither firm in the market could penetrate the other's market, whereas in circular competition firms could penetrate rival markets. Papandreou admitted that the coefficient of penetration, being an unknown function of cost and demand elasticity, was not easily measurable, and that this was a challenge that would have to be faced by microeconomists.

Contributing to the theory of the firm, Papandreou (1952, 184) tried to broaden the theory of the firm, by viewing the firm as an institution of society. He rejected profit maximization as a framework of analysis. He argued that the firm was a system of communication and coordination under the authority of a peak coordinator, who determined its ends according to "preference-function maximization" – a concept that would need further development, when an economist would consider the firm as a part of the operating market system. The organizational theory of the firm was said to broaden the scope of existing theory by including motivation, uncertainty, and other sociological and psychological dimensions into the analysis. For this reason, it was considered by Papandreou as a superior and more promising way of analyzing the firm. The conclusions of his survey were in line with the results of his thesis, namely that management, unions, and regulators had more power than firm shareholders and financial groups, leading to new structures in the economy and a "new society" (1952, 217).

The concept of workable competition, or "qualified free competition," in the economic system lay at the heart of the textbook written jointly by Papandreou and John Wheeler in 1954. The authors attempted to relate economic analysis, institutional description, and legal interpretation in the study of competitive behavior in markets and its regulation by government authorities. They offered a classification of types of behavior and indicated how each type of behavior corresponded to market forms. The classification included independence, horizontal and vertical coalitions, fusions, and interference of corporations in the market. According to the authors, it would be aggressive behavior, firm size, and conscious cooperation between existing firms, which would call for more government action in the economic system in the future.

Studying the Greek economy in the early 1960s, Papandreou found that "in some sense there is too much government on the Greek economic scene, while there is too little research and too little planning" (1962, 103). Greece's association agreement with the EEC posed the challenge of reallocating resources for the modernization of the country. The whole economy had to become more efficient, and the means to achieve this was the introduction of reforms in education and administration. Industry shouldn't be protected as much as it was, and the oligopolistic structure of the banking system should be dealt with. Papandreou pointed out that two Greek banking complexes controlled 97% of commercial banking and channeled 70% of total credits to the 30 bigger industrial concerns. The existing negative balance of payments was "a symptom of resource misallocation" (102). The limit to growth was due to lack of external financing (101) in times of sluggishness of exports. Income inequalities should be alleviated, and human capital encouraged to flourish (1965). Import substitution seemed the most appropriate strategy for fostering economic growth in Greece, and it could alter the long-run structure of the economy. The striking privileges offered to attract foreign capital to Greece didn't benefit the economy and should be discontinued. Large-scale programmed structural change, based on democratic principles and on criteria of economic efficiency, held the key to future prosperity and growth (1966).

When the Papandreou proposals were partially introduced between 1964–5 in the country, they met with the disapproval of what Papandreou called "the establishment" of Greek political life and led to the overthrow of his father's government. This "establishment" was also present in Papandreou's autobiographical account of Greece in the 1960s, where it was used to account for opposition to attempts by the Center Union to rationalize the rules of the political game and modernize the economy. To Papandreou's mind, the establishment included the palace, the American Embassy, the CIA, and major Greek economic interests. Along with some Greek politicians he labeled as "wholesalers of influence" (Papandreou 1973), the culprits behind the political derailment and the imposition of the junta in 1967.

Papandreou's erudition, rhetoric, and ability to engage in debate set in motion a new kind of economic reasoning in the country. He personified a paradigm followed by many economists. Through the establishment of KEPE, he accelerated economic literacy and set the stage for the internationalization of Greek economics that was to follow in the next decade.

6.8 Camps of Thought

The most important issue for the Greek economists in the post-1945 era was the economic development of the country. The more appropriate strategy to remove obstacles and set accelerated growth in motion was at the heart of articles, books, and pamphlets. In the early 1960s, and up to the late 1970s, the association with the EEC was a further issue of great importance and provoked exchanges of arguments and debates. Three camps or schools of thought, a continuation of the state of economic thought of the interwar years, can be identified concerning these issues: a liberal-dirigiste, a structuralist-interventionist, and a Marxist.

6.8.1 The Liberal Camp

The liberal camp considered economic development as an inevitable process if the institutional framework of the Greek economy was adjusted to principles governed by the logic of the market. Reliance on foreign technical and financial assistance was, for this camp, important in the development process because of the lack of native capital that could be used in the service of large investment projects. Even if there would be a high price to pay in terms of profit repatriation from investment in the country, foreign capital was welcome.

Greek liberals, however, always kept in the back of their minds the idea of strong government action, if needed, in the economy, as the example of Panagis Papaligouras demonstrated. This notion was based mainly on the generally affirmative leaning of postgraduate-trained Greek economists in interwar Germany. Greek liberalism was, to quote Schumpeter, a "political liberalism" (Schumpeter 1954, 394). Policy could be undogmatically interventionist if the outcome would benefit private initiative. Greek liberals, facing the economic misery of the country after the great depression and the Nazi occupation, had developed a broad sense of social policy to include whatever action was necessary, if the financial means to implement it existed. Xenophon Zolotas with his analyses contributed to the flexibility of liberals in their recommendations and approaches.

As expected, this liberal camp espoused Greece's association and later full membership in the EEC, minimizing in various degrees possible negative effects, like the gradual loss of protection of Greek industry and the rights of autonomous economic action in future circumstances. The major figure for this camp was again Professor Zolotas. His journal *EPOE* disseminated these ideas.

There were two distinct phases of editorial policy and contributors: one that lasted from 1944 to the mid-1950s and a second from then until 1967. In the first phase, and especially in the first years of publication, papers in *EPOE* tended to share the then prevailing vision of "full employment in a free society," and were critical of mainstream economics, sometimes even "socialist." In the second phase, which coincided with the editor's tenure as governor of the Central Bank, the pages of the journal got shorter, and the articles were technical and written by economists of the new generation. The views expressed by Zolotas were reproduced by other authors.

Addressing himself to opponents of the Central Bank's policy who pointed out still high rates of unemployment and low productivity of labor in Greek agriculture and services, central bank economist and later Governor, Dimitrios Chalikias, suggested such phenomena could be eliminated by the growth of productive capacity. For him, unemployment in Greece was "of a very different kind than the one which is due to ineffective demand" (Chalikias 1958, 13). The so-called Greek economic problem consisted in "an inability of the economic system to fully employ the available workforce, whatever high monetary demand may be" (Ibid.). Therefore, demand expansion was "wrong and implied high risks" (Ibid., 15) for the economy. What was needed was the elimination of the scarcity of capital through a policy that would encourage saving and promote investment.

The Central Bank, supervising the development process, regarded the tendency of consumption to grow with suspicion in 1956 and considered a possible budget deficit "not acceptable" (Bank of Greece 1959, 22). It tried to adjust the magnitude of total effective demand to the production possibilities of the economy, and not the opposite. The liberal camp formed the majority in the Hellenic Society of Economic Sciences, founded in 1950. The Society numbered 67 full and 56 adjunct members in 1962. Female economists were underrepresented with three and four members respectively. The Society held occasional meetings and published volumes of conferences it hosted every two years. It dissolved after 1974.

6.8.2 The Structuralist Camp

The structuralist-interventionist camp identified Greece not as a less developed European country but rather as a third-world one, torn between political dependence on the Great Powers and economic underdevelopment. What was needed for this camp was strong government action in all fields of social life. If administrative reforms, especially in human capital, were implemented, then a huge developmental potential would reveal itself. Greece could thus create an industrial sector that would upgrade the economy, transforming it to a "European" one. "Fair" external economic relations became, in this scenario, very crucial, and this camp espoused Raul Prebish's Economic Commission for Latin America findings that the terms of trade between rich and poor countries favored the former. Democratic planning on a large scale could make the vision of a modern industrialized Greece a reality.

The first steps toward forming this camp were undertaken by Angelos Angelopoulos. Immediately after his return to Greece in 1959, he was instrumental in the inauguration *of The Greek Society of Planning* that immediately attracted 76 members. In its appeal, the Society defined Greece as being in a state of crisis. Because of huge unemployment/underemployment, Greece was stuck at a very low-income level. It could only become viable with economic planning. In April 1959, the Society published a first ten-year plan for Greece. One year later, the commercial policy of Greece was scrutinized to demonstrate the need for a more positive management of both internal and external economic relations of the country. A further study on the economic and political state of communities in Greece followed in June 1960.

Throughout its existence, the Society was extremely active in making its views heard and engaged young economists to support them. Works of important economists such as Ragnar Nurkse, Oscar Lange, John Hicks, Nicholas Kaldor, and Gottfried Haberler were translated, as well as studies of the International Labor Organization. In April 1965, a conference was held, and the topics "Planning the free economy and democracy," "Common market and economic development of Greece," and "Administrative reform and institutions of economic development" were discussed. It is worth mentioning that the Society was open to all views and approaches, and on the topic of the association with the EEC, Angelopoulos, who was critical of the treaty, debated and exchanged arguments with the chief negotiator of the agreement for the Greek side, Ioannis Pesmazoglou.

The journal *New Economy* was a pluralist scholarly journal that supported broadly the aims of the Society. Here, too, two phases of editorial policy can be distinguished. The first, from 1949 up to 1958–9 was more pro-third world oriented, and planning successes in real existing socialism were praised. The second was characterized by the inclusion of many young economists on the editorial board who had completed or were doing at the time postgraduate studies in the UK. *New Economy* was critical of certain aspects of government policies, especially of concessions to foreign capital. On the EEC question, the line was more flexible. *New Economy* advocated association, but under other economic circumstances when the Greek economy would be more competitive and better suited to compete on an equal basis with the industrialized European nations.

Some authors of the *New Economy* assembled in the "Papanastassiou Club," an influential group of young center-left intellectuals. For them, a factor adversely affecting economic growth in Greece was the vested interests of the privileged. Political action was needed to curtail their influence in economic policymaking (Papanastasiou Club 1966, 28). According to this group, Greece faced a dual problem: high unemployment and low income on the one hand, and lack of quality and quantity of capital on the other. No institutions with the declared aim to assist the developmental effort existed, and the Greek administration was not supportive of growth. The Club admitted that there was economic progress between 1953–63, but, despite this betterment, agriculture was still the most important sector of the economy and industry was playing a small part. The emigration of the labor force was going to add to existing problems, especially the scarcity of capital. Vested interests needed to be confronted with these tendencies, and the economic paradigm ought to change, despite their opposition. What was needed was a close collaboration between government and private initiative to foster growth. The planning of the economy was particularly important because the price mechanism could not allocate resources efficiently, especially in Greece, due to monopolistic situations (Karagiorgas 1965, 1022).

6.8.3 Heterodox/Marxist Thought

The heterodox camp supported the idea that Greek underdevelopment was due to the political dependence of the country on the West. Shortly after Greek liberation, Dimitris Batsis with his *The Heavy Industry in Greece* (1947) offered an alternative to Greek capitalist development. He advocated the idea that, to overcome underdevelopment, Greece had to promote all possible industrial sectors and exploit every possible raw material in the country, imitating thus the example of the Soviet Union after 1930. His very detailed plan was divided into three parts dealing with the exploitation of productive resources, an industrialization plan, and an analysis about the viability of Greek industry. It set the stage for a lively exchange of arguments in the left-leaning Society *Science and Rebuilding* (that published around 30 contributions on the topic) and the scholarly review *Antaios*. Common to most contributions was the thesis that there were enough financial resources and technical skills in Greece to build up a heavy industry, if there was only the political will to tame the bourgeois class that opposed the project (Batsis 1947, xx). These publications slowed down during the civil war and ended after the defeat of the communist left in 1949. Batsis was arrested in 1952, accused of being a Soviet spy, and was executed in March 1952.

After the communist defeat, the Marxist camp had a difficult time finding means of expression. *Modern Issues* (Synchrona Themata) was a Marxist review of letters and social sciences. Economic contributions therein applauded economic successes in real existing socialism and were critical of all aspects of government policy in Greece. So did authors in *Communist Review* and *New World*, periodicals that were published outside Greece and were not legally circulating in the country.

The left got a boost in the 1958 elections when EDA, a legal left party, got 25% of the vote and became the main opposition. This success resurrected many of the arguments about the Greek economic viability of the late-1940s. At that time, the association with the EEC was brewing, and EDA took a very negative position on the issue. For the leader of the party, Ilias Iliou, the agreement was like throwing the Greek economy in "the lion's den" (Kitsikis 1962, 355). Iliou was very critical toward the EEC and cited in support of his arguments Dimosthenis Stefanidis and the reservations of both the export chamber and the commercial and industrial chamber of Greece against aspects of this agreement. The Greek side had lacked competent advisors to hold serious negotiations, he opined. The comprador mentality of Greek businessmen was another negative element for the Greek economic future, and last, not least Greek exports to Eastern Europe would be negatively affected instead of being supportive of Greek growth. Consequently, and based on political assumptions about the role of the EEC in the bipolar era against the Soviet camp, Greek Marxists were opposed to Greece's association with the EEC. This negative stance was continued by KKE after 1974, but was abandoned by reformist Marxists who supported the full integration to the EU in 1981.

6.9 Elaborations on Keynes

An interesting thread in the post-World War II evolution of economic thought in Greece was the confrontation of Greek economists with Keynesian theory and the popularization of Keynesianism in particular.

There was an established professorial authority in Greece which was, as we already saw, negative about the General Theory. Established economists such as Zolotas and Christodoulopoulos recognized the importance of Keynes as a personality but were distant to his thought. So did Angelopoulos and Kalitsounakis from a different ideological angle. An authority of the Papanastasiou club, Professor Vassilis Filias, explicitly denounced the search of elements helpful in understanding the problems of underdeveloped countries, like Greece, in Keynes' work as "both wrong and unfair to this great man" (Filias 1967, 78). The relevance of Keynes for the problems of developing countries (Kurihara 1959; Singer 1985) was alien to these circles.

Younger economists such as the late Spiros Katiforis, Marina Goudi, Rena Zafiriou, and Ioannis Pesmazoglou were literate in Keynesian economics and promoted through their works insights and elements of his approach. However, whereas internationally the "neoclassical synthesis," had found a welcome reception, in Greece due to the dominance of the interwar generation at the university level, the new gospel of modern economics had to wait until 1975 to be praised. This started in 1975 with a book by the newly elected Professor Giorgos Krimpas (Krimpas 1975). Other economists of the new generation who worked toward making Keynesian theory known and deserve mention include, among others, Georgios Kanas and Apostolos Vogiatzis.

Kanas did his PhD in Thessaloniki in 1953 on fiscal policy and national income. He also wrote *Controlled Inflation and Fiscal Policy* (1957), where he argued that a little inflation may be stimulating in the economy and careful monitoring can assure progress instead of regression. Apostolos Vogiatzis worked as a legal counselor of the General Confederation of Workers Union (GSEE) and wrote in 1957 *Full Employment as Social Policy in Greece.* He argued that, in defiance of international developments, full employment was not an issue in Greece, and he thought that this was the case because most economists considered the law of scarcity to have higher importance than achieving full employment (1957, 3). Agrarian reform in Greece had given property rights to peasants, he stressed, but no funds to access modern technology. Therefore, agriculture had low productivity and could not solve the employment problem. Industry also possessed unproductive horizons, technicians had no incentives, and the danger of internal migration to cities was real. The rate of industrial growth was far greater than the rate of employment in industry, resulting in an ever-growing pool of unemployed. International experience had demonstrated, in his view, that an expansionary policy could boost growth and reduce unemployment, and the workers union was in favor of such initiatives.

To conclude, Greek post-World War II interventionism was not Keynesian either from the point of view of its intellectual origins or from that of its overall philosophy. In fact, it can be better understood in terms of the peculiarities of the Greek political system, which is usually referred to as clientelism (Legg 1969, 154–75). Greek liberals considered Keynesianism as dangerous to monetary stability, structuralists thought it was irrelevant for the reforms needed, and heterodox economists had other visions, such as central economic planning. This was the situation for Keynes in Greece at the time of the restoration of democracy.

7 The Internationalization of Greek Economics after 1971

7.1 Overview of Economic and Institutional Developments

The breakdown of the Bretton Woods system marked the end of an era of continuous growth with low inflation for Greece. It found the governing dictatorship unprepared and isolated, not having a plan to guide the country in the new global realities. The economy went into a prolonged turbulence, starting with a huge inflation rate of 35% in 1973.

The restoration of democracy marked the beginning of a new phase of policy interventions. National defense, economic stabilization, and regional development were priorities amid stagflation. Three big private sector companies, Olympic Airways, the Skaramangas Shipyards, and the Commercial Bank of Greece Group, were nationalized during the following years (Psalidopoulos 2023). The reorientation of economic policy under the National Unity government led to a partial recovery and the drachma to a steady depreciation vis-à-vis major European currencies that continued until 2002 when the Euro became the state currency.

The National Unity government also dealt successfully with market liquidity. Economic activity staged a mild recovery after 1976 when Greece applied for membership in the European Communities. The drachma was definitively unpegged from the US dollar, and the Bank of Greece began to set the exchange rate of the drachma with reference to an algorithm based on a basket of currencies. This effort coincided with the second oil shock, and the economy stuck again in anemic growth rates (Bank of Greece 1992).

From 1 January 1981, Greece became a full member of the EEC/EU.[1] This agreement was initially opposed by the socialist party PASOK and its leader, Andreas Papandreou, who became Prime Minister that year. By appointing Gerasimos Arsenis as Governor of the Bank of Greece, a new era of stronger state involvement in the economy was inaugurated with the aim of achieving broader economic and social objectives. After 1983, however, the policy focus shifted to the need to stabilize the economy, contain inflation, and current account deficits. Inflation reached 24.5% in 1981 and remained at double digits until the mid-1990s. The general government deficit rose sharply from 2.6% of GDP in 1980 to 11.6% in 1985. The Currency Committee that oversaw monetary policy had been abolished in 1981.

To tackle the problems in the balance of payments, a stabilization program was launched in January 1983, accompanied by further devaluation. This effort

DOI: 10.4324/9781315413419-8

failed to deliver long-term positive effects on the economy. On the other hand, EEC participation had worsened the balance of payments (Giannitsis 1985). This development, combined with higher labor costs due to an increase in minimum wages by 32% in 1982, aggravated the financial problems of many businesses and led to the emergence of the "ailing firms" that were taken over by the public sector. With Law 1386/1983, an attempt was made to manage them in principle to avoid job losses. In the same period, investment as a percentage of GDP fell from 19.1% in 1980 to 16% in 1984. To assist the efforts of the government, public debt started rising.

In the face of these developments, the second Papandreou government, in October 1985, introduced a new stabilization program that was submitted to the European Commission. The program provided for a new devaluation of the drachma, cuts in government public spending for 1986, and a legislative restriction on nominal wage increases. The Automatic Wage Indexation system was now based on inflation forecasts (instead of past inflation) and excluded imported inflation. Assisted by falling international oil prices, the program brought about a remarkable improvement in macroeconomic indicators but was discontinued after 1987. The budget deficit was on average 10% of GDP.

With the growth rates of the Greek economy slightly above zero for several years, and with market deregulation measures having been decided at the European level, the Bank of Greece started the "hard drachma" policy. The drachma depreciated less than the inflation rate to contain the increase of public debt. This policy had positive results, but at the cost of a higher external deficit, which rose from 0.8% of GDP in 1987 to 4.3% in 1989.

New elections in 1989 amid extreme polarization led to a short-lived national unity government under Xenophon Zolotas, who used his authority to achieve a minimum of consensus. He assigned the Angelopoulos committee the task of offering an outline of future action needed for the economy to remain on its European path.

Following the transition to a right-wing government in 1990, efforts were resumed to reduce the fiscal deficit, as well as to restructure domestic production through a new program of gradual macroeconomic adjustment. This was necessary due to the completion of the EU internal market by 31 December 1992. This entailed a full deregulation of the banking system, a process that was consistently implemented, especially after 1994 (Garganas & Tavlas 2001, 108–14). All of this led to the conversion of macroeconomic aggregates to European standards.

Meanwhile, at the European level, the Maastricht Treaty was signed. The Greek economic policy had to adjust to this new fact as well. Deficit reduction, deregulation, and privatizations became priorities once more. Inflation dropped to single digits, reaching 2.1% in 1999. Furthermore, growth was satisfactory throughout the second half of the 1990s, while fiscal deficits declined. The high bank interest rates in Greece, compared with the rest of Europe, encouraged capital inflows. The debt-to-GDP ratio remained constant at around 90%.

Early in 2000, the drachma conversion rate to the euro was fixed at 340.75 drachmas per euro, a level close to its trading rate since its entry into ERM and thus presumably seen by the market as fair. Soon afterward, Greece applied to join EMU and was accepted as its 12th member (Psalidopoulos 2018).

GDP performance was satisfactory until the outbreak of the global financial crisis of 2008. Following the drastic declines in lending rates for Greek bonds after 2002, the country entered a cycle of excessive foreign borrowing, imports, and consumption; price developments were partly under control, but ample liquidity caused overheating. Towards the end of the decade, against the backdrop of the Lehman collapse and as Greece's budgetary statistics figures were publicly challenged –f or the second time since 2004– the country faced a problem of strong macroeconomic imbalances. At the same time, harbingers of the financial crisis began to be felt in the economy. This crisis marked the end of an era and the entry of Greece, from 2009 onward, into a phase of unprecedented economic contraction (see Stournaras & Albani 2008). Faced with a budget, a balance of payments, and a debt crisis, the country lost 25% of its GDP in 2011–12, unemployment rose to 25%, and internal austerity was proclaimed by the government, the EU authorities, and the IMF due to the country sharing the same currency with other EU countries.

In the following sections, we will discuss the evolution of economic thought, starting with a reference to new academic appointments over time. Because we gradually approach the present, we will proceed in a selective way, focusing on names and works that set a precedent from our perspective. We will refer again to important names such as Zolotas, Papaligouras, and Papandreou and then move to journals, associations, and exchanges that took place as the economy was moving from EU full membership to Euro adoption. We will close with developments after 2010 when the global financial crisis hit Greece.

7.2 Developments in Academia

The internationalization of economics in Greece started, as already mentioned, with the introduction of an autonomous degree in economics in 1971. This meant that special subfields of economics as practiced internationally needed to be included in the curriculum, and professors who would teach these in a detailed manner had to be hired. It also meant the inclusion of econometric analysis next to statistics as a part of the degree and, in general, the teaching of mathematical economics. This internationalization process homogenized curricula of studies on a world scale, based on the mathematical modeling of economic problems and on Anglo-Saxon textbooks (Coats 1996, 395–6). Teaching in Greece adapted gradually to these UK/American standards, and so did research by Greek economists, who grew in numbers and became more extroverted. The transition to the new normal occurred gradually, but the path was irreversible.

The process got underway during the dictatorship. The generation that had conquered academia during the interwar period and set the tone in academic life until the late 60s/early 70s retired and gave way to new appointments. Former KEPE economists formed the core group of these new hirings. After the fall of the dictatorship, some academics who had identified themselves with the junta were dismissed from their positions (Balopoulos, Eleftheriou, Panas), while others were suspended for shorter periods (Coutsoumaris, Agapitidis).

These new appointments were taken to another level when PASOK won the parliamentary majority in 1981. Existing University Chairs and the positions of ifigites were canceled, and professors, together with other faculty, now belonged, according to the new university law, to departments and sections thereof. Then, in 1985, Departments of Business and Economics were created at the Universities of The Aegean and of Patras. Two years later, the University of Crete inaugurated an Economics Department and in 1989, all existing Highest Schools were renamed to universities. The University of Thrace and of Ioannina followed. Toward the middle of the 1990s, full postgraduate education was introduced in all these institutions, making thus new hirings and specializations necessary. The new universities offered combined economics degrees and, in some cases, degrees in economics were linked with European studies, whereas in others with Political Science.

7.2.1 University of Athens

At the University of Athens and next to Marina Goudi, Panagiotis Pavlopoulos, and numerous assistants, the faculty was briefly enriched with Nikolaos Devletoglou, holder of a PhD from the LSE and co-author with James Buchanan of *Academia in Anarchy* in 1970. This book was a public choice analysis of higher education in the USA, arguing in a conservative manner for high tuition fees and market rules in tertiary education. After the restoration of democracy in Greece and in the wake of the rise of a radical student movement in the country, Devletoglou resigned. In 1976, the department elected two new members, Petros Gemtos who held a PhD from Tuebingen, Germany, and specialized in economic methodology and epistemology, and Giorgos Krimpas, the first Greek academic to explicitly praise Keynesian economics, who had studied philosophy at the University of Texas and then proceeded to get his PhD from Brunel in 1974. Both went on to become full professors some years later. In 1979, Constantine Vaitsos, a Yale graduate with a PhD from Harvard, who was an internationally renowned development economist with vast experience in Latin America, was elected. (For all academic appointments, see Karakostas 2010; see also Gavroglou et al., 2014).

Other professors elected in the 1980s included Anastasios Giannitsis (who started his tenure as an "epimelitis" in 1974), Nikos Petralias (a former professor in Berlin and at Panteion who joined in 1986), Stavros Thomadakis (who held a PhD from MIT and taught at the City University of New York before joining the department in 1987), Louka Katseli (a Princeton PhD holder and a professor at Yale, elected in 1987), Loukas Papademos (an MIT PhD holder and former professor at Columbia, elected in 1988), and Yiannis Samaras (with a doctorate from Budapest who was elected to teach Marxian economics in 1988). In 1990, new faculty hirings followed with Vassilis Droukopoulos in 1990, Vassilis Rapanos in 1992, Giorgos Provopoulos (who rose to professorship from the rank of epimelitis), Yannis Stournaras, and others. The department reached a maximum of 55 faculty members in 2008.

7.2.2 ASOEE

In ASOEE and next to Chalkiopoulos and Coutsoumaris, the profile of new academics included a first degree from this university, then work for KEPE, and later graduate studies in the USA or the UK. A selective list of names includes the following:

In 1970, Ilias Balopoulos, with a PhD degree from Manchester since 1963, was appointed as a professor. His thesis that won professional acclaim was on *Fiscal Policy Models of the British Economy*. He had served at KEPE and became its scientific director in 1966. He served during the dictatorship as a Minister, and after 1975, he was dismissed from public service and went on to work in the private sector.

In 1971 (and up to 1974, when he left for the USA), Alexandros Kondonassis, with a PhD from the University of Indiana, joined briefly the faculty. In the same year, Emmanouil Drandakis, with a PhD from Rochester, became a full professor, after a brief academic career in the US. He had a strong quantitative background and was instrumental in the route of ASOEE to the internationalization era.

In 1972, Efstathios Panas became a professor, and so did in 1973 Triantafyllos Eleftheriou. They were both dismissed from public service in 1975 for having served the dictatorship. Eleftheriou obtained his first degree from ASOEE and after a brief tenure as an employee at the Ministry of Coordination received a scholarship and completed his PhD in Manchester in 1968. Upon his return, he was hired at KEPE. Efstathios Panas was appointed as vice governor of the Bank of Greece in 1969 and he wrote *Problems of Control of Aggregate Demand* and *Collected Papers on Economic Planning in 1971*, where he endorsed the management of the economy according to neoclassical synthesis standards.

In 1973, three new professors were elected: Georgios Chiotis, with a PhD from Manchester, whose field was spatial economics, Theodoros Lianos with a PhD from North Carolina at Raleigh, who was elected to teach macroeconomics and rose to become one of the most distinguished members of the faculty, and Theodoros Georgakopoulos with a PhD from York, to teach public finance.

After the restoration of democracy, Giogios Kottis, with studies in Geneva, the LSE, and Wayne State University, joined the faculty, as did (his spouse) Athena Petraki-Kotti, who held graduate titles from the same universities. Another woman to be elected full professor in the same year was Maria Konstantopoulou, with graduate studies in Paris and the LSE.

Riginos Theocharis, holder of a PhD from the LSE supervised by Lionel Robbins, was elected in 1975 to teach the History of Economic Thought. The next years saw Georgios Dimopoulos, with a PhD from the State University of New York at Buffalo, Kyprianos Prodromidis, who had a PhD from Wayne State University, and Panagiotis Korliras, who did his PhD in 1972 at the University of Rochester, also join. Finally, in 1979, Georgios Bitros, with a PhD from New York University, was elected.

In the next two decades, new appointments followed and they all bore the same characteristics: graduate degrees mostly from the USA and the UK and substantial publications in foreign journals. Some of them came from the Greek banking sector, such as Ioannis Levendakis and Sofoklis Brissimis. Others moved from ASOEE to other Universities in Greece, such as Iosif Hassid, or went abroad to continue their careers like Giannis Ioannidis, Kostas Azariadis, and Iraklis Polemarchakis. Anika Charalambidou joined the faculty to teach heterodox economics. The early 1990s saw the appointments of professors who went on to play important roles in government and in policy making. They included Giorgos Alogoskoufis, a PhD holder from the LSE, Giorgos Zannias from Oxford, Eleni Louri from Oxford, Tryfon Kollintzas from Northwestern, Nikos Christodoulakis from Cambridge, and Efklidis Tsakalotos from Oxford.

As was the case with the University of Athens, ASOEE hosted in its departments far more economists than the ones referred to above (For a full list, see Barkoula 2020).

7.2.3 University of Thessaloniki (AUTH)

At the University of Thessaloniki next to Dimitrios Delivanis and Vasilios Vogiatzis, Stylianos Poulopoulos was elected in 1969 to teach Economic Geography. In 1972, Nikolaos Marmatakis started his academic career teaching micro- and macroeconomics. Loukas Theocharopoulos was appointed to teach Public Finance and Fiscal Legislation in 1973. In the same year, Triantafyllos Raftis, holder of a PhD from Tuebingen, Germany, became ifigitis and went on to become a full professor. Alexandros Gianniotis became a professor in 1974, and one year later, Thanassis Argyris, with a PhD in Berlin, joined the faculty.

7.2.4 Other Universities

In the Highest School of Industrial Studies in Thessaloniki, and next to Psilos, Negreponti Delivani, and Sepentzis, Giannis Tsekouras (PhD from Basel) and Michalis Chatziprokopiou (PhD from Rochester) were elected in 1974. Theofanis Benos was elected in 1976, and all the above led the School in the new era.

In the Highest School of Industrial Studies in Piraeus, new faculty in the 1970s and later included Stylianos Sarantidis, Vasilios Sarsentis, Theodoros Gamaletsos, Theodoros Skoutzos, Athanasios Kanelopoulos, Lazaros Houmanidis, Georgios Drakos, and Nikolaos Giannakopoulos (see Kalafatis 2009).

At Panteios Highest School of Political Sciences and next to LSE graduate Dionysios ("Sakis") Karagiorgas, who returned after his imprisonment by the junta to his position, economic theory was taught by Nikos Petralias (Heidelberg), economic policy by Stavros Theofanidis (Manchester), and regional economics by Ieronimos Pintos (Munich).

This enormous expansion changed the landscape of economic education in Greece completely. The internationalization of post-war economics meant, as already mentioned, primarily, the coming of age of the UK- or American-trained economist in Greece (Psalidopoulos 2000). Since the 1980s, all schools of economic thought have been represented in every economics department, and the history of economics itself is taught (as it used to be) either as a compulsory or as an optional course in all universities. This plurality in numbers has destroyed the existing sense of a close community of the 1960s. The Hellenic Association of Economic Science became defunct after 1974, and no efforts to recreate it were undertaken. Greek economists are members of foreign economic associations and societies and publish both in Greek and other languages. Most of them are devoted to teaching and publishing, whereas some others, mainly from the UoA and from ASOEE, got involved in politics, as ministers, governors, and consultants with Greek authorities.[2]

7.3 The Liberal Camp: Politicians and Academics

The restoration of democracy in the country brought back to power and influence the persons who dominated economic discourse in Greece during the period before the dictatorship, most notably the liberal thinkers X. Zolotas and P. Papaligouras. Initially, they set the tone and articulated arguments in favor of a liberal economic approach to economic policy. In the early 1980s, a younger generation of liberal economists entered the scene.

Papaligouras defended during this period a careful discretionary policy mix that would honor the unique, stagflationary circumstances of the period. He advocated less government intervention in the banking sector, more competition in the economy, and at the same time warned against big economic interests exploiting the economy for their short-term profit. Now he defined his policy as "radical liberalism," a synthesis of accommodating private sector intentions with overall government objectives. The government in a developing economy performed a balancing act by supporting the markets without fulfilling whatever private interests demanded. According to him, by incentivizing initiatives and monitoring outcomes during the turbulent times of stagflation, an optimum recovery path could be found. The international setting and European integration were developments that needed to remain the primary focus of economic policy, and globalization was the trend toward the future. In agreement with Prime Minister Karamanlis, he pushed for immediate access to the EC, and after demanding negotiations, the desired agreement was reached (Psalidopoulos 2023, 166–206).

The negative balance of payments of Greece was a reason of main concern for Papaligouras. He embarked on a plan to ensure all possible Greek energy resources to possibly minimize the dependence on oil. As of March 1975, the drachma started fluctuating, as we mentioned, with its value set through monitoring of the movements of foreign currencies that mattered to Greek exports. Regional development was targeted, indicative economic planning was further promoted, and the public sector proceeded to nationalize private sector companies that either were selling their assets or had violated the law. This policy mix was declared by Papaligouras as a child of necessity. Social dimensions of government policies should remain within the limits of the financially feasible. At the same time, he repeatedly stressed that what mattered most was not just accessing European financial resources but co-authoring and co-deciding future European policies to the benefit of all European citizens. Due to illness, he resigned in 1978 from politics and did not intervene in public policy until his passing in 1993.

Zolotas, on the other hand, criticizing the economic policy of the dictatorship, stressed that "the tactics of sustaining a high level of economic activity through additional programs of public investment isn't right in the long run" (Zolotas 1973, 5). However, due to the freezing of wages during the dictatorship, he confirmed after the restoration of democracy that it was "generally acceptable that we shouldn't let real wages fall in times of depression" (Zolotas 1975, 18). Facing the challenge of containing stagflation, Zolotas recommended, in agreement with the government, an expansionary monetary policy in 1975–7. He believed that existing structural problems could be solved as the economy would adjust to the other European economies of the EC. He was therefore in favor of the proposal to fully integrate Greece into the European economy.

The second oil crisis led to a further relaxation of monetary policy, and in numerous publications, Zolotas analyzed energy resources, industrial policy, and export promotion as vehicles for Greek growth without rigid ideological lenses. Aware as he was of the need for economic policy to adapt to novel realities, he warned against excessive government intervention and spoke of a "peculiar face of (economic) Greece" (Zolotas 1978). The country needed to remain extroverted and aim at exporting more. Policies aimed at domestic market expansion would not result, in his opinion, to sustained growth.

In the 1980s, Zolotas turned his interest to global developments and with his *Economic Growth and Declining Social Welfare* (1981), he accepted that growth based on profit-seeking only didn't lead to maximum welfare. Questions about the quality of life and other social indicators should be included in the metrics of success of economic policy, he opined. At a national level, he was critical of Papandreou's policies because of their failure to combat stagflation. He recommended the opening of a dialogue that would bring together all Greek economists and lead to the adoption of measures that would make the public sector more effective. As this did not materialize, Zolotas sounded alarmist in 1986. The Greek economy was "an economy of subventions, ... deficits and avaricious spending" (as cited in Psalidopoulos 2008, 118), he stressed. As the economy was not adapting to European best practices, opportunities were lost and the vicious circle of inflation with low productivity and balance of payments issues continued to burden the economy, he stressed. Despite the austerity program of 1985–7, the economy was torn between a restrictive, hard drachma monetary policy and an expansionary expenditure policy, when in Europe monetary stability and future monetary integration were top priorities.

Zolotas became Prime Minister in 1989. The fiscal deficit and the rate of exchange were the two major issues his government faced and tried to reconcile. He stressed that his government could not produce miracles and that the accumulated deficits couldn't be brought to zero in a short time. In his words, the economy needed "long term treatment and not irresponsibilities" (as cited in Psalidopoulos 2008, 119). The Angelopoulos Committee's report focused on the stabilization and the future development of the economy. It was short but comprehensive and set the necessary steps forward to adjust to EU monetary goals. They included next the achievement of fiscal and external balance, issues such as privatizations, the liberalization of the labor market, and the shrinking of government activity in the economy. The need to arrive at a reform of the tax system that would increase revenue out of undeclared incomes was a substantial part of the report. Zolotas did not have the time to implement the suggestions of the report but endorsed fully the restrictive policies that were adopted after 1991 by the New Democracy government. The bottom line was that the report signaled the convergence of right- and left-leaning economists around the necessity for Greece to become a part of the EU economic project. Zolotas remained until his passing in 2004 a believer in practical liberalism, a follower of policies that suited concrete circumstances.

During the late 1970s, a younger generation of Greek politicians who clearly identified themselves as liberals emerged. Their most prominent members were Stefanos Manos and Ioannis Palaiokrassas.

Manos studied engineering in Zurich and received an MBA from Harvard. After a career in the private sector, he entered politics with the right-wing New Democracy Party in 1977 and was Economy Minister between 1992 and 1993. Despite opposition from his own party, he insisted on a policy that would see state economic activity shrink. This, according to him, would increase productivity. Manos was an eloquent speaker, and his interventions in discussions concerning the future of the Greek economy were very influential. In 1998, he left New Democracy to form his own Liberal Party, which was unsuccessful in elections. Manos articulated the most liberal discourse among younger Greek politicians, and with lots of publications, he urged public opinion toward accepting a greater role for the market in questions related to economic policy. He remains active until the present.

Ioannis Palaiokrassas held degrees in Economics from the LSE and after a successful career in the private sector, he became involved in politics and was an MP and Minister of Finance between 1990 and 1992. Palaiokrassas was also very vocal in transplanting in Greece the basic postulates of Reaganomics and of Thatcherism, but lost however political leverage after 1995, as Manos had.

Manos, Palaiokrassas, Evangelos Devletoglou, and Stavros Dimas, as well as other younger Greek liberals, distanced themselves from the economic policy of their party in the 1970s. They thought it was a mistake not to turn immediately after the restoration of democracy to privatizations and not to attack inflation as other countries had done to overcome stagflation. They were also critical of the nationalizations of the three big companies that Papaligouras had promoted, as they thought that they had alienated private initiatives and introduced investment abstention of the private sector.

This break with the Zolotas-Papaligouras tradition in liberal thought occurred mainly through the Center of Political Research and Communication (KPEE) that published in the bimonthly journal *Epikentra*. *Epikentra* started circulating in

March 1978 with the aim of influencing public opinion and promoting economic liberalism. The articles were short and informative, aiming to disseminate liberal thought to the wider public. Main contributors to economic issues included, among others, politician Andreas Andrianopoulos, lawyer Kostas Christidis, journalist Kostas Kolmer, communicator Giannis Loulis, and economist Nicolas Tsioris.

The journal published surveys about modern tendencies of the market economy and identified the Greek economic problem as situated in the neglect of the supply side (Issue 16, 1980). Inflation was the consequence of state intervention, and the views of Hayek and Friedman were quoted for support. Interviews with British politicians serving in the government of Margaret Thatcher and comments from France, Sweden, and other European countries underlined that the quest for more market and less state intervention was a pan-European demand, and not a simple, temporary slogan aiming at local circumstances.

Supply-side economics featured prominently (19, 1981) and, ironically, at the time that Andreas Papandreou was beginning his first premiership, in a special issue (23, 1981). The Laffer curve was featured next to an article about the "death of Keynes" in economics. A special symposium with Greek and foreign speakers was hosted in May 1981 and covered topics such as the extent of the market and state intervention, interest rates and inflation, and the real meaning of liberalism in the current epoch (20, 1981). In another special issue (25, 1982), the government budget was scrutinized and an alternative non-inflationary budget for Greece was proposed, a budget that would include spending cuts, but also rationalize spending. The British experience under Margaret Thatcher was continuously hailed (39, 1984), and developments in Poland and the transition of the Soviet economy to perestroika were discussed with the aim of demonstrating the limits and the decline of collectivism.

Epikentra continued advocating and disseminating liberal ideas in an environment that favored Andreas Papandreou's policy mix. Tensions arose between KPEE and the mother party of New Democracy, and in 1983, the party inaugurated the Institute of Democracy as its own think tank. The three years of ND in power (1990–93) would not bring the adoption of supply-side liberal policies due, as already mentioned, to different views within the party. The Adam Smith Club and later the Liberal Forum were created by Professor Georgios Bitros and his colleague at ASOEE Tryphon Kollintzas. The two professors edited a book aimed at offering an alternative view of Greek economic problems (Bitros & Kollintzas 1992). New periodicals of the same persuasion started circulating, *Overview* (Epopteia) and *Free Choice* (Eleftheri Epilogi) among others. Policy measures of the ND governments were heavily criticized by some of these liberals.

Next to Kollintzas and Bitros, another liberal intellectual became active from that period onward, their ASOEE colleague Giorgos Alogoskoufis. KPEE had already started losing momentum and *Epikentra* stopped circulating. New subgroups and periodicals emerged, but the autonomous political representation of the liberal camp as a separate party was not successful. Monetarism and supply-side recommendations could have resurrected when New Democracy returned to power in 2004, and Alogoskoufis became an Economy Minister. Despite his liberal credentials and his early work in rational expectations, Alogoskoufis oversaw during his watch the expansion of debt and deficits. This drew criticism from other liberals such as Bitros. After the financial crisis hit Greece in 2010, the Center for Liberal Studies (KEFIM) became the focal point for the dissemination of liberal ideas, carrying on to the present the tradition that started in the 1970s.

7.4 The Interventionist Camp: From Dependency Theory to Reformist Socialism

After his arrest by the junta in 1967, Papandreou was freed and allowed to leave the country. He was offered a position at Stockholm University and shortly thereafter at York University, Toronto, where he stayed until 1974. During these years of exile, Papandreou evaluated his political experiences in the light of the theoretical contributions of radical political economy that became fashionable after 1968. He wrote two books on contemporary capitalism (Papandreou 1970, 1972), in which he sought to redefine the relationship between individual and business interests in late capitalism. He also wrote an autobiographical history of Greece (Papandreou 1973). He finally co-authored a book on development planning (Papandreou & Zohar 1974). After the restoration of democracy, he returned to Greece and resumed his political career. Upon his return, he wrote – exclusively in Greek – books on economic development (1975) and on the transition to socialism (1977, 1978). In 1981, he became Prime Minister. He won another election in 1985, but in 1989, PASOK moved into opposition for three years. It is perhaps worth noting that during his eight years in office, he never took immediate personal responsibility for any ministry dealing with economic affairs. In October 1993, Papandreou won the elections again, but his health was fragile, and he passed away in 1996.

The experience of Papandreou in Greek politics in the years 1965–74 (when out of power and in exile) caused a shift in his approach to economics. It is for this reason that his earlier academic economics exerted little influence on economic policymaking in Greece during his term in office. The latter was influenced much more by his later works in radical political economy, and this was the part of his thought that influenced the discourse of his followers.

In *Man's Freedom* (1970), Papandreou made the case for the citizens against the omnipotent government of the day, which evaded popular control. Capitalist society was, for Papandreou, deeply pluralistic but had become a society of power enclaves and oligopolies. These enclaves of power constituted in every country the ruling coalition which Papandreou called the "establishment." The establishment was, for him, a more flexible concept than the Marxian "ruling class," for it allowed changes in the balance of power – provided of course that there was a change in the vision of those who possessed power. In societies that didn't develop rapidly, the establishment often demonstrated structural rigidity. Changing the establishment entailed deep political rift and crisis, as forces that did not belong to it, tried to join in. Sometimes they didn't succeed, not least due to foreign intervention.

Extrapolating from the Greek experience, he defined the "para-government" as the conduit of influence from the establishment to the state (high government officials, secret services, etc.). To return to a more democratic system of government, Papandreou pleaded for a decentralization of state power, the suppression of the establishment's political machinery, which operated behind the scenes, and the politicization of the organizations through which citizens exercise their influence in a pluralist society.

Big business was, of course an integral part of the establishment, especially those corporations that came to exert decisive influence over national defense and foreign policy, not least through public procurement contracts. The big corporation, according to Papandreou, had rendered the economic process irrational. Under the prevailing "monopolistic capitalism," the ends of consumers and those of the country were not being served by the industrial system (Papandreou 1970).

Man's Freedom also had an internationalist dimension. In the age of the two superpowers and bipolarity of the late 1960s, smaller states were integrated within the existing camps and were not allowed to go their own way. Greece in 1967, within the Western alliance, and Czechoslovakia in 1968, within the Warsaw Pact, were cases in point. For this reason, it was necessary to support and demonstrate solidarity with nationalist/revolutionary movements around the globe that fought against oppression.

In *Paternalistic Capitalism* (1973), Papandreou placed emphasis on understanding the power structures that dominated political life in contemporary Western societies. He relied heavily on Paul Baran's and Paul Sweezy's analysis in *Monopoly Capital* and on John Kenneth Galbraith's *New Industrial State* and called for decentralized popular control of any authority. The "region," a country unit with balanced natural resources, self-sufficient in technical and administrative terms, was, for him, the proper platform of social planning under existing circumstances. Regions could challenge central government authority and provide an alternative conduit of democratic control. The central government would thus be weakened, and a more democratic society might emerge out of this social struggle.

Papandreou accepted the analysis of the *Monthly Review School* about contemporary capitalism, as well as their North/South analysis of the world economy based on the notion of unequal exchanges in trade. Drawing from the Prebish-Singer analysis of the causes perpetuating underdevelopment, Papandreou declared the economic plan to be an ideological tool for political action. This plan would be guided by democratic principles and was to be based on the Lange/Lerner proposals of decentralized decision-making (28).

For Papandreou, neoclassical development theory was ahistorical and its gospel in Greece consisted of a mix of relying on private decisions plus free trade plus monetary stability,an unconvicing mix. Underdevelopment could be best explained through the dependency of some states on other states, dating back to colonial times. Imperialism was how the industrialized nations held underdeveloped nations' independence in the post-colonial era (Cardoso 1970; Frank 1970; Howard-King 1992). Keynesian economics, on the other hand, aimed at restoring deficiencies of the capitalist system. Papandreou, as he declared, wanted to lead Greece in "the third way," meaning something between capitalism and real existing socialism. Therefore, Keynesian insights were irrelevant for him.

The world system was characterized by the contradiction between the countries of the Metropolis and the countries of the Periphery (Amin 1972). The state of dependence on the latter grew out of the fact that the development path of the periphery reflected the demands of the metropolis, not native decisions. Growth could occur without affecting the structure of dependence. Popular forces that came to power should be ready to change this situation. Social planning in a truly democratic, participatory society had to be decentralized, with the region functioning as the key planning unit (Papandreou 1975). Unequal exchange, the transfer of surplus from the periphery to the metropolis (Baran & Sweezy 1968), and the dominance of the economy of the periphery from metropolitan decision-making had to be stopped (Papandreou 1977). Development projects had to have what Papandreou (and his co-author Uri Zohar) named the "impact approach" to development planning (Papandreou & Zohar 1974). According to it, investment projects should be judged not by profit maximization, but by their overall impact on the economy. If the metropolis didn't allow the capitalist development of the periphery, then the popular forces living in these countries had no other choice but to follow a socialist path. "Socialism in Greece" (1977a) and "The Way to Socialism" (1977b) popularized these ideas and became sacrosanct texts for his followers.

A very important concern for Papandreou was the issue of political support of any government wanting to implement "change" in the Greek economy. This was of absolute importance as the "establishment" would try to overthrow people's rule, as they had done in 1967. To secure the loyalty of the popular masses, Papandreou wanted what he called "social consumption" to grow. This meant big raises in wage income, especially in the public sector. The public sector was a tool to control the economy, to boost growth, and to absorb the unemployed, he declared. Next to social consumption, the banking system had to be nationalized and supply not only the private economy but the public sector as well. Public enterprises and agricultural cooperatives should have full access to credit to finance their activities. Papandreou called this a "socialization" of the banking system, since the oversight of banking activity was relegated to boards of overseers that included trade unionists and trade representatives. Finally, foreign trade had to be centrally controlled for the national economy to remain immune from global economic imbalances.

Papandreou, as a politician went at length to emphasize that his party was *socialist* and not *social-democratic*. In his view, Greece was a peripheral country in the capitalist world. In the past, the "establishment" had hindered the pursuit of an alternative development path. This meant a struggle for national liberation by the Greeks and a battle against imperialism. Both presupposed the choice of the path to socialism (Papandreou 1977a). If PASOK were to win popular support and come to power, it would have to break the bonds of economic, military, and cultural dependence on the West. The prime target of a socialist government would be the widening, as already mentioned, of social consumption (1977b, 68). This would broaden the coalition of power between PASOK and various social classes and strata in the country. The socialist government would have to implement structural changes. Coordinated public investment projects should guarantee the balanced growth of strategic sectors of the economy. Economic policy should be based on three principles (Papandreou 1977b):

1. The socialization of the financial and credit system that would secure the appropriate channeling of funds for investment projects.
2. The centralized control of foreign trade, making it capable of manipulating and circumventing foreign exchange constraints.
3. The socialization of strategic monopoly/industrial units, to curb the influence of big business in political affairs.

Despite his plea for the socialization of the credit system, he rejected, as we mentioned, Keynesian theory as politically belonging to social democracy, whereas his party, being socialist, had nothing in common with theories correcting weaknesses of the capitalist system (Papandreou 1974, 211). His supporters should endorse dependency theory as it was pronounced for Latin America by Samir Amin, Andre Gunder Frank, and other authors (Papandreou 1975, 54). Employing Marxism in a creative and not in a Marxist-Leninist way was an accepted research method (1977a, 37). The most important issue of the socialist experience would be the participation of the working man in decision-making, social planning, and other self-governing bodies. Political life "would not be controlled, if not run by the U.S." (Papandreou 1976, 53) and "Greece would belong to the Greeks," according to one of his most popular slogans.

What then PASOK as a government initially tried to do was to use the state apparatus to provoke structural changes in the direction of a different kind of development. What happened was a substitution of private investment activity by public expenditure and transfer payments, which is meant to establish a new coalition of interests in society (Petras 1987). In the years 1981–3, a huge increase in wages was introduced amidst a recession. This led to a widening of the deficit of the balance of payments and to the introduction of an austerity policy in the years 1985–7. Efforts were undertaken to reform the existing channels of middlemen and intermediaries who dominated internal trade, with marginal success. To finance the real economy, public debt was increased. Over time, especially after 1985, economic policy became more in tune with European Union directives and priorities. This was also true after Papandreou returned to power in 1993 (for evaluations of his years in office, see, from a friendly view, Tsakalotos (1991); and from a critical one, Petras (1987), and Thomadakis and Seremetis (1992)).

When PASOK won the elections in 1993, Papandreou decried the already huge public debt he had helped create and famously declared in a statement on 2 December 1993, that "either the debt will be tamed by the nation, or it will destroy it." Shortly thereafter, he passed away.

Andreas Papandreou's contribution to Greek economic thought and policy was unique. His formation as an economist was stellar. Economic theory, either in the form of neoclassical microeconomics or in the guise of Keynesian macroeconomics, was not his main scientific preoccupation, and neither was Schumpeterian dynamics – even though he was literate in them all. His early desire that economics should keep close ties with the other social sciences and his plea for empirical relevance and operationally meaningful theorems in economics distinguished him within the critical mainstream of American economics of the 1950s and 1960s.

An enlightened liberal with a rational mind, he came back to his mother country in the early 1960s and faced a challenge as an economist, a citizen, and a professional. In the experimental field of Greece, Papandreou proposed some obvious reforms and provoked political reaction. His propositions were defeated in the 1960s, not because they were lacking in logic or coherence, but because they couldn't be sustained by the politics of the day. His traumatic experience of imprisonment and exile led to a shift in his research interests and way of thinking. He became a political economist, applying Galbraithian insights combined with the *Monthly Review School*'s analyses to shape a very peculiar "school" of economic thought that espoused interventionism.

The most influential PASOK economists until 1985 were Apostolos Lazaris, the University of Pireaus academic we referred to above, and Gerasimos Arsenis. Arsenis had a first degree in Law from the University of Athens and got a PhD from MIT. He worked at the Secretariat of the UN and was a member of the team that set up UNCTAD. From New York, he moved to the OECD in Paris to become its director of the research department. He returned as a senior economist at UNCTAD in 1967 and later became its director at the time when discussions about world trade at international organizations were peaking (Rist 1997, 140–70). He was part of the bodies that helped introduce the Special Drawing Rights and oversaw the modernization of the World Bank and the IMF in the 1970s.

Following the invitation of Papandreou, Arsenis returned to Greece and became Governor of the Central Bank and later, simultaneously, Minister of the National Economy. By 1986, his relationship with Papandreou deteriorated as the latter turned to more mainstream positions in Arsenis' view, and he resigned from PASOK (Arsenis 1987). As his effort to create his own party was unsuccessful, he returned to PASOK in 1993 and served as Defense Minister and later as Minister of Education.

Arsenis was an erudite technocrat, who belonged to the "structuralist developmentalist school" (see his autobiographical interview in Arsenis 1987, 16–27). He shared the view that a "good" administration of the existing situation in any developing country couldn't lead to the overcoming of poverty and crises (17). He adopted the Singer/Prebish approach and injected insights from Mihal Kalecki and Joan Robinson in his studies for UNCTAD concerning the role of competition in an open economy (21). He shared Papandreou's vision for an alternative development path for Greece and tried to implement the development program of 1983–7 during times of economic turbulence. During this time, he collaborated with economists as Dimitris Koulourianos, Vasso Papandreou, Manolis Drettakis, and the academics Kostis Vaitsos, the outstanding development economist, and Panagiotis Roumeliotis, an expert on strategies to confront multinational corporations. Roumeliotis later served in the European parliament and the IMF. He held a doctorate from Paris and was and still is a prolific author. In periodicals such as *Economy and Society* and *Antitheseis,* intellectuals wrote supportive or critical essays on the economic policy of the period.

After 1985, the man in charge of the economy became Kostas Simitis, a Commercial Law professor at Panteios. After Papandreou's passing, Simitis became party leader and Prime Minister. During his tenure, economic policy was fine-tuned with the need to converge with requirements posed by EU policies. His Minister for Economy and Finance from 1994 to 2001 was Yiannos Papantoniou, a Cambridge PhD holder with experience in the OECD and the European parliament. He was succeeded by ASOEE Professor Nikos Christodoulakis, another Cambridge PhD and academic who had served as a Minister of Development before serving as the Economy Minister during the transition to the Euro *The Association to Reflect on the Modernization of Society* (the Greek acronym OPEK) was the forum where intellectuals supporting these policies gathered and debated.

The Central bank that became part of the ECB during these times was governed by UoA professor Loukas Papademos. Nicolas Garganas (a UCL PhD holder) was the Vice Governor and later Governor of the Bank and Georgios Tavlas (an NYU economist with a strong academic record and work experience at the IMF) was the top advisor. Other UoA academics who served the Simitis governments were Tassos Giannitsis, economic advisor to Papandreou and Simitis, who was Foreign and Labor Minister, and Vassilis Rapanos (PhD Queen's University, Kingston, Canada) who held important positions in the banking sector and advisory positions relating to Europe. John Spraos, a UCL professor, wrote an important report on the future of the Greek insurance system and warned that Greece might catch something like a "Dutch disease," if it failed to reform its pension system. Spraos went on to represent Greece at the Executive Board of the IMF. Professor Louka Katseli served in various positions including the OECD before becoming a Minister under Georgios Papandreou in 2010. So did Giorgos Papakonstantinou (PhD LSE). Katseli and Papakonstantinou were in charge when the crisis hit Greece.

7.5 The Heterodox Camp

After 1974, the Communist party (KKE) was legalized, and Marxist analyses of the Greek economy started getting published. They all rested on the theory of state monopoly capitalism that had developed in the Eastern block and among Western Marxists as an explanation of the situation prevailing in Western Europe after World War II (Boccara et al. 1971; Hardach et al. 1987, 63–8). According to this theory, government and big business interests, monopolies, had merged. With the consent of reformist trade unions, they agreed and implemented policies that secured growth with a great degree of inclusivity, avoiding strikes, crises, and social tensions. What was needed was to fight against this new reality to "democratize" the state and introduce policies in favor of all other interests in society that were sidelined.

Michalis Mallios was the first author who provided a Marxist analysis of contemporary Greek capitalism after the return of democracy. In his book, *The Contemporary Phase of Development of Greek Capitalism* (1975), he proceeded to analyze the Greek economy. According to him, Greece was, during the interwar period, a country in transition to full-blown capitalism. It enjoyed a middle level of capitalist development and unfortunately, during those times, KKE followed the analysis of the Third International, thus making several analytical mistakes. It espoused the thesis that Greece was imperialist and set as an interwar goal the dictatorship of the proletariat, by overthrowing the existing order. However, in 1934, KKE corrected this mistake. It declared that Greece was a medium-level economic power, and politically, the aim of the party was to advance the bourgeois-democratic character of the Greek economy. This would lead to a transformation that would make a proletarian-socialist takeover possible sometime in the future (15). The basic problem of the development of capitalism in Greece since the 1960s was to identify the precise state of the relations between the economy and society as well as the reasons for the appearance of state monopoly capitalism in the country (19).

Before Greek Independence, commercial capitalism accumulated capital, but the overthrow of the Ottomans was accompanied by foreign intervention, he reminded. Therefore, foreign capital started dominating and dictating policies in Greece with the result that capitalism was developing in the commercial and banking sector, with industry remaining at an infant stage, not able to expand its full potential (30). This led the Greek bourgeois class to orient itself not towards secondary production, but towards services (34) and did not allow the country to develop as it would have if foreign capital had not penetrated the economy. Mallios went on to compare Greece with Latin America and concluded that Greece stood somewhere in the middle as it didn't have the feudal characteristics of South America, even though foreign penetration had destructed the economic structure of both. Following the economic performance of the country in the last 30 years, Mallios admitted that capitalism had developed in almost all sectors of economic activity (116).

However, the overall picture of the economic structure had not changed, as foreign capital continued to dominate the economy and keep it on a narrow path, not allowing it to advance based on national capital interests. A few big Greek companies of monopolistic nature had assimilated with the state apparatus for reciprocal benefits (134), relegating workers, peasants, and small capital owners to a secondary rank. This reality dictated for Mallios the need for an allied political action that would change the economic structure of the country, with the Communist party playing a leading, supportive role in this struggle.

Giannis Samaras, who was elected as a professor at the UoA, offered a similar analysis of *State and Capital in Greece* (1977). Greece was a country where monopolistic capitalism was dominant and omnipotent (82–97). Government and monopolies were interwoven through the government budget (99–152), and the reproduction of the economy was highly dependent on government investment and the inflation process. Inflation complicated the management of the economy due to a "right-wing Keynesian dogma" (322), followed by the Greek bourgeoisie. The non-monopolistic capitalist class was torn between submission to the establishment and the search for a different perspective. Arguing in a similar way as Mallios, Samaras predicted that political developments could lead to a new coalition of power in society and government and change the path of Greek capitalism bringing it in line with socialist ideals.

A further treatise written by Stergios Babanasis and Kostas Soulas (1976) led to similar conclusions. The two authors focused on economic developments in the past two decades, in industry and agriculture. Greece was again described as a country where state monopoly capitalism was the dominant form of production (91–106). The balance of payments was next to the government budget, a mirror of foreign penetration in the Greek economy, with foreign investment and invisible receipts being necessary to keep the economy rolling. The association agreement with the EEC made Greece "enter decisively in the orbit of international unification" (151) and was, in general a positive step. It could also lead to drawbacks if the state apparatus could not master the opportunities and obligations associated with it. Greece was a semi-developed country, with a median degree of capitalization, an "assistant laboratory of the advanced capitalist nations" (182). Despite its growth, the Greek economy was not as stable as the rest of the European economies. It lacked self-sustained industry, native research, and development potential, giving the economy "a comprador, non-productive, parasitic character" (197). A political change to move things in a productive direction could be a solution to the Greek economic problem.

Grigoris Farakos was an author and a communist who became the general secretary of KKE between 1989 and 1991. In his *Topics on Greek State Monopoly Capitalism* (1978) and offering case studies, he repeated the analysis of other Marxists of the period that big companies dominated not only the economy but also dictated government decisions. Small business interests should form an alliance with the working class to change this situation, and this was the political message conveyed as PASOK, the Socialist Party, was heading toward becoming the ruling party.

During the 1980s, PASOK's policies were criticized by other heterodox economists and Marxists for not providing the path needed for the Greek economy. The *Center for Marxist studies* and the journal *Scientific Thought* (Epistimoniki Skepsi) were close to orthodox Marxist analyses. *Contemporary Themes* (Synchrona Themata) and *The Citizen* (O Politis) offered contributions reflecting Eurocommunist ideas. Positions (Thesis) also followed a critical path of analysis, and heterodox thought entered Greek academia during this period.

After 1990, the Eurocommunist camp became very pro-European in its policy recommendations. Michalis Papagiannakis was one of its advocates and espoused the ongoing globalization of the world economy. The global arena was better than a national one for the promotion of workers' rights, he stressed. This analysis led Greek Euro-communists to approve the ratification of the Maastricht Treaty in the Greek parliament, whereas KKE voted against it.

Other left-wing economists following political careers were Grigoris Giannaros and Giannis Dragasakis. Their opinion articles and political interventions were quite influential. Dragasakis' activity reaches contemporary times.

7.6 Economic Thought after 2010

Since the mid-1980s, when Papandreou and PASOK stopped challenging Greece's EU participation, most Greek economists accepted the EU as the institutional anchor for the future of the economy and questioned only marginally

European policies that affected the economic development of the country. At the same time, it was clear that industry was losing market shares due to EU competition and its participation in GDP fell. Many economists called for government action aiming to prevent industrial decline in the ongoing process of the economic and financial unification of Europe (Giannitsis 1991). Others analyzed developments in the balance of payments and concluded that competitiveness losses led to the decline of exports and lower rates of growth. Finally, other authors pointed out that government expenditure as a percentage of GNP had increased from 29.8% in the 70s to 36% in 1981, and to 50.1% in 1989. Their conclusion was that state activity crowded out private initiatives, with high rates of inflation as an outcome and consequently, declining rates of growth (Nikolaou 1991).

Other topics of debate included the Maastricht criteria, the effectiveness of the policy of the "hard drachma," and the prospect of joining the Euro as a currency. The persistence of budget deficits continued in the 2000s despite warnings spelled out by the central bank. The non-compliance with the Stability and Growth Pact didn't sound alarm bells in the belief that "this time was different." And indeed, growth rates were moderate, and inflation was kept at bay. Then, the global financial crisis changed everything.

In May 2010, interest rates for Greek bonds climbed to 35%. Faced with an enormous budget deficit, 15.8% of GDP, an equally big deficit in the balance of payments, with 13.8%, and Greek banks in distress, the government appealed to the EU and the IMF. It was bailed out through a long and torturous process. Other EU members were also in distress, and the Eurozone crisis was a reality. In the end banks were saved. On the other hand, Greece had no currency of its own that could be devalued. Forced austerity in the country to ensure euro participation led to a 25% loss of GDP in 2011–13. Unemployment rose to 25%. After a long period of distress, in 2018, the country returned to relative normalcy.

This decade was full of contributions about the ongoing economic crisis and distress. A Greek Society for Political Economy (GSPE) was called into life and its members contributed a volume of 22 articles on the crisis (GSPE 2011). Topics such as forced austerity, wage cuts, the reduction of the public sector, unemployment, heavy taxation, and others provoked many publications that tried to analyze the state of the Greek economy.

Neoclassical, Keynesian, and Marxist writers and all other variants of economic thought competed to win the hearts and minds of the public, and possibly influence the Greek electorate. It is impossible to do justice to this extensive literature, so the following is a selective summary.

Three different camps can be identified in the writings of this period. One espouses a return to a national currency that would enable the country to regain, through devaluation its international competitiveness; a variant in this camp was extremely nationalistic and xenophobic, and espoused conspiracy theories to explain conditions in Greece. A second camp called for a new Marshall Plan type of aid to Greece that would foster investment and growth, and thus the repayment of public debt soon; this camp identified the Eurozone crisis as stemming from a surplus North versus a deficit South divide and saw a solution in the issuing of Eurobonds if this could be made possible. A third group agreed that the extent of austerity in the country was based on false premises but recognized that Greece ought to bring its finances back to order so that the country would be able in the future to renegotiate any changes to existing agreements.

Yanis Varoufakis, professor at the University of Athens since 2000, rose to fame during this period for his many books and his effort as a Finance Minister in 2015 to renegotiate the agreement between Greece and the EU/IMF. He was the most outspoken defender of the second group mentioned above. His 2010 *A Modest Proposal,* co-authored with Stuart Holland, proposed reforms that would help the global and the European economy cope with the financial crisis. In subsequent editions, the book profited from inputs from James Galbraith and Michel Rocard. In *The Global Minotaur* (2011), he explained the crisis as a late consequence of the post-1945 dollar-based Bretton Woods system. The USA absorbed until 2008 through its investment banks the global financial surpluses that were entrusted to them for high private profits. These capitals were therefore not available to finance productive investment around the world so that poverty and underdevelopment could be overcome. Varoufakis was not able to convince his fellow finance ministers of the Eurogroup to change their policies toward Greece.

As the Greek economy still struggles to regain its past levels of income, these exchanges by Greek economists are a good and healthy sign. Economic thought in Greece still is and needs to remain pluralist to contribute to the welfare of the country.

Notes

1 For rules, transition periods, tax and tariff harmonization clauses, see Mitsos 1981.
2 For an extensive discussion of their careers, see Souliotis 2021.

Concluding Summary

In the foregoing chapters, we investigated the evolution of economic thought in modern Greece. To fulfill our aim, we used authors with scholarly contributions about the Greek economy and the conduct of economic policy as the country was transitioning from low to higher income levels. These contributions were important to create a common language and a body of explanatory common understanding, which eventually led to the forming of camps of economic thought. These were formed with inputs received from abroad, so foreign ideas and policy recommendations were also important in this process. The discussions about the right path for the Greek economy had their roots in a specific relationship between transmitters of economic theories in different European countries and Greek recipients, the latter facing national realities and adjusting their positions and enriching or changed economic paradigms.

Economic thought in Greece in the beginning of the 19th century was rudimentary and shallow. It evolved through a prolonged period of preparation when development was slow, society was pre-modern, and only a handful of people practiced the "economics profession." As this period was crucial for the take-off of economics in Greece, we devoted a great part of our attention to it.

Then, an almost 50-year-long period of the institutionalization of economics followed. Economics was taught and studied at the university level, even if combined with Law or Political Science. Academic economists entered the scene and economic discourse became more sophisticated and robust. Associations of economists were created, periodicals appeared, and literacy in economics was expanded without losing its national, Greek, character.

A new, third, era was launched with the introduction of the autonomous degree of economics at Greek universities in 1971. This became the period of the internationalization of Greek economics, of the multiplication of economists working on all fields of academic expertise, of the breakthrough of the economist as a professional. The whole process, from small increments of thought to the internationalization of economics, was slow and accompanied the evolution of the Greek economy from subsistence levels to EU modernity.

Our investigation into the History of Modern Greek economic thought started before Greek Independence. Greek space was an Orthodox Christian province of the Ottoman Empire and economics followed religious, non-materialistic thought, in fact anti-capitalist thought. This attitude was in tune with Ottoman economic

DOI: 10.4324/9781315413419-9

thought, which had central government and its needs as the principal decision maker in economy and society. Mercantilist theories aimed at the strengthening of the nationstate were not transmitted, or not fully understood, among intellectuals and state administrators of the late Ottoman Empire. The reality for peoples in the Balkans was that the state was entitled to intervene in the economy and shape society, but without a wealth-creating philosophy to assist private wealth-seeking efforts.

Commerce thrived and shipping flourished among Greeks, and sympathy for the Enlightenment and the French Revolution grew, along with them ideas associated with economic freedom, individual rights, and private property. On the eve of and immediately after the Greek Revolution, a mix of encyclopedias, translations of French economists, mixed with the presence of Benthamites from Britain and Saint-Simonians from France, disseminated utilitarianism and industrialism despite the Orthodox Church's hostility towards some of these teachings.

Foreign intervention after the assassination of the first Greek ruler brought German cameralism to the country, which introduced an administrative system of economic governance. Cameralism aimed at the satisfaction of the revenue needs of the imposed King, the paternalistic guidance of economic processes, and national self-sufficiency. It was an administrative practice of the existing order at the lowest denominator possible. Cameralism ultimately did not strengthen the Bavarian king and withered slowly without achieving the economic progress of the country. Nevertheless, it left its mark on the formation of the neo-Hellenic state with an administrative mentality prevailing among Greek politicians and administrators.

Meanwhile, at the University of Athens, a variant of French economic liberalism flourished and opposed the economic policies of Greek governments until 1893, which remained of an administrative/voluntarist nature. During the entire 19th century, the community of economists was very small, and Economics was embedded in law.

Liberal economic thought was introduced in Greece by Ioannis Soutsos, who was at the same time original and quite heavily influenced by French academics and writers. Intellectuals followed mostly his steps, with politicians staying distanced and practicing an adhoc administration. British classical political economy was not followed by anyone due to its rigid class-oriented distribution analysis and its pessimism identified by the stationary state. The shock of the military defeat in 1897 led to the rethinking of the past and to proposals about the economic future of Greece, with the German Historical School becoming the ruling economic paradigm around the turn of the century. This became reality because of the choice of a young generation to study economics in Germany and the methodological avenues opened by German economic thought to analysis and policy making in less developed countries.

Greece entered modernity in 1910 when the historical approach of German-trained Greek economists, combined with the new liberal agenda of Prime Minister Venizelos, coincided with a period of territorial expansion and economic growth. At this juncture, the importance of personality in historical evolution is proven. Andreas Andreadis acted as a bridge between liberal economics and historical methodology, and in the process of the post-1920s institutionalization of Greek economics, he assisted a young generation of economists to reach positions of authority in academia without questioning their personal beliefs about their methodological or political stance. Economics became thus a university discipline, economists grew in numbers, and attempted to analyze issues such as monetary stabilization, public infrastructural works, and the relation between government priorities and the free market. Two different camps, a neoclassical and an interventionist, were formed and debated on the right path to growth. Then the Wall Street Crash followed, and this brought all economists in agreement about the need of the public sector to support private initiative and dampen social conflicts by protecting and regulating the economy. These two camps of thought were challenged by Marxism. An interesting and revealing episode in the evolution of economic thought during this time was the negative reception of John Maynard Keynes and his ideas by the established generation of Greek economists, as opposed to some younger economists who couldn't influence policy much. Left-leaning interventionists also found Keynesian economics suited for a developed economy, and not offering tools to cope with the Greek case. This attitude continued until the internationalization of economics in Greece.

The novelty in Greek economics after World War II was the advent of Anglo-Saxon economics through British and US economists offering financial assistance to Greece. The "generation of 1930" in academia continued their careers and the two schools of thought from interwar resurfaced. Economists believing in the primacy of monetary stability fought against those who pleaded for policies in the direction of structural changes in the economy. Both camps advocated the association of Greece with the EEC, contributing thus to a minimum of mutual convergence. Marxist and heterodox voices were not able to articulate their ideas/arguments explicitly.

The liberal camp during this period was led by Xenophon Zolotas in academia and central bank policy and Panagis Papaligouras in politics. A moderate monetarism, combined with regulation, oversight, and a mix of ordoliberal ideas with social justice and the use of economic planning to sustain growth, set the standard followed by other economists of similar persuasions.

The interventionist camp was led by Andreas Papandreou. Creating KEPE, he set the basis of the internationalization of Greek economics by introducing mathematical techniques, a policy-orientated economic analysis, and neoclassical synthesis Keynesianism. Scholarships awarded to young economists of KEPE led to them being trained in the UK and the USA. These economists came to hold academic appointments in the country in the 1970s.

The internationalization process in economics after 1971 created a market for economists in the country and broadened significantly the academic field. Neoclassical and Keynesian economics were taught to an ever-growing audience of students, scholars, and professionals. The 1980s saw Andreas Papandreou, whose views shifted from the mainstream of the 1960s to more radical positions in the 1970s, become Prime Minister. Papandreou opposed neoclassical economics openly and endorsed dependency theory. His economic policies were interventionist and, despite mixed economic results, they were supported by the electorate due to their social inclusiveness. State-developmentalist economic thought dominated economic discourse in Greece until the crisis of 2010, with liberals and Marxists expressing their reservations. Successive governments after 1990 did not significantly challenge the fundamentals of government intervention; they rather brought it in line with the necessities of the country's European Union membership. Low interest rates after the adoption of the euro added a further boost to foreign borrowing and led to crisis in 2010, when, after the global financial crisis of 2008, the actual state of Greek statistics was revealed.

Economic thought in modern Greece offered to policymakers instruments to rationalize their policies, to frame new visions in development strategies, to pursue nationalistic and equality-based platforms of action, to follow class-specific preferences and demands. In this process, policymakers remained relatively autonomous from academic economics even if the distance that existed in the 19th century was somehow closed in the 20th.

Economic thought after 2010 is at a crossroads due to the extended economic crisis and distress of 2010–18. The economic downturn of the country and forced austerity led to many publications that try to analyze the current situation of the Greek economy from different angles. Neoclassical, Keynesian, and Marxist writers and all other variants of economic thought analyze aspects of the "Greek variety of capitalism" and compete to win the hearts and minds of the interested public. Historians of economics, an older guard, and a young generation, are active in this process. This reality is likely to continue.

Bibliography

About, E. (1855). *La Grèce Contemporaine*, Paris: Hachette.

Agapitidis, S. (1935). *Le corporatisme en Italie*, Paris: Lipschitz.

Agapitidis, S. (1940). *Policy of Economic Autarchy*, Athens: Pyrsos (in Greek).

Agriantoni, C. (1986). *The Origins of Industrialisation in Greece in the 19th Century*, Athens: Commercial Bank of Greece (in Greek).

Agriantoni, C. (2006). Venizelos and Economic Policy. In: Kitromilidis, P. (Ed.), *Eleftherios Venizelos: The Trials of Statesmanship*, Edinburgh: Edinburgh University Press, 284–318.

Alysandratos, G. (2006). *Radicalism in the Ionian Islands*, Argostoli: Etairia Keffaliniakon Meleton (in Greek).

Amin, S. (1972). *Accumulation on a World Scale*, New York: Monthly Review Press.

Anastasopoulos, G. (1947). *History of Greek Industry*, 3 vols, Athens: Elliniki Ekdotiki (in Greek).

Andreades, A. (1904). *L'Impôt Direct en Grèce et son Évolution*, Paris: Giard et Brière.

Andreades, A. (1906). *Lectures in Public Finance*, Athens (in Greek).

Andreades, A. (1909). *History of the Bank of England, 1640 to 1903*, London: King.

Andreades, A. (1927). Griechenland. In Mayer, H. (Ed.), *Die Wirtschaftstheorie der Gegenwart*, Vienna: Springer, 236–246

Andreades, A. (1928). *Les Effets Économiques et Sociaux de la Guerre en Grèce*, Paris: Presses Universitaires de France.

Andreades, A. (1933). *A History of Greek Public Finance*, Cambridge, MA: Harvard University Press.

Andreou, Ap. (1933). *The External Trade Policy of Greece, 1830–1933*, Athens (in Greek).

Angelomati-Tsougaraki, E. (1990). *The Eve of the Greek Revival: British Travelers' Perceptions of Early 18th Century Greece*, London: Routledge.

Angelopoulos, A. (1928). *Societes Anonymes in Greece from an Economic and a Fiscal Point of View* [Ph.D. thesis, ASOEE] (in Greek).

Angelopoulos, A. (1931). *Die Einkommensbesteurung im Lichte der Einkommenssteuerstatistik* [Ph.D. thesis, University of Leipzig].

Angelopoulos, A. (1932). *Charges Fiscales and Depenses publiques*, Paris.

Angelopoulos, A. (1933). *Direct Taxation in Greece*, Athens: Eleftheroudakis (in Greek).

Angelopoulos, A. (1937). *The Public Debt of Greece*, Athens: Eleftheroudakis (in Greek).

Angelopoulos, A. (1939). *Fiscal Policy and Economic Fluctuations*, Athens: Eleftheroudakis (in Greek).

Angelopoulos, A. (1942). *Public Finance*, Athens: Papazissis (in Greek).

Angelopoulos, A. (1953). *The Programmed Economy Versus Liberalism, New Economy*, 8, 490–495, 531–535 (in Greek).

Anónimos o Éllin (1973). *Hellenic Nomarchy, or Discourse on Freedom*, Athens: Kalvos (in Greek).
Anonymous (1837). *Wealth. Combined Lessons in Geography, History and Science Applied to Trade, the Arts, and Industrial Occupations*, Smyrna (in Greek).
Anonymous (1839). *Lives of Benjamin Franklin and Adamantios Korais and Poor Richard's Almanac for Greek Juniors*, Hermoupolis (in Greek).
Anthimos (1798). *Fatherly Teaching*, Constantinople: Pogos (in Greek).
Apostolopoulos, G. (1868). *On Agriculture in Greece, in Particular on the Agricultural Achool of Tyrins*, Nafplion: Ioannidis (in Greek).
Arena, R. (2000). J.B. Say and the French Liberal School of the Nineteenth Century: Outside the Canon. In: Forget, E. & Peart, S. (Eds.), *Reflection on the Classical Canon in Economics*, London: Routledge, 205–223.
Argyriadis, P. (1892–3). Contemporary Socialism, *The Socialist*, 12–38 (in Greek).
Argyropoulou, R. (1995). *Philosophical Thought in Greece*, Athens: Gnósi (in Greek).
Arndt, H. W. (1987). *Economic Development. The History of an Idea*, Chicago: University of Chicago Press.
Arsenis (1987). *Political testament*, Athens: Odysseas (in Greek).
Augello, M. & Guidi, M. (Eds.). (2001). *The Spread of Political Economy and the Professionalization of Economists*, London and New York: Routledge.
Augello, M. & Guidi, M. (Eds.). (2005). *Economists in Parliament in the Liberal Age (1848–1920)*, London: Ashgate.
Babanasis, S. & Soulas, K. (1976). *Greece in the Periphery of Developed Countries*, Athens: Themelio.
Backhouse, R. (1988). *Economists and the Economy: The Evolution of Economic Ideas, 1600 to the Present Day*, Oxford: Blackwell.
Backhouse, R. & Tribe, K. (Eds.). (2018). *The History of Economics*, Agenda: Newcastle.
Baeck, L. (1994). *The Mediterranean Tradition in Economic Thought*, London: Routledge.
Bairoch, P. (1976). Europe's Gross National Product 1800–1975, *The Journal of European Economic History*, 5, 273–340.
Bakopoulos, N. (1920). *On Banks of Issue*, Athens:Vitsikounakis (in Greek).
Bank of Greece (1992). *Long-Term Statistical Series of the Greek Economy*, Athens: Bank of Greece.
Bank of Greece (2020). *Statistical Series of the Greek Economy*, Athens: Bank of Greece.
Baran, P. & Sweezy, P. (1968). *Monopoly Capital*, New York: Monthly Review Press.
Barker, E. (1957). *Social and Political thought in Byzantium from Justinian I to the Last Palaeologus*, Oxford: Clarendon Press.
Barkoula, H. (2020). *Economic University of Athens, 100 Years of History, 1920–2020*, Athens: Mavrogenis (in Greek).
Barrau, Th. H. (1869). *Counsel to Workers on the Means which Make them Happy*, Athens: Vilaras (in Greek).
Bateman, B. W. (2011). German Influences in the Making of American Economists 1885–1935. In: Kurz, H. D., Nishizawa, T. & Tribe, K. (Eds.), *The Dissemination of Economic Ideas*, Cheltenham: Edward Elgar, 108–124.
Batsis, D. (1947). *Heavy Industry in Greece*, Athens: Nea Vivlia (in Greek).
Beaulieu, P. (1902). *Precis d' Économie Politique*, translated by K. Kypriadis, Athens: Estia (in Greek).
Bentham, J. (1948) [1789]. *An Introduction to the Principles of Morals and Legislation*, New York: Hafner Press.
Berend, I. & Ranki, G. (1982). *The European Periphery and Industrialization, 1780–1914*, Cambridge: Cambridge University Press.

Bernstein, E. (1921). *Der Streik. Sein Wesen und Wirken*, translated by S. Koronis, Athens: Eleftheroudakis (in Greek).
Bitsaxis, E. (1943). A Critical Analysis on Unemployment in the Theory of Keynes, *EKDO*, 11, 57–85.
Blaug, M. (1986). *Who's Who in Economics: A Biographical Dictionary of Major Economists, 1700–1986*, Cambridge: MIT Press.
Blaug, M. (1980). *The Methodology of Economics, or How Economists Explain*, Cambridge: Cambridge University Press.
Block, M. (1882). *Petit Manuel d' Économie Politique*, translated by K. Kypriadis, Athens: Enosis (in Greek).
Boccara, P. et al. (1971). *Le Capitalisme Monopoliste d' Etat*, 2 vols, Paris: Editions Sociales.
Bougatsos, N. (1980). *The Social Teaching of the Greek Fathers*, 3 vols, Athens: Apostoliki Diakonia (in Greek).
Brandt, K. (1992–1993). *Geschichte der Deutschen Volkswirtschaftslehre (vols. 1–2)*, Freiburg/Breisgau: Haufe.
Bredimas, A. (2021). *International Law and Diplomacy During the Years of the Revolution of 1821*, Athens: Sakkoulas (in Greek).
Breton, Y & Lutfalla, M. (1991). *L' Économie Politique en France au XIXe Siècle*, Paris: Economica.
Candilis, W. (1968). *The Economy of Greece*, Washington: Praeger.
Carabott, P. (Ed.). (1997). *Greek Society in the Making, 1863–1913: Realities, Symbols and Visions*, Aldershot: Ashgate.
Cardoso, F. (1970). Dependency and Development in L. America, *New Left Review*, No. 74.
Cardoso, J. L. (2003). The International Diffusion of Economic Thought. In: Samuels, W. J., Biddle, J. E. & Davis, J. B. (Eds.). *A Companion to the History of Economic Thought*, Malden, MA: Blackwell, 622–633.
Chalikias, D. (1958). *The Industrialization of Greece*, Athens: Bank of Greece (in Greek).
Chalikiopoulos, P. (1863–4). *Thoughts on Greece*, 2 vols, Patras: M. Georgiadis (in Greek).
Chalikiopoulos, P. (1880). *On the Improvement and Encouragement of Greek Agriculture*, Athens:Metarythmissis (in Greek).
Chalkiopoulos, G. (1943). *On the Theory of Wage Policy*, Athens: Papazissis (in Greek).
Chalkiopoulos, G. (1945). *The Price Mechanism in a Socialist Society*, Athens: Papazissis (in Greek).
Chalkiopoulos, G. (Ed.). (1967). *Long-term Trends of the Greek Economy*, Athens: Ethniko Idryma Erevnon (in Greek).
Charitakis, G. P. (1927). *Die Heutige griechische Industrie*, Hamburg: de Gruyter.
Charitakis, G. P. (1928). State and Economy, *Review of Local Government*, 7 (1–2), 17–29 (in Greek).
Charitakis, G. P. (1932). Individualism or Socialism? *EKDO*, 1, 1–25 (in Greek).
Charitakis, G. P. (1930). *Lectures in Social Economics*, Athens (in Greek).
Christidis, K. (1870). Speech Delivered at the Ceremony of the Second Period of Olympia, *Aion*, November 5 (in Greek).
Christodoulopoulos, P. (1930a). Die Finanzierung des beginnenden Aufschwungs, *Jahrbuecher fuer Nationaloekonomie und Statistik*, 133, 213–224.
Christodoulopoulos, P. (1930b). Die Konjunkturschwankugen der Aktienkurse, *Allgemeines Statistisches Archiv*, 20, 225–254.
Christodoulopoulos, P. (1930c). *Credit Policy and Reoccurring Crises*, Athens: Pyrsos, (in Greek).
Christodoulopoulos, P. (1930d). *Savings at the Bank of Issue*, in: Peitharchia in Greek8-9.
Christodoulopoulos, P. (1931). *Elasticity of Demand for Greek Tobacco* (in Greek).

Christodoulopoulos, P. (1935). *The Rebalancing of International Payments* (in Greek).
Christodoulopoulos, P. (1939). Unemployment and Saving. A Critical Essay on Keynes' Theory of Unemployment, *AKOE*, Winter 305–320 and Spring 1–99 (in Greek).
Christodoulopoulos, P. (1945). *Theoretical Political Economy: Introductory Lessons*, Athens: Papazissis (in Greek).
Christoula, R. (1946). *The Labor Theory of Value and Marxism*, Athens: Papazissis (in Greek).
Clarke, P. (1988). *The Keynesian Revolution in the Making, 1924–36*, Oxford: Clarendon Press.
Clogg, R. (1969). The Dhidaskalia Patriki 1798: An Orthodox Reaction to French Revolutionary Propaganda, *Middle Eastern Studies*, May, 87–115.
Clogg, R. (Ed.). (1973). *The Struggle for Greek Independence*, London: MacMillan Press.
Clogg, R. (2002). *A Concise History of Greece*, Cambridge: Cambridge University Press.
Club A. Papanastassiou (1966). *The Social-Political Forces in Greece*, Athens: Club Papanastassiou (in Greek).
Coats, A. W. (Ed.). (1996). The Post-1945 Internationalization of Economics, *History of Political Economy Annual Supplement*, 28, 1-11.
Coats, A. W. & Colander, D. (1989). An Introduction to the Spread of Economic Ideas. In: Colander, D. & Coats, A. W. (Eds.), *The Spread of Economic Ideas*, Cambridge: Cambridge University Press, 1–22.
Collison Black, R. (1987). T. C. Banfield. In: Eatwell, J., Milgate, M. & Newman, P. (Eds.), *The New Palgrave Dictionary of Economics*, vol. 1, London: Macmilan, 182.
Cooper, W. (1919). *The Claims of Labor and Capital*, translated by K. Dosios, Athens: Sideris (in Greek).
Dakin, D. (1972). *The Unification of Greece, 1770–1923*, London: Ernst Benn.
Damalas, V. (1946). The General Theory by Keynes, *EOPE*, 1, 191–204 (in Greek).
Damiris, C. (1920). *Le Systeme Monetaire Greque et la Change*, 3 vols, Paris: Giard.
Darvaris, D. (1796). *True Road to Happiness*, Vienna: Vendotis (in Greek).
Daunou, P. C. F. (1825). *Essay on Personal Insurance*, Athens: Didotou (in Greek).
Decasos, P. (1904). *Die Landwirtschaft im Heutigen Griechenland*, Berlin: Parey.
D'Eichtal, G. (1974) [1866]. *Economic and Social Situation in Greece after the Revolution*, Athens: Byron (in Greek).
Delivanis, D. (1931). *La Politique des Bankes Allemandes en Matière de Credit a Court Terme* [Ph.D. thesis, University of Paris].
Delivanis, D. (1935). *The Relationship Between the Internal and the External Value of the Currency in Greek*, Athens: Pyrsos (in Greek).
Delivanis, D. (1938). *On International Economic Relations and the Influence of Direct Government Measures on Them*, Athens: Pyrsos (in Greek).
Delivanis, D. (1939a). The Views of Mr. J.M. Keynes on Employment, Interest and Money, *EKDO*, Fall, 202–220, (in Greek).
Delivanis, D. (1939b). Economic Policy before and after August 4th, *Neon Kratos*, 21, May (in Greek).
Delivanis, D. (1940). The Instruments of Modern Economic Policy, *Neon Kratos*, 29, January (in Greek).
Delivanis, D. (1941). The Economic and Fiscal Policy of Ioannis Metaxas, *Neon Kratos*, 42, February (in Greek).
Demos, R. (1958). The Neo-Hellenic Enlightenment 1750–1821. A General Survey, *Journal of the History of Ideas*, XIX, 523–541.

Dertilis, G. B. (1980). *The Question of Banks, 1871–1873*, Athens: NBG (in Greek).

Dertilis, G. B. (1988). *Banquiers, Usuriers et Paysans*, Paris: La Decouverte.

Dertilis, G. B. (1993). *Taxes and Power in the Modern Hellenic State*, Athens: Alexandria (in Greek).

Dertilis, P. (1929). *La Reconstruction Financiere de la Grece et la Societe des Nations*, Paris: Rosseau.

Dertilis, P. (1930). *The Economics of Local Government*, Athens: Margaritis (in Greek).

Dertilis, P. (1936a). *La Dette de l'Emigration Greco-Bulgare et les Reparations*, Paris: Rodstein.

Dertilis, P. (1936b). *The State Budget*, Athens: Etaireia Dioikitikon Meleton (in Greek).

Dertilis, P. (1950). *Lessons in Sociology*, Thessaloniki: Sakkoulas (in Greek).

Dertilis, P. (1951). The Financial Clauses of Greek Constitutions, *EOPE*, 6 (4), 349–394 (in Greek).

Dertilis, P. (1953). *History of Economic Life*, Thessaloniki: Sakkoulas (in Greek).

Devletoglou, N. & Buchanan, J. (1970). *Academia in Anarchy: An Economic Diagnosis*, New York: Basic Books.

Diamantopoulos, A. (1861). *On Changes in Taxes*, Athens: To mellon tis patridos (in Greek).

Diomidis, A. (1905). *The Budget*, Athens: Raftanis (in Greek).

Dorfman, J. (1955). The Role of the German Historical School in American Economic Thought, *American Economic Review, Papers and Proceedings*, 45 (2), 17–28.

Dosios, A. (1867). *Les Limites d'Économie Politique*, Paris: Dentu.

Dosios, L. (1871). *On Industry in Greece*, Athens: Efimeris ton Sizitiseon (in Greek).

Drakoulis, P. (1893). *The Manual of the Labourer, or the Basis of Socialism*, Athens: Leonis (in Greek).

Droz, J. (1833) [1829]. *Economie politique ou principes de la science des richesses*, translated by A. Polyzoidis, Nafplio: Tombras (in Greek).

Duesenberry, J. (1949). *Income, Saving and the Theory of Consumer Behavior*, Cambridge, MA: Harvard University Press.

Eagly, R. (1968). *Events, Ideology and Economic Theory*, Detroit: Wayne State University Press.

EEPO (2011). *Economic Crisis and Greece*, Athens: Gutenberg (in Greek).

EEPOS (1916–17). *Minutes of the Society of Political Economy and Statistics*, Athens (in Greek).

Economos, Al. (1950). *Three Men*, Athens: Elliniki Ekdotiki (in Greek).

Economos, Ar. (1869). *The Freedom of Trade and Greek Industry*, Athens: Koromilas (in Greek).

Economos, Ar. (1872). *Lavrion*, Athens: Themis (in Greek).

Efmorfopoulos, L. (1863). *Few Words as an Answer to the Customs' Report of Mr Sotiropoulos*, Syros: Syros Chamber of Commerce (in Greek).

Efmorfopoulos, L. (1864). *On the Abolition of Custom Offices in Greece*, Athens: National Printing Office (in Greek).

Efmorfopoulos, L. (1865). The Society for the Freedom of Trade: A Speech, *Hermoupolis*, 24, January 30.

Ermis, F. (2013). *A History of Ottoman Economic Thought*, London: Routledge.

Evelpidis, C. (1930). *Les Etats Balkaniques*, Paris: Rousseau.

Evelpidis, C. (1935). *National Income*, Athens: Papazissis (in Greek).

Evelpidis, C. (1944). *Agriculture in Greece*, Athens: Logos (in Greek).

Evelpidis, C. (1948). *An Introduction to the Social Sciences, in Particular Economics*, Athens: Papazissis (in Greek).

Evelpidis, C. (1949). *Utopias and Realities*, Athens: Papazissis (in Greek).
Evelpidis, C. (1952). *Economic and Social History of Greece*, Athens: Papazissis (in Greek).
Evlambios, M. (1930–1931). *Efthymios I. Kehayias in the National Bank of Greece and His Parliamentary Activity*, 2 vols, Athens: Vlastos (in Greek).
Faccarello, G. & Steiner, P. (1990). *La Pensée Économique Pendant la Révolution Française*, Grenoble: Presses Universitaires de Grenoble.
Farakos, G. (1978). *Topics on Greek State Monopoly Capitalism*, Athens: Synchroni Epochi (in Greek).
Fawcett, M. (1881). *Political Economy for Beginners*, Athens: Iasemidis (in Greek).
Fetter, F. W. (1980). *The Economist in Parliament: 1780–1868*, Durham: Duke University Press.
Feyerabend, P. (1970). *Against Method*, London: Verso.
Filias, V. (1967). *The Problem of Productive Capital Formation in Underdeveloped Economies*, Athens: Papazissis (in Greek).
Forget, E. (1993). J.B. Say and Adam Smith: An Essay in the Transmission of Ideas, *Canadian Journal of Economics*, 26 (1), 121–133.
Forget, E. (1999). *The Social Economics of Jean-Baptiste Say*, London: Routledge.
Forget, E. (2001). Jean-Baptiste Say and Spontaneous Order, *History of Political Economy*, 33.2, 193–198.
Frank, A. (1970). *Capitalism and Underdevelopment in Latin America*, New York: Modern Reader.
Franklin, B. (1823). *Poor Richard's Almanac*, translated by F. Fournarakis, Paris (in Greek).
Franklin, B. (1831). *The Way to Wealth*, translated by I. Manesis, Triest (in Greek).
Freeden, M. (1978). *The New Liberalism: An Ideology of Social Reform*, Oxford: Oxford University Press.
Freris, A. F. (1986). *The Greek Economy in the Twentieth Century*, London: Croom Helm.
Friedman, M. (1967). *Money and Economic Development*, New York: Praeger.
Garganas, N. C. & Tavlas, G. S. (2001). *Monetary Regimes and Inflation Performance: The Case of Greece, in: Greece's Economic Performance and Prospects*, Athens: Bank of Greece, 43–95.
Garnier, J. (1869). *Éléments de l'Économie Politique*, translated by D. Despotopoulos, Athens: Passaris (in Greek).
Gaston, R. (1919). *Le Socialisme et la Science Sociale*, translated by I. Oikonomopoulos, Athens: Fexis (in Greek).
Gavriilidis, V. (1918). *Labouring Greece*, 3 vols, Athens: Akropolis (in Greek).
Gavroglou, K., Karamanolakis, V. & Barkoula, H. (2014). *The University of Athens and its History*, Herakleion: Crete University Press (in Greek).
Gedeon, M. I. (2010). *The Nation's Spiritual Movement during 18th and 19th Century*, Athens: Hermes (In Greek).
Gekas, S. (2016). *Xenocracy: State Class and Colonialism in the Ionian Islands*, New York: Berghan Books.
Genc, M. (1994). Ottoman Industry in the Eighteenth Century: General Framework, Characteristics and Main Trends. In: Quataert, D. (Ed.). *Manufacturing in the Ottoman Empire and Turkey 1500–1950*, Albany: State University of New York Press, 59–86.
Georgiadis, G. (no year). *Socialism. Problems of Theory, Application and Practice*, I & II, Athens: Papazisis (in Greek).
Ghazanfar, S. M. (Ed.). (2003). *Medieval Islamic Economic Thought: Filling the "Great Gap" in European Economics*, London: Routledge.

Giannakopoulos, N. (1969). *The Application of Solutions of Neumann, Morgenstern and Nash on Bilateral Monopoly*, Athens: Papazissis (in Greek).

Giannios, N. (1914). *Socialism of the State*, Athens: Sosialistiko Kentro (in Greek).

Giannitsis, T. (1985). *The Greek Industry, Development and Crisis*, Athens: Gutenberg (in Greek).

Giannitsis, T. (1991). Economic Integration and Development: The Experience of a Newly Industrializing Economy, Greece 1981–87, *Rivista Internazionale di Scienze Economiche e Commerciali*, 1, 55–79.

Gide, C. (1923). *Principes d'Economie Politique*, translated by E. Tsouderos, Athens: Eleftheroudakis (in Greek).

Giouras, T. (2000). *Taxation and Politics*, Athens: Karagiorgas Foundation (in Greek).

Goodwin, C. (1972). Economic Theory and Society. A Plea for Process Analysis, *American Economic Review, Papers and Proceedings*, 62 (1/2), 409–415.

Goodwin, C. D. W. & Holley Jr., I. B., (Eds.). (1968). *The Transfer of Ideas: Historical Essays*, Durham: Duke University Press.

Gordon, B. (1975). *Economic Analysis Before Adam Smith. Hesiod to Lessius*, London: Macmillan.

Gordon, B. (1976). *Political Economy in Parliament 1819–1823*, New York: Barnes and Noble.

Gordon, S. (1991). *The History and Philosophy of Social Science*, London: Routledge.

Goudas, A. N. (1874). *Parallel Lives of Distinguished Men During the Renaissance of Greece*, 2nd ed. 2011, Athens: Passaris (in Greek).

Goudi, M. (1946). The General Theory as an Explanation of the Economic Cycle, *EPOE*, 1, 205–223 (in Greek).

Goudi, M. (1947). *Indifference Curve Analysis According to J. R. Hicks*, *EPOE*, 2, 297–333 (in Greek).

Goudi, M. (1950). *Observations on the Problem of Exports After the Readjustment*, Athens: Papazissis (in Greek).

Goudi, M. (1953). *The Readjustment of the Exchange Rate Parity*, Athens: Papazissis (in Greek).

Goudi, M. (1962). *How General is Contemporary Theory of Economic Development?* Athens: Papazissis (in Greek).

Goudi, M. (1968). *On Money*, Athens: Sakkoulas (in Greek).

Gounarakis, N. (1882). *On Metallic Legal Money, in Particular on Bimetallism*, Athens: Enosis (in Greek).

Gounarakis, N. (1890). *Inaugural Lecture on Political Economy*, Athens: Paliggenesia (in Greek).

Gounarakis, N. (1918). *Elements of Political Economy*, 3rd ed., vol. 1, Athens: Paliggenesia.

Grampp, W. (1965). On the History of Thought and Policy, *American Economic Review*, 55, 128–135.

Grapsas, C. M. (1948). *Greek Political Encyclopedia*, 2 vols, Athens: Vouli ton Ellinon (in Greek).

Grimmer-Solem, E. (2003). *The Rise of Historical Economics and Social Reform in Germany: 1864–1894*, Oxford: Oxford University Press.

Grimmer-Solem, E. & Romani, R. (1999). In Search of Full Empirical Reality: Historical Political Economy, 1870–1900, *European Journal of the History of Economic Thought*, 6 (3), 333–364.

Halevy, E. (1928). *The Growth of English Radicalism*, translated by M. Morris, London: Faber and Faber.

Haney, L. (1927). *History of Economic Thought*, New York: Macmillan.
Hardach, G., Karras, D. & Fine, B. (1978). *A Short History of Socialist Economic Thought*, London: Arnold.
Harlaftis, G. (1996). *History of Greek Owned Shipping*, London: Routledge.
Harrison, R. (1983). *Bentham*. London: Routledge.
Henderson, G. P. (1970). *The Revival of Greek Thought, 1620–1830*, Albany: State University of New York Press.
Herbst, J. (1965). *The German Historical School in American Scholarship: A Study in the Transfer of Culture*. Ithaca: Cornell University Press.
Hering, G. (1992). *Die Politischen Parteien in Griechenland 1821–1936*, München: Oldenbourg.
Herkner, H. (1919). *The Labor Issue*, Athens: Eleftheroudakis (in Greek).
Hobhouse, L. (1994) [1911]. *Liberalism and Other Writings*, Cambridge: Cambridge University Press.
Howard, M. & King, J. (1992). *A History of Marxian Economics*, 2 vols, Princeton: Princeton University Press.
Hutchison, T. W. (1956). Bentham as an Economist. *The Economic Journal*, 66(262), 288–306.
Hutchison, T. W. (1988). *Before Adam Smith: The Emergence of Political Economy, 1662–1776*, Oxford: Basil Blackwell.
Iliou, I. (1962). *The Truth About the Common Market*, Athens: Oikonomia-Politiki) (in Greek).
Inalcik, H. (1970). The Ottoman Economic Mind and Aspects of the Ottoman Economy. In: Cook, M. A. (Ed.), *Studies in the Economic History of the Middle East*, London: Oxford University Press, 207–218.
Inalcik, H. & Quataert, D. (1995). *An Economic and Social History of the Ottoman Empire, 1300–1914*, Cambridge: Cambridge University Press.
Ionescu, G. (1976). *The Political Thought of Saint-Simon*, Oxford: Oxford University Press.
Ithakissios, D. (1992). John A. Soutsos (1804–1890): Greece's First Academic Economist, *Quaderni di Storia dell Economia Politica*, 2, 136–148.
Jacoud, G. (2010). *Political Economy and Industrialism: Banks in Saint-Simonian Economic Thought*, London: Routledge.
Kakridis, A. (2017). *Kyriakos Varvaressos*, Athens: Bank of Greece (in Greek).
Kalafatis, T. (Ed.). (2009). *70 Years University of Piraeus*, Piraeus: University of Piraeus (in Greek).
Kalitsounakis, D. (1921). The Present Trend Towards Nationalization, *AOKE*, 1, 49–72 (in Greek).
Kalitsounakis, D. (1925). *Political Science: Characterisations, Economic, and Social Studies*, Athens: Eleftheroudakis & Barth (in Greek).
Kalitsounakis, D. (1926). *Theory of Money*, Athens: Vassiliou (in Greek).
Kalitsounakis, D. (1929). *History of Political Economy: Economic History and History of Economic Doctrines*, Athens: Eleftheroudakis (in Greek).
Kalitsounakis, D. (1930). Sombart and the Systematization of Political Economy, *AOKE*, 10, 165–212 (in Greek).
Kalitsounakis, D. (1932). *Tobacco*, Athens: Zacharopoulos (in Greek).
Kalitsounakis, D. (1936). Eleftherios K. Venizelos (1864–1936), *AOKE*, 16, 99–101 (in Greek).
Kalitsounakis, D. (1943). *Economic Forecast: Contribution to the Morphology of the Capitalist Society*, Athens: Papazissis (in Greek).

Kalitsounakis, D. (1946). Prospects for the Future in the Economy, *Nea Oikonomia*, 1, 52–53. (in Greek).
Kalitsounakis, D. (1952a). Keynesian and Antikeynesian Views on Economic Equilibrium. In: *Yearbook of the Panteios Graduate School of Political Sciences*, 183–198, Athens (in Greek).
Kalitsounakis, D. (1952b). Bookreview, W. Eucken Grundsaetze der Wirschaftspolitik, *AOKE*, 32, 199–201 (in Greek).
Kalitsounakis, D. (1957). The Relation of Monetary and Fiscal Policy in Keynesian Theory. In: *Yearbook of the Panteios Graduate School of Political Sciences 1957*, 97–110, Athens (in Greek).
Kallergis, S. (1893a). *Vademecum for the Laborer*, Athens (in Greek).
Kallergis, S. (1893b). *A Letter to all Greek Socialists*, Athens: Sosialistiko Kentro (in Greek).
Kalostypis, I. (1885). *National Industry*, Athens: Efimeris (in Greek).
Karagiorgas, D. (1965). The Role of the State in the Five-Year Plan for Economic Development, *Spoudai*, 16, 1022–1032 (in Greek).
Karakostas, I. (Ed.). (2010). *The Law School 1837–1982*, Athens: Sakkoulas (in Greek).
Karanikolas, G. (1963). *Illegitimate Elections in Greece 1844–1961*, Athens: Antoniadis (in Greek).
Karayiannis, A. (1994). The Eastern Christian Fathers (350–400 A.D.) on the Redistribution of Wealth, *History of Political Economy*, 26 (1), 39–67.
Karayiannis, A. & Ithakissios, D. (1999). Hellenic Nomarchy: A Discourse on Freedom. An Early 19th Century Greek Humanist Treatise, *Storia del Pensiero Economico*, 38, 137–144.
Kassimatis, S. (1865). A Speech by S. Kassimatis. *Eleftheria tou Emporiou*, 8, 197–207, 9, 217–227, 10, 249–261, 11: 282–291, 12, 31–39.
Katiforis, S. (1938). *Theory of Monetary Policy*, Athens: Zacharopoulos (in Greek).
Katiforis, S. (1939). *Retrospect and Additions to the Theory of Distribution*, Athens: Pyrsos (in Greek).
Katiforis, S. (1941). *Reward of Capital and Interest Rate*, Athens: Vasileiou (in Greek).
Katselidis, G. (1902). *The Currency*, Athens: Estia (in Greek).
Kazazis, N. (1894). *General Principles of Political Economy*, Athens: Saliveros.
Kehagias, E. (1875). *The New Monetary System*, Athens: Papalexandris (in Greek).
Kerofilas, K. (1915). *Eleftherios Venizelos. His Life and Work*, London: Murray (in Greek).
Keynes, J. M. (1935). Andrew Andréadès, *Economic Journal*: 45, September, 597-9.
Keynes, J. M. (1936). *The General Theory of Employment, Interest and Money*, London: Macmillan.
Kitromilidis, P. (1988). European Political Thought in the Making of Greek Liberalism: The Second National Assembly of 1862–1864 and the Reception of John Stuart Mill's Ideas in Greece, *Parliaments, Estates and Representation*, 8 (1), 11–21.
Kitromilidis, P. (1992). *The Enlightenment as Social Criticism*, Princeton: Princeton University Press.
Kitromilidis, P. M. (1999). *Neohellenic Enlightment*, Athens: MIET (in Greek).
Kitromilidis, P. (Ed.). (2006). *Eleftherios Venizelos: The Trials of Statesmanship*, Edinburgh: Edinburgh University Press.
KKE (1975). *Official Texts*, 4 vols, Athens: Synchroni Epochi (in Greek).
Kofas, J. (1981). *Financial Relations of Greece and the Great Powers*, New York: Columbia University Press.
Kofinas, G. (1901). *Interpretation of Tariff Legislation*, Athens: Konstantinides (in Greek).
Kokkalis, A. (1934). *The Economic Crisis*, Thessaloniki: Alexios kai Pikopoulos (in Greek).

Kokkalis, A. (1950). *Introduction to the Total Theory of Labor: New Positive Foundation of Economics*, Athens (in Greek).

Kokkinos, G. (1996). *Political Irrationalism in Greece. The Work and Thought of Neoklis Kazazis*, Athens: Trochalia (in Greek).

Koliopoulos, J. & Veremis, T. (2002). *Greece: The Modern Sequel. From 1831 to the Present*, London: Hurst.

Korais, A. (1798). *Brotherly Teaching to all Greeks Found in the Ottoman State*, Rome (in Greek).

Korais, A. (1803). *Mémoire sur l'état actuel de la civilisation dans la Grèce*, Paris: Societe des observateurs de l' homme.

Kordatos, G. (1924). *The Social Meaning of the Greek Revolution of 1821*, Athens: Papadogiannis (in Greek).

Kordatos, G. (1930). *Introduction in the History of Greek Capitalism*, Athens: Vivliothiki Koinonikon Erevnon (in Greek).

Kordatos, G. (1932). *History of the Greek Labor Movement*, 2 vols, Athens: Karavakos (in Greek).

Koromilas, L. (1894). Revenues and Taxes. In: Syrmaloglou, A. (2021). *Taxation, Democracy and State Formation*, Athens: Metamesonychties ekdoseis, 125–405 (in Greek).

Koronis, S. (1914). *Greek Railways and Railway Policy*, Athens: Eleftheroudakis (in Greek).

Koronis, S. (1920). *Technique and Economy*, Athens: Vergiannitis (in Greek).

Koronis, S. (1931). *International Commercial Policy can't Save Europe*, Athens: Papazissis (in Greek).

Koronis, S. (1944). *The Labor Policy of 1909–1918*, Athens: Papazissis (in Greek).

Kostelenos, G. (1995). *Money and Output in Modern Greece, 1858–1938*, Athens: KEPE (in Greek).

Kostelenos, G. (2003). Historical Estimates of National Accounts Magnitudes in Greece, 1837–1939, *Spoudai*, 53 (1), 37–64.

Kostelenos, G. & Kazis, D. (2011). *50 Years of the Centre of Planning and Economic Research*, Athens: KEPE.

Kotsowilis, K. (1995). *Die griechischen Studenten in München unter Koenig Ludwig I von Bayern von 1826 bis 1844*, Uni München: Magisterarbeit.

Koulis, I. (1943). *Wirtschaftliche Grundfragen des Staatskredits* [Ph.D. thesis, Univesity of Munich].

Koulis, I. (1948). *Social Arrangement of Taxation or Economic Tax Policy*, Athens: Sakkoulas (in Greek).

Koulis, I. (1950). *The Tax Burden in Greece*, Athens: Sakkoulas (in Greek).

Koulis, I. (1954). *Public Finance and Fiscal Policy*, Athens: Sakkoulas (in Greek).

Kountouris, M. (1998). *The Evolution of Economic Thought in Greece: 1837–1942* [Unpublished Ph.D. thesis, University of Athens] (in Greek).

Koutoupis, Th. (1908). *Economics of the Greeks*, Athens: Tarousopoulos (in Greek).

Koutoupis, Th. (1933). *Political Economy*, 2 vols, Athens: Dimitrakos (in Greek).

Koutoupis, Th. (1935). *Public Finance*, 2 vols, Athens: Dimitrakos (in Greek).

Koutsoyiannis, A. (1973). *Theory of Econometrics*, Basingstoke: Macmillan.

Koutsoyiannis, A. (1975). *Modern Microeconomics*, Basingstoke: Macmillan.

Koutsoyiannis, A & A. Gana (1967). *Input-output Table of the Greek Economy 1960*, Athens: KEPE (in Greek).

Krimpas, G. (1975). *Keynes' General Theory*, Athens: Papazissis (in Greek).

Kuhn, T. (1962). *The Structure of Scientific Revolutions*, Chicago: University of Chicago Press.

Kurihara, K. (1959). *The Keynesian Theory of Economic Development*, London, New York: Columbia University Press.
Laiou, A. & Morrison, C. (Eds.). (2007). *The Byzantine Economy*, Cambridge: Cambridge University Press.
Laiou, A., Morrisson, C. & Dorin, R. (Eds.). (2013). *Economic Thought and Economic Life in Byzantium*, London: Routledge.
Lakatos, I. & Musgrave, A. (Eds.). (1970). *Criticism and the Growth of Knowledge*, Cambridge: Cambridge University Press.
Lampe, J. R. & Jackson, M. R. (1982). *Balkan Economic History, 1550–1950*, Indiana: Indiana University Press.
La Nauze, J. (1972). Hearn, William Edward (1826–1888). In *Australian Dictionary of Biography*, vol. 4. Melbourne: Melbourne University Press, 370–372.
Langholm, O. (1992). *Economics in Medieval Schools*, Leiden: Brill.
Laskaridis, C. & Syrmaloglou, A. (2019). Two Sticks and One Carrot: Public Debt and the International Financial Commission in Greece, 1854–1859, *Œconomia*, 9 (4), 797–829.
De Laveleye, E. (1894). *Elements d'Economie Politique*, Athens: Vlastos (in Greek).
Legg, K. R. (1969). *Politics in Modern Greece*, Stanford: Stanford University Press.
Leroux, R. (Ed.). (2012). *French Liberalism in the 19th Century: An Anthology*, Routledge.
Levandis, J. (1944). *The Greek Foreign Debt and the Great Powers, 1821–1898*, New York: Columbia University Press.
Loules, D. (1985). *The Financial and Economic Policies of President Ioannis Capodistrias, 1828–1831* [Ph.D. thesis, King's College London].
Loverdos, Sp. (1901–2). *The National Wealth*, 2 vols, Athens: Syllogos pros diadosin ofelimon vivlion (in Greek).
Loverdos, Sp. (1916). *War and the Economic Intervention of the State*, Athens:Tarousopoulos (in Greek).
Lowry, S. T. & Gordon, B. (Eds.). (1998). *Ancient and Medieval Economic Ideas and Concepts of Social Justice*, New York: Brill.
Macrakis, M. (2000). *Andreas Papandreou. The Beginning*, Athens: Katoptro (in Greek).
Maddison, A. (1995). *Monitoring the World Economy, 1820–1992*, Paris: OECD.
Maddison, A. (1997). The Nature and Functioning of European Capitalism: A Historical and Comparative Perspective, *Banca Nazionale del Lavoro Quarterly Review*, 203, 431–479.
Magliulo, A. (2022). *A History of European Economic Thought*, London: Routledge.
Magnusson, L. (1994). *Mercantilism: The Shaping of an Economic Language*, London: Routledge.
Malamatianos, K. (1931). *On the Economic Problem of Greece*, Athens: Leonis (in Greek).
Mallios, M. (1975). *The Modern Phase of Development of Capitalism in Greece*, Athens: Synchroni Epochi (in Greek).
Maloney, J. (1985). *Marshall, Orthodoxy and the Professonalization of Economics*, Cambridge: Cambridge University Press.
Manuel, F. E. (1956). *The New World of Henri Saint-Simon*, Cambridge, MA: Harvard University Press.
Mason, E. (1982). The Harvard Department of Economics from the Beginning to World War II, *Quarterly Journal of Economics*, 97, 383–433.
Masson-Vincourt, M. (2000). *Paul Calligas (1814–1896) et la Fondation de l'État Grec*, Paris: Harmattan.
Mathas, Z. (1847). *Historical Catalogue of the First Bishops and the Patriarchs of the Holy and Great Church of Constantinople*, Nafplion: Koromilas (in Greek).

Maurer, G. L. [1835] (1976). *The Greek People*, Athens: Tolidis (in Greek).
Mavrokordatos, G. (1838). *A Manual of Greek Commercial Legislation*, vol. 1, Athens (in Greek).
Maximos, S. (1930). *Parliament, or Dictatorship?* Athens: Karavias (in Greek).
Maximos, S. (1940). *The Greek Merchant Marine in the 18th Century*, Athens: Flamma (in Greek).
Maximos, S. (1943). *Theoretical Economics and Economic Lack of Judgement*, Athens: Loukatos (in Greek).
Maximos, S. (1945). *The Dawn of Greek Capitalism. Turkish Rule 1685–1789*, Athens: Karavias (in Greek).
McGrew, W. (1985). *Land and Revolution in Modern Greece, 1800–1881*, Kent: Kent University Press.
Melas, K. (1848). *Treatise on Commerce, Industry, Shipping and on Trade Transactions in Particular*, Athens (in Greek).
Milward, A. & Saul, J. (1977). *The Development of the Economies of Continental Europe*, London: Allen & Unwin.
Mitchell, B. R. (1978). *European Historical Statistics, 1750–1950*, Cambridge: Columbia University Press.
Mitrofanis, G. (1992). *Taxation of Primary Production in Greece (1828–1862)* [Ph.D. thesis, University of Athens] (in Greek).
Mitsos, A. (Ed). (1981). *The Accession in the European Communities*, Athens: Synchrona Themata (in Greek).
Mommen, A. (2011). *Stalin's Economist. The Economic Contributions of Jeno Varga*, London: Routledge.
Mueller-Armack, A. (1947). *Wirtschaftslenkung und Marktwirtschaft*, Berlin: Haupt.
Naftalin, A., Nelson, B., Sibley, M., Calhoun, D. & Papandreou, A. (1953). *An Introduction to Social Science*, Chicago: Lippincott.
Naftis, G. (1859). *General Principles of Trade*, Athens: Mavromatis (in Greek).
Negreponti–Delivani, M. (1960). *L'Influence du Developpment Economique sur l'Allocation des Revenues*, Paris: SEDES.
Negreponti–Delivani, M. (1962). *Le Développement de la Grèce du Nord Depuis 1912*, Thessaloniki: Etairia Makedonikon Spoudon.
Negreponti–Delivani, M. (1965). *Lectures on the History of Economic Thought*, Thessaloniki: Sakkoulas (in Greek).
Negreponti–Delivani, M. (1969). *Economic Analysis*, Thessaloniki: Sakkoulas (in Greek).
Negreponti–Delivani, M. (1970). *La Contribution des Investissements Publics au Developpment Regional de la Grece*, The Hague.
Nelson, R. (1987). The Economics Profession and the Making of Public Policy, *Journal of Economic Literature*, XXV, 49–91.
von Neumann, J. & Morgenstern, O. (1947). *Theory of Games and Economic Behavior*, Princeton: Princeton University Press.
Nikolaou, N. (1991). The Economic Policy of the Last Decade is Responsible for Today's Dead-End, *Economicos Tachidromos*, April 4 (in Greek).
Nokkala, E. & Miller, N. B. (Eds.). (2019). *Cameralism and the Enlightenment*, New York: Routledge.
Noutsos, P. (1992–93). *Socialist Thought in Greece, from 1875 to 1974*, 5 vols, Athens: Gnosi (in Greek).
Nowack, J. (1809). *Grundriss der Handlungsgeschichte*, Vienna: Johann Zweck (in Greek).

O'Brien, D. P. (2004). *The Classical Economists Revisited*, Princeton: Princeton University Press.

Özveren, E. (2002). Ottoman Economic Thought and Economic Policy in Transition: Rethinking the Nineteenth Century. In: Psalidopoulos, M. & Mata, M. (Eds.). *Economic Thought and Policy in Less Developed Europe*, London: Routledge, 129–144.

Palairet, M. (1997). *The Balkan Economies, c. 1880–1914: Evolution Without Development*, Cambridge: Cambridge University Press.

Paleologos, G. (1833–1835). *Agricultural and Home Economics*, Nafplio: Royal Printing House (in Greek).

Pamuk, Ş. (1987). *The Ottoman Empire and European Capitalism, 1820–1913*, Cambridge: Cambridge University Press.

Panas, E. (1971). *Problems of Control of Aggregate Demand*. Athens: Bank of Greece (in Greek).

Panas, E. (1972). *Collected Papers on Economic Planning*. Athens: Bank of Greece (in Greek).

Pantelakis, N. (2018). *Alexandros Diomidis*, Athens: Metamesonychties Ekdoseis (in Greek).

Papaderos, A. (1970). *Metakenosis. Griechenlands Kulturelle Herausfordetrung Durch die Aufklaerung*, Meisenheim: Hein.

Papadopoulos, N. (1815). *Ermathini, or Business Studies*, Venice: Glykis (in Greek).

Papadopoulos, N. (1815–17). *The Gainful Hermes, A Commercial Encyclopedia*, Venice: Glykis (In Greek).

Papageorgiou, K. (2012). *Jeremy Bentham and the Greek Revolution*, Athens: Foundation of Greek Parliament (in Greek).

Papaligouras, P. (1996). *Speeches-Articles*, edited by M. Psalidopoulos, Athens: Aiolos (in Greek).

Papanastasiou, A. (1972). *Political Writings*, 2 vols, Athens: Byron (in Greek).

Papandreou, A. (1943). *The Location and Scope of the Entrepreneurial Function* [Ph.D. thesis, Harvard University].

Papandreou, A. (1949). Market Structure and Monopoly Power, *American Economic Review*, 39, 883–897.

Papandreou, A. (1950). Economics and the Social Sciences, *Economic Journal*, 60, 715–723.

Papandreou, A. (1952). Some Basic Problems in the Theory of the Firm. In: Haley, B. (Ed.), *A Survey of Contemporary Economics*, Homewood: Irwin, 183–222.

Papandreou, A. (1953). An Experimental Test of an Axiom in the Theory of Choice, *Econometrica*, 21, 477.

Papandreou, A. (1957). *A Test of a Stochastic Theory of Choice*, Los Angeles: University of California Press.

Papandreou, A. (1958). *Economics as a Science*, Chicago: Lippincott.

Papandreou, A. (1962a). *A Strategy for Greek Economic Development*, Athens: Center of Economic Research.

Papandreou, A. (1962b). *Fundamentals of Model Construction in Macroeconomics*, Athens: Center of Economic Research.

Papandreou, A. (1963). Theory Construction and Empirical Meaning in Economics. *American Economic Review, Papers and Proceedings*, 53, 205–210.

Papandreou, A. (1965a). A New Economic Policy for Greece, *To Vima*, January 30 (in Greek).

Papandreou, A. (1965b). *The Political Element in Economic Development*, Stockholm: The Wicksell Lectures.

Papandreou, A. (1970). *Man's Freedom*, New York: Columbia University Press.

Papandreou, A. (1971). *Paternalistic Capitalism*, Minneapolis: University of Minnesota Press.

Papandreou, A. (1973). *Democracy at Gunpoint*, Harmondsworth: Penguin.

Papandreou, A. (1975). *Imperialism and Economic Development*, Athens: Nea Sinora (In Greek).

Papandreou, A. (1976a). *From PAK to PASOK*, Athens: Ladias (In Greek).

Papandreou, A. (1976b). *Greece to the Greeks*, Athens: Karanasis (In Greek).

Papandreou, A. (1977a). *For a Socialist Society*, Athens: Echmi (In Greek).

Papandreou, A. (1977b). *Transition to Socialism*, Athens: Echmi (In Greek).

Papandreou, A. & Wheeler, J. (1954). *Competition and its Regulation*, New York: Prentice Hall.

Papandreou, A. & Zohar, U. (1974). *Project Selection for National Plans*, New York: Praeger.

Paraskevopoulos, I. (1936). *Economic Credit*, (in Greek).Athens: Zacharopoulos.

Parios, A. (1802). *Antiphonisis*, Ermoupolis: Ethnos (in Greek).

Parios, A. (Ed.) (2015). *Christian Teaching*, Athens: Grigori (in Greek).

Parish, H. (1838). *The Diplomatic History of the Monarchy of Greece*, London: Hatchard.

Parsons, T. (1949). *The Structure of Social Action*, Glencoe: The Free Press.

Pavlopoulos, P. (2022). *The Constitutional Foundations of the Modern Greek State*, Athens: Evrasia (in Greek).

Perakis, M. (2000). The Replacement of Tithe by the Tax on Animals Used in Agriculture. In: Aroni-Tsichli, K. & Tricha, L. (Eds.). *Harilaos Trikoupis and His Era*, Athens: Papazissis (in Greek).

Perry, G. & Tobin, J. (Eds). (2000). *Economic Events, Ideas and Policies*, Washington, DC: Brookings.

Pesmazoglou, I. (1939). *The Subjective Theory of Value*, Athens: University of Athens (in Greek).

Pesmazoglou, I. (1945). *Labor Market and Labor Employment* [Ph.D. thesis, University of Athens] (in Greek).

Pesmazoglou, I. (1945). *On Transports in General and Especially in Greece*, Athens: Papazissis (in Greek).

Pesmazoglou, I. (1949). *Certain Aspects of the International Transmission of Cyclical Fluctuations, 1870–1913* [Ph.D thesis, University of Cambridge].

Pesmazoglou, I. (1957). *Developments and Prospects for the Greek Economy*, Athens: Bank of Greece (in Greek).

Pesmazoglou, I. (1958). *Greece Facing the Tendencies of European Economic Unification*, Athens: Bank of Greece (in Greek).

Pesmazoglou, I. (1962). *The Association of Greece with the EEC*, Athens: Bank of Greece (in Greek).

Pesmazoglou, I. (1965). *The Relation Between Monetary and Fiscal Policy*, Athens: Bank of Greece (in Greek).

Petras, J. (1987). The Contradictions of Greek Socialism, *New Left Review*, 163, 3–25.

Petropulos, J. (1968). *Politics and Statecraft in the Kingdom of Greece, 1833–1843*, Princeton: Princeton University Press.

Petropulos, J. (1981). The Greek Economy during the First Decade of Othonian Rule, *Bulletin of Historical and Ethnological Society of Greece*, 24, 142–228.

Petrou, I. (1992). *Church and Politics in Greece (1750–1909)*, Thessaloniki: Kyriakidis (in Greek).

Pintos, I. (1934). *Preisbildung im unvollkommenen Monopol* [Ph.D. Thesis, University of Munich].

Pintos, I. (1936). *The Theoretical Analysis of Price Changes in the Modern Economy*, Athens: Sakkoulas (in Greek).

Pintos, I. (1939). The Equation of Saving and Investment in Modern Economic Theory, *EKDO*, Spring, 78–89, Summer 129–142 (in Greek).

Pipinelis, P. (1932). *The Monarchy in Greece, 1833–43*, Athens: Vartsos (in Greek).

Plamenatz, J. (1973). *Liberalism, Dictionary of the History of Ideas*, vol. 3, New York: Charles Scribner, 36–61.

Platis, K. (1840). *Treatise on Commerce and Commercial Laws*, Hermoupolis: N.K. (in Greek).

Politis, T. (2011). *IOBE and the Greek Economy, 1974–2010. 35 Years of Co-Existence*, Athens: IOBE (in Greek).

Potier, J. P. & Tiran, A. (Eds.). (2003). *Jean Baptiste Say. Nouveaux Regards sur son œuvre*, Paris: Economica.

Pouliopoulos, P. (1924). Greek Menshevikism, *KOMEP*, 7, 9–10 (in Greek).

Pouliopoulos, P. (1934a). *Democratic or Socialist Revolution in Greece?* Athens: Govostis (in Greek).

Pouliopoulos, P. (1934b). Stalinist Underconsumption of Economic Thought, *Spartakos*, 23 (5), 14–19 (in Greek).

Poulopoulos, S. (1943). *Economic Science in Greece*, Athens (in Greek).

Psalidopoulos, M. (1989). *The Crisis of 1929 and the Greek Economists*, Athens: Foundation of the Commercial Bank of Greece (in Greek).

Psalidopoulos, M. (Ed.). (1994). *Essays on Greek Industry in the 19th Century*, Athens: ETBA (in Greek).

Psalidopoulos, M. (1996a). Aristides Economos and the "Oikonomiki Epitheorissis": The Rise and Fall of an Economic Journal in 19th Century Greece, *History of Economic Ideas*, 4 (3), 149–167.

Psalidopoulos, M. (1996b). Keynesianism Across Nations: The Case of Greece, *European Journal for the History of Economic Thought*, 3 (3), 449–462.

Psalidopoulos, M. (1999). *Political Economy and Greek Intellectuals*, Athens: Typothito-Dardanos (in Greek).

Psalidopoulos, M. (2000). Institutional Constraints and the Internationalization of Economics: The Case of Greece. In: A. W. Bob Coats (Ed.), *The Development of Economics in Western Europe*, London: Routledge, 227–245.

Psalidopoulos, M. (2005). The Greek "Society for the Freedoms of Trade" (1865–7): Rise, Activities, Decline, *Journal of the History of Economic Thought*, 27 (4), 383–398.

Psalidopoulos, M. (2006). Economic Thought and Policies. In Kostis, K. & Petmezas, S. (Eds.), *The Development of Greek Economy During the 19th Century*, Athens: Historical Archive of Alpha Bank, 337–377 (in Greek).

Psalidopoulos, M. (2008). *Xenophon Zolotas and the Greek Economy*, Athens: Metamesonychties ekdoseis (in Greek).

Psalidopoulos, M. (2010). *Economists and Economic Policy in Modern Greece*, Athens: Metamesonychties ekdoseis (in Greek).

Psalidopoulos, M. (2014), "New liberalismand the economic policy of Eleftherios Venizelos," Athens: Idryma tis Voulis tn Ellinon (in Greek), p. 171–192.

Psalidopoulos, M. (2015a). Greece. In: Barnett, V. (Ed.), *Handbook of the History of Global Economic Thought*, London: Routledge, 68–76.

Psalidopoulos, M. (2019). *The Greek Loans*, Athens: Papadopoulos (in Greek).

Psalidopoulos, M. (2023). *Panagis Papaligouras. An Intellectual in Politics*, Athens: Foundation of Greek Parliament (in Greek).

Psalidopoulos, M. & Mata, M. (Eds.) (2002). *Economic Thought and Policy in Less Developed Europe*. London: Routledge.
Psalidopoulos, M. & Stassinopoulos, Y. (2009). A Liberal Economist and Economic Reform in Nineteenth Century Greece: The Case of Ioannis Soutsos, *History of Political Economy*, 41 (3), 491–517.
Psalidopoulos, M. & Syrmaloglou, A. (2005). Economists in the Greek Parliament (1862–1910). In: Augello, M. & Guidi, M. (Eds.), *The Economist in Parliament in the Liberal Age: A Comparative Perspective*, Aldershot: Ashgate, 227–256.
Psalidopoulos, M. & Theocarakis, N. (2011). The Dissemination of Economic Thought in South-Eastern Europe in the Nineteenth Century. In: Kurz, H., Nishizawa, T., & Tribe, K. (Eds.), *The Dissemination of Economic Ideas*, Cheltenham: Elgar, 161–191.
Psalidopoulos, M. & Theocarakis, N. (2015b). Disparaging Liberal Economics in 19th Century Greece: The Case of the "Economist's Duck," *European Journal for the History of Economic Thought*, 22, 949–977.
Psilos, D. (1964). *Capital Market in Greece*, Athens: KEPE.
Psilos, D. & Westebbe, R. (1964). *Public International Development Financing in Greece*, New York: Columbia University School of Law.
Psimmenos, N. (1988). *Greek Philosophy*, Athens: Gnosis (in Greek).
Pylarinos, F. (1833). *Political Lectures*, Nafplio (in Greek).
Pylarinos, O. (1860). *Inaugural on Social Economics*, Corfu (in Greek).
Raftanis, S. (1853). *Interest Rate Calculator: Or Interest Bringing Charts on a Given Capital, Time and Interest Rate*, Zakynthos (in Greek).
Rapet, J. (1865). *Manuel de Morale et d'Économie Politique à l'Usage des Classes Ouvrières*, translated by M Kanellopoulos and A. SkalidisAthens, Filomousos Lesxi (in Greek).
Rhigas, F. (1790). *School of Delicate Lovers*, Vienna: Adelfoi Varvarigou (in Greek).
Rhigas, F. (1797). *New Political Administration*, Vienna: Poulios (in Greek).
Rist, G. (1997). *The History of Development*, London: Zed.
Robbins, L. (1930). The Present Position of Economic Science, *Economica*, 28, 14–24.
Robbins, L. (1952). *The Theory of Economic Policy in English Classical Political Economy*, London: Macmillan.
Rontiris, A. (1868). Agriculture, *Aion*, November 14 (in Greek).
Rorty, R. (1984). The Historiography of Philosophy. In: Rorty, R., Schnewind, J. & Skinner, Q., *Philosophy in History*, Cambridge: Cambridge University Press.
Rosen, F. (1992). *Bentham, Byron, and Greece*, Oxford: Clarendon Press.
de Ruggiero, G. (1927). *The History of European Liberalism*, London: Oxford University Press.
Russell, H. B. (1898). *International Monetary Conferences: Their Purposes, Character and Results*, London: Harper & Brothers.
Sabine, B. E. V. (1966). *A History of Income Tax*, London: George Allen and Unwin.
Samaras, G. (1977). *State and Capital in Greece*, Athens: Synchroni Epochi (in Greek).
Samuelson, P. (1947). *Foundations of Economic Analysis*, Cambridge, MA: Harvard University Press.
Samuelson, P. (1948). *Economics, an Introductory Analysis*, New York: McGraw-Hill.
Saounatsos, A. (1928). The Stabilization of the Drachma, *AOKE*, 159–190 (in Greek).
Saounatsos, A. (1935). *The Long-term Fluctuations* [Ph.D. thesis, University of Athens] (in Greek).
Say, J. B. (1828). *Catechism of Political Economy*, Aegina (in Greek).
Sbarounis, A. (1945). *Thoughts on a Post-War Viable Greece*, Athens: Ethniko Typografeio (in Greek).

Sbarounis, A. (1950). *Studies and Reminiscences from the Second World War*, Athens: Ethniko Typografeio (in Greek).
Sbarounis, A. (1953). *The Economy of the Marshall Plan and of the Mutual Security Program*, Istanbul: Universite d'Istanbul.
Scherer, A. (1968) *Suedosteuropa Dissertationen*,1918–60, Graz: Boehlau.
Schoenhaerl, K. (2017). *Finanziers in Sehnsuchtstraeumen*, Goettingen: Vandenhoek und Ruprecht.
Schoorl, E. (2013). *J. B. Say. Entrepreneur and Economist*, London: Routledge.
Schumpeter, J. A. (1954). *History of Economic Analysis*, New York: Oxford University Press.
Senior, N. W. (1859). *A Journal Kept in Turkey and Greece in the Autumn of 1857 and the Beginning of 1858*, London: Longman.
Seppel, M. & Tribe, K. (Eds.). (2017). *Cameralism in Practice*, Woodbridge: Boydell & Brewer.
Shehab, F. (1953). *Progressive Taxation*, Clarendon: Oxford University Press.
Sherman, D. (1974). The Meaning of Economic Liberalism in mid-Nineteenth Century France, *History of Political Economy*, 6 (2), 171–199.
Shionoya, Y. (Ed.). (2001). *The German Historical School: The Historical and Ethical Approach to Economics*, London: Routledge.
Sideris, A. (1921). The Paris Commune, *KOMEP*, A, 70–79 (in Greek).
Sideris, A. (1924). On the Crisis, *Nea Epochi*, March 15 (in Greek).
Sideris, A. (1926). The Revision of the Economic Ideas of Karl Marx, *AOKE*, 6, 111–129, (in Greek).
Sideris, A. (1931). The Historical Evolution of Agricultural Taxation, *AOKE*, 11, 355–412 (in Greek).
Sigalos, K. (1865). A Speech Held Before the General Assembly, *FT*, 2, 25–34 (in Greek).
Simantiras, I. (1905). *The Issue of Forced Circulation*, Athens: Vergiannitis (in Greek).
Simpson, J. (1976). The Origin of the United States' Academic Interest in Foreign Economic Development, *Economic Development and Cultural Change*, 24, 633–644.
Singer, H. (1985). Relevance of Keynes for Developing Countries. In: Wattel, H. (Ed.). *The Policy Consequences of J.M. Keynes*, Basingstoke: Macmillan, 128–144.
de Sismondi, S. (1846). *On the Constitutions of Free People*, Athens: Nikolaidou Filadelfeos (in Greek).
Skaltsounis, I. (1868). *Thoughts on Industry in Greece*, Athens: Ktenas kai Soutsas (in Greek).
Sklavenitis, T. (1991). *The Commercial Manuals of the Venetian and Turkish Periods and the Commercial Encyclopedia of N. Papadopoulos*, Athens: EMNE Mnimon (in Greek).
Sklavenitis, T. (1994). Spyridon Valletas and the Translation of J. B. Say's Political Economy, *Mnimon*, 9, 107–156 (in Greek).
Skliros, G. (1907). *Our Social Question*, Athens: Konstantinidis (in Greek).
Skliros, G. (1917). *The Philosophy of War and Peace*, Alexandria: Grammata (in Greek).
Skliros, G. (1919). *Contemporary Problems of Hellenism*, Alexandria: Grammata (in Greek).
Skopetea, E. (1988). *The "Model Kingdom" and the Great Idea. Aspects of the National Problem in Greece (1830–1880)*, Athens: Polytypo (in Greek).
Slobodian, Q. (2018). *Globalists*, Cambridge, MA: Harvard University Press.
Small, A. (1909). *The Cameralists*, Chicago: Chicago University Press.
Sockwell, W. D. (1994). *Popularizing Classical Economics*, Basingstoke: Macmillan.

Sombart, W. (1921). *Das Proletariat. Bilder und Studien*, Athens: Eleftheroudakis (in Greek).
Sorokiadis, N. (1887). Greek Industry and Mr Emile Burnouf, *Evdomas*, April 26.
Sotiropoulos, M. (2023). *Liberalism after the Revolution*, Cambridge: Cambridge University Press.
Sotiropoulos, S. (1861). *Treatise on Land Taxation in Greece*, Athens: Mavromatis (in Greek).
Sotiropoulos, S. (1861). *Report on the Change of the Tax System*, Athens: Mavromatis (in Greek).
Souliotis, N. (2021). *Economists-Technocrats in the Greek Political Scene*, Athens: Alexandreia (in Greek).
Soutsos, I. A. (1843). *Draft for a Political Constitution for Greece*, Athens: Mantsarakis (in Greek).
Soutsos, I. A. (1851). *Treatise on the Production and Distribution of Wealth*, Athens: Koromilas (in Greek).
Soutsos, I. A. (1853). *Reply of a Greek to an Easterner*, Athens: Koromilas (in Greek).
Soutsos, I. A. (1861). Faits Économiques qui se Sont Produits en Grèce de 1833 en 1860, *Journal des économistes*, 29 (3), 373–386.
Soutsos, I. A. (1863). *An Essay on Economic Reforms*, Athens: Passaris (in Greek).
Soutsos, I. A. (1864). *Manual of Public Finance, or Theory of the Budget*, Athens: Passaris (in Greek).
Soutsos, I. A. (1874). *Ploutological Studies*, Athens: Passaris (in Greek).
Soutsos, I. A. (1876). *Economic Review: 1876 Budget and Tax Bills*, Athens: Aion (in Greek).
Soutsos, I. A. (1879a). The Tax Bills of 1876, *Economic Review*, 7, 204–223 (in Greek).
Soutsos, I. A. (1879b). *The Economic Issue*, Athens: Passaris (in Greek).
Soutsos, I. A. (1882–85) [1868-9]. *Ploutology*, Athens: Passaris (in Greek).
Soutsos, I. A. (1890). *Manual of Public Finance*, Athens: Passaris (in Greek).
Spengler, J. J. (1970). Notes on the International Transmission of Economic Ideas, *History of Political Economy*, 2 (1), 133–151.
St. Clair, W. (1972). *That Greece Might Still be Free*, London: Oxford University Press.
St. Simon, H. (1821). *Du systeme industriel*, Paris: Renouard.
Stassinopoulos, Y. (2000). *Monetary Theory and Policy in 19th-Century Greece*, Athens: Typothyto [in Greek].
Stassinopoulos, Y. (2021). Andreas Andreadis: Economic Liberalism's Dilemmas in the Interwar Period, *European Journal of the History of Economic Thought*, 28 (61), 1–24.
Staum, M. (1998). French Lecturers in Political Economy, 1815–1848: Varieties of Liberalism, *History of Political Economy*, 30 (1), 95–120.
Stavrianos, L. (2000). *The Balkans Since 1453*, New York: New York University Press.
Stefanidis, D. S. (1926a). *Chambers of Commerce in Greece in Particular*, Athens: Denaxas (in Greek).
Stefanidis, D. S. (1926b). *Economic Studies*, Athens: Koronaios (in Greek).
Stefanidis, D. S. (1927). *Imperialism. Its Nature, the Means for its Strength and its Most Important Manifestation* [Ph.D. thesis, University of Athens] (in Greek).
Stefanidis, D. S. (1930). The *Inflow of Foreign Capital in Greece and its Economic and Political Consequences*, Thessaloniki: Triantafyllou (in Greek).
Stefanidis, D. S. (1932). *The World Economic Crisis and Greece*, Thessaloniki (in Greek).
Stefanidis, D. S. (1935). *The New Directionsin Foreign Commercial Policy*, Thessaloniki: University of Thessaloniki (in Greek).

Stefanidis, D. S. (1937). *Introduction in Applied Social Economics*, Thessaloniki: Ekdoseis Ellinikis Iatrikis (in Greek).
Stefanidis, D. S. (1938). *The Position of Industry in our Social Economy*, Thessaloniki (in Greek).
Stefanidis, D. S. (1939). The Social Question under the Light of National Socialism, *Neon Kratos*, 17–18, 1487–1507, 1588–1619 (in Greek).
Stefanidis, D. S. (1945). *Greeks and Bulgarians as Economic Agents in the Balkans*, Athens: Aetos (in Greek).
Stefanidis, D. S. (1948–50). *Social Economics in its Historical Evolution*, 3 vols, Athens: Loukas (in Greek).
Stefanidis, D. S. (1961). *National Economic Policy*, Athens (in Greek).
Steil, B. (2013). *The Battle of Bretton Woods*, Princeton: Princeton University Press.
Steiner, P. (1998). The Structure of Say's Economic Writings, *European Journal of the History of Economic Thought*, 5 (2), 227–249.
Stigler, G. J. (1965). *Essays in the History of Economics*, Chicago: Chicago University Press.
Stigler, G. J. (1969). Does Economics Have a Useful Past? *History of Political Economy*, 1 (2), 217–230.
Stournaras, Y. and Albani, M. (2008). *The Greek Economy After the Crisis: In Search of a New Growth Model*, Athens: ICBE.
Strong, F. (1842). *Greece as a Kingdom*, London: Longman.
Suzanne, P. H. (1849). *Principes Généraux d'Économie Publique et Industrielle*, translated by M. Vernardos, Athens: Antoniadis (in Greek).
Svolos, A. (1972) [1998]. The Constitutional History of Greece. In: Axelos, L. (Ed.), *The Greek Constitutions 1822-1975/1986*, Athens: Stochastis (in Greek).
Syrmaloglou, A. (2007). *Taxation or Bankruptcy? Fiscal Policy in the Greek Parliament, 1862–1910*, Athens: Metamesonykties Ekdoseis (in Greek).
Syrmaloglou, A. (2015). Parliamentary Economists and Social Reform: The Case of the 'Japanese' in the Hellenic Parliament (1906–1908), *The History of Economic Thought*, 56 (2), 47–66.
Syrmaloglou, A. (2016). Panagiotis Halikiopoulos and Greek Agriculture. In: Psalidopoulos, M. (Ed.), *Development Models in Greece. Past, Present and Future*, Athens: Metamesonykties Ekdoseis, 29–52 (in Greek).
Tarshis, L. (1947). *The Elements of Economics. An Introduction to the Theory of Price and Employment*, Cambridge: Houghton Mifflin.
Theocarakis, N. (2013). The Reception of Adam Smith in Greece: A Most Peculiar Metakenosis, *Adam Smith Review*, 7, 148–164.
Theocarakis, N. (2018). Addendum: The Reception of Adam Smith in Greece. In: Adam Smith (Ed.), *An Inquiry on the Nature and the Causes of the Wealth of Nations*, translation of books I–II, Athens: Pedio, 471–527 (in Greek).
Thiersch, H. J. (1866). *Friedrich Thiersch's Leben*, 2 vols, Heidelberg: Winter.
Thiersch, F. [1833] (1972). *The Greece of Kapodistrias. The Present Situation of Greece (1828–1833) and the Means to Achieve its Reconstruction*, Athens: Tolidis (in Greek).
Thomadakis, S. & Seremetis, D. (1992). Fiscal Management, Social Agenda and Structural Deficits. In: Kariotis, T. (Ed.), *The Greek Socialist Experiment*, New York: Pella 203-255.
Tournakis, I. (1923). *Commercial Policy and Currency Policy*, Athens: Petris (in Greek).
Tournakis, I. (1924). *About the Concentration of Wealth and its Economic and Social Outcomes* [Ph.D. thesis, University of Athens] (in Greek).
Tournakis, I. (1930). *International Emigration Movements and Emigration Policy*, Athens: Petris (in Greek).

Tournakis, I. (1937–39). Study on the Greek Problem, *Nea Politiki*, 1 and 10/1937, 3 (286–309) and 9/1938(905-929) and 2/1939(157-187) (in Greek).
Tribe, K. (1984). Cameralism and the Science of Government, *The Journal of Modern History*, 2 (56), 263–284.
Tribe, K. (1995). *Strategies of Economic Order: German Economic Discourse, 1750–1950*, Cambridge: Cambridge University Press.
Tribe, K. (2003). Continental Political Economy from the Physiocrats to the Marginal Revolution. In: Porter, Th. M. & Ross, D. (Eds.), *The Cambridge History of Science Volume 7*, Cambridge: Cambridge University Press, 154–170.
Tribe, K. (2017). *Governing Economy: The Reformation of German Economic Discourse 1750–1840*, Newbury: Threshold Press.
Triffin, R. (1940). *Monopolistic Competition and General Equilibrium Theory*, Cambridge: Cambridge University Press.
Trikaliotis, S. (1863). *On the Organization of a System of National Production and the Ways to do it*, Athens: Sakellariou (in Greek).
Trikaliotis, S. (1865). *Treatise on the Most Suitable Economic and Political Organization for Greece*, Athens: Sakellariou (in Greek).
Trikaliotis, S. (1866). *Inaugural Lecture on Political Economy*, Athens: Sakellariou (in Greek).
Trikaliotis, S. (1871). *Manual of Political Economy*, Athens: National Printing Office (in Greek).
Tsakalotos, E. (1991). *Alternative Economic Strategies: The Case of Greece*, Aldershot: Gower.
Tsopotos, D. (1912). *Land and Peasants in Thessaly*, Volos: Thessalia (in Greek).
Turczynski, E. (2009). *Sozial und Kulturgeschichte Griechenlands im 19 Jahrhundert*, Muenchen: Harrasowitz.
Typaldos-Bassias, A. (1893). *La Protection Industrielle et Le Nouveau Regime Douanier*, Paris: Nabu.
Varoufakis, Y. (2011). *The Global Minotaur*, New York: Zed Books.
Varoufakis, Y. & S. Holland. (2010). *A Modest Proposal for Overcoming the Euro Crisis*, New York: Levy Institute.
Varvaressos, K. (1912). *The Theory of Population*, Athens: Raftanis (in Greek).
Varvaressos, K. (1920). *The Meaning of the Economic Clauses of the Peace Treaty*, Anthropotis: April (in Greek).
Varvaressos, K. (1923). *Trade Agreements and the Clause of the Most Favoured Nation*, Athens: Makris (in Greek).
Varvaressos, K. (1937). The Problem of Economic Organization, *Journal of Greek Legal Experts*, May 16, Athens (in Greek).
Varvaressos, K. (1938a). Zum Problem der Wirtschaftsordnung, *Jahrbuecher fuer Nationaloekonomie und Statistik*, 148, 513–524.
Varvaressos, K. (1938b). Entwicklung und Probleme der griechischen Waehrung, *Bericht Ueber den Tag der Deutschen Wirtschaftswissenschaft*, 239–260.
Varvaressos, K. (1939a). Some Thoughts about the Problem of Value. *Etudes dedies a la memoire de A. Andreadis*, 337–347.
Varvaressos, K. (1939b), *History and Problems of the Greek Monetary System*, Athens: Pyrsos (in Greek).
Varvaressos, K. (1941). *The Greek Battle: Economic Interests and Moral Factors*, London: Royal Institute of International Affairs.
Varvaressos, K. (1952). *Report on the Economic Problem of Greece*, Athens (in Greek).
Varvaressos, K. (1954). *Interview 25/1*, Washington, DC: Ethnos.

Varvaressos, K., Petropoulos, G. & Pintos, I. (Eds.). (1938). *Works of Andeas Andreades*, Athens: University of Athens (in Greek).
Venizelos, E. (1969). *Political Testaments*, 2 vols, Athens: Leschi Fileleftheron (in Greek).
Vergopoulos, K. (1975). *The Agrarian Question in Greece*, Athens: Exandas (in Greek).
Vergopoulos, K. (1978). *State and Economic Policy in the 19th Century*, Athens: Exandas (in Greek).
Vernardakis, A. (1884). The New Tariff System, *Aion*, July 10 (in Greek).
Vesanis, S. (1895). *Ueber das Verhaeltnis der Vermehrung der Zinskapitalinhaber und der Zinskapitalien*, Berlin: Puttkammer.
Vesanis, S. (1897). *The Right to Live*, Athens Estia (in Greek).
Vlagalis, N. (1913). *Memorandum on the Encouragement of Local Industry*, Athens: Estia (in Greek).
Vogiatzis, A. (1957). *Full Employment as Social Policy in Greece*, Athens: Evropaikos Organismos Paragogikotitas (in Greek).
Vogiatzis, V. (1938). *People Without Space*, Thessaloniki: Society for Makedonian Studies (in Greek).
Vogiatzis, V. (1949a). *Theory and Meaning of Social Policy*, Thessaloniki: Sakoulas (in Greek).
Vogiatzis, V. (1949b). *Some Problems of Theoretical Economics from the Perspective of Social Policy*, Thessaloniki (in Greek).
Vogiatzis, V. (1970). *The Importance of the Human Factor in Economic Development*, Thessaloniki: Emporiko kai viomichaniko epimelitirio Thessalonikis (in Greek).
Vorios, S. (1943). *Theoretical Economics and Economic Absence of Judgment*, Athens: Loukatos (in Greek).
Vournazos, K. (1896). *On the Freedom of Activity*, Athens: Syllivriotis (in Greek).
Vournazos, K. (1904). *System of Political Economy*, Athens: Kousoulinos (In Greek).
Vournazos, K. (1910). Une Position Particuliere du Change en Grece, *Revue d'Economique Internationale*, 7, 324–343.
Vrailas-Armenis, P. (1846). *On the Subject and the Limits of Political Economy*, Corfu: Praktika Etaireias Filomathon (in Greek).
Vryonis, N. (1831). *On Shipping, A Teaching Manual*, Syros: Gravinos (in Greek).
Vryonis, N. (1839). *Lessons in the Science of Shipping*, Hermoupolis: Melistagas (in Greek).
Wade Hands, D. (2001). *Reflection Without Rules*, Cambridge: Cambridge University Press.
Wagner, A. (1892). *Grundlegung der Politischen Oekonomie*, Leipzig: Wintersche Verlagsbuchhandlung.
Wakefield, A. (2012). *The Disordered Police State. German Cameralism as Science and Practice*, Chicago: Chicago University Press.
Wattel, E. (1831). *Rights of Nations; or Principles of Natural Law*, Nafplion: Typografion tis Dioikiseos (in Greek).
Whatmore, R. (1998). Everybody's Business: Jean-Baptiste Say's "General Fact" Conception of Political Economy, *History of Political Economy*, 30 (3), 451–468.
Willis, H. P. (1901). *A History of the Latin Monetary Union: A Study of International Monetary Action*, Chicago: University of Chicago Press.
Winkel, H. (1997). *Die Deutsche Nationaloekonomie im 19. Jahrhundert*, Darmstadt: Wissenschaftliche Buchgesellschaft.
Woodhouse, C. M. (1973). *Capodistria: The Founder of Greek Independence*, London: Oxford University Press.
Woodhouse, C. M. (1986). *George Gemistos Plethon. The Last of the Hellenes*, Oxford: Oxford University Press.

X., A. (1839). *Life of Benjamin Franklin and Adamantios Korais*, Hermoupolis: Polymeris (in Greek).
Zafiriou, R. (1942). The Contemporary Status of the Theory of Monopolistic Competition, *EKDO* 11, 211–239 (in Greek).
Zafiriou, R. (1945). *The Concept of Capital in Economic Theory. A Critique of Orthodox Economics* [Unpublished Ph.D. thesis], London School of Economics.
Zakynthinos D. (1976). *The Making of Modern Greece*, London: Blackwell.
Zallony, M. F. (1824). *Essai sur the Phanariotes*, Marseille: Ricard.
Zeggelis, I. (1894). *On Progressive Taxation*, Athens: Konstantinidis (in Greek).
Zeggelis, I. (1895). *On Usury and Measures to Combat it*, Athens:Paligennesia (in Greek).
Zeggelis, I. (1901). *Current Political Affairs*, Athens: Kostantinidis (in Greek).
Zografos, I. (1876). *Essay on Money*, Athens: Eleftheroudakis (in Greek).
Zografos, I. (1878). *The Value of Paper Money in Greece*, Athens: Eleftheroudakis (in Greek).
Zografos, I. (1882). *Public Finance, i.e., the Science of Managing Public Money*, Athens: Perris.
Zografos, I. (1925–6). *Fiscal Studies, I-III*, 2nd ed. Athens: Eleftheroudakis (in Greek).
Zografos, K. (1895). *The Development of National Production*, Athens (in Greek).
Zografos, K. (1906). *On Land Rent*, Athens (in Greek).
Zolotas, X. (1926). *Griechenland auf dem Wege zur Industrialisierung*, Leipzig: Teubner.
Zolotas, X. (1927a). The Quantity Theory of Money and the Fluctuation in Prices, *AOKE*, 7, 139–150 (in Greek).
Zolotas, X. (1927b). Currency Theories, *AOKE*, 7, 310–336 (in Greek).
Zolotas, X. (1928). *Monetary and Currency Phenomena in Greece, 1910–27*, Athens: Greca (in Greek).
Zolotas, X. (1929a), *The New Trends in Theoretical Social Economics*, Athens: Greca (in Greek).
Zolotas, X. (1929b), *Monetary Stabilization*, Athens: Greca (in Greek).
Zolotas, X. (1939). Taxation, Saving and Investment. In: *Studies Dedicated to A. Andreades*, Athens: University of Athens, 252–283 (in Greek).
Zolotas, X. (1942). *Theoretical Economics*, Athens: Papazisis (in Greek).
Zolotas, X. (1944a). *Economic Fluctuations*, Athens: Papazissis (in Greek).
Zolotas, X. (1944b). *Creative Socialism*, Athens: Papazissis (in Greek).
Zolotas, X. (1945). *Greece Ought to Become Viable*, Athens: Papazissis (in Greek).
Zolotas, X. (1947). Distribution of Income and Social Exploitation, *EPOE*, 1, 55–64 (in Greek).
Zolotas, X. (1948). *Reconstruction and Viability*, Athens: Papazissis (in Greek).
Zolotas, X. (1952). The Varvaressos Report and Economic Development, *EOPE*, 7, 1–24 (in Greek).
Zolotas, X. (1953). *The Transformation of Capitalism*, Athens: Academy of Athens (in Greek).
Zolotas, X. (1954). *Full Employment and Inflationary Pressures*, Athens: Academy of Athens (in Greek).
Zolotas, X. (1959). *Economic Development and Technical Education*, Athens: Bank of Greece (in Greek).
Zolotas, X. (1967). *Monetary Planning*, Athens: Bank of Greece (in Greek).
Zolotas, X. (1965). *Monetary Equilibrium and Economic Development*, Princeton: Princeton University Press.
Zolotas, X. (1973). *The Orientation of the Economy*, Athens: EDIK (in Greek).

Zolotas, X. (1975). *Our Economic Problem*, Athens: Bank of Greece (in Greek).
Zoumboulakis, M. (2023). A.G. Papandreou's Economic Thought, 1943–63, *Journal for the History of Economic Thought*, 45 (3), 486–502.
Zweynert, J. (2002). *Geschichte des Oekonomischen Denkens in Russland, 1805–1905*, Marburg: Metropolis.
Zygouras, X. (1870). *Greek Commercial Correspondence*, Constantinople: Anatoli (in Greek).
Zygouras, X. (1874). *History of Commerce in General*, Constantinople: Voutiras (in Greek).
Zygouras, X. (1876). *Elements of Ploutology, Theoretical and Practical*, Constantinople: Voutiras.
Zygouras, X. (1877). *On General Industry*, Constantinople:Voutiras (in Greek).

Index

For Product Safety Concerns and Information please contact our EU representative GPSR@taylorandfrancis.com
Taylor & Francis Verlag GmbH, Kaufingerstraße 24, 80331 München, Germany

www.ingramcontent.com/pod-product-compliance
Ingram Content Group UK Ltd.
Pitfield, Milton Keynes, MK11 3LW, UK
UKHW020150200926
475702UK00016B/2634

9781032738116